Securing Storage

Securing Storage

A PRACTICAL GUIDE TO SAN AND NAS SECURITY

Himanshu Dwivedi

✦✦Addison-Wesley

Upper Saddle River, NJ • Boston • Indianapolis • San Francisco
New York • Toronto • Montreal • London • Munich • Paris • Madrid
Capetown • Sydney • Tokyo • Singapore • Mexico City

The publisher offers excellent discounts on this book when ordered in quantity for bulk purchases or special sales, which may include electronic versions and/or custom covers and content particular to your business, training goals, marketing focus, and branding interests. For more information, please contact:

      U. S. Corporate and Government Sales
      (800) 382-3419
      corpsales@pearsontechgroup.com

For sales outside the U. S., please contact:

      International Sales
      international@pearsoned.com

Visit us on the Web: www.awprofessional.com

ISBN 0-32-134995-4
Text printed in the United States on recycled paper at Courier in Westford, Massachusetts.
First printing, November 2005

Library of Congress Cataloging-in-Publication Data

Dwivedi, Himanshu.
  Securing storage : a practical guide to SAN and NAS security / Himanshu Dwivedi.
    p. cm.
  Includes bibliographical references and index.
  ISBN 0-321-34995-4 (hc. : alk. paper)

  1. Storage area networks (Computer networks)—Security measures. 2. Fibre Channel (Standard) 3. iSCSI (Computer network protocol) I. Title: Practical guide to SAN and NAS security. II. Title: SAN and NAS security. III. Title.

TK5105.86.D95 2005
005.8—dc22

               2005021323

THE HEART OF THIS BOOK IS DEDICATED TO MY VERY SUPPORTIVE WIFE, KUSUM, WHOSE ACTIONS, INTELLIGENCE, AND SIGNIFICANT SACRIFICES THROUGHOUT MY CAREER HAVE BEEN ACCOMPANIED ONLY BY THE UTMOST HUMILITY AND SUPPORT. KUSUM, I LOVE YOU, I THANK YOU, AND I'M VERY GLAD TO BE WITH YOU.

THE WORK ETHIC OF THIS BOOK IS DEDICATE TO MY FATHER, CHANDRADHAR DWIVEDI, WHOSE WORK ETHIC, DEDICATION TO HIS FIELD, LOYALTY TO HIS FAMILY, AND PATIENCE/PERSISTENCE IN THE WORKPLACE HAVE SHOWN ME LESSONS FOR A LIFETIME. DAD, I THANK YOU VERY MUCH.

THE PASSION OF THIS BOOK IS DEDICATED TO MY MOTHER, PRABHA DWIVEDI, WHOSE SUPPORT, SMILES, AND OVERWHELMING LOVE HAS ALWAYS CREATED A COMFORTING ENVIRONMENT FOR ME. THANKS, MOM!

THE EXPERIENCE OF THIS BOOK IS DEDICATED TO MY BROTHER AND SISTER, SUDHANSHU AND NEERAJA DWIVEDI, WHOSE GUIDANCE, EXPERIENCES, UNDERSTANDING, AND ADVICE HAVE ALWAYS PAVED THE WAY FOR ME DOWN A VERY SAFE AND STEADY ROAD.

THE COMPLETION OF THIS BOOK IS DEDICATED TO THE WORKING PEOPLE IN THE WORLD. THE PEOPLE WHO SHOW UP EARLY AND LEAVE LATE, THE PEOPLE WHO DO NOT HAVE A FLEXIBLE WORK SCHEDULE, THE PEOPLE WHO ARE WORKING SEVERAL JOBS AT ONCE, THE PARENTS SUPPORTING THEIR ENTIRE FAMILIES WHILE SUPPORTING EVERY PROJECT AT THEIR WORK, THE VETERANS OF THE WORKFORCE WHO HAVEN'T SPECIALIZED IN KNOWING THE RIGHT PERSON BUT ALLOWING THEIR WORK TO SPEAK FOR ITSELF, THE PEOPLE WHO WORK FIRST AND RELAX LATER (IF AT ALL), THE PEOPLE WHO FINISH JOBS RATHER THAN GATHERING EXCUSES, THE NON-SQUEAKY WHEEL, THE PEOPLE WHO "DO" BEFORE THEY "SAY," AND THE PEOPLE WHO HAVE PROVEN THAT THE SECRET TO SUCCESS WITHOUT HARD WORK IS STILL A SECRET.

Contents

Preface

Storage security is the two-ton secret in your data center. It is the big white elephant that you walk by every day—you can see it from your desktop, you look for it on your servers, and you even rest your coffee mug on it every now and then. Despite the fact that the elephant is very large, heavy (two tons), albino (white), and sitting in the middle of the data center, it is the dirty little secret that no one speaks about. So why do people ignore such a large entity that can significantly damage their enterprise? The answers, as well as the solutions, are addressed in this book.

The storage industry is missing the mark in terms of security, data protection, availability, integrity, and compliance. The absence of security in storage makes it an open target for unauthorized access and data compromise. The most prominent security control for storage networks is the lack of knowledge many attackers have about the technology. Lack of knowledge, or better known as security by obscurity, never stands the test of time as shown in other technologies affected by security, such as application development, voice over IP, wireless, and even electronic voting stations. Furthermore, security by obscurity never passes a governmental compliance test for data protection or integrity.

The book's primary goal is to discuss security weaknesses and acceptable solutions for Storage Area Networks (SANs) and Network Attached Storage (NAS). The book will discuss the mechanisms to evaluate your own storage network, design security into storage networks, and implement security settings on common storage devices. The book will also cover the standard practices for securing storage by discussing strategies that will minimize security weaknesses in SAN and NAS architectures.

Before we dive deeper, let's define storage security for a moment. Security is an entity that can be applied to different things, such hosts, devices, networks, and communication mediums. Security can also be applied in several methods, such as encryption, access controls, authentication, checksums, logging, or dedicated products. Similarly, storage is an entity that is also applied in many ways. It can be applied as media (tapes, CD-ROMs, disk drives, USB drives), a communications medium (Internet Protocol, Fibre Channel, iSCSI), or even a network (Network Attached Storage or Storage Area Networks). Based on their different descriptions, security and storage traditionally are two items that are not usually paired together. Storage concentrates on holding data, while security concentrates on protecting data. Nevertheless, it is interesting that both entities address data needs and concerns, yet have not been addressed in a complementary fashion.

There are several reasons why security and storage are two strangers. One incorrect assumption is that storage does not need security because it already has been addressed elsewhere in a network, which unfortunately is not true. It is often unnoticed that it is easier for internal attackers to compromise storage devices when compared to applications or operating systems. For example, unlike most applications and operating systems, many storage devices do not even require authentication to get access to large volumes of data, a fact that would never pass on most security audits. Furthermore, if an internal server has ever been affect by a virus or worm, the perimeter of the network is probably not as secure as a Visio document may picture it to look. The fact is the network perimeter has disappeared with the advent of wireless networks, remote VPN users, site-to-site VPNs with business partners, back-end support connections, and internal unauthorized users such as contractors/consultants. This fact, combined with the large amount of internal data heists occurring every month, make storage a prime target of attackers. Compliance entities have also realized that data is not protected adequately and its integrity is at risk on the storage network.

It is often overlooked that perimeter security controls are easily subverted to gain access to entities connected to the storage network, thus creating an open gateway. It is also assumed that unauthorized users attack from their own machines, but actually they attack from compromised management servers, administrator workstations, or compromised applications. Another assumption is that if any entity, such as an application data owner, can gain access to the stored data, they must have been authorized to do so; thus, having the ability to access data equates into the authorization to access data, again simply not true (especially for regulated data). For example, if an Exchange administrator has access to the Exchange server, it does not mean that he or she is authorized to read everyone's email. Furthermore, the ability for unauthenticated users to connect directly to the storage network and view, copy, and delete data does not mean all users should have that authority. The assumptions also carry over to different organizational groups. Security groups are often preoccupied with network and application attacks to fully understand the high risks of insecure storage. Additionally, the storage group's lack of information security background combined with their focus on performance and capacity concerns make security a neglected entity. All these assumptions and groups make it hard to realize that a large amount of data is sitting wide open in the storage network for anyone to compromise.

WHAT DOES IT MEAN TO SECURE STORAGE?

What does it mean to secure storage? For the purposes of this book, *securing storage* is the process of assessing, implementing, and testing security on existing SAN and NAS architectures. The book will focus on the following items:

- How do I assess my storage network for best practices?
- How do I test my storage network from attacks and compliance breaches?
- How do I implement security on my storage network based on industry standards?

The book will cover three primary themes. The first theme is to provide guidance and assessment techniques for storage networks. The second theme is to provide testing procedures for SAN and NAS architectures. The third theme of this book will discuss the security solutions for each attack class and security exposure currently presented on storage networks and devices. The book will discuss many security specifications and industry standards and how they affect storage security overall.

SAN AND NAS SECURITY

Storage Area Networks (SANs) and Network Attached Storage (NAS) are two types of storage networks. SANs have been based primarily on Fibre Channel (FC), with iSCSI becoming more popular, and NAS architectures have primarily been based on IP using CIFS or NFS. Both types of storage networks have one thing in common: SANs and NAS are not used for backup anymore.

Data from the storage network is being presented to applications and hosts in all parts of the network, which do not hold a high level of security. For example, a Fibre Channel SAN may be connected to a web or database cluster that is available to the Internet or internal network, allowing a single comprised web/database server to be the gateway to the SAN. If the SAN was using iSCSI, the storage device would be easier to break into. The attacker would only need to connect to the IP network and connect to the iSCSI storage device, bypassing the database application and web server all together. Furthermore, a NAS device might be holding medical data (patient information) that can be assessed by authorized doctors; however, it is also stored in clear-text, allowing any system administrator to access the sensitive data.

The need for SAN and NAS security is long overdue. This book will describe the specific implementation steps to deploy SAN and NAS security options, while also discussing the different ways to fully optimize current storage architectures. This book can also be used by organizations that have deployed a storage network and are interested in learning more ways to secure it.

BLOCK DATA VERSUS FILE DATA

In order to understand security threats for storage networks, it is important to understand the differences between file-level data and block-level data. NAS storage devices support file-level data, which is the traditional type of data we are accustomed to on PC systems. NAS devices using file-level data present file systems remotely over the network. An entire file system, a partial file system, or even a single individual file can be presented to a remote server over the network. File-level data using NFS and CIFS (SMB) are the traditional methods of deployment. SAN storage devices use block data, where an entire SCSI partition is presented over the network. Unlike file-level data, block data does not present individual files, folders, or even file systems, but the entire drive (block) itself (usually 50 to 100 gigabytes in size at a time). For example, think of file-level data as an access to the remote file system (partial or full); however, think of block-level data as an access to the entire hard drive (regardless of file system type) over the network. Block data is like having two or three more hard drives inside a server, but presented to the server over the network using iSCSI or Fibre Channel and not installed inside the machine using IDE or SCSI ribbons.

The other difference between file-level data and block-level data is that file-level data (NAS devices) contain multi-system support and block data blocks usually do not. Multiple machines or users can access the same remote file system (NFS or CIFS) at the same time as long as it is formatted to the correct file system time (such as NTFS or FAT for Windows). On the other hand, block data is not necessarily meant to have multiple systems connected to a single block of data at the same time. (Note: Some Fibre Channel and iSCSI SANs do support multiple connections to the same block data, but it is not the default.) It would be difficult for a single hard drive to have two IDE or SCSI ribbons connected to two separate servers; similarly, block data does not usually have multiple servers connected to it at the same time. It is possible for multiple systems to connect to the same block data repository over iSCSI or Fibre Channel; however, it results in a denial-of-service problem because two separate servers are trying to mount the same block data. Until one of the servers stops sending requests for the block data, the other will not be able to access it either.

The key idea to understand with either file or block data is that they are both data targets that contain large amounts of data viewable to any attacker or unauthorized user. File data is what most systems are accustomed to. Block data, however, is just as valuable to an attacker (if not more) since it contains large volumes of data but in block format, which is just as easy to mount and read as file-level data but requires different mounting and reading steps.

The following table briefly summarizes the difference between block and file data.

Block Data	File Data
SANs	NASs
Block format (hard drive)	File format (file system)
Usually one system per block	Multiple systems per folder
SCSI via iSCSI or Fibre Channel	NFS or CIFS via IP
New hard drives over the network	New file systems over the network

The top figure shows a mounted drive (Disk 1) for block data. The bottom figure shows a mounted file system (X:\) for file data.

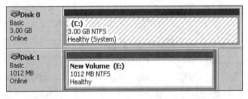

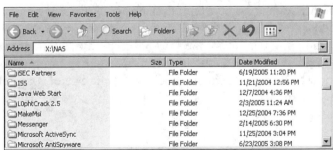

WHY STORAGE SECURITY?

The necessity for storage security is similar to the need for security on any other entity of high value in your organization. For example, the popularity of patching utilities and anti-virus applications are not necessarily for their ability to provide security protection (even though that is an important benefit), but rather their ability to improve uptime and availability of computer systems, networks, and data integrity. Similarly, the unavailability of a storage network or the lack of integrity of data, which would leave an organization in a state of disarray, has a much bigger impact than an infected laptop or an offline application. A good example of this is the SASSER-RPC worm released in 2004 that targeted Microsoft operating systems. Although the worm was intended for Windows, many storage devices that support Windows protocols, such as CIFS and SMB, were also vulnerable, which essentially made the storage device unusable until a full system reboot and patch. The risk of data being unavailable, corrupted, abused, or even deleted will cause tremendous financial harm and storage downtime for many organizations. Furthermore, the regulatory issues that involve storage networks are confusing at best, requiring a resource to guide everyone through the process.

This book's primary attraction is its ability to discuss, demonstrate, and prioritize the storage security issues that every organization faces. The book will not use high-level or abstract language and fail to provide any details, but rather provide an abundant amount of security details to allow readers to finally understand what the real issues are with storage security and how they can asses the risk for themselves. The book will also provide details to distinguish the high-risk/high-impact issues versus low-risk/nominal-impact issues.

A key purpose for the book is to provide a clear understanding of the technology. Storage security is a relatively new industry and can be an overwhelming topic. Several years ago when I began researching storage and security, there were no storage security products, web sites, or whitepapers about storage security. There were only a few people willing to talk to me about the seriousness of storage security. Years later, there is not only an entire industry on securing storage, with large companies like Symantec and Veritas merging together, but with its new popularity, there is a lot more confusion.

The need to secure storage is important on many levels. From a security perspective, many organizations (and their security departments), are not aware of the data protection issues surrounding storage. From the storage perspective, many storage administrators are unaware of the security issues that will affect system uptime and data availability.

Another reason why storage security is needed is for the ease of comprehension. There are many sources that discuss attack classes in storage, but a few actually provide risk exposure descriptions. A key goal of this book is not to force arbitrary risk levels on your organizations, but to describe the threat vector and attack surface in detail and allow readers to deduce their own risk based on the outcomes of these possible attacks. Readers will find out that security attacks don't change, but get modified and improved (just like viruses and worms). History has shown that attack classes that affected networks in the 1990s will also affect applications in the 2000s. Similarly, the same attack classes, such as segmentation weakness, poor session maintenance, and poor authentication, have also affected storage networks. However, a successful attack on storage equates to data loss or outright compromise.

The completion of this book will provide a very detailed guide of securing storage and understanding attacks.

REGULATIONS AND STORAGE

Regulatory issues facing storage have created significant legal issues for many financial, e-commerce, and medical organizations. New acts and policies such as the Health Insurance Portability and Accountability Act (HIPAA), Sarbanes-Oxley, Gramm-Leach Bliley Act (GLBA), SEC Rule 17a-4, DOD (Department of Defense) 5015, and California's SB1386 (Senate Bill 1386) are making a sizable impact on how the storage of data must be protected from unauthorized users, even if those unauthorized users are not hackers but internal employees. Furthermore, as internal audit groups and external IT auditors begin to understand that sensitive data is residing in the storage network/ devices (as opposed to servers or desktops), the focus will shift away from operating system security to storage networking security.

Government regulations primarily focus on security controls and auditing practices. A key issue for many storage networks, devices, and protocols is their lack of any security controls to protect data at-rest or in-flight. Additionally, government regulations don't decipher the difference between controls against outside attackers versus malicious internal employees. The fact that data is easier to compromise on a storage filer versus an operating system only adds to the storage security problem.

Regulations have highlighted an overlying issue of data protection. Data, whether it is financial data, non-public private information, or medical data, needs to be protected from unauthorized external and internal entities at all times. Government regulations have only helped raise the concerns that have existed since the first SAN or NAS network.

BEST-PRACTICE BENEFITS

Parts of certain chapters in this book are solely dedicated to best practices. Best practices are important in order to understand standard methods of secure deployment; however, they should not be used as inflexible guidelines. Implementation of security standards and practices will depend on the details and specifics of a storage network.

Best practices can be best described as items that are a prerequisite in order to deploy an acceptable amount of security in any given entity. Some of the sample best practices to secure storage are as follows:

- High-level architecture (defense in depth)
- Multi-layer architecture
- Authentication with authorization
- Encryption
- Integrity
- Auditing
- Detailed implementation guidelines
- Node hardening
- Zoning
- LUN masking
- CT/CHAP authentication
- SSL and IPSec encryption
- At-rest (AES or SHA1) encryption
- Management access

WHO SHOULD READ THIS BOOK

This book targets individuals who are responsible for IT infrastructure. Examples of these individuals are IT managers, storage administrators, network designers, architects, and engineers who want to evaluate security in storage architectures. It will also serve the needs of security consultants, engineers, architects, managers, auditors, trainers, and technical marketing managers who want to update their backgrounds in storage security.

The book is targeted toward readers who want to learn the common "how-tos" of securing storage. Readers requiring an essential reference guide can use the book as their primary resource. Generally speaking, this book is targeted for three types of individuals:

- Individuals who are interested in establishing or expanding their knowledge of securing storage
- Individuals who are interested in learning how to assess and audit their own storage networks
- Individuals who are looking for best practices or new strategies for storage security

The book's audience will range from novice readers who are looking for the basics behind storage architectures, networking, and LANs, to moderately skilled administrators looking to gain information on Fibre Channel communication, iSCSI, and Internet Protocol.

Readers will benefit from the book in several different ways. First, readers will be able to remove the confusion from securing storage. Readers will be able to qualify the risk of their storage network with a clear description of the security issues in storage. Readers will also learn the security principles for designing, testing, and evaluating storage networks. Several chapters have hands-on self-assessment steps for critical security threats and vulnerabilities. Additionally, best practices security measures are discussed in the context of data availability, integrity, and compliance requirements. Finally, readers will understand the security concerns for storage and be able to determine the impact of each issue.

This book will provide readers with the data center's guide to analyzing, testing, and implement SAN and NAS security. This book will cover common "how-tos," provide the all-essential "reference steps," and provide recommendations for storage security best practices.

The book is not necessarily meant to be read from start to finish, but instead can be a quick reference, where individual chapters are self supporting without knowledge of prior chapters. For example, if a reader needs to understand how to secure a brocade Fibre Channel switch, he can turn directly to Chapter 4, "SANs: Zone and Switch Security." The book can provide insight for the following types of individuals:

- Individuals interested in a practical method to secure SAN and NAS networks
- Individuals interested in assessing the security of their existing SAN and NAS networks

- Individuals interested in testing the security of their existing SAN and NAS networks
- Individuals interested in expanding their security knowledge on emerging storage technologies, such as encryption, authentication, and management
- Individuals interested in understanding how governmental regulations and compliance requirements affect storage

How This Book Is Organized

This book is organized into five parts consisting of fourteen chapters that include details on SAN security, NAS security, iSCSI security, storage defenses, polices, trends, and case studies.

The first three parts discuss core issues with SAN and NAS security, attacks against SAN and NAS devices, and SAN and NAS security solutions. These chapters target some of the most important topics in securing storage, as well as testing procedures for each attack class.

Chapter 1 begins with an overview of storage security, covering its basic premise, the problems encountered, typical uses, and future trends. Additionally, an overview of security and storage standards is discussed.

Chapters 2 through 4 discuss SAN security risks, including weaknesses of Fibre Channel (FC) and adjoining devices, such as switches and host-bus adapters (HBAs). Additionally, these chapters discuss SAN attacks, self-assessment steps (which allow readers to perform checks against their storage architecture), and mitigating solutions.

Chapters 5 and 7 are similar to Chapters 2 through 4, but focus on NAS architectures instead of SANs. Chapter 5 discusses the risks associated with NAS storage devices using IP protocols such as NFS and CIFS.

Chapters 6 and 7 discuss CIFS and NFS security issues, attacks, self-assessment steps, and mitigating solutions for storage architectures.

Chapter 8 discusses iSCSI security, including an overview of iSCSI communication, risks associated with iSCSI storage devices, and a discussion of the iSCSI attacks.

Part Four of the book focuses on storage defenses. Chapter 9 is a discussion on securing Fibre Channel SANs, Chapter 10 discusses the security of NFS/CIFS NAS, and Chapter 11 discusses the methods to secure iSCSI SANs. These chapters concentrate on how to take existing storage devices and ensure that they secure themselves. Part Five of the book shifts focus from SAN and NAS security risks and attacks, to larger storage security issues, such as emerging security technologies, regulations, and case studies.

These three chapters discuss security from the adherence perspective, both from the governmental aspect as well as from best practices. Chapter 12 discusses some of the major governmental policies that affect storage architectures. Chapter 13 discusses how to audit your storage network based on the government compliances and security best practices. Finally, Chapter 14 is a discussion of real-world case studies in storage environments. Examples describe SAN and NAS architectures with the optimal amount of security and functionality.

How This Book Is Written

The book is written to address the topic of securing storage from a technology perspective. It does not discuss the proper paper policies and procedures that should be in place, nor does it describe the human processes of security as it pertains to storage. It also does not discuss storage security at a high level, but does specifically discuss how storage systems, networks, and protocols are affected by security. The key difference this book will offer is not to generically say storage has security problems and glaze over the details, but to start with the details first.

The book discusses the security weaknesses, threats, exploits, and attacks of storage systems, networks, and technologies in Chapters 2 through 8. After the discussion is complete, the book discusses the mitigating solutions of each prior attack identified in Chapters 9 through 14. The reason for a deep discussion of the attacks is because it is very difficult to discuss solutions only without any context of the problem. Although some vendors will not appreciate the fact that this book exposes problems, it is not written to embarrass any vendor or to prevent end-users from adopting storage devices, but instead to show organizations why certain security mitigations and solutions need to be in place when deploying a storage network. For example, after a virus infects a user's machine, it is easier to discuss why anti-virus software and host hardening procedures are very important items. The same idea applies to storage. Organizations will understand why taking active steps to secure storage is important after reviewing the attacks in Fibre Channel, iSCSI, CIFS, and NFS.

The book makes an attempt to classify the risk of each identified problem; however, the discussion is limited because risk is best measured when applied to specific scenarios and not generic examples. Many attacks shown in this book can be classified as low risk, but they are still discussed to expose the reader to the security problem. Conversely, many attacks shown in the book are also high risk and are shown to its full extent and detail.

The book is not vendor specific, but rather protocol specific (Fibre Channel and iSCSI for SANs and NFS and CIFS for IP NAS).

The book holds storage systems, networks, and protocols to the same standard of security as operating systems, wireless networks, and application security. Storage security strengths are discussed to show the reader the positive security aspects of storage; however, it also shows failed or poor security attempts in storage systems, networks, and protocols. The book does not give storage devices/networks any "breaks" since it is an emerging technology. Any system and/or network that controls a large portion of an organization's data must be held to the same high security standard expected from operating system vendors or even application product vendors.

Finally, the book is written in the context of full disclosure. The goal is to allow each reader to receive enough information to read, perform, and analyze each security problem and each discussion about the mitigating solution. This model should allow the reader to make risk acceptability decisions based on their own storage environment.

"Whatever you do will be insignificant,
but it is very important that you do it."

—*Mahatma Gandhi*

Acknowledgments

I would like to personally thank and acknowledge several people who have helped me with my storage security research. These people have assisted me in several ways, allowing me to make this book better than what I could have done alone. To these people, I would like to say…**Thank You**. These people are Andy Hubbard, Kevin Rich, Anthony Barkley, John Blumenthal, John Donovan, Chris Odhner, Curtis Preston, and Mike LaRette. I would like to acknowledge the people at the Storage Security Industry Forum (SSIF) who continue to create awareness on storage security, including Leroy Budnik and Eric Riedel. I would also like to thank to Dr. Lance Leventhal, who guided me early on with this book, and Jessica Goldstein, who was willing to take a chance on storage security and was very integral in getting the book established.

Last, I would like to thank the people at iSEC Partners, including Joel Wallenstrom, Alex Stamos, Jesse Burns, and Scott Stender for being great partners.

About the Author

Himanshu Dwivedi is a founding partner of iSEC Partners, a digital security services and products organization. Before forming iSEC Partners (www.isecpartners.com), Himanshu was the Technical Director for @stake's San Francisco security practice, a leader in application and network security. His professional experience includes application programming, infrastructure security, and secure product design with an emphasis on storage risk assessment.

Himanshu is considered to be an industry expert in storage security. He has been published in major journals, magazines, and news articles regarding his storage security research. Himanshu has been invited to speak at several security and storage conferences in the United States and in Asia, such as BlackHat and Storage Networking World. Although specializing in SAN and NAS security, Himanshu's research includes storage technologies such as Fibre Channel, iSCSI, NFS, and CIFS as well as storage devices such as Fibre Channel switches, host bus adapters, storage controllers, iSCSI initiators, NAS filers, iSNS servers, NAS gateways, and encryption appliances. Himanshu has also written several tools for storage security assessment, including the iSCSI CHAP Password Tester and the Storage Port Scanner.

Himanshu currently has a patent pending on a storage design architecture that he co-developed with other professionals (U.S. Patent Serial No. 10/198,728). The patent is a security design for Fibre Channel storage networks. Himanshu has also published two other books, including *Storage Networks: The Complete Reference*, the "Security Considerations" chapter (McGraw-Hill/Osborne), and *Implementing SSH: Strategies for Optimizing the Secure Shell* (Wiley Publishing). Furthermore, Himanshu has also published two security white papers, including "Securing Intellectual Property" (http://www.vsi.org/resources/specs/ippwp310.pdf) and "Storage Security" (http://www.atstake.com/research/reports/acrobat/atstake_storage_networks.pdf).

Introduction to Storage Security

In the motion picture *Sneakers*, Ben Kingsley (known as Cosmo) stated, "The world is not run by weapons anymore, or energy, or money; it's run by little 1s and 0s, little bits of data." Mr. Kingsley was so very right. Data, and lots of it, is out there. It is on your desktop, on servers, inside applications, and even flying through the network. This data, which holds medical information, financial statements, trade secrets, credit card numbers, military records, social security numbers, source code, defense designs, confidential documents, intellectual property, and even private customer information, is the backbone to your organization. Despite where the data has been or what form it holds, it will end up in one place: the storage network. In order for the data to be protected, significant efforts need to be in place to adequately secure storage.

Securing storage is the process of assessing systems, testing networks, identifying gaps, and implementing security solutions. The following topics will help start the discussion of all these categories:

- Secure storage
- The demands of storage
- Risk management and data classification
- Security basics
- Storage attacks
- Questions from a storage administrator

SECURE STORAGE

Securing storage is a major problem that few people are discussing. Organizations are paying a great deal of attention to computer network security; however, valuable data spends most of its lifetime in storage devices, not on computers, servers, or networks. If local failures or outside intruders can change, destroy, or otherwise compromise stored data, the security of computers or networks is of little importance.

IT departments responsible for data protection are failing to see the issues. Storage groups do not fully understand the security problems, the external auditors are asking more questions on data protection, and the security team is preoccupied with operating systems and application security. Oddly enough, the item that ultimately holds all types of confidential information is overlooked in terms of data security.

While security has gained attention in several areas of information technology, such as perimeter networks and application security, it has been ignored in the storage network. The idea of protecting information and maintaining network uptime is nothing new for most organizations; however, it has not carried over to the entity that could impact the organization the most.

The current state of security in storage is mainly due to the recent emergence of Storage Area Networks (SANs) and Network Attached Storage (NAS) as new markets. In the early stages, vendors have focused on making the products perform well and have ignored secondary requirements such as security. The product features currently available are unable to support the security policies of most entities, such as the use of standard authentication processes. Furthermore, most storage architectures barely support any security, leaving the systems with no native defenses to protect themselves. This situation invites problems for the storage network.

To help explain the need for storage security, let's consider the analogy of a bank robber and a bank. A bank robber can steal money from bank teller drawers or valuables from the vault. Think of the money in teller drawers as data on servers/workstations. Additionally, think of the valuables in the vault as data in storage architectures. While there is a significant amount of money in the bank teller drawer, it does not compare to the jackpot in the bank vault. Similarly, while the data on servers/workstations is significant, it does not compare to the amount of information in the storage network. The comparison ends when banks have added security to protect the vault, yet storage networks contain little security to protect the vast amount of information on their systems. A storage network that has little security and also contains a large amount of data becomes a key target for attackers.

Issues such as unauthorized access and data compromise is only part the problem for storage. Regulatory requirements, viruses, worms, configuration mistakes, human errors, and disgruntled employees all can cause security problems in storage. The lack of focus on security affects several items, including availability, uptime, and compliance.

THE DEMANDS ON STORAGE

In 1981, Bill Gates, chairman of Microsoft Corporation, stated that 640K of memory, roughly half the size of a megabyte, ought to be enough for anybody. Not only have we found that statement to be untrue, but similar predictions of storage capacities have simply not been enough. The growing demands for more data in the enterprise at anytime, anywhere, and anyhow will only be satisfied by networked storage solutions using SANs or NAS.

The information age has amplified the need for storage and has caused it to increase tremendously. End-user information requirements continue to rise almost by the week. For example, storage capacities for laptops, personal computers (PCs), USB drives, digital cameras, digital video recorders, MP3 players, iPods, and personal email seem to have a never-ending upward trend. In fact, in 2004, Google, Inc. revolutionized web mail storage capacities by granting 2000MB (2 gigabytes) of free email storage for its Gmail users, which were over 10 times the current amounts from Yahoo! or Hotmail.

Similar to end-user and compliance requirements, organizational storage requirements are tripling for business email, office files, operational/business applications, databases, software development, and server systems. Furthermore, data storage requirements for government and legal regulations are being set for a minimum of seven years, requiring a considerable amount of increased storage for several organizations. In fact, text messages sent over mobile phones possibly holding sensitive information are kept in storage years after the communication, allowing subpoenas and warrants to access the data well into the future.

With the arrival of the paperless workplace, the need for digital storage will continue to rise. Furthermore, with the need for high storage capacities, local operating systems cannot meet the demanding need. Storage networks using SANs and NAS have become the norm in many organizations and will continue to grow in a manner similar to how networks and databases grew in the 1990s and wireless networks grew in the early 2000s.

The trend to network storage is telling in only the last five years. In the 1990s, the number of SANs and NAS were minor compared to direct attached storage (storage local on a PC or on a server operating system). However, according to the IDC, in 2003 over half (55 percent) of all storage has become networked (10.9 percent is NAS and 44.1 percent is SANs). The IDC also reports that by 2007, only 22 percent of storage will be directly attached, increasing NAS solutions to approximately 18.8 percent and SAN solutions to 59.2 percent, creating an estimated $6.5 billion market for SAN hardware

(Gartner) and another $7 billion associated with NAS (IDC). This raises the bar for net-worked storage solutions in the enterprise environment. Furthermore, another indica-tion of the storage-networking trend is its penetration into the home market. Several SOHO (Small Office/Home Office) vendors, such as Linksys and Netgear, are selling storage devices to meet the needs of personal home users.

The future for network storage is tremendous, but its security pitfalls leave us with a case of déjà vu all over again. Only this time, it's Fibre Channel Protocol and iSCSI (Internet SCSI), as well as IP (Internet Protocol) using CIFS/NFS. The storage industry has repeated the mistakes of the past decade in IP networking by failing to implement security in product and network design.

The attacks on critical infrastructure have begun already to hit the major government and financial organizations. In 2005 alone, Bank of America, Ameritrade, Iron Mountain, ChoicePoint, Citibank, LexisNexis, TimeWarner, FDIC, CitiBank, and Stanford University have admitted the malicious compromise or accidental loss of stor-age data/tapes that contain sensitive information. The trend will go on as attackers con-tinue to realize that networked storage devices are easier to compromise and have more access to data than any operating system or application[1]. In fact, in July of 2004, Los Alamos National Laboratory shut down all operations due to the loss of storage disks containing classified information that affects national security[2]. Furthermore, on July 22, 2004, a hacker was found guilty of stealing personal information from the database of an Arkansas-based financial company during a 16-month period, creating 7 million dollars in damages for the organization[3]. In 2003, hackers made off with more than 8 million credit-card numbers from an Omaha-based company responsible for handling online transactions[4]. And finally, in March of 2003, the University of Texas lost the personal information, including social security numbers, of 55,000 of its students and faculty.[5] These are just a few of the incidences that have been reported, and this will continue to rise as new government regulations force organizations with poor storage security stan-dards to reveal their security compromises publicly (for example, California Senate Bill 1386).

1. http://www.nwc.com/showArticle.jhtml?articleID=160500416

2. http://www.eweek.com/article2/0,1759,1824710,00.asp

3. http://www.computerworld.com/securitytopics/security/story/0,10801,94673,00.html?SKC=security-94673

4. http://www.byteandswitch.com/document.asp?doc_id=40508

5. http://www.byteandswitch.com/document.asp?doc_id=40508

RISK MANAGEMENT AND DATA CLASSIFICATION

Risk management and security both concern data protection. Security cannot mandate that organizations protect storage data at all times, but rather manage an organization's acceptable risk level for the type of data residing in storage networks.

A healthy risk management lifecycle is important for a strong security posture. Risk management allows an organization to understand what type of data is priceless, such as trade secrets and source code, and what type of data would not highly affect an organization financially.

The process of risk management starts with data classification. It is important to understand what type of data classifies as sensitive or confidential and what type is classified as internally public or externally public. For example, Human Resource data would probably be classified as sensitive with the risk acceptability level as low, therefore requiring the data to be protected at a high level. Conversely, web site marketing data can be classified as externally public since the compromise of the data does not equate to financial or strategic losses. This type of data would have a low risk level and a low level of protection. See Figure 1.1 for a risk management acceptance chart.

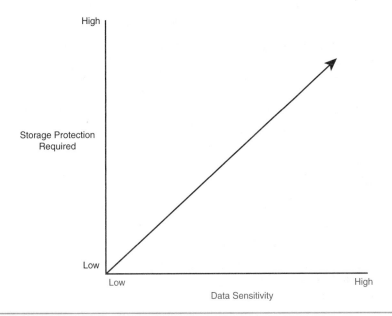

Figure 1.1   Risk management acceptance chart.

A healthy storage security posture requires organizations to address risk management and data classification. As organizations begin to address SAN and NAS security issues, the sensitivity of the data needs to be identified. Once data classification has been completed, the level of acceptable risk for each type of data class should ultimately provide the level of security required for SAN and NAS architectures. The process is not very quick; however, organizations that commit to risk management and data classification are able to make their data available and function without undermining its security or integrity.

SECURITY BASICS

Before we dive into the topic of SAN and NAS security, it is important to establish some security basics. Security basics revolve around six major concepts: authentication, authorization, auditing, integrity, encryption, and availability. A brief definition of each of these concepts follows:

- **Authentication**—Verifying an entity's identity.
- **Authorization**—Determining the rights granted to a trusted entity.
- **Auditing**—Capturing and retaining events that occur within an entity.
- **Integrity**—Assuring that the protected resources and/or data have not been modified by unauthorized entities or in unauthorized ways.
- **Encryption**—The process of obfuscating information in order to protect it from unauthorized access or modification.
- **Availability**—The ability to ensure resources are available to legitimate users, applications, or network devices when requested.

AUTHENTICATION

Authentication is the process of validating the identity of an entity. Since authentication procedures are often the first line of defense against potential attackers, it also becomes one of the first things attackers attempt to subvert.

An example of weak authentication usually involves a single entity, such as the use of a standard username and password combination. While the existence of some type of authentication is always more favorable than its absence (discussed later with SAN authentication models), poor authentication models often grant end users a false sense of security.

Stronger examples of authentication include two types of authentication levels (such as a username and password), followed by an additional verification request, such as a certificate, token, or public key. This type of authentication—username and password followed by a verification request—is known as two-factor authentication and is regarded as best practice. Not only does two-factor authentication protect against common attacks, such as brute forcing an authentication method, but also strongly defends against the constant problem of poor passwords. Since two-factor authentication requires a token, certificate, or public key, the use of a weak or guessable password does not become the weakest link for a given network.

Authentication processes and SANs don't really have a long history together. In fact, while DH-CHAP is just now supported for Fibre Channel and CHAP is supported for iSCSI, many SANs are often deployed without any type of authentication. Most SAN architectures and products rely on other aspects of the network to perform authentication, such as databases or operating systems. Most SAN architectures assume that if a host is connected to the SAN and can make a SAN request, it must have permission to do so. If that were the case, anyone who can make a telephone call to you must be someone you know and trust; otherwise, how would they have your phone number? As we all know, there are plenty of telemarketers who we do not know or trust that make telephone calls to us all the time! Obviously, most SANs do not follow a best practice in terms of authentication.

Authentication processes and NAS architectures are somewhat different from their SAN counterparts. NAS architectures usually deploy NFS or CIFS, where NFS (Network File System) is primarily for UNIX-based systems and CIFS (Common Internet File System) is for Windows-based systems. Similar to SANs, traditional NFS architectures (version 4 and before) in NAS networks do not use any type of authentication, but rather rely on other authorization processes to validate an entity. Many NFS NAS devices do not require authentication by default. A common "mount" command on an NFS NAS device may get you to the file you need. Nevertheless, later implementations of NFS, specifically NFS version 4, do offer authentication process with Kerberos, an industry standard authentication process. While Kerberos does not offer two-factor authentication, Kerberos does offer a very strong authentication architecture with session tickets, ticket-granting services, and ticket-granting tickets (for more information on Kerberos, visit web.mit.edu/Kerberos/www).

Unlike NFS, CIFS does offer an authentication process in all its implementations. If a NAS device is using CIFS in a Windows 2000 or 2003 architecture, Kerberos is used for the authentication process. Similar to NFS, the Windows 2000 Kerberos authentication process also uses the session tickets, ticket-granting services, and ticket-granting tickets to authenticate an entity. On the other hand, if a NAS device is using CIFS in a Windows NT 4.0 or below architecture, then NTLM is being used for the authentication process.

While NTLM is significantly weaker and full of security issues, it does provide a level of authentication for the NAS architecture.

Finally, authentication is also available with iSCSI storage networks. iSCSI uses CHAP for authentication between an iSCSI client and an iSCSI server. Some of the problems with iSCSI authentication is that it uses CHAP, which has several significant security weaknesses, it is clear-text, and it is disabled by default on several products. Furthermore, some iSCSI client drivers store passwords in the clear on the operating system, allowing attackers to simply take what they want. A major problem with iSCSI authentication is not only that it uses CHAP, but also the fact that the authentication is optional. Authentication should not be optional for an iSCSI storage network that controls the access to terabytes of data.

AUTHORIZATION

Authorization is the process of granting rights and privileges to an entity that is considered trusted, which is usually after authentication has been completed successfully. Trust is usually determined from an entity's identification value. Authorization is often confused with authentication, but is very different. Authorization recognizes an entity by a particular value and grants or denies access to that entity based on trust allocations. Authentication verifies an entity is really who they say they are. Unlike authentication, where there may be multiple steps in the process, the authorization model is usually a Boolean process—yes or no.

Strong authorization methods usually involve a value that cannot be spoofed, changed, or forged by another entity. Strong authorization values will ensure that once authorization permissions have been granted, it can only be accessed by the correct entity.

Weaker authorization methods usually involve a value that can be spoofed or forged by another entity. For example, IP addresses can be spoofed, making it a weak authorization parameter. If a web application contains security controls that state a system must contain the source IP of 172.16.11.17, then any attacker can change his IP address and access the protected site. If the authorizing entity grants access to another entity based solely on its IP address, then the authorization parameters should be considered weak. In this example, there is no guarantee that the entity requesting system is authorized to view the projected site since anyone can change their IP address to the required value. Using an IP address for authorization would be similar to using the return address in a postal letter. The return address listed by a sender is not necessarily correct and therefore cannot be trusted. Furthermore, any return address can be written by a sender with any validation of the address.

Authorization methods in iSCSI/Fibre Channel SANs apply to hardware. None of them allow limitations by username, which is a major weakness. The authorization processes in Fibre Channel SANs involve World Wide Names (WWNs). If a node's Host-Bus Adapter (HBA) contains the correct value for its WWN, then the authorizing entity, usually a fibre channel switch, will grant access to the node. There is no secondary check once the WWN is verified since the WWN is the sole value that is queried for authorization. Since WWN are easily modifiable (spoofable), as will be demonstrated later in this book, WWN-based authorization procedures are weak.

Authorization processes in NAS architecture are somewhat similar to SANs. NFS-based NAS architectures usually use an IP address for their authorization value. If the requesting entity contains the correct IP address, then the authorizing entity, usually an NFS NAS device, will grant access to the requester. Similar to WWNs, IP addresses are easily spoofable in IPv4 networks, making them a weak authorization entity.

Unlike NFS NAS architectures, CIFS NAS architectures do not really use authorization methods for granting access. Since authentication is heavily relied upon in CIFS-based NAS architecture, by default, most CIFS NFS devices do not use any authorization process. If the authentication process is subverted in a CIFS NAS device, there is usually no authorization process to ensure the entity should be granted a certain type of access. Nevertheless, there are options in place to add authorization checks in CIFS NAS architectures, but similar to NFS NAS architecture, CIFS NAS architectures also rely on IP addresses, which are easily spoofable and therefore considered a weak authorization procedure.

Finally, the authorization process for iSCSI is also similar to SANs. iSCSI clients contain an iSCSI Qualifier Name (IQN), also referred to as the Initiator Node Name, that is used to authorize client nodes by iSCSI storage devices. Similar to WWNs in fibre channel SANs, IQNs are easily spoofable by iSCSI client drivers. Furthermore, IQNs pass through the network in clear-text, requiring an unauthorized entity to simply sniff an IQN over the network on port 3260 or 3205. After an IQN is sniffed over the network, an attacker can change his existing IQN to the captured IQN and subvert the authorization parameters placed by the iSCSI storage device. Furthermore, most iSCSI device drivers allow the capability to change your IQN right in the software.

AUDITING

Auditing is the process of capturing and retaining events for current and future analysis. The ability to capture and retain event information about architectures, networks, products, and communication—for both security related events and non-security related events—is essential for security awareness and overall stability. Auditing is also a very important security aspect for forensics purposes and incident response, especially where there is a need to retrace possible compromised security involving regulated or confidential data.

While auditing is not the most interesting security aspect, it could be the most important. Without the proper use of auditing and event correlation, key security attacks and unauthorized probes could go undetected. Furthermore, many government regulations require several types of audit logs, causing many storage product vendors to design better logging methods to meet standards.

Without proper use of auditing, attacks will go unnoticed. Unnoticed attacks or security breaches cannot be controlled, fixed, or even evaluated due to the lack of awareness of the issue. This grants a false sense of security to many administrators and engineers, allowing them to think that no security issues have arisen. In fact, many storage administrators may comment that there have not been any security breaches in their storage network. The statement may be true on the documentation part, but the fact is there have been several security breaches due to poor storage security; however, storage networks are not equipped well enough today to detect such attacks.

All components of the storage network must be able to capture and maintain log information, either remotely or locally. This includes networking components, network communication, hosts, storage devices, host adapters, and storage applications. While various components of the storage environment may capture and record log information in different ways, they must have the capability to log pertinent information in the context of security.

Auditing in both SAN and NAS architectures are quite similar; both architectures usually provide device- or application-specific auditing parameters. There is no centralized or consolidated logging infrastructure that falls outside the storage management products used to manage the SAN, such as SANPoint Control, EMC Control Center (ECC), and Computer Associates (CA), which is a significant gap in the industry. While these products, and many more like them, are excellent for managing and administering SAN and NAS architectures, they do not provide an overwhelming amount of options for auditing and tracking of events—especially any events that may relate to security.

It would be fair to say that both SAN and NAS architectures contain only the traditional auditing capabilities for network monitoring and maintenance, such as Simple Network Management Protocol (SNMP), SCSI Enclosure Services (SES Storage Management Initiative Specification (SMI-S). A significant gap needs to be fulfilled due to the absence of security awareness, unauthorized events, or suspicious activities for security management.

INTEGRITY

Integrity is the process of ensuring that an entity can be trusted. Specific to the storage industry, integrity is the process of assuring that data can be trusted and there has not been any unauthorized modification or tampering of the data.

Data integrity in SAN and NAS networks is imperative, to say the least. If any type of data would be classified as corrupt, an entire data store could be deemed as useless or unavailable. As viruses and worms become more complex, a corrupt data store could result in numerous dollars in lost revenue or countless person-hours in data retrieval.

The simplest example of data integrity is hashing. Data hashing has been used in several aspects. The idea behind data hashing is that a hash algorithm is used to create a virtual fingerprint for the piece of data. For example, if a document called "Kusum.txt" existed on your hard drive, a hash could be taken on that file as it stands today. If there were any modifications to Kusum.txt, such as if someone edited the document or added a single character to the document, then the hash would be different because the document, Kusum.txt, has changed.

MD5 (Message Digest 5) and SHA-1 (Secure Hash Algorithm 1) are common hash algorithms that are used for data integrity. MD5 hashes (RFC 1321—www.faqs.org/rfcs/rfc1321.html) and SHA-1 hashes (RFC 3174—www.faqs.org/rfcs/rfc3174.html) are algorithms to verify the data's integrity and to ensure that any data that is presented can be used in a trusted manner.

For example, using a Windows environment, you can download SHA-1.exe from the Internet. The SHA-1.exe utility will take a SHA-1 hash on any file. After you have downloaded SHA-1.exe, make a test file called Kusum.txt. Open the file, type **LYNUS** in the body of the file, and then save and close the file. After you have made the test file, type the following on a command-line client:

```
c:\SHA-1.exe Kusum.txt
```

After you hit Enter, you should see the SHA-1 hash of the file:

```
C1D34418 DE708FFD 6F965CC3 4DACA540 353607FE
```

Now, open Kusum.txt and add the number 1 after the word LYNUS (e.g., LYNUS1) and then save. After you have saved the file, type the same command as done previously to get the SHA-1 hash:

```
C:\SHA-1.exe Kusum.txt
```

After you hit Enter, you should see the SHA-1 hash of the file:

```
AAB6992E F745F11A A0F031ED 2EBA871F 164CBD85
```

Notice now the SHA-1 hash is different due to the fact that the file has been changed. You can now verify the integrity of the file with the SHA-1 hash. For example, for every email attachment you send in clear-text, you could also make an SHA-1 hash of the attachment to make sure it has not been tampered with in transit. There are many utilities to do this for you, such as PGP (Pretty Good Privacy), located at www.pgp.com.

In addition to MD5 and SHA-1 hashing, IPSec (IP Security) can be used. The Authentication Header (AH) in IPSec is used for the hashing of packets as they traverse a network. AH is a great option when encrypting the data cannot be completed due to performance reasons, but the integrity of the data needs to be verified. While this does not prevent unauthorized users from viewing the data, it does allow authorized users to verify that the data has not been tampered with.

The way integrity is used for data in SAN and NAS architectures will determine how healthy a storage network will be. When data resides in the SAN or NAS network, there must be methods to ensure that the data's integrity has not been compromised. There are several emerging methods and technologies to complete this; however, none of them are standard. Several major NAS organizations, such as EMC and NetApp, are implementing solutions that do check for data integrity using propriety and industry standard hashed algorithms. In the SAN industry, there are not as many options, since many of the SAN data is actually block data not at the file level. Nevertheless, certain organizations, such as NeoScale and Decru, are developing solutions to provide more integrity checking processes in SAN architectures.

ENCRYPTION

Encryption is the ability to obfuscate an entity, which is usually some type of data. Encryption is often used to disguise information in order to protect it from unauthorized presentation, access, or modification.

Encryption can be used in two aspects: in-line encryption (over-the-wire encryption) and encryption of data on a disk (at-rest encryption). Both types of encryption play an integral role in SAN and NAS security aspects.

The use of encryption in NAS architectures varies between in-line and at-rest encryption. In-line encryption standards such as IPSec can be commonly used to protect storage data from unauthorized users over a public or untrusted network, such as the

Internet, DMZ, internal corporate network, or Extranet. For example, if NAS filers are used for Human Resources (HR) data, it would be wise to use encryption from the HR end users accessing the data to the HR NAS filers over the corporate public network. At-rest encryption in NAS architectures would not encrypt the data over the wire, but would contain encrypted payload, allowing the data transmitted to be already encrypted from the disk. However, the at-rest encryption would normally take place from the NAS device to tape device or from an operating system to the NAS device. Either method still exposes the data from the desktop/laptop PC to the NAS device, where most attackers target systems.

A strong example of the need for encryption is the use of consolidated data stores. If a NAS device holds data for the entire organization, such as HR, IT, Engineering, and Finance, there may be unauthorized administrators able to view all the data on the NAS device. It may be cost prohibitive to purchase a separate NAS device for each department, but also a security risk to hold all types of information on a single NAS system. If the data has been encrypted before it reaches the NAS filer (between the server and the NAS device), then this risk is mitigated since the data sitting on the NAS disk is available to everyone, but not useable/readable to everyone. Encrypted data does not protect against denial-of-service (DOS) attacks, allowing malicious users to destroy encrypted data without the need to view its contents.

The use of encryption in SANs is different than NAS due to the use of Fibre Channel (FC) or iSCSI communication with block data as opposed to file-level data. The need for the encryption in SANs is rising fast. For example, many SAN architectures need to have redundant locations for business continuity and disaster recovery. While many SAN architectures use backbone networks do create redundant SANs datacenters, many of the backbones are not private but use public infrastructures. Although there is a small attack surface, the fact that data is transmitted in the clear across a public backbone is high-risk. Similarly, data at-rest encryption is very important in SAN architectures. Many SANs are backed up to tape using third-party storage companies and third-party courier services, all of which are not authorized to view the data they control. If the SAN is holding data for all backup systems within the company and the data has not been encrypted at-rest, the possibility of an unauthorized user gaining access to data is high (described further in Chapter 9 "Securing Fibre Channel SANs"). Conversely, if the data at-rest is encrypted, the attack possibilities for the unauthorized user are significantly more difficult.

The use of encryption is highly dependent on how and where it has been deployed. Due to the fact that most storage networks are becoming more widely deployed throughout the corporate network, encryption will become a very popular aspect in securing storage in the short-term.

AVAILABILITY

Availability is simply the process of making data accessible in a secure manner. Availability allows data that is stored in a SAN and NAS to be available to authorized end users, applications, operating systems (servers), or network devices when requested.

Often, availability is not commonly thought of as a security aspect; however, consider the fact that if a denial-of-service attack was successful, the availability of any entity, including any Oracle databases and Exchange servers, would be at risk. Unlike many other entities in a data center, any attack that affects availability of the storage network could be the most devastating attack on a SAN or NAS and any server they are connected to. The problem gets amplified with the fact that denial-of-service attacks are easy to write, deploy, and execute on most storage targets, despite the fact that they may not give an attacker any type of remote control.

In the security industry, a denial-of-service attack is, quite frankly, amateur hour. Most denial-of-service attacks don't compromise any systems, don't gain access to data, and don't reveal any type of sensitive data that could be used to escalate another attack. That is not to say that denial-of-service attacks are not important; many denial-of-service attacks can reveal vulnerabilities in network devices and applications that are fairly significant (such as the SQL Slammer worm of 2002). The fact that denial-of-service attacks don't result in a remote root compromise give them a lot less attention than other possible security attacks. Nevertheless, a denial-of-service attack in a SAN or NAS network, and each server that is connected to the storage network, is not only highly sensitive and important, but denial-of-service attacks are probably the most devastating type of attack in a storage network.

The idea of a SAN or NAS storage system being vulnerable to a denial-of-service attack is possibly the worst attack that could happen in a storage network (maybe even greater than data compromise for some storage administrators). Availability of SAN and NAS networks and connected servers is one of the most crucial aspects of securing storage. If the SAN or NAS architecture is unavailable, how much money would that cost an organization? How much downtime would that cause end-users and executive officers? How much revenue would that translate to an organization if email and all databases were unavailable for an hour, a day, or even a week?

Making storage networks available and functional are the two most dominant requirements for many storage administrators. Security is often regarded as data compromise, but with SAN and NAS architectures, administrators should start thinking of security as data availability during sensitive attacks, unforeseen natural disasters, and business continuity planning.

STORAGE ATTACKS—SCENARIOS

In order to fully understand the importance of securing storage, a discussion of the SAN and NAS attacks needs to take place. A thorough description of several different SAN and NAS attacks occur throughout the book; it is imperative to answer the questions that many storage administrators have about storage security threats. A few questions about these attacks are as follows:

- What are the attacks against the storage network?
- What is the likelihood that the real attacks against storage networks will succeed?
- What are the points of vulnerability in my storage network?

The next sections will address these two primary questions about storage attacks:

- What are the attacks against a storage network?
- Storage Area Network (SAN) attacks

The following is a list of the SAN attacks that can be used by unauthorized internal and external attackers. All attacks will be discussed further in Chapters 2 through 4 in this book.

- **World Wide Name (WWN) spoofing**—World Wide Name spoofing is the act of bypassing authorization methods in a SAN. Many SANs allocate data resources based on a node's WWN. If an attacker spoofs (changes) a WWN of an HBA to the WWN of another authorized HBA (which is quite easy), data allocated to the authorized HBA will be granted to the unauthorized attacker.
- **Name server pollution**—Name server pollution is the process of corrupting the name server information on a Fibre Channel switch during a fabric PLOGI (Port Login) by a client node to a SAN fabric. An attacker can spoof (change) his 24-bit address and correlated valid WWNs to invalid 24-bit addresses. Once the name server information is polluted, frames can be sent to an unauthorized entity.
- **Session hijacking**—Session hijacking is the act of intercepting Fibre Channel sessions between two trusting entities by guessing the predictable sequence control number (SEQ_CNT) and static sequence ID (SEQ_ID) of a Fibre Channel frame that controls the session. Once an unauthorized user has hijacked the session, sessions (such as management sessions) can be controlled from an unauthorized resource.

- **Man-in-the-Middle**—A Man-in-the-Middle is the act of redirecting frames from an authorized node to an unauthorized node with the use of name server pollution. Once the name server has been corrupted, the key to send frames to an unauthorized entity (the node in the middle) would be possible.

- **Zone hopping**—Zone hopping is the act of hopping across switch zones that allow a node to access another zone to which they should not have access. This is possible by using route-based attacks and WWN spoofing.

- **E-port replication**—E-port replication is the act of a single Fibre Channel switch transferring all fabric information—such as name server information, router information, and zone information—to another switch without any type of authentication or authorization process by connecting two e-ports together.

- **LUN mask subversion**—LUN (Logical Unit Number) subversion is the act of undermining the masking properties that have been implemented on a particular node by spoofing (changing) a node's WWN or simply changing LUN masking properties on the management client, which does not require authentication.

- **Management**—Management attacks on SAN devices can vary between several items; most notably, attacks can web (HTTP) management consoles on SAN switches. These attacks use brute force and often leak a tremendous amount of information about the SAN fabric without any authentication required.

- **F-port replication**—F-port replication occurs when an attacker can copy all the data from one host port to another host port that he or she controls using intelligent switch features, which does not required authentication.

NETWORK ATTACHED STORAGE (NAS) ATTACKS

The following is a list of the NAS attacks that can be used by unauthorized internal and external attackers. All attacks will be discussed further in Chapters 5 through 7 of this book. Unlike SAN attacks, NAS attacks are divided into two categories: CIFS (Common Internet File System), which is primarily used in Windows environments; and NFS (Network File System), which is commonly used in UNIX environments.

COMMON INTERNET FILE SYSTEM (CIFS) ATTACKS

The following is a list of the CIFS attacks that can be used by unauthorized internal and external attackers.

- **CIFS enumeration**—CIFS enumeration is the ability to enumerate sensitive information from a NAS device, such as usernames, groups, shares, passwords authentication methods, services, and so on. This type of information leakage significantly helps an attacker gain access to a NAS system.

- **CIFS share-level passwords**—Share-level passwords attacks are brute-force attacks against a single password that it used to protect an entire share for a NAS device. Additionally, any implementation of a share-level password uses plain-text passwords, which can be sniffed over any network connection.

- **CIFS LANMAN and NTLM**—LANMAN and NTLM password hashes are susceptible to several types of attacks, including brute-forcing, password decryption, and replay attacks.

- **CIFS Kerberos**—Kerberos tickets can also be compromised and allow unauthorized access to NAS devices. The use of Kerberos tickets and Windows CIFS Active Directory architecture could allow passwords to be compromised.

NETWORK FILE SYSTEM (NFS) ATTACKS

The following is a list of the NFS attacks that can be used by unauthorized internal and external attackers.

- **Authorization**—NFS uses an exports file, located in /etc/exports, to determine which hosts are authorized to attempt to login. The contents of the exports file can be an IP address, an IP address range, a hostname, a hostname variable, or an IP address with variables. The attack with NFS authorization is not so much on the protocol itself, but an attack on IPv4. Because it is relatively easy to spoof an IP address or hostname in IPv4, combined with the fact that NFS may solely rely on hostname or IP address for authorization, this makes the process of subverting the authorization controls that NFS-enabled devices hold relatively easy.

- **Authentication**—NFS exports can be enumerated fairly easy and the UID/GIDs can be subverted. Once NFS exports are enumerated, an attacker can change their UID and GID on their own system to match the UID/GID from the NAS device. Once the mount command is made with the change UID/GIDs, access is granted to the unauthorized user.

- **Encryption**—Because many NFS implementations use the clear-text version of NFS, all communication between two legitimate NFS devices can be sniffed, monitored, and possibly modified by a passive third-party attacker.

- **Access controls**—This NFS attack exposes NFS directories to unauthorized users by using the UID and GID values for access control instead of some type of authentication process.

INTERNET SCSI (ISCSI) ATTACKS

The following is a list of the iSCSI attacks that can be used by unauthorized internal and external attackers.

- **iSCSI Qualifier Name (IQN) spoofing**—iSCSI Qualifier Name spoofing is the act of bypassing authorization methods in an iSCSI storage network. iSCSI networks allocate data resources based on a node's IQN (also referred to as the Initiator Node Name). If an attacker spoofs (changes) an IQN, which can be sniffed over the network in clear-text on ports 3260 and 3205, to the IQN of another authorized iSCSI adapter, data allocated to the authorized node will be granted to the unauthorized attacker.

- **Authentication**—Authentication is optional in iSCSI storage networks. If iSCSI authentication is disabled, which is the default, then there is no need to perform an attack. If iSCSI authentication is enabled, it uses CHAP for its authentication method. CHAP is known to have security weaknesses associated with it, all of which can be performed in an iSCSI network.

- **CHAP offline password brute forcing**—Offline brute-forcing attacks involve an attacker sniffing iSCSI communication, including the CHAP challenge, ID, and Hash, which is quite simple since they traverse the network in clear-text. Once captured, an attacker can attempt hundreds or thousands of words until the password is identified. The attack is offline, allowing the attacker to continue the brute-forcing indefinitely until most, if not all, weak dictionary passwords or moderately complex passwords are cracked.

- **CHAP message reflection**—Message reflection attacks involve an attacker submitting the message challenge and ID received from one connection back to the iSCSI target on a second connection. If the iSCSI target responds to the challenge and ID with a message hash, the attacker can present the hash back to the target on the first connection and get authenticated without knowing the password.

- **CHAP username sniffing**—CHAP authentication sends usernames in clear-text over the network, which can be sniffed by an attacker and used in a brute-force password attack. While a client's password is encrypted with a random key from the server, the server sends the key to the user once it receives an authentication request, which has the username in the clear.

- **Authorization**—Authorization is required in iSCSI networks, but the ability to brute force IQN is not difficult. For example, the only unknown variable of an IQN is the end string. As such, the default IQN for Microsoft's, Cisco's, and IBM's IQNs are iqn.1991-05.com.microsoft:HOSTNAME, iqn.1987-05.com.cisco:xxxxxx, and iqn.1992-08.com.ibm:xxxxxx, respectively. An attacker would just have to brute force a hostname, if using a Microsoft iSCSI client, or brute force the last six characters, if using a Cisco or IBM client. Furthermore, all IQNs traverse the network in clear-text, so many times brute forcing will not be necessary.

- **Encryption**—iSCSI provides the ability to use IPSec to encrypt communication from an iSCSI client to an iSCSI device. There are no weaknesses associated with IPSec encryption in iSCSI networks. The issue is that IPSec is an optional component that is disabled by default. Additionally, the fact that the use of IPSec will cause performance penalties to the network usually means it won't be turned on very often.

- **Management**— Management attacks on iSCSI devices can vary between several items; most notably, attacks can web (HTTP) management consoles. These attacks use brute force and often leak a tremendous amount of information about the iSCSI network without any authentication required.

WHAT ARE THE ATTACK SURFACES (ENTRY POINTS) OF MY STORAGE NETWORK?

SAN

- Any operating system that has an IP connection (NIC) and a Fibre Channel connection (HBA) can be a gateway to the FC SAN.
- If any server has been infected with a virus, worm, or Trojan, then it can also be compromised by an attacker and be used as the gateway into the SAN.

- Any management server (desktop that runs Vertias, EMC, or CA software) can be used to attack the SAN, which usually sits on the insecure internal network.
- Ethernet interfaces on all fibre channel switches are attack entry points for SAN enumeration.
- Any application that uses systems connected to the SAN can be used to target SAN data.

iSCSI SANs or IP NAS

- Any IP network connection, either external (Internet, business extranets, wireless networks, etc) or any segment inside the internal network.
- An iSCSI target or IP NAS appliance is just as accessible as any desktop, laptop, network device, or server operating system on the IP network.

QUESTIONS FROM A SAN ADMINISTRATOR

Securing storage is a new topic for many SAN administrators; therefore, it is important to discuss the common questions about the topic. Following are some example questions from actual SAN administrators. The answers are meant to provide specific details about each topic:

1. **Isn't SAN security really about physical security? Wouldn't someone have to phys-ically access a SAN in order to perform any attacks? How would they even access the Fibre Channel connections?**

   SAN security is definitely not about physical security. SANs are exposed to untrusted IP networks of all types, such as the internal network (corporate network), a DMZ, a business partner network, a backup network, and even a management station. Any insecure SAN component, such as a server with an HBA or a Fibre Channel switch with the IP interface, that is connected to an untrusted network can be the gateway to the SAN. The key issue is if the security of the Windows or UNIX server is strong enough to protect the SAN. An organization should always ensure that terabytes of data do not solely rely on an operating systems' security.

2. **Most people are not aware of Fibre Channel, right? While there may be security issues with a Fibre Channel SAN, how many individuals are actually capable of exploiting them?**

   Security by obscurity never stands the test of time—just ask application developers in the Northeast. For example, let's say a home's front door is unlocked, but it is one of 30 homes in a neighborhood. Does the fact that there are several houses in a neighborhood make the home any more secure? No. The house is insecure as soon as the front door is left unlocked. The idea of leaving a house unlocked because it is one of 30 houses in a neighborhood makes it only statistically harder to find. There is no denying why storage administrators assume that security issues are an IP issue due to the fact that IP security issues are more susceptible to attack than Fibre Channel networks. Nevertheless, when addressing entities such as intellectual property, propriety information, trade secrets, and governmental regulations (GLBA, SB1386, Sarbanes-Oxley, HIPAA, SEC Rule 17a4), all aspects of data security must be addressed. Many times, invalid or unconfirmed assumptions, especially ones that pertain to security by obscurity, are the entities targeted by attackers.

3. **We have firewalls, router ACLs, and encryption devices on our IP network, so wouldn't it be virtually impossible for a hacker to get into our SAN?**

   Probably not, but it depends on your architecture. SANs often bridge several security zones (DMZ, internal, application, and database networks) that are segmented on the IP network. Without some type of segmentation on the Fibre Channel network, the segmentation on the IP network could be negated, allowing a single compromised server to open the gateway to the SAN. If you have any server accessible from the
   outside Internet, such a web server in a DMZ or a management server with Windows terminal services, then a single application or brute-force attack could render all your firewalls, ACLs, and encryption devices useless. Additionally, external attackers are not the only issue; an unauthorized person may be able to attack the storage network, such as internal employees and VPN users.

4. **What tool(s) would a hacker need in order to gather information about the SAN connections that our servers have?**

   The tools would be the native management tools provided by vendors. When doing a SAN assessment, you can use a combination of vendor tools, such as ECC, SANPoint, and Emulex HBA software drive toolkit. All three of these applications have unauthenticated query commands that can enumerate the SAN and its nodes with ease. From the IP perspective, you can use tools to enumerate the IP interface on FC switches, such as SNMP tools (GetIF), a web-admin tool for web administration of FC switches (Grinder), IP or FC sniffers such as Ethereal, and many more. The key here is to compromise any server (W2K or Solaris) that has an HBA. If that is not possible, then find the IP interfaces to any SAN-connected device—and there are plenty.

5. Once that information is gathered, what software would the hacker use to manipulate the SAN?

The same from number 4.You can use the management software itself on a switch. For example, a compromised Brocade switch can change the zoning information, which allows an unauthorized host to have access to several data LUNs in the SAN.

6. Wouldn't the hacker need to use expensive proprietary software specific to a vendor's SAN (such as EMC or Hitachi) in order to make changes?

Yes and no. Any storage software can talk FC, right? The cost of the software is not the issue, since copies are easy (somewhat) to come by. Also, defense is not necessarily defending against hackers, but unauthorized users. The unauthorized user could be an internal employee who can access all that software and management consoles quite easily. If the unauthorized employee decides to be curious and get more information than he should, the organization could be liable for potential Sarbanes-Oxley, HIPAA, SB1386, or GLBA issues.

7. We have web servers and database servers that are in the DMZ and connected to a SAN, as well as internal servers connected to the same SAN. Is this an issue?

Yes, this is an issue. Any segmentation you have on your IP network, such as firewalls and router ACLs separating your DMZ from your internal network, is virtually negated because the SAN is connecting all the servers to one big flat fabric. If proper zoning, LUN masking, separate fabrics, zone-member allocation, port locking, and so on is not used, then potentially one compromised web server can be a gateway to the SAN.

8. The prevailing attitude among the IT network administrators is that the data in the SAN is safe because it is not going across as IP traffic, the servers' data are safe because they are connected by Fibre Channel, and individual data in the SAN can only be seen by the individual server that it is attached to. For these reasons, hackers could only get to one server's data if they somehow got through to it, right?

If any server connected to the SAN has never been infected with a virus, then this perspective would be correct. However, if any operating system that is connected to the SAN has ever been infected with a virus, worm, or Trojan, then an attacker can do the same. For example, if a web server in your DMZ was compromised and it is connected to the SAN, then an attacker can now directly attack the SAN. WWN spoofing is the simplest and easiest attack in a SAN at this point. Once the attacker has enumerated all the WWNs in the SAN with any HBA software, he can change the node WWN and hop across zones.

9. **What advice can you offer on setting up security for SANs in a DMZ?**

A DMZ using SANs needs to be isolated, separate fabrics if possible. If separate fabrics are not possible, ensure that hard zoning, port-based zone allocation, port locking, port-type locking, and fabric membership authorization are used. If you are using Cisco's MDS switches, use their VSAN technologies.

10. **What are some proper white-hat penetration tests to identify vulnerabilities in a SAN?**

Here are some steps:

1. Use HBA driver software to enumerate all the WWNs in the SAN.
2. Certain FC switches will display all WWNs by simply pointing a browser to the IP address of the switch.
3. Change (spoof) the node WWN to a WWN attached to a LUN that you wish to access.
4. Reboot your system or reinitialize your software.
5. Once you reboot/reinitialize, you will have access to data in a different LUN in an unauthorized manner.

BE CAREFUL—DO NOT PERFORM THIS TEST IN A PRODUCTION ENVIRONMENT.

This attack may damage your data, creating a denial-of-service attack also.

QUESTIONS FROM A **NAS** ADMINISTRATOR

Similar to the questions from a SAN administrator, NAS security also needs to be addressed. The following are questions that many NAS administrators may be asking:

1. **Don't most attacks in IP concern operating systems and not network devices, such as a NAS storage device?**

   No. Most NAS devices are running some type of UNIX-based operating systems that may be vulnerable to buffer overflow attacks, just like any operating system. While many of these devices contain a stripped-down operating system (some form of Linux), the dangerous services, such as SNMP, are always on. Furthermore, many of the devices support either NFS or CIFS, making the storage devices and the data they contain susceptible to all weaknesses in the CIFS and NFS protocols.

2. **We have firewalls, router ACLs, and encryption devices on our front-end IP network, so wouldn't it be virtually impossible for a hacker to get into our NAS storage system?**

   Probably not. NAS storage systems are often connected together by internal and back-end networks. NAS devices connected to internal networks can be accessed by VPN users, Trojans, viruses, worms, contractors, consultants, and so on. NAS devices connected to backup storage networks usually bridge several security zones (DMZ, internal, application, and database networks) and do not contain firewalls or ACLs for segmentation. While operating systems in a DMZ and internal network are separated by a firewall, they also contain another interface that connects them directly to a storage network. Without some type of segmentation on the storage network (often called the backup network), the segmentation on the front-end IP network will be negated.

3. **Are there actually any tools that a hacker could use in order to gather information about the NAS connections that our servers have?**

   There are plenty of tools. Most of the tools are made for operating systems running UNIX or Windows, since the tools target protocols, such as CIFS and NFS. For example, tools such as showmount, winfo, GetIF, mount, net use, and enum can all be used to attack a NAS device.

4. **What types of attacks could actually affect the storage network?**

   Authentication, authorization, and encryption weaknesses—such as Kerberos, NFS UID/GIDs, CIFS LANMAN hashes, weak passwords (brute-force attacks), web server management, and sniffing—could all be exploited on a NAS device.

5. **Wouldn't a hacker need a significant amount of information to actually attack my NAS storage architecture?**

   Security by obscurity never works. Critical SNMP issues, such as the one from June 2002, would leave every device vulnerable to a remote compromise. A hacker would not need to know anything but the fact that SNMP services have been enabled by the NAS device, which is easily enumerated by a port scanner on port 161.

6. **We have web servers and database servers that are in the DMZ and connected to several NAS devices shared internally. Are we vulnerable?**

   Yes. Any segmentation you have on your front-end IP network, such as firewalls and router ACLs, separating your DMZ from your internal network, is virtually negated with the back-end connections. If a web server is compromised, the attacker could use the back-end storage network to attack all devices without filters. Ensure that back-end networks are using some type of VLAN or segmentation technology to remain consistent with the front-end network's security.

7. **The prevailing attitude among the storage administrators is that security is not our problem, but rather a perimeter defense issue. Why do you say it is not?**

   If any server that is connected to the internal network has never been infected with a virus, worm, or Trojan, then this perspective is correct. However, if any internal operating system has ever been infected with a virus, worm, or Trojan, then an attacker can also exploit the machine. (If the SQL slammer worm infected your databases, your storage devices are probably vulnerable to the next generation of worms targeting storage devices and applications.) Many servers, including ones on the perimeter (web servers and database servers), partner networks (servers running SAP and Bann software), and management servers (backup servers) are often either directly connected to the storage network or also have network access to it, allowing attackers to target the storage systems. There is more data to be compromised in a storage device than 20 different servers and workstations. Furthermore, CIFS shares and NFS mounts are usually easier attack targets because authentication is often not required in order to mount data or uses a weak authentication protocol (e.g. NTLM).

8. **What advice can you offer on setting up security for NAS devices in a DMZ?**

   DMZs connected to back-end NAS devices need to be isolated using any type of technology for segmentation, such as Cisco's VLAN technology. VLANs can be used to segment servers into private isolated VLANs for each individual port or private community VLANs for each group of ports.

9. **What are some proper white-hat penetration tests to identify vulnerabilities in a NAS?**

   1. Download a tool called Winfo, written by Arne Vindstrom (www.ntsecurity.nu) that can enumerate CIFS share points, services, accounts, and groups on any servers running CIFS, including NAS devices.

   2. Run the tool against a NAS device running CIFS, which will produce usernames and shares of the device.

   3. Use the windows `net use` command to connect to the NAS share with a null username and null password:

```
net use * \\dns.nas.device\sharename "" /user:""
```

   You will now have an unauthenticated connection to the NAS share. For more manual tests, refer to Chapters 5, 6, and 7.

QUESTIONS FROM AN iSCSI ADMINISTRATOR

1. **Isn't iSCSI already secure?**

   IPSec is a good thing, but it is not a magic band-aid that solves all of iSCSI's security problems. There is no question that IPSec will strengthen iSCSI storage networks, but there is also no question that it will often not be used due to the performance penalties it will add and the administrative overhead of deploying shared secrets across hundreds of iSCSI targets and initiators. Performance demands will always beat security requirements, which is why IPsec will not be enabled as much as people would like it to be.

2. **Won't the availability of authentication significantly improve iSCSI's security?**

   CHAP authentication does add significantly to iSCSI security; however, CHAP authentication is probably the weakest of the three non-FC storage technologies (NFS, CIFS, and iSCS). CHAP is and has been vulnerable to several attacks for many years before it was chosen by iSCSI, such as username sniffing, offline password brute-forcing, and message reflection attacks (to name a few). Additionally, authentication is optional—not required. The fact that authentication is optional to protect several hundred terabytes of data is a ridiculous notion. An end user or administrator would not choose to have authentication optional for their own online banking system or even a database inside the network; therefore, there are no reasons for authentication to be optional for large amounts of storage data.

3. **My network is protected by firewalls, so my iSCSI storage network is protected, right?**

   No. iSCSI is not protected by firewalls. In fact, storage has never been protected by firewalls; however, due to the fact that any entity connected to an IP network, such as the internal network or even the Internet, is able to connect to large amounts of iSCSI storage from any laptop, desktop, or server, iSCSI needs to protect itself. Additionally, many storage architectures show designs using a three-tier model, where a client connected to a server, the server is connected to a switch, and the switch is connected to an iSCSI storage device. Although the design is optional, there is nothing to prevent a client from connecting directly to an iSCSI storage device, whether or not it is authorized. The fact is that any client, laptop, or desktop, can connect directly to an iSCSI storage device without any server in-between, which allows any node connected to the internal network as a possible attacker. In fact, if you ever had a virus on your desktop, then you know that any firewall will protect you. Imagine the same thing but the virus spreading to the iSCSI drive install of your local hard drive.

4. **Isn't iSCSI security enforced by Initiator node names and LUN groups?**

   No. iSCSI does require authorization, which is the only type of security it requires, by the use of Initiator Node Names and LUN groups. However, this form of authorization is spoofable, which means that any node on the IP network can spoof another authorized Initiator Node Name and get access. This would be similar to using your phone number as your ATM pin number. Your phone number is unique, but easy to get from a variety of places. Additionally, iSCSI communication is sniffable, allowing any attacker to sniff Initiator Node Names of the network, which make them very easy to capture and spoof. The fact that authorization for iSCSI storage is spoofable, uses clear-text communication (sniffable), and is the only thing required to get LUN access, makes the only security enforced on iSCSI storage quite weak.

SUMMARY

The tip of the iceberg for storage and security was covered in this chapter. Discussions about the key aspects about security—such as authentication, authorization, auditing, encryption, integrity, and availability—were the primary security areas covered.

The next several sections of this chapter addressed many of the common questions from both SAN and NAS administrators. Many of the questions are not out of doubt or disagreement with security issues in storage, but rather explain the pertinent issues of security.

When deciding whether SAN and NAS security is important for your organization, the idea of data classification is very important. Without fully knowing the value of any stored data, both in terms of financial loss or organization threat, it is a very difficult task to address the issues of storage security. Risk management and security go hand-in-hand, which starts with understanding what type of data you are willing to lose and what type of data would cripple your organization.

From this point forward, the reader should have a high-level understanding of the purpose of security and SAN and NAS architectures; however, the rest of the chapters provide more details on the aspects of security, such as attacks and practical defenses.

PART I
SAN Security

SANs: Fibre Channel Security

The emergence of SAN technology combined with data protection, privacy, and regulatory concerns has made storage security an important topic. SAN security risks are often misunderstood and/or underestimated. Furthermore, the critical issues associated with SANs, combined with the lack of communication concerning defenses, has created a security gap in storage.

The purpose of this chapter is to discuss Fibre Channel SAN security risks (iSCSI security risks will be discussed in Chapter 8). Each risk will be described and then fully discussed to allow organizations to make decisions based on their SAN data, its implementation, and the organization's risk-tolerance level.

Chapter 2 is the first of three chapters (Chapters 2, 3, and 4) where SAN security risks and the correlating attacks will be discussed. After a detailed description of the security risks, we discuss the details of the SAN attacks. Several sections in the next three chapters will be followed by a self-assessment exercise, allowing administrators to test their own exposures, vulnerabilities, and exploits.

The following topics are the primary focus of this chapter:

- SAN risks
- Risks of Fibre Channel
- Fibre Channel frame weaknesses (session hijacking)
- Fibre Channel address weaknesses (Man-in-the-Middle attacks)

SAN RISKS

In order to discuss the risks in SAN architectures, we must evaluate it on the six areas of security discussed in Chapter 1, "Introduction to Storage Security." Table 2.1 lists each of the sections, as well as their security presence in SANs.

Table 2.1   SAN Risk and Security

Security	SAN Risk
Authentication	Authentication aspects in most SAN environments do not exist. Fibre Channel Authentication Protocol (FCAP), DH-CHAP (Diffie-Hielman CHAP), and Fibre Channel Security Protocol (FC-SP) have emerged to fulfill a significant gap for authentication; however, most SANs are designed with the assumption that authentication has taken place elsewhere in the architecture. For example, organizations often assume authentication occurring at file/record layers (databases) should be enough, which ignores network authentication at lower network levels. This would be similar to requiring authentication on a web application but not requiring authentication for a telnet or SSH connection to the web server. In both scenarios, data can be compromised fully.
	Authentication is indirectly available through some of the applications that have access to the SAN. Management applications, which can be used to administer storage data, usually require some type of username and password.
	CT Authentication, DH-CHAP, FCAP, and FC-SP, as well as some other authentication modules, have been developed to authenticate node to node, node to switch, and switch to switch (discussed further in Chapter 9, "Securing Fibre Channel SANs").
Authorization	Authorization parameters are usually provided with World Wide Names (WWNs) from the Fibre Channel host bus adapters. WWNs can be port WWNs, which identify the port, or node WWNs, which identify the node on the fabric.
Encryption	Encryption aspects in most SAN environments do not exist unless some third-party at-rest encryption device is used. Natively, Fibre Channel does not use any encryption in any of its layers (layer 0 thru layer 4).
Auditing	Auditing aspects in most SANs are enabled only at the device or application level, such as a Fibre Channel switch or a management application. There is error management via the fabric; however, nothing for typical security auditing.
Integrity	There are currently no native methods for integrity checking in Fibre Channel frames.
Availability	Availability or Quality of Service (QoS) is indirectly available in layer 2 Fibre Channel frames in the Error Control fields of the frame. This aspect provides more QoS aspects than data availability. Availability is arguably the most important aspect of SAN security. If the storage data becomes unavailable, networks as well as applications melt down quickly.

RISKS OF FIBRE CHANNEL

Risks in Fibre Channel? There are no risks in Fibre Channel, right? Wrong. The Fibre Channel communications medium is absent of several entities that are required for secure transmission. Several of the weaknesses are similar to the weaknesses in IP version 4 (IPv4) and have been repeated in Fibre Channel. This section discusses the following topics:

- Description of Fibre Channel
- Clear-text communication

DESCRIPTION OF FIBRE CHANNEL

In order to understand the security issues with Fibre Channel SANs, we should discuss the architecture of Fibre Channel communications. Fibre Channel uses frames between one node to the other (similar to how IP networks use packets). Each frame contains five layers. The layers within each frame work with the layer below and the layer above to provide different functions within a Fibre Channel topology. Most SANs use either a switched Fibre Channel topology, similar to what we use in an IP-enabled switch network, or a Fibre Channel arbitrated loop (FC-AL). In either topology, each layer performs a specific function depending on the architecture that has been deployed. The five different layers of Fibre Channel frames are as follows:

- Upper Layer Protocol Mapping—FC Layer 4
- Common Services Layer—FC Layer 3
- Signaling/Framing Layer—FC Layer 2
- Transmission Layer—FC Layer 1
- Physical Layer—FC Layer 0

Similar to an IP network, Fibre Channel frames work from the physical layer, layer 0, to the upper layers. The similarities of the two communication methods primarily end at the physical layer; however, they do share similar security weaknesses and both have absent security controls. Several IP weaknesses have translated to vulnerabilities and exploits. Unfortunately, several of these attack types are also available in Fibre Channel frames. The weaknesses in Fibre Channel frames specifically target Fibre Channel layer 2, known as the framing/flow control layer (layer 2 in Fibre Channel and the Data/Networking (layer 2/layer 3) layer in an IP packet). The similarities are close in terms of security weaknesses and the lack of authentication, authorization, integrity, and encryption. Figure 2.1 shows the five different layers of a Fibre Channel frame.

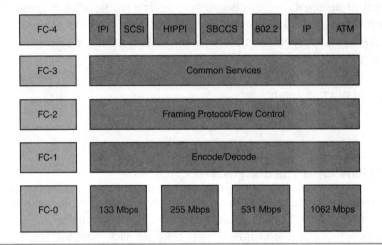

Figure 2.1 Five layers of a Fibre Channel frame.

Fibre Channel layer 2, the Framing Protocol/Flow Control layer, is the primary target when addressing frame security weaknesses. Fibre Channel layer 2 contains the header information for each frame. The header information is the location of several security weaknesses. The contents of the header include a 24-bit address (also known as the port ID) of the source node, the 24-bit address of the destination node, the sequence control number, the sequence identification number, and the exchange information. The following entities are located within the frame header:

- **Source Address (S_ID)**—A 24-bit fabric address used to identify the source address when routing frames.
- **Destination Address (D_ID)**—A 24-bit fabric address used to identify the destination address when routing frames.
- **Sequence ID (SEQ_ID)**—A static number transmitted with each frame in a sequence that identifies the frame as part of a session. Each frame in the same session has the same sequence ID.
- **Sequence Count (SEQ_CNT)**—A number that identifies individual frames within a sequence. For each frame transmitted in a sequence, SEQ_CNT is incremented by 1, allowing the frames to be arranged in the correct order.

- **Exchange ID**—Information that specifies how many frames a node can accept at one time. This information is passed from one node to another.
- **Originator Exchange ID (OX_ID)**—The exchange information of the sender.
- **Recipient Exchange ID (RX_ID)**—The exchange information of the receiver.
- **Type**—The Upper Layer Protocol byte section.
- **Routing Control (R_CTL)**—Contains information such as the routing bits, which contain data values, and the information category, which tells the receiver what type of data is contained in the frame.

Each node on a SAN fabric has a 24-bit fabric address that is used for a variety of things, including routing and name server information. (Note: Do not confuse the 24-bit fabric address with the 64-bit WWN address from the HBA.) Similar to how an IP packet is used to route packets, the 24-bit address is used to route frames from one node to the other. Figure 2.2 shows an example of the header information in Fibre Channel layer 2.

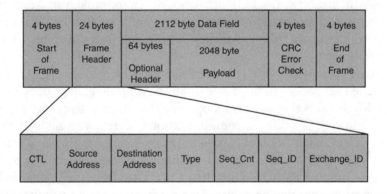

Figure 2.2   Fibre Channel layer 2.

CLEAR-TEXT COMMUNICATION

Fibre Channel communication is clear-text. The lack of security built into the different layers of Fibre Channel frames combined with the fact that it is clear-text allows for certain security threats to be very successful.

The lack of encryption at the frame level is not a significant negative issue, considering the amount of performance impact the storage network would have if all frames were encrypted. Furthermore, sniffing is a difficult task in a Fibre Channel SAN since it can only take place if a hardware device is connected to a node in the SAN or if a Cisco MDS switch is comprised and configured to send traffic remotely to the software only sniffer called Ethereal. Nevertheless, the lack of data obfuscation that contains sensitive information can allow unauthorized users to view information that is required to complete an attack. In fact, a key starting point for successful attackers is the ability to sniff clear-text communication, which can be conducted with any traffic analyzer.

Clear-text communication can be viewed as the Achilles' heel of data networks. It satisfies the enormous performance and capacity issues, but it also exposes untrusted entities to sensitive information, including SAN information. For example, clear-text protocols in IP networks, such as Rsh, Rsysnc, Rlogin, FTP, Telnet, SNMP, POP3, SMTP, ARP, and even iSCSI, allow many IP risks and attacks to either be possible or escalated. The fact that sensitive information, such as usernames/password, community strings, message challenges/hashes, and/or route information, traverse clear-text communication mediums allow untrusted users to gain sensitive information without doing anything but tapping the connection.

Many IPv4 administrators overlook clear-text communication due to the false sense of security of switched networks. In IP networks, switch technology makes it more difficult to sniff network communication; however, many attacks, such as the Man-in-the-Middle (MITM) attack, can subvert switched networking, including Fibre Channel switched networking.

Fibre Channel networks can use Fibre Channel Arbitrated Loops (FC-AL) or Fibre Channel switched networks. Sniffing Fibre Channel Arbitrated Loops does not require any MITM tricks because the fabric is a loop (ring) topology, where every connected node on the same loop can view the communication of every other node on the loop. Furthermore, using similar techniques used in IPv4 network, sniffing on a Fibre Channel switch fabric is not an impossible task, but significantly more difficult than an IPv4 network. More discussion of the MITM attacks are discussed later in this chapter, but it is important to note that sniffing on a Fibre Channel fabric is a security risk that may expose the sensitive information that traverses the network in clear-text.

The risk and weaknesses of Fibre Channel start with the clear-text transmission of sensitive information, which directly results in enumeration (the first basic step for an attacker). Enumeration is a phase where an unauthorized user would gather information about the network, architecture, device, or application they want to compromise. The result from this phase is the actual fuel that is used to perform an attack. You'll notice that the enumeration phase is not something shown in Hollywood security films, but the truth is that the enumeration phase of an attack is usually 60 to 80 percent of the process itself. The actual act of performing an attack is less than a quarter of the work. As stated earlier, sniffing the network is the first step in the enumeration phase of attacks, which is used to reveal weaknesses in the network itself.

The results of the enumeration phase determine how triumphant the actual attack will be. For example, if the enumeration phase was able to gain significant information about the network, devices, applications, operating systems, routers, WWNs, and IQNs, then the penetration phase will not only be successful, but might also be far more damaging. Conversely, if the enumeration phase does not yield favorable results for an attacker, the actual penetration phase would be short and probably unsuccessful. Figure 2.3 is a graph that shows the relationship of the enumeration and penetration phase of an attack.

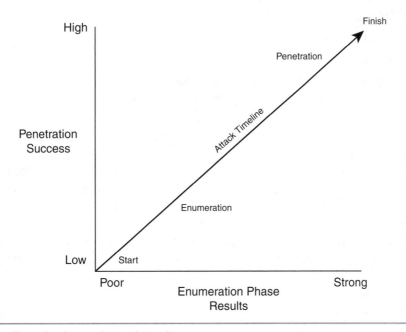

Figure 2.3 Example of a sample attack timeline.

In Figure 2.3, notice the direct relationship between the enumeration phase results and the attack success. As more success occurs in the enumeration phase, the likelihood of success in the attack process increases.

Now that we have established that enumeration is a very critical step in an attack, the problems with clear-text communication leaking an abundance of sensitive information should be understood. The next question to address is exactly what sensitive information in the Fibre Channel frame can actually be used in a possible attack? The following list describes several of the items that an unauthorized user can enumerate from a node connected to the SAN. Each of these entities gives ammunition to attackers to complete a successful attack:

- Fabric name
- Domain identification
- Switch name server information
- Session sequence control number
- Session sequence IDs
- World Wide Names used in the fabric
- Layer-2 frame information
- 24-bit addresses
- Routing information (destination and source IDs)
- Management information (such as SES and FC-SNMP)

The enumeration of a Fibre Channel SAN does not equate into data compromise, but it does significantly help the process. As an attacker tries to gain enough information to perform an attack, he or she will need to enumerate the target before any attack can be executed. Conversely, not all enumeration is negative. An organization may send clear-text information over the network that is not considered to be sensitive; such as Exchange IDs from Fibre Channel frames. The proper exercise of data classification should be conducted, as discussed in Chapter 1, "Introduction to Storage Security," to determine what type of data that traverses the network is consider public or private.

HACKING THE SAN

Hacking the SAN translates to unauthorized access to an entity or data in a storage area network. In the next three chapters, we discuss the following items.

- Session hijacking
- Man-in-the-Middle attacks
- Name server pollution
- WWN spoofing
- LUN masking attacks
- Zone hopping
- Switch attacks

Table 2.2 is summary of the weaknesses that are discussed in the next three chapters and their correlating attacks.

Table 2.2 SAN Security Weaknesses and Correlation SAN Attacks

SAN Weaknesses	SAN Attacks
Sequence weaknesses	Session hijacking
Fabric address weaknesses	Man-in-the-Middle attacks
FLOGI/PLOGI weaknesses	Name server pollution
HBA weaknesses	LUN masking attacks/WWN spoofing
FC switch weaknesses	Zone hopping

A key idea to introduce at this time before we begin our discussion on SAN attacks is the difference between a valid attack and a valid risk. In a given network, there are several hundred attacks that are fully possible to execute, but only a handful of them may actually pose a valid risk due to the nature of the network or the business. Hence, for each attack described in this section, a chart is used to describe how easy or difficult the execution of the attack will be, and its risk level also will be discussed. See Figure 2.4 for the example chart.

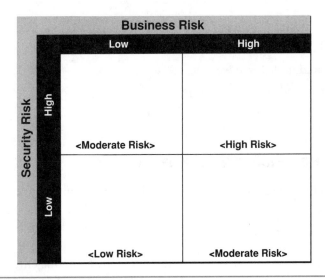

Figure 2.4 Security and Business Risk chart.

The primary purpose of the SBR chart is to place each threat described in some type of security risk context. This chapter covers many risks and threats in Fibre Channel SANs; many of the threats are easy to perform, but many are very difficult to execute due to the need for physical access to the network or a hardware analyzer for sniffing. It would not be in the best interest of the book to simply skip the threats that are hard to actually perform, but use the SBR chart to appropriately show the risk level of each attack after it has been described.

In Figure 2.4, notice that each area of the chart represents a different security and business risk value. Items in the upper-left corner are high security risk, but low business risk. Risks in this area should be technically mitigated from a security perspective only since the business risk is low. Items in the upper-right corner are high security risk and high business risk. Risks in this area should be resolved immediately since they present a high business and security risk. Conversely, items in the lower-left corner are low security risk and low business risk. Risks in this area can often be accepted (bearable) since the impact is relatively low. Finally, items in the lower-right corner are low security risk and high business risk. Risks in this often need a process solution rather than a technical solution. The type of summary in the Security and Business Risk (SBR) chart will help readers understand what valid attacks are and the risks associated with them.

Now that we understand the architecture of Fibre Channel frames and the problems associated with clear-text communication, we will now discuss the security weaknesses with Fibre Channel frames. The following list describes each weakness that we will discuss:

- Sequence weaknesses
- Address weaknesses
- Fabric, port, and node login weaknesses
- FLOGI, PLOGI, and address spoofing

FIBRE CHANNEL FRAME WEAKNESSES

The following sections discuss the weaknesses with Fibre Channel at the frame level.

SEQUENCE WEAKNESSES

A *sequence* is a set of frames transmitted unidirectionally from one entity to another in order to maintain a session between two nodes. A frame uses a Sequence ID (Seq_ID) and a Sequence Count (Seq_CNT) in each frame to identify, control, and maintain the session. Each frame includes the Sequence ID (Seq_ID) that identifies the unique session that the frame belongs to. For example, if a node were communicating with several different entities, each session would have a unique Seq_ID to identify which frame belongs to which session. In addition to the Sequence ID, the Sequence Count is used also. The Sequence Count is used to ensure frames are placed in the right order by the entities. Each Seq_CNT is incremented by 1 for each subsequent data frame.

The Sequence ID and Sequence Count have similar responsibilities in a Fibre Channel frame as the Initial Sequence Number (ISN) in an IP packet. The ISN in an IP packet is also responsible for maintaining a session between two nodes on an IP network.

In order for a session to be maintained between two nodes, all session information must be maintained. The security weakness with IP networks is the predictable (guessable) ISN. An ISN is the core component to allow packets to become a part of an established session. If the ISN is predictable, it would potentially allow unauthorized packets to join or hijack the session. A third-party entity could inject packets with the next relevant ISN and take control of the established session. For example, for simplicity's sake, let's say two of the first three packets in a session have the ISN of 123 for packet number one and 456 for packet number two. An attacker could probably predict that the third packet should have an ISN of 789 to be part of the existing session. If the attacker sends their packet to the target first and uses the ISN of 789, the session will then be handed over to the attacker and not the legitimate node. This means that if an entity was able to guess the next ISN in the sequence and the entity was able to inject packets in an established session, the entity would own the session. See Figure 2.5 for more details.

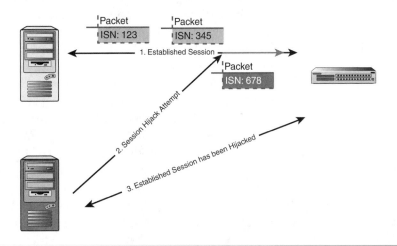

Figure 2.5   ISN session hijacking attack.

As shown in Figure 2.5, a weak or predictable ISN can leave an established and trusted session vulnerable to a session hijacking attack. A predictable value to allow/deny entities into a trusted session should not be used. ISN values must be unpredictable *and* unique, not unpredictable *or* unique. This premise has also plagued HTTP (web) applications. Session identifiers in cookies used in HTTP applications, known as the Session ID, are being used to maintain sessions in the stateless HTTP protocols. While applications distribute cookies with unique Session IDs, the Session IDs are not necessarily unpredictable. This allowed unauthorized users to guess or predict the Session ID and log into applications using another user's existing sessions. For example, if a legitimate user and a malicious user logged on to their favorite webmail service, they would receive a cookie from the webmail site that contains a Session ID. Both users would present their cookie to the site each time they want to check email. If the site granted a Session ID of 100 to the legitimate user and 101 to the malicious user, then an attacker could guess/predict that the Session IDs is a three-character digit being incremented by one for any new session. The attacker could access the site under the legitimate user's profile by changing their Session ID in their cookie to 100 and send it to the site. Once the site receives the cookie from the malicious user that contains the Session ID of 100, it would recognize the attacker as the legitimate user because the site recognizes the user based on the Session ID in a user's cookie. This would allow the attacker to log to the legitimate user's session and give them access to profile pages, credit card pages, and account information.

As stated in the Preface, attacks don't change, but they do get modified. Similar to the session hijacking weaknesses in IP ISN packets, which was introduced over 15 years ago, and Session IDs in HTTP cookies, the Sequence ID and Sequence Counts in Fibre Channel frames are unique values, but they are predictable. The Sequence Count value is incremented by one, a very predictable pattern. Furthermore, the Sequence ID is a unique number, but is also a static number that does not change within the session. Therefore, of the two entities that maintain the session in a Fibre Channel frame, one is a static value and the other is a value that increments by one, both of which can allow an unauthorized entity to predict or guess values and inject their own frames to hijack a session. For example, let's say two nodes are communicating on a Fibre Channel network—they have a Sequence ID of 12, and the first frame has a Sequence Count of 1117171342 and the second frame has a Sequence Count of 1117171343. An unauthorized node could inject frames to the target node with the Sequence ID of 12, since the frame is in clear-text and the value does not change, and predict the next Sequence Count of 1117171344 in order to hijack the session. Notice that although 1117171342 is a long and unique number, the first four digits is the date (November 17th or 1117) and the last six digits is time (5:13 and 42 seconds or 17:13:42). By doing some simple pattern matching and predictions, it is easy to figure out that the next few frames will have the Sequence Count of 1117171344, 1117171345, and 1117171346.

What does this mean? Well, this does not mean that you can go download Hunt, Ettercap, or WebProxy and begin to perform session hijack attacks on Fibre Channel SANs (Hunt, Ettercap, and WebProxy are IP/Application tools to hijack sessions in IP networks or web applications). Although the weaknesses are there in a Fibre Channel frame, the threat and exposure is relatively low. A Fibre Channel analyzer is required to modify frames and inject them into established session. With speeds up to 2gb/sec, this is not an easy task. Nonetheless, the weakness of session management with the Seq_ID and Seq_CNT fields in a Fibre Channel frame do exist, which tells us that security may have not been a significant factor when developing session management for Fibre Channel or Fibre Channel-enabled products.

SESSION HIJACKING

Session hijacking is the act of an untrusted third party intercepting and controlling (hijacking) a valid session between two trusted entities. Telnet is a good example of a trusted session between two entities that can be hijacked by an anonymous third party on the segment if weak ISNs are being used for the TCP packets. Figure 2.6 shows a high-level example of session hijacking.

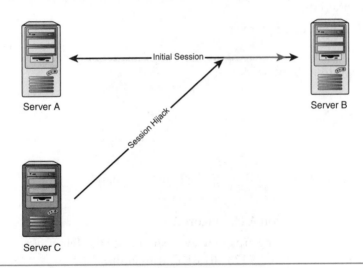

Figure 2.6 Sample session hijacking between two trusted entities.

Session hijacking was first introduced many years ago in the IP networking world for weak and predictable Initial Sequence Numbers in TCP headers for IP packets.

The attack became quite easy to execute with IP tools such as Hunt (http://lin.fsid. cvut.cz/~kra/#HUNT) and Ettercap (http://ettercap.sourceforge.net/). Session hijacking resurfaced in the application world when weak and predictable session IDs became apparent in application cookies to maintain state in web (HTTP) communication. Similar to our discussion in Chapter 1 on how several attacks don't change, but get modified, the idea of session hijacking can be applied to Fibre Channel frames also.

ASSESSMENT EXERCISE

In order to better understand session hijacking, we will demonstrate an example using an IP network and also using the tool called Hunt, which works solely on the Unix/ Linux platform. While Hunt is a great tool, you might have to try it several times to get it to work correctly. Based on Figure 2.6, server C will be the malicious user hijacking a session from server A to server B. The following steps outline the method to perform session hijacking:

1. On server C, download Hunt from http://lin.fsid.cvut.cz/~kra/#HUNT.
2. Unzip Hunt:
    a. cd /usr/local/bin
    b. gunzip --c hunt.tar.gz | tar xvf --
3. Compile Hunt:
    c. cd /usr/local/bin/hunt-1.5
    d. make
    e. make install
4. Execute Hunt:
    f. ./hunt
5. On server A, telnet to server B, using the telnet command:
    g. telnet serverB
6. On server C, choose option A (see Figure 2.7).
7. On a hub (or a switch using arpspoof), you should see the Telnet session from server A (10.10.80.122) to server C (128.101.81.1) with Hunt.
8. At the choose conn> prompt, enter **0** to hijack the session (see Figure 2.8).

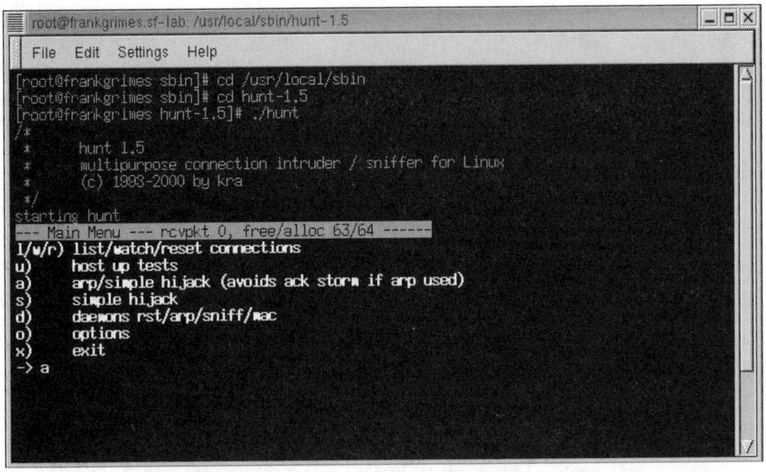

Figure 2.7 Hunt's options.

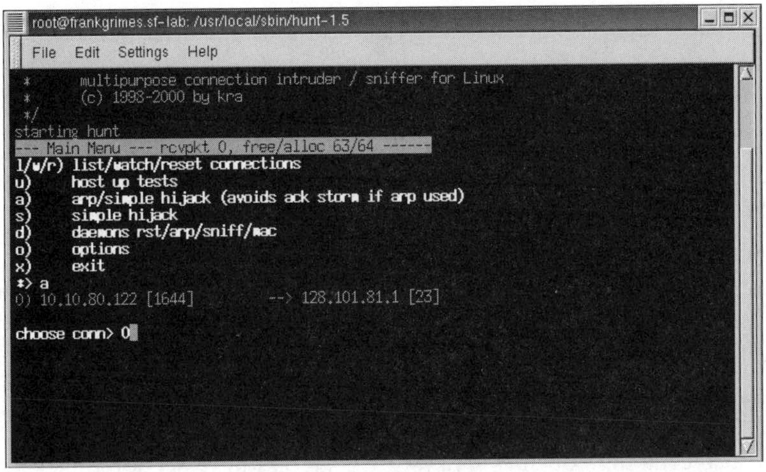

Figure 2.8 Telnet session with Hunt.

9. Accept all the defaults (labeled in brackets) until you see the target session (see Figure 2.9).

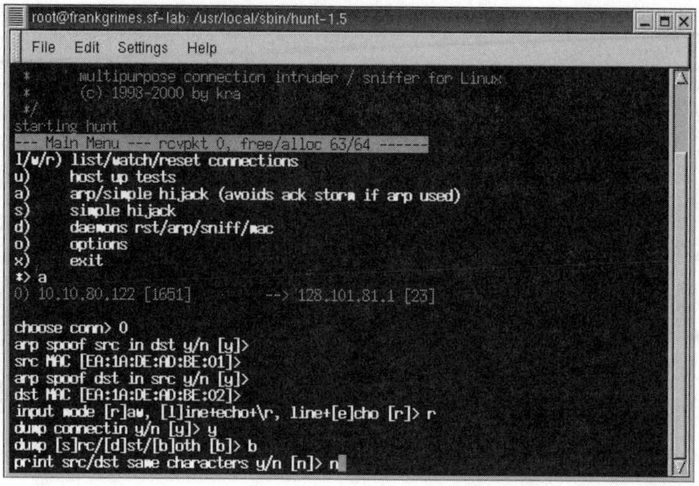

Figure 2.9   Hunt's defaults.

10. Ensure the user on server A continues to type and is not sitting idle with the telnet prompt.

11. Back on server C, if the user on server A is using the Telnet session, you will be able to either watch the session or hijack it at any time by pressing the Enter key a couple of times (preferably after the user has su to root!!!). Once you have hijacked the session, Hunt will inform you that "you took over the connection."

12. Done. Server C has now hijacked the Telnet session from server A to server B due to poor session information in the Initial Sequence Number of the TCP header (see Figure 2.10).

Based on our attack here, the IP session hijacking will be classified as a high security risk, since authentication can be subverted from a malicious attacker. Additionally, the attacker will also get a high business risk, since a successful IP session hijack attack will allow an unauthorized user to gain access to machines containing sensitive data. See Figure 2.11 for an SBR chart.

Figure 2.10 Successful hijacked session from server A.

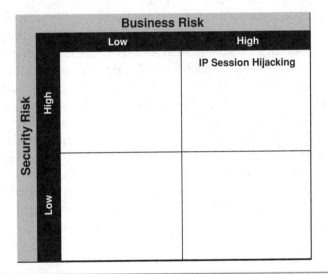

Figure 2.11 SBR chart for IP session hijacking.

SESSION HIJACKING—FIBRE CHANNEL

In a Fibre Channel architecture, in order for two Fibre Channel nodes to communicate with each other, an established session must be made. The session information is managed by the Sequence Count number (Seq_CNT) and the Sequence Identification number (SEQ_ID). The definitions for Sequence Count numbers and Sequence Identification numbers are as follows:

- **Sequence Count (SEQ_CNT)**—A number identifies individual frames within a sequence. For each frame transmitted in a sequence, SEQ_CNT is incremented by 1, allowing the frames to be arranged in the correct order.
- **Sequence ID (SEQ_ID)**—A static number transmitted with each frame in a sequence that identifies the frame as part of a session. Each frame in the same session has the same Sequence ID.

The session information between two FC nodes is the entity that is in charge of maintaining a session. For example, if 100 frames were delivered from several nodes to another single node, there needs to be a method to understand which frame came from which node and to organize the frames in their correct order. In order to complete this, the Seq_ID and Seq_CNT are used. The Seq_ID and Seq_CNT will tie each frame to a particular session and place it in its correct order.

The issue with session management starts with the lack of Fibre Channel authentication when sending or receiving frames. Similar to the IP and Hunt example earlier, in order to break in and hijack a session, a malicious user could send frames to an authorized node with the correct Seq_ID and Seq_CNT (using the source address (S_ID) as the attacker and not the original session holder), thus, transferring the session's control to the malicious user. Furthermore, since the Seq_ID never changes (which makes it very easy to guess), and the Seq_CNT number increments by the value of one (which makes it very easy to predict), the hijacking process of the session is quite trivial.

Although the attack is very trivial, as demonstrated with IP/Hunt as well as web applications and session identifiers, currently there are no automated tools to perform this type of attack. A Fibre channel analyzer would have to be used to actually perform session hijacking on FC frames, rendering the attack as a high security threat, but a low risk item (see Figure 2.12).

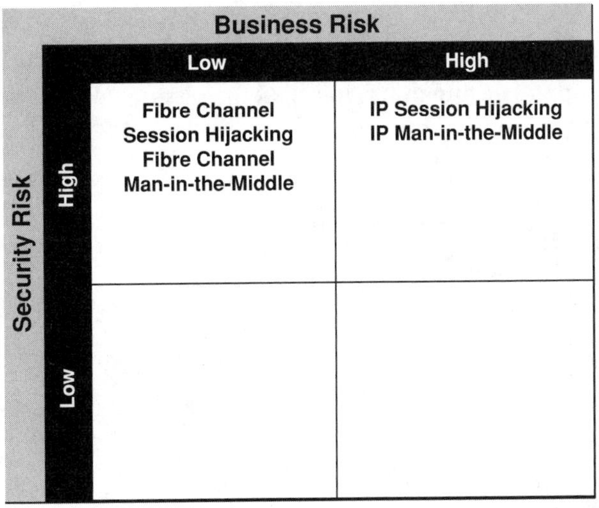

Figure 2.12   SBR chart for Fibre Channel session hijacking.

ASSESSMENT EXERCISE

In order to fully understand the Fibre Channel hijacking attack, the following steps describe the attack process according to Figure 2.13:

1. Node Kusum makes an established connection with node Neeraja.
2. Node Kusum and node Neeraja exchange frames for communication.
3. Using a Fibre Channel traffic analyzer, the malicious user, Lakshman, identifies the static value for the Seq_ID and the Seq_CNT number.
4. Lakshman then injects frames to Neeraja with the Seq_ID, taken from the frames between Kusum and Neeraja, and then increments the Seq_CNT number by one, which will identify the next frame in the session.
5. Neeraja receives the frame(s) from Lakshman, and because the frames have the correct Seq_ID and the correct value for the Seq_CNT, the frames are regarded as the next set of frames in the session.
6. Because the S_ID of the Lakshman's frames are from a different address, the session is then handed to that node wherever the session last left off.

7. Lakshman has hijacked the session from Kusum and now has an established connection to Neeraja without any authentication or authorization.

8. Despite the fact that Lakshman has hijacked the session, Neeraja still thinks the established connection is with Kusum.

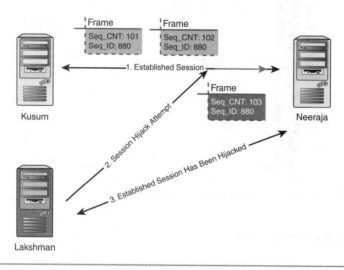

Figure 2.13 Topology for session hijacking.

The technical details of the attack are obviously more complicated, but generally follow the steps outlined beforehand. The first step would be to enumerate the frame information from the two trusted entities. Using any type of Fibre Channel fabric analyzer or IP sniffer with an IP to Fibre Channel connector, there are a variety of methods to do this attack depending on the type of architecture. For example, if a fabric loop topology had been deployed (FC_AL), the analyzer can see all the traffic in the loop of every node connected to the fabric. In a switched architecture, the analyzer would need to be connected to the core FC switch and also within the same routing segment of the target. Once the targets have been identified and enumerated by the traffic analyzer, the following fields in the header part of the frame are important for the attack: S_ID, D_ID, OX_ID, RX_ID, Seq_ID, and Seq_CNT.

Within Fibre Channel layer 2, you would modify the header information with your traffic analyzer of the frame that you will generate in order to complete the attack. When crafting the frame, the S_ID would change from the original source fabric address to the fabric address of the attacker. The D_ID would remain the same, which is the fabric address of the target (while both entities are technically targets, the entity that is on the receiving end of the session is the real target). The OX_ID and RX_ID values would have to be consistent with the original source (Kusum in our previous example) since the malicious node would need to be able to send and receive the same amount of frames as the original source and consequently send the correct amount of frames to the target specified in the original RX_ID field. The Seq_ID field will also need to remain identical to the original in order to ensure the target node considers the frame(s) as part as the legitimate session. Unlike the Seq_ID, the Seq_CNT field will not remain identical but rather will need to be incremented by one in order for the target to consider that frame as the next legitimate frame in the session. This is probably the trickiest part of the attack; even though the act of incrementing the Seq_CNT by one is a trivial procedure, it is not as easy to determine what Seq_CNT is the last one. For example, using your traffic analyzer, you are able to view the Seq_CNT number of all sessions, but by the time you send your frame(s), the legitimate source may already have sent a frame with that Seq_CNT, thus leaving your frame useless. Although this attack takes some trial and error, a good way to ensure that the attack works correctly is to estimate what the Seq_CNT number will be by the time you have the opportunity to send your frame(s) and to set up multiple instances of malicious frames, each using a Seq_CNT that could possibly be the next legitimate one by the time it reaches the target. After you have successfully done this with your traffic analyzer, you will notice that your node will start receiving the frames from the target with the same Seq_ID and Seq_CNT from the original session, despite the fact that you have not officially logged into the node (NLOGIN).

ATTACK SUMMARY: SESSION HIJACKING

Attack description—Hijacking a data or management session by guessing the sequence control number (SEQ_CNT) and the sequence identification number (SEQ_ID) of a Fibre Channel frame.

Risk level—High. An unauthorized entity could gain access to an authorized management session or simply modify the sequence numbers randomly and attempt to perform a denial-of-service attack.

Difficulty—High. This is a sophisticated attack that requires deep knowledge of Fibre Channel frames and the use of a hardware and software traffic analyzer.

Best practice—None to date; however, the use of strong or unpredictable SEQ_CNT or SEQ_ID would mitigate this issue in the future. Ask your storage vendor about frame authentication or integrity options.

FIBRE CHANNEL ADDRESS WEAKNESSES

Now that we have established that attacks don't change, but they do get modified, let's discuss another attack that stems network and application history. Manipulation of the 24-bit fabric address can cause significant damage and denial of service in a SAN.

Each node in a SAN has a 24-bit fabric address that is used for routing, among other things. Along with routing frames correctly to/from their source and destinations, the 24-bit address is also used for name server information. The name server is a logical database in each Fibre Channel switch that correlates a node's 24-bit fabric address to their 64-bit WWN. Additionally, the name server is also responsible for other items, such as mapping the 24-bit fabric address and 64-bit WWN to the authorized LUNs in the SAN. Furthermore, address information is also used for soft and hard zoning procedures (discussed in the Chapter 4, "SANs: Zone and Switch Security"). The 24-bit fabric address of a node determines route functions with soft and hard zoning procedures, specifically if a frame is allowed to pass from one zone to the other. While there are several other uses of the 24-bit address, the use of the address in name servers and zoning procedures are by far the most important in terms of security.

The major issues with the 24-bit address is that it is used for identification purposes for both name server information and soft/hard zone routing, almost like an authorization process, but it is an entity that can be easily spoofed. Using any traffic analyzer, the 24-bit source address of a Fibre Channel frame could be spoofed as it performs both PLOGI (Port Login) and FLOGI (Fabric Login) procedures.

In Fibre Channel, there are three different types of login—Port Login, Fabric Login, and Node Login. Two can be corrupted with a spoofed 24-bit fabric address. Before we discuss how spoofing disrupts these processes, let's discuss the login types first.

FABRIC LOGIN (FLOGI), PORT LOGIN (PLOGI), AND NODE LOGIN (NLOGI)

The Fabric Login (FLOGI) process allows a node to log in to the fabric and receive an assigned address from a switch. The FLOGI occurs with any node (N_Port or NL_Port) that is attached to the fabric. The N_Port or NL_Port will carry out the FLOGI with a nearby switch. The node (N_Port or NL_Port) will send a FLOGI frame that contains its node name, its N_Port name, and any service parameters. When the node sends its information to the address of 0xFFFFFE, it uses the 24-bit source address of 0x000000 because it hasn't received a legitimate 24-bit address from the fabric yet. The FLOGI will be sent to the well-known fabric address of 0xFFFFFE, which is similar to the broadcast address in an IP network (though not the same). The FC switches and fabric will receive the FLOGI at the address of 0xFFFFFE. After a switch receives the FLOGI, it will give the

N_Port or NL_Port a 24-bit address that pertains to the fabric itself. This 24-bit address with be in the form of Domain-Area-Port address from, where the Domain is the unique domain name (ID) of the fabric, Area is the unique area name (ID) of the switch within the domain, and Port is the unique name (ID) of each port within the switch in the fabric. Table 2.3 shows how the 24-bit address is made.

Table 2.3 24-Bit Addresses

24-Bit Address Type	Description
8-bit domain name	Unique domain ID in a fabric. Valid domain IDs are between 1 and 239.
8-bit area name	Unique area ID on a switch within a fabric. Valid area IDs are between 0 and 255.
8-bit port name	Unique port ID within a switch in a fabric. Valid port IDs are between 0 and 255.

A 24-bit address (port ID) uses the following formula to determine a node's address:

```
Domain_ID x 65536 + Area_ID x 256 + Port_ID = 24 bit Address
```

An example address for and node on the first domain (domain ID of 1), on the first switch (area ID of 0), and the first port (port ID of 1), would be the following:

```
1 x 65536 + 0 x 256 + 1 = 65537 (Hex: 0x10001)
```

After the node has completed the FLOGI and has a valid 24-bit fabric address, it will perform a Port Login (PLOGI) to the well-known address of 0xFFFFFC to register its new 24-bit address with the switch's name server, as well as submit information on its 64-bit port WWN, 64-bit node WWN, port type, and class of service. The switch then registers that 24-bit fabric address, along with all the other information submitted, to the name server and replicates that information to other name servers on the switch fabric. Figures 2.14 and 2.15 show the FLOGI and PLOGI processes.

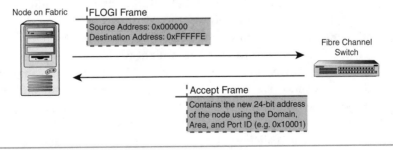

Figure 2.14 FLOGI process.

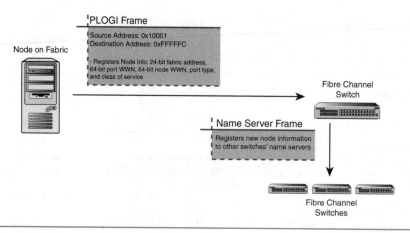

Figure 2.15   PLOGI process.

A Node Login is somewhat similar to a Fabric Login, but instead of logging in to the fabric, the node would log in to another node directly (node to node communication). The node will not receive any information from the fabric, but will receive information from the other node as it relates to Exchange IDs (OX_ID and RX_ID) and session information (Seq_ID and Seq_CNT). After this information has been exchanged, the two nodes will begin to communicate with each other directly.

FLOGI, PLOGI, AND ADDRESS SPOOFING

Now that we have established facts concerning FLOGI, PLOGI, and address spoofing, let's understand how the weaknesses interrelate them. After performing the FLOGI process, an FC node needs to perform a PLOGI to the well-known address of 0xFFFFFC. The PLOGI then registers the 24-bit address of the node to the Name Server (also referred to as a Simple Name Server) of the switch. If an entity were to spoof their 24-bit fabric address and send it to the address of 0xFFFFFC, the switches would see a node performing a PLOGI. Once the switch receives the information from the PLOGI frame, it will register the spoofed 24-bit address of the node to the name server—thus, polluting the name server with incorrect information. You might wonder what the big deal is since the node has corrupted its own information; however, consider the fact that the 24-bit address is used for hard and soft zoning. For example, let's say the 24-bit address of 65537 (Hex: 0x10001) was allowed to route to nodes in zone A and no other addresses can access that zone. A malicious attacker has the address of 65541 (Hex: 0x10005) and cannot access that zone. The malicious attacker can spoof (change) their 24-bit address to match 65537 (0x10001) and then route frames to the restricted zone A, despite being unauthorized to do so. Spoofing the 24-bit address during PLOGI negates any route-based zoning rules that may have been applied. The simple process of spoofing now creates the ability to route (hop) across hard and soft zoning rules. Figure 2.16 shows the FLOGI/PLOGI spoofing process.

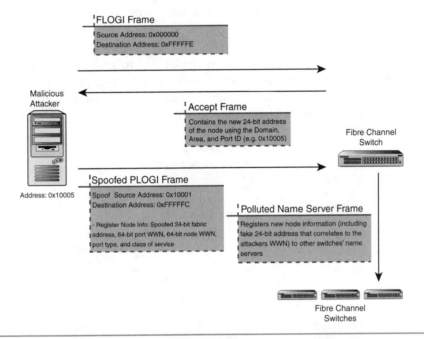

Figure 2.16 FLOGI/PLOGI spoofing process.

We will take this idea a bit further in the next section, "Man-in-the-Middle Attacks," when I discuss the issues of spoofing the 24-bit fabric address and spoofing a node WWN. The fact is that this attack is very severe by breaking the integrity of any hard or soft zoning rules. However, a traffic analyzer is required to perform this attack, thus creating barriers to perform the attack itself.

MAN-IN-THE-MIDDLE ATTACKS

A *Man-in-the-Middle (MITM) attack* is the act of an untrusted third party intercepting communication between two trusted entities. For example, when you call a friend on the telephone, you dial his or her phone number and wait for an answer. When your friend picks up the phone, you then begin communicating with him or her. In a MITM attack, a malicious user would intercept the connection between you and your friend. Instead of talking to your friend directly, you would actually be communicating through a malicious third party. The malicious third party would then connect you to your friend. Both you and your friend would begin communicating, not knowing that an unauthorized entity has connected you both and is listening to every word of the conversation. It is like a three-way call, but two of the three callers don't know that there is a third person listening.

In the digital world, the untrusted third party plays the role of a router, but unlike an authorized router, the untrusted third party should not have permission to view, modify, or intercept any of the communication between the two trusted entities. Figure 2.17 shows a high-level example of a Man-in-the-Middle attack.

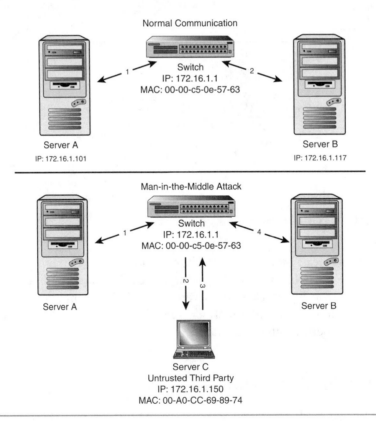

Figure 2.17   Sample Man-in-the-Middle attack.

Man-in-the-Middle attacks were first introduced many years ago in the IP networking world. Unauthenticated OSI layer 2 Address Resolution Protocol (ARP) packets could update ARP tables (tables that match a node's IP address to their machine (MAC) address) in switches and/or operating systems. The purpose of the MITM is to sniff on a switch. A switch will only transmit information to the correct port, not allowing any other ports to see any communication that is not theirs. On the other hand, a hub is a dumber device that allows all ports to see all communication, making it quite easy to sniff a neighbor's traffic. Many switches are layer 2 devices, meaning that they can transmit packets from one port on a switch to another without the need for an IP address, but with a node's machine address (MAC). For example, on a Windows operating system, type **ipconfig /all** from the command line and then press Enter. Notice the physical address is the machine address of your node, which is actually the MAC address of your Network Interface Card (NIC). The MAC address comes from the manufacturer of the NIC to identify it. If your node wanted to speak to another node via a layer 2 switch, it would use the MAC address and not your IP address. Layer 2 routing is common for performance reasons, allowing switches to transfer packets quickly across the network. Once the packets get to a layer 3 device, such as a router, then a node's IP address can be used.

Since ARP is a layer 2 protocol, it uses a node's MAC address to identify nodes and transfer packets. ARP is similar to Name Servers in the Fibre Channel world, where Name Servers match the WWN of HBAs to the 24-bit fabric address (as well as a few other items, such as zones and LUN access).

MAN-IN-THE-MIDDLE ATTACKS—IP

Before we can begin to understand the idea about a Fibre Channel Man-in-the-Middle attack, let's first understand the concept using the IP protocol. An entity using IP, such as a switch or an operating system, will send out ARP requests when it is trying to communicate with other entities. For example, if server A wanted to communicate with server B, which has the IP address of 172.16.1.1 and the MAC address of 00-0A-CC-69-89-74, server A would send out an ARP request asking, "Who is 172.16.1.1?" Then the switch or the operating system would respond, replying with its MAC address, which is 00-0A-CC-69-89-74. The issue with ARP, which we will also address with Fibre Channel name servers, is that any malicious entity could send out an ARP reply instead of the actual server. For example, if you stepped outside your home and yelled out, "What is the address of the post-office," a malicious neighbor could say, "I am the post-office; please send your mail to me." If you believed this malicious neighbor without asking for proof, then your mail would be compromised. This is how ARP works, without any authentication. A malicious user could send out ARP replies with the incorrect information.

Since there is no authentication with ARP, similar to how there is no authentication with PLOGI in Fibre Channel fabrics, an entity receiving an ARP reply from an attacker would update their routing table with the incorrect information. Furthermore, even if a node did not send out an ARP request, which would request the MAC address of a specific IP address, it doesn't mean it won't receive an ARP reply and update its own routing table. For example, a malicious user could send out ARP replies to the entire network segment, telling each entity that the MAC address of the router, which is 172.16.1.1, is actually the MAC address of the malicious entity. When one node tries to communicate to any other node by going through the default router, it will actually be going to the malicious entity first, since it is using the MAC address of the malicious entity for layer 2 routing.

ASSESSMENT EXERCISE

Let's attempt an IP Man-in-the-Middle attack using the following steps to better understand the issue:

1. Ensure you are on a test network and you have full permission from your network administrator because a Man-in-the-Middle attack will cause network disruption.
2. In our example using Figure 2.17, servers A and B will try to communicate with one another and server C will intercept that traffic.
3. Download Cain and Abel to server C from http://www.oxid.it/cain.html.
4. Type **ipconfig** on server A. Notice that is the default route listed as "Gateway Address." In our example, the default gateway is 172.16.1.1. Therefore, when server A tries to communicate to server B, it would go through its router first, which is 172.16.1.1 (see Figure 2.18).
5. Still on server A, ping its gateway address by typing **ping <default gateway>**, such as ping 172.16.1.1. See Figure 2.19. Now that server A has pinged the router, it will have its MAC address in its ARP table. Type **arp –a** to see the dynamic ARP table in the system (see Figure 2.19).
6. Switch to server C (the malicious user). Use Cain and Abel to enable server C to send out ARP replies to the network segment, telling everyone that the address of 172.16.1.1 is actually associated with the MAC address of 00-00-86-59-C8-94, which is the MAC address of server C, not the MAC address of the router. The MAC address of the router is 00-00-C5-0E-57-63, which we know from the arp –a command that told us the MAC address of the default router (172.16.1.1). Perform the steps in the next exercise on server C.

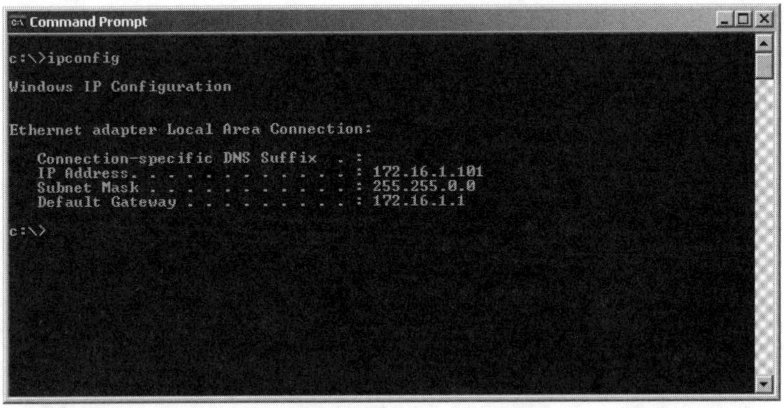

Figure 2.18 Server A's IP address and gateway.

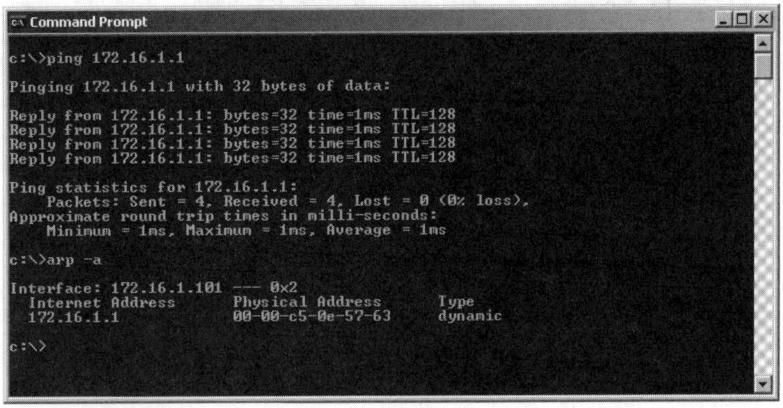

Figure 2.19 Server A's ARP table.

ASSESSMENT EXERCISE

Complete the following steps to perform a MITM attack according to Figure 2.17 with Cain and Abel:

1. Install the Cain and Abel program using its defaults.
2. Install the WinPCap packet driver, if you don't already have one installed.

3. Reboot.

4. Launch Cain and Abel (Start -> Programs -> Cain).

5. Select the icon in the upper-left corner that looks like a green Network Interface Card.

6. Ensure that your NIC card has been identified and enabled correctly by Cain.

7. Select the Sniffer tab.

8. Select the + symbol in the toolbar.

9. The MAC Address Scanner window appears. This enumerates all the MAC addresses on the local subnet. Hit OK. See Figure 2.20 for the results.

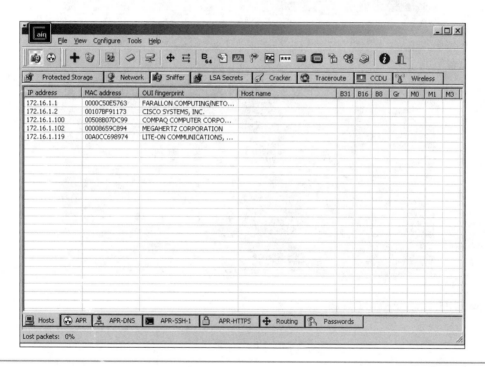

Figure 2.20 MAC Address Scanner results.

10. Select the APR tab on the bottom of the tool to switch to the ARP Pollution Routing tab.

11. Select the + symbol on the toolbar to show all the IP addresses and their MACs (see Figure 2.21).

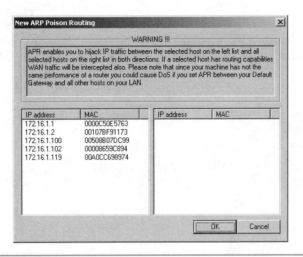

Figure 2.21 IP addresses and their MACs.

12. On the left hand side of Figure 2.22, choose the target for your MITM attack. Most likely this will be the default gateway in your subnet, so all packets will go through you first before the real gateway of the subnet.

13. Once you select your target, which is 172.16.1.1 in our example, you then select the hosts on the right side that you want to intercept traffic. This value can be all the hosts in the subnet or one particular host. We will choose one host, which will be 172.16.1.119. Select OK (see Figure 2.22).

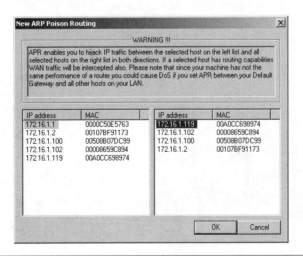

Figure 2.22 Man-in-the-Middle targets.

14. Now select the yellow and black icon (second one from the left) to officially start the MITM attack. This will allow server C to start sending out ARP responses on the network subnet, telling 172.16.1.119 that the MAC address of 172.16.1.1 has been updated to 00-00-86-59-C8-94 (see Figure 2.23).

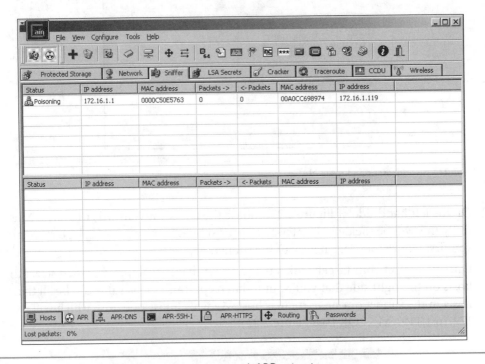

Figure 2.23   Man-in-the-Middle attack in process with ARP poisoning.

15. At this point, all traffic from server A to server B is going to server C first and then on its appropriate route. Server C can open up a network sniffer to view all the traffic. Additionally, Cain has a Passwords tab at the bottom that will capture the password of major protocols such as FTP, HTTP, IMAP, POP3, Telnet, and VNC. It will also capture password hashes such as Kerberos and IPsec using IKE (see Figure 2.24).

Layer 2 in the OSI model (Ethernet) is a key target for attackers. The attack becomes quite easy to execute with IP tools such as Windoze Interceptor, Dsniff, and Cain and Abel. Man-in-the-Middle attacks have also resurfaced in the application world using the same preceding techniques, but with cookies and certificates instead of ARP packets.

Similar to our discussion in Chapter 1 on how several attacks don't change but instead get modified, the idea of Man-in-the-Middle attacks can be applied to Fibre Channel frames also.

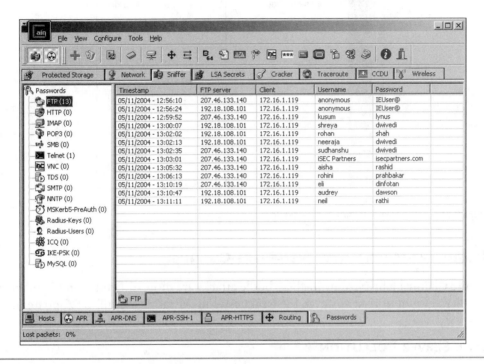

Figure 2.24   Capture password hashes due to the Man-in-the-Middle attack.

The MITM attack is possible due to the lack of authentication in ARP packets as well as the insecurities of IPv4. As demonstrated with Cain and Abel, the attack can be quite trivial, rendering the attack as a high security threat, but a high-risk item (see the SBR chart in Figure 2.25).

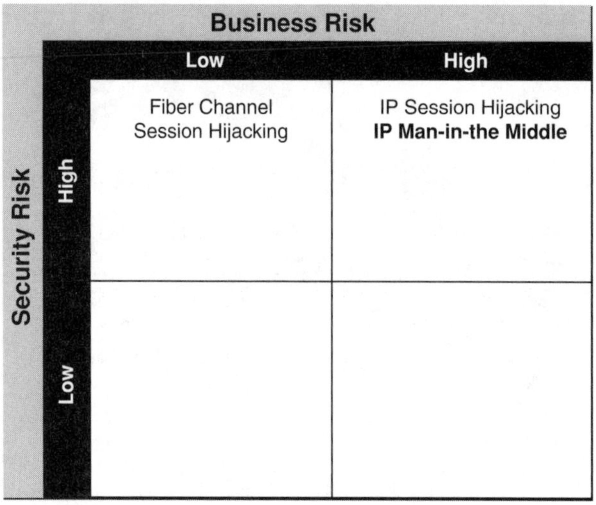

Figure 2.25   SBR chart—IP Man-in-the-Middle.

MAN-IN-THE-MIDDLE ATTACKS—FIBRE CHANNEL

In Fibre Channel fabrics, Man-in-the-Middle attacks are more difficult than IP and bear a smaller amount of risk; however, the weaknesses in the fabric are still very apparent.

NAME SERVER POLLUTION

In order to conduct a MITM attack on a Fibre Channel network, name server pollution is required. Described earlier in this chapter, there are significant weaknesses in the FLOGI and PLOGI processes that can be used to pollute the name server.

When performing a FLOGI, a Fibre Channel node will use the source address of 0x000000 because it does not have a valid S_ID yet. The node will send its frame to the destination address (D_ID) of 0xFFFFFE, which is similar to a broadcast address for Fibre Channel fabrics. After the switches receive the frame at the address of 0xFFFFFE, it will return an Accept frame, known as an ACC, to the node with its new 24-bit address, giving the node a valid fabric address. After the node has received the ACC frame and its new 24-bit address, it will then perform a PLOGI. The PLOGI will send its new 24-bit address to the address of 0xFFFFFC, registering its new address to the switch's name servers.

The security weakness is that a malicious node can craft a spoofed PLOGI frame and send it to the address of 0xFFFFFC. The malicious node could complete the FLOGI process, but instead of responding with its real 24-bit address, it could use a spoofed 24-bit address of a target during the PLOGI. Since the malicious node knows the address to send PLOGI responses to (0xFFFFFC), the act of inserting the 24-bit address is not a challenge. The switch name server would receive the spoofed PLOGI frame at the address 0xFFFFFC and will update its name server with the incorrect information. For a persistent attack, the malicious node would continue to send PLOGI frames at the address of 0xFFFFFC, continuously updating the name server with incorrect information and leaving the target with the actual 24-bit address completely out of the process. A detailed description of the contents of each frame is depicted in Figure 2.26.

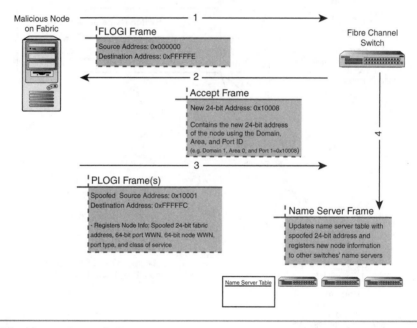

Figure 2.26 Name server pollution process.

MITM ATTACK

In order for two Fibre Channel nodes to communicate with each other, they must know the others' 24-bit address and port ID on the fabric. The fabric address is given and updated during the FLOGI and PLOGI processes, which also has no authentication process (similar to ARP). The port ID is the physical port number that the node is connected to on the switch. If one node wanted to communicate to another node, it would then send frames to the other node's 24-bit address, which would be the Destination address (D_ID) in a frame header. The switch would receive the frame, match the 24-bit address to the correct port ID, which is completed via the switches' name server table, in order to find the correct physical port of the destination node, and then pass the frame on to the correct port. See Figure 2.27 for normal communication in a fabric.

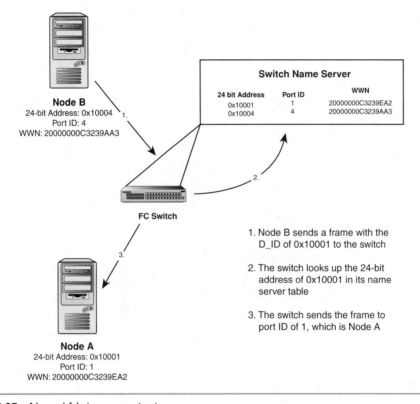

Figure 2.27   Normal fabric communication.

In order to perform a Fibre Channel MITM attack, a malicious node would spoof its 24-bit address to match the address of its target node (Node A). Because name server information can be automatically updated during the PLOGI process (remember that the FLOGI and PLOGI processes update name server information without authentication), the malicious user would then perform a PLOGI, sending their port ID, WWN, and spoofed 24-bit address to the fabric address of 0xFFFFFC for all the switches in the fabric to accept. The switches, with the incorrect information for the 24-bit address, would update their name servers with the port ID, WWN, and the spoofed 24-bit address. When another node wants to communicate to the real node, the switch's routing table will map the 24-bit address, which was spoofed, to a different port ID—hence, routing the frame to a different node. See Figure 2.28 for details.

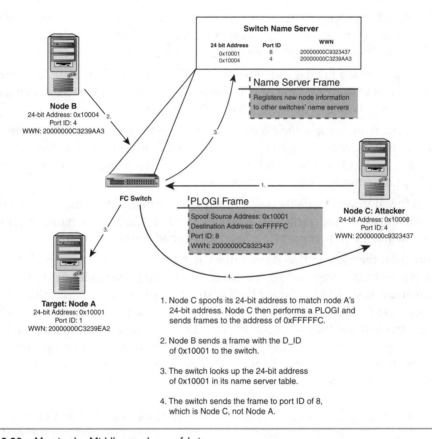

Figure 2.28   Man-in-the-Middle attack on a fabric.

The primary security weakness is the lack of authentication when sending FLOGI or PLOGI frames that consequently update name server information on switches. In Figure 2.28, node A has a 24-bit fabric address of 0x10001 and node B has a 24-bit fabric address of 0x10002. Fabric routing tables and rules would allow the two entities to communicate with each other quite easily using port ID 1 and port ID 2. When the malicious node, node C, performed a Man-in-the-Middle attack to intercept the traffic between node A and node B, the following steps were performed:

1. Node C did not perform a FLOGI, because it does not care to have a real 24-bit fabric address, but will be using the 24-bit address of its target, which is node A.
2. Using a traffic analyzer, node C crafts a frame mimicking a PLOGI frame, as if it were registering its own 24-bit address to the fabric and adjoining switches, but actually updating its spoofed 24-bit address to the authorized name server.
3. Node C performs a PLOGI using the 24-bit fabric address of 0x10001, allowing name servers to think that the 24-bit address of 0x10001 now correlates to node C, port ID 8, and WWN of 20000000c9323437.
4. Once the switches update their name servers, correlating the 24-bit address of 0x10001 with node C, any traffic destined to the 24-bit address of 0x10001, which should be node A but now is node C, will be redirected to the malicious node for interception, enumeration, and compromise.
5. When the address of 0x10004 (node B) tries to communicate to the 24-bit address of 0x10001 (node A), the traffic will actually go to node C, since the name server table in the switch thinks that port ID 8 has the 24-bit address of 0x10001.
6. In order for the Man-in-the-Middle attack to be fully complete, once node C receives the traffic from node B, it must then actually route the frames to the real destination (node A) in order for both parties to continue communication without any suspicion and for node C to continue to receive traffic from node B. If node C fails to transmit the traffic to node A, node B will realize the communication it is trying to perform is not working and stop sending frames, thus leaving node C without any frames to compromise. (Note: The last routing portion of the attack is extremely difficult due to the speeds of 2gb/sec.)

The Fibre Channel MITM attack is possible due to the lack of authentication in PLOGI frames, as well as the security weaknesses during the name server update process. As demonstrated with the preceding examples, the attack is quite possible in SAN fabrics; however, it is significantly difficult due to the speeds that an attacker would have to emulate in order to switch frames in the SAN at 2gb/sec. The throughput/performance part of the attacks makes its risk value lower, rendering the attack as a high security threat, but a low-risk item (see Figure 2.29).

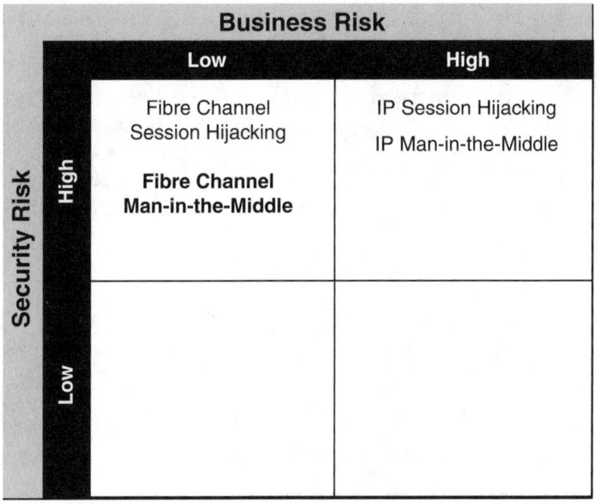

Business Risk		
	Low	**High**
High	Fibre Channel Session Hijacking **Fibre Channel Man-in-the-Middle**	IP Session Hijacking IP Man-in-the-Middle
Low		

Figure 2.29 SBR chart—Fibre Channel Man-in-the-Middle.

Attack Summary: Man-in-the-Middle

Attack description—Sending a fake PLOGI frame to the switch in order to register a target's 24-bit address to the attacker's WWN and port ID; hence, pollute the name server to route traffic incorrectly to the malicious node.

Risk level—Low. An unauthorized entity could gain access to unauthorized frames.

Difficulty—High. This is a sophisticated attack that requires deep knowledge of Fibre Channel frames and the use of a hardware and software traffic analyzer.

Best practice—None to date; however, the use of authenticated FLOGI and PLOGI frames would mitigate this issue in the future. Ask your storage vendor about frame authentication or integrity options.

Attack Summary: Name Server Pollution

Attack description—Corrupting the name server information on Fibre Channel switches where an attacker registers its 24-bit address to a target's WWN. If any legitimate node attempts to communicate to the target, the traffic is redirected to the attacker's machine by the incorrect name server information (similar to a Man-in-the-Middle attack in the IP architecture).

Risk level—High. An unauthorized entity could gain access to sensitive data with trivial attacks.

Difficulty—High. This is a sophisticated attack that requires deep knowledge of Fibre Channel frames and the use of a hardware and software traffic analyzer.

Best practice—Ensure malicious PLOGI frames, which are used to update switch name servers, cannot corrupt name server tables. Ask your storage vendor about frame authentication or integrity options.

SUMMARY

In this chapter, we discussed the risks of Fibre Channel communication in SANs. This chapter is the first of three chapters that will describe the risks of SANs and describe how to actually expose each risk identified.

Three different aspects of security were addressed that are important for any entity, including the overall risks of the entity, the method of communication that is used within the entity, and the objects that are used in the entity. Fibre Channel security risks were addressed overall, including risks of Fibre Channel as a medium of networking and risks of devices that are used in Fibre Channel storage networks.

The chapter was able to identify some of the key overall issues of Fibre Channel as they pertain to the six areas of security that can be applied to any entity, including authentication, authorization, encryption, auditing, integrity, and availability. The chapter also identified the security strengths and weaknesses of each category in order to determine the level of risks that can be exposed. Unfortunately, most SANs are missing some of the major security entities that are required for proper security, including authentication, encryption, and integrity. Furthermore, many security entities do not exist, such as authorization, are not ideal, and do not hold up to many SAN attacks, such as spoofing.

This chapter was also able to discuss some of the risks associated with Fibre Channel as a medium of communication and networking. The chapter demonstrated how clear-text communication can be a big issue in terms of SAN protection. Furthermore, the weaknesses in Fibre Channel frames can hurt the overall security of a SAN architecture. The chapter also discussed Fibre Channel layer 2 as a target for various attacks on Fibre Channel frames, including spoofing, man-in-the-middle, session hijacking, PLOGI/FLOGI attacks, and name server corruption.

In the next chapter, we will describe the details of the risks identified with HBA and LUN masking. The next chapter will also describe the details of each risk and what factors need to exist in order to perform any attacks that lead to data compromise.

SANs: LUN Masking and HBA Security

In order to discuss the risks that currently exist in SAN architectures, we must evaluate the key devices and applications that exist in SANs. The critical entities in SANs that address security are Host Bus Adapters (HBAs), storage controllers, storage switches (discussed in Chapter 4, "SANs: Zone and Switch Security"), and storage management consoles that house storage applications for management purposes (such as Veritas SANPoint or EMC Control Center management consoles). While most of these devices play an integral role for data storage and availability in SANs, each of them also play a very important role in terms of data security and availability. The following sections discuss risk in these Fibre Channel devices as they pertain to data and storage security:

- Host Bus Adapters (HBA)
- WWN spoofing
- Storage controllers
- LUN masking
- LUN masking attacks
- Storage management consoles

HOST BUS ADAPTERS

Host Bus Adapters (HBAs) are similar to Network Interface Cards (NICs) in IP networks. All NICs have Machine Address Codes (MACs) that are granted by the manufacturer, such as 3Com or Xircom, to identify a NIC. Similarly, Host Bus Adapters have a World Wide Name (WWN) that is also granted by the manufacturer, such as QLogic, Emulex, or LSILogic, which identifies the node on the fabric. Unlike MACs in IP networks, WWNs hold a lot more power and security responsibility in SANs. Remembering back to Chapter 1, "Introduction to Storage Security," and the six aspects of security, including authentication, authorization, encryption, integrity, auditing, and availability, WWNs are heavily relied upon for authorization of storage nodes in a SAN. With the absence of true authentication in SANs, authorization parameters using WWNs becomes very significant. For example, if a Fibre Channel zone is set up on a switch, it would most probably use a node's WWN for its zone membership, known as WWN-based zoning (not the same as soft zoning, which is explained later in this chapter). Similar to MACs on NICs, WWNs can be changed or spoofed quite easily. In fact, unlike most NIC drivers; many device drivers that are installed with HBAs contain a feature to change the WWN (this feature is actually very useful for the management and configuration flexibility for SAN administrators). The function is granted to end users to manage SANs significantly easier. This feature also allows the ability for a malicious entity to spoof its World Wide Names. Furthermore, with the absence of authentication, spoofing (changing) a WWN would allow a malicious user to steal another node's identity in the SAN. If a malicious entity spoofed their WWN to the WWN of another trusted entity belonging to a protected zone, then the malicious node would be able to access the protected zone and any LUNs that may be present. Figure 3.1 shows this attack in more detail.

The real issue here is that another spoofable resource, the WWN of an HBA, is used as a completely trusted entity. While this is similar to the 24-bit fabric address being trusted by a name server, this attack is far more severe because large volumes of data can be damaged or compromised from a single spoofed attack. Since zones use WWNs as an authorization tool (to grant and restrict access to data LUNs), the ability to change an identity and gain access or damage data is trivial. The fact that an attacker must have control of a server that is connected to the SAN in order to commit such an attack is true and reduces the threat, but does not remove the risk. This equates to the reliance of operating system security, which is usually installed very poorly by default, as the entity that is responsible for the security of terabytes of data in the SAN. Are organizations willing to trust Microsoft, Solaris, or even Linux variants to protect the terabytes of data in their SANs?

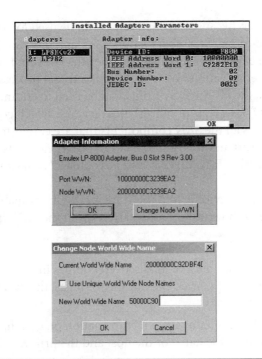

Figure 3.1 Changing a node WWN of an HBA .

WWN SPOOFING

WWNs are an entity that is used to identify a node in a SAN by its HBA information. WWNs are great entities to be used for segmentation purposes, but since WWNs are spoofable (changeable), similar to how a MAC address can be changed in an IP NIC, they are not the best security tool. Unfortunately, SANs have a strong reliance on WWNs as their sole security entity, which make SAN security, or the lack there of, a big issue. While the ability to change (spoof) a WWN is simple enough to understand, you might be wondering how you would find the WWN information of a targeted node. There are several ways to do this, none of which offer any strong obstacles for an attacker. The first method is to simply enumerate other HBAs connected to the fabric via the HBA driver software, which all HBA manufacturers provide as a feature. The next method is to simply connect to the IP interface of a Fibre Channel switch (without any type of authentication) and view the switch's configuration, including all the WWNs of each node connected to the SAN. The last method would be to use pattern matching with brute forcing. All WWNs have 16 characters; however, of the 16 characters, only 2 to 6 are different from each other. Because only hex values can be used for WWNs, an attacker could attempt to brute-force 16 numbers/letters (A–F and 0–9) for 2 to 5 key spaces. Although that is not the most efficient method, the attack is simple enough to do.

The ability to enumerate valid WWNs to spoof is a trivial process. For example, if using an Emulex HBA, the HBAnyware utility can be used to enumerate the SAN. The HBAnyware utility has a feature called Discovery tree, which goes out into the SAN fabric and discovers all the SAN components that are connected to the SAN. Furthermore, an abundant amount of information on the elements in the SAN can be enumerated, such as all HBAs, WWNs, and possible LUNs in storage controllers connected to the SAN.

Using the same Emulex device driver, there are many tabs available on the software utility that can enumerate a wealth of information about the SAN, including the following tabs:

- **Discovery tab**—Contains a list of all discovered nodes in the SAN, including information on the number of fabrics, the number of hosts, the number of adapters, and the number of LUNs.

- **Host Attributes tab**—Contains specific information on each host identity from the discovery tab, including the name of the host and the firmware being used.

- **Fabric Attributes tab**—Contains information on the fabric address of the fabric identified.

- **Target Attributes tab**—Contains information on a highlighted target, such as vendor/product ID, Fibre Channel ID, LUNs mapped to the highlight target, WWN of the target, device name of the target, and so on.

- **General tab**—Contains specific information on all identified adapters enumerated in the SAN, such as WWN, firmware, hostname, link status, and so on.

- **Details tab**—Contains detailed information on a highlight target, such as its WWN, number of ports on the adapter, description, driver version, and so on.

- **Port Attributes tab**—Contains information of all ports identified in the fabric, including WWN, FC ID, port types, port state, support class of ports, and so on.

- **Port Statistics tab**—Contains information on details and statistics of each port enumerated in the fabric, such as Tx frames, Tx words, Tx KB counts, and Tx Sequences.

- **Firmware tab**—Contains information on how to download the latest firmware of the Emulex device driver.

Not only can a WWN be enumerated without authentication via the SAN fabric or the switch itself, but the ability to guess an HBA's WWN is not too difficult either. The HBAs that are being used in the many SANs are using a predictable WWN. For example, let's say a database server has a WWN of 10000000c869de17 and a test server has a WWN of 10000000c86335d3. Assuming servers in the test environment do not have production-level security controls applied to them, an unauthorized user could have a good chance of compromising the database server's SAN data. If the unauthorized user was interested in production database information and not the test information, then a WWN spoofing attack could take place. Looking at both servers' WWNs, a lot of similarities exist in the identities:

```
10000000c869de17
10000000c86335d3
```

Notice that of the 16 characters in the WWN, only five of them are different, considerably reducing the amount of attempts to execute a successful spoofing attack. Furthermore, since WWNs can only be hex values, the possible values to spoof are only 16 characters (A–F and 0–9). This type of WWN usage (brute forcing only five characters with up to 16 possible values) will leave the WWN vulnerable to spoofing relatively easily. Reverting back to security best practices, the minimum length for strong passwords is eight characters. Furthermore, the use of numbers, letters, special characters, and spaces is highly encouraged for passwords. For example, a simple word like "jumanji" could be turned into a strong password by changing the letter "a" to 4, changing the letter "i" to 1, and finally adding a space after the word, making it an eight-character word instead of a seven-character word. The new password would be "jum4nj1 " (with a space at the end), making this alphanumeric with spaces. Going back to WWNs, we already know that special characters and/or spaces are not allowed or possible in WWNs, so the attacker would know that only valid characters and numbers need to be used. That makes the possibility of brute forcing the WWN of an HBA very likely and possible over a given period of time. This would be similar to using a simple dictionary word for your bank password. It would take time, but if someone really wanted to access your bank account, he or she could eventually do it with a 15-dollar purchase or Webster's dictionary. Furthermore, if any data in the SAN requires HIPAA, GLBA, Sarbanes-Oxley, and/or SB1386 protection, then the choice of weak and brute forceable WWNs for the sole security entity may not be wise.

Many administrators might think if the ability to enumerate WWNs is limited, the attackers' ability to spoof a valid WWN is more difficult. In security terms, this would be classified as security by obscurity, where all the weaknesses still remain (by the reliance of WWN for security), but the ability to perform the attack is consider to be obscure. Although this may be a sufficient short-term mitigation step, it is a bad long-term security practice. Whether you are defending against LUN masking attacks or zone hopping attacks, the idea of using a WWN for the sole security entity that grants or denies access is poor. The mitigation discussed here would be similar to an individual using her home telephone number as her PIN for the bank account, but then to ensure no one can access the bank account, she decides not to list the number in the phone book. Would you feel comfortable using your home telephone number as your bank access PIN because of the fact that your number is unlisted? I should hope not. The same idea applies to WWNs.

As you can probably guess, the HBA device drivers contain a plethora of tools and utilities that we can use to perform our LUN masking and zone hopping attacks described previously. To download the latest version of the Emulex device driver, go to http://www.emulex.com/ts/dds.html.

ASSESSMENT EXERCISE

Complete the following steps to perform WWN spoofing at the client node, using the elxcfg software driver from Emulex:

1. Enumerate the WWN of a client node that you want to spoof.
   a. Using any browser, type the IP address of the Fibre Channel switch that is used in the fabric.
   b. Click on the Name Server button.
   c. Select a WWN of a client node that appears on the name server table that you want to target. In this example, we target a node connected to port 1 with the WWN of 510070e876a16886. Our system is connected to port 15 with the WWN of 510020250590225c.

2. Open the Emulex Configuration Software:
   a. Start -> Programs -> Emulex -> elxcfg.

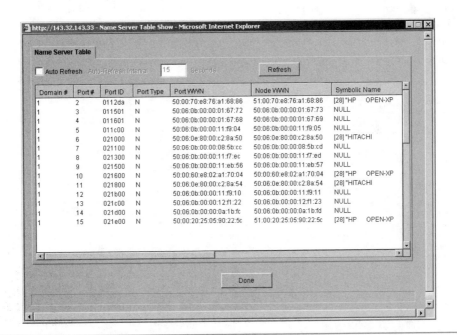

Figure 3.2 Name Server Table.

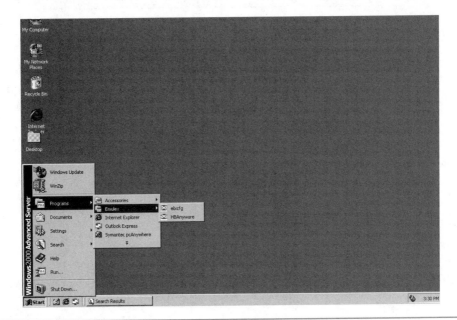

Figure 3.3 Emulex HBA Configuration.

3. Double-click on the adapter in the Available Adapters section of the driver software. This will be the HBA you want to change to match the WWN of the target you identified in step 1.

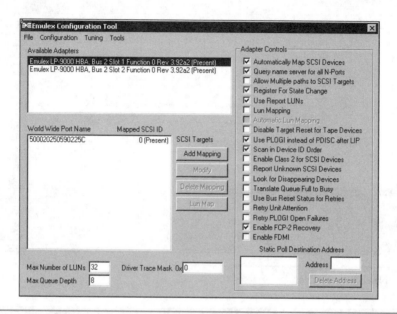

Figure 3.4   Emulex Configuration Tool.

4. After you double-click on the adapter, the Adapter Information window should appear. Click on the Change Node WWN button and enter the node WWN of the HBA identified in step 1, which would be 510070e876a16886.

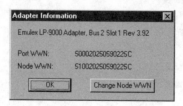

Figure 3.5   The Adapter Information window.

5. After you have changed the node WWN of your adapter to match the node WWN of your target, reboot the machines and reconnect to the fabric.

6. After the HBA driver connects to the fabric, the target LUN associated with the spoofed WWN should now appear.

7. Done! WWN spoofing is now complete.

At this point, there are two WWN node names, the original and the spoofed one, trying to access the same volume (LUN). Fibre Channel storage devices are not built to have two WWN node names connect to the same LUN at the same time. Unlike CIFS and NFS mounts where multiple users/machines can access the same mount point, Fibre Channel and iSCSI SANs are built to only have one machine at a time. At this point, both Fibre Channel clients will be unable to access the SAN volume, confusing the Fibre Channel storage device. This equates into a successful denial-of-service attack for the storage controller volume. The legitimate node names do not relinquish control of the volume; however, it doesn't maintain full control either. The original node name will have intermittent access to the remote drive and possibly lose all real-time access to it. Furthermore, the spoofed node names don't have full access to the drive either—only the ability to make it unavailable to the network. If this was a database server, this would be a severe problem because all database tables will suddenly disappear from the server. In most situations, the actual SAN administrator will troubleshoot the machine and possibly reboot or reinitialize the service. Once the legitimate server reboots or reinitializes the service, it relinquishes control of the Fibre Channel LUN. Once the original client relinquishes control (via reboot or restarted the service), the spoofed client captures full control of the volume since there are not two requestors anymore but just one. While this may only last 5 or 10 minutes until the legitimate machine reboots or attempts to reconnect, the attacker is given full access to the data drive and can browse the volume freely.

ASSESSMENT EXERCISE

WWNs on HBAs are similar to MAC on NICs. If you don't have an HBA handy to perform the previous exercise, you can complete the following steps to change (spoof) your MAC address on your Network Interface Card (NIC), which is similar to changing a WWN (shown in Figures 3.6–3.12). While this is not a SAN-specific attack, we will perform this exercise to show how trivial it is to change a hardware setting on interface cards using operating system software.

1. Download Etherchange from http://www.ntsecurity.nu/toolbox/etherchange/, written by Arne Vindstrom.

2. Place etherchange.exe in your Windows path, such as the Windows\system32\.

3. Open a command prompt:

   a. Start -> Run -> cmd.exe.

4. Type **ipconfig/all** and enter.

   a. Note the physical address row, which states the MAC address of your network adapter (in Figure 3.6, the MAC is 00-0D-60-FC-F6-43).

      i. The MAC address is the value you will be changing.

```
Command Prompt                                                        _ □ ×
c:\>ipconfig /all

Windows IP Configuration

        Host Name . . . . . . . . . . . . . : Storage
        Primary Dns Suffix  . . . . . . . :
        Node Type . . . . . . . . . . . . : Hybrid
        IP Routing Enabled. . . . . . . . : No
        WINS Proxy Enabled. . . . . . . . : No
        DNS Suffix Search List. . . . . . : Aum, Inc.

Ethernet adapter Intel:

        Connection-specific DNS Suffix  . : Aum, Inc.
        Description . . . . . . . . . . . : Intel(R) PRO/1000 MT Mobile Connecti
on
        Physical Address. . . . . . . . . : 00-0D-60-FC-F6-43
        Dhcp Enabled. . . . . . . . . . . : Yes
        Autoconfiguration Enabled . . . . : Yes
        IP Address. . . . . . . . . . . . : 172.16.1.101
        Subnet Mask . . . . . . . . . . . : 255.255.0.0
        Default Gateway . . . . . . . . . : 172.16.1.2
        DHCP Server . . . . . . . . . . . : 172.16.1.100
        DNS Servers . . . . . . . . . . . : 206.13.28.12
                                            172.16.1.100
                                            206.13.31.13
        Lease Obtained. . . . . . . . . . : Saturday, January 01, 2005 4:58:33 P
M
        Lease Expires . . . . . . . . . . : Saturday, January 08, 2005 4:58:33 P
M
c:\>
```

Figure 3.6 MAC Address of local system.

5. Now type **etherchange.exe** on the command prompt.

6. If you have multiple adapters on your PC, you will be asked which adapter you want to change the MAC address.

7. Choose the number for the adapter you want to modify the MAC.

8. You will now be asked whether you want to specify a new MAC (Ethernet) address or go back to your original MAC address (the latter setting should be used only after you have changed your MAC address and you now want to go back to the original [real] address).

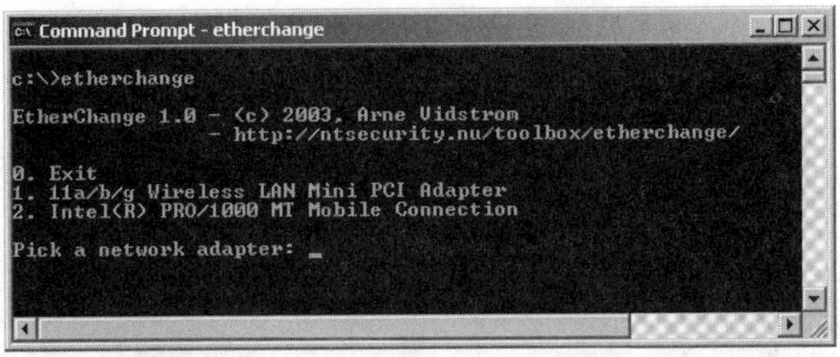

Figure 3.7 Select Interface to change the MAC.

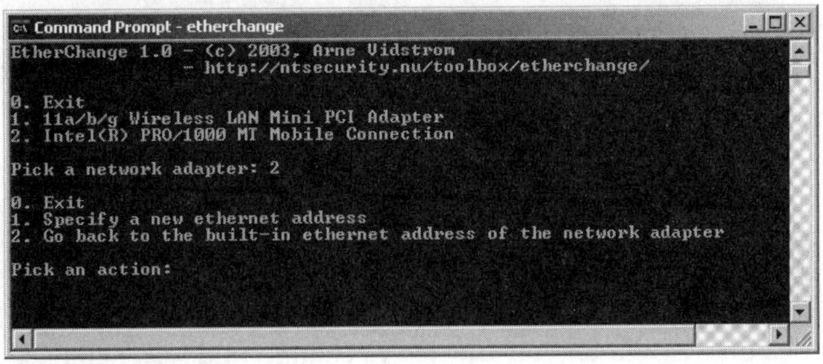

Figure 3.8 Changing the MAC address.

9. Select option number 1 to create a new MAC (Ethernet) address for your specific NIC.

10. Enter your new MAC (Ethernet) address, which is 12 characters long, in hex format (A–F and 0–9 characters only) with no separations:

   a. Enter **0000070147CD**.

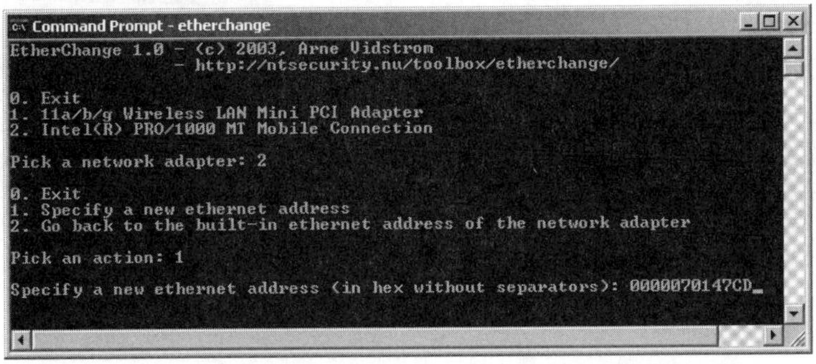

Figure 3.9 Specifying the new MAC address.

11. The interface should now be disabled and re-enabled in order for the setting to take place.

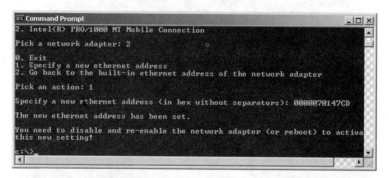

Figure 3.10   Confirming the new MAC address.

12. Disable and re-enable the select adapter:

a. Start -> Settings Network Connections.

b. Right-click on the adapter you selected to change, and select disable.

c. Right-click on the adapter you selected to change, and select enable.

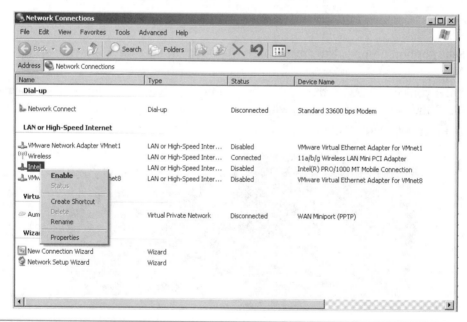

Figure 3.11   Disable and re-enable the interface.

13. Once the adapter has been re-enabled, the MAC address should now be changed:

    a. Open a command prompt (Start -> Run -> cmd.exe).

    b. Type **ipconfig /all**.

    c. Notice that the MAC address is now 00-00-07-01-47-CD.

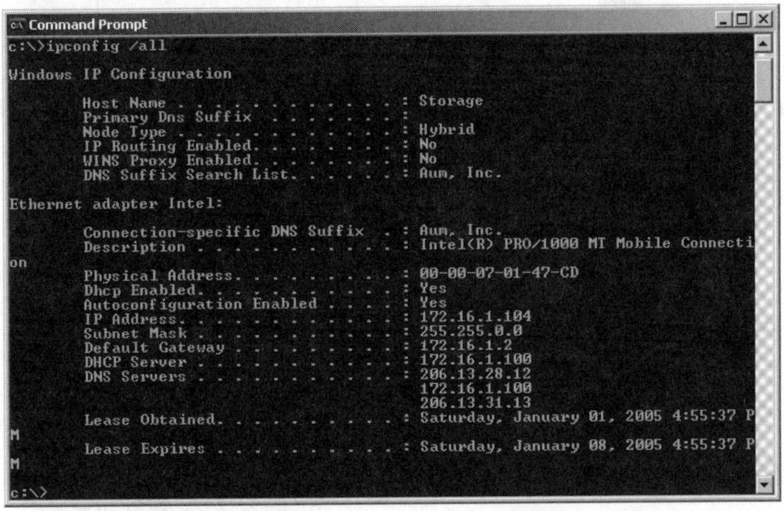

Figure 3.12 Display of the new MAC address.

14. Done!

15. To change the address back to the original, follow the next steps:

    a. Etherchange.

    b. Select the adapter to change back to the original.

    c. Select option 2 to go back to the original MAC address.

    d. Disable and re-enable the network adapter.

16. Done!

WWN spoofing is not only very trivial, but also contains various methods to execute the attack. Additionally, the reliance of WWNs in SANs creates a significant security exposure for SAN architectures solely depending on WWNs for authorization. The WWN spoofing attack has a high security threat and also is a high-risk item (see Figure 3.13).

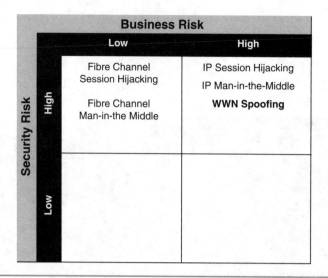

Figure 3.13   SBR chart—WWN spoofing.

ATTACK SUMMARY: WWN SPOOFING

Attack description—An unauthorized entity changes the WWN of a storage node and attempts to gain access to another node's data.

Risk level—High. An unauthorized entity could gain access to sensitive data with trivial attacks.

Difficulty—Low. Changing a WWN is available with most device drivers of HBAs.

Best practice—Fibre Channel switches should isolate and restrict unauthorized nodes from access to each other. Hard zoning can be used to enforce restriction parameters on zone settings. Port WWN can be used instead of node WWN for zoning parameters.

STORAGE CONTROLLERS

Storage devices also play an important role in terms of security and risk management. Fibre Channel storage devices such as EMC, HP, IBM, Compaq, Sun Microsystems, and DEC are usually ignored when it comes to risk and security. While most of these devices are not directly accessible to untrusted entities, they are vulnerable to the same types of attacks that were described previously (such as spoofing).

On most SAN storage devices, the only security mechanism provided is LUN masking. SAN vendors provide the ability to use LUN masking for data security, which is really only data segmentation. Most SAN vendors assume that security will be provided by other areas of the SAN or the general network, either on the Fibre Channel switch or the HBAs on the client machines themselves. Next, we describe some of the security risks associated with LUN masking.

LUN MASKING

A LUN is a Logical Unit Number that is used as the unique SCSI identifier that specifies a logical unit of data. For simplicity sake, think of a 100GB disk drive divided into four parts. Each logical part of the drive would be a separate LUN with a separate identifier representing 25GB of storage space. For example, an EMC Symmetrix may have several LUNs with associated identifiers. LUN 0000 and 0001 could be data stores associated to zone 1 on the switch, which connects the NT machine to a SAN. LUN 0002 and 0003 could be in another zone that connects on the Unix machines in a SAN. Each LUN is presented to operating systems based on the logical segmentation of the storage device.

LUN masking is the process of allocating LUNs to the right servers by the way of the HBA's WWN. Each server will be granted access to a LUN and then masked (hidden) from the other LUNs that they should not have access to. LUN masking can be done at four different areas within the SAN, including the storage controller, the HBA, the Fibre Channel switch, or a third-party application.

Storage controllers offer LUN masking as a segmentation/security tool by mapping storage LUN to servers. See Figure 3.14 for a LUN masking table at the storage controller.

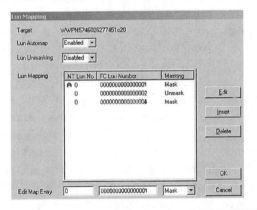

Figure 3.14 LUN Masking at the storage controller.

The process of using LUN masking at the storage controller creates a security risk since LUN masking relies on WWNs of a HBA. The WWN of the HBA is used as the identifier when allocating LUNs to a node. For example, if LUN numbers 0001, 0002, and 0003 on a storage controller are required for a Windows file server, the WWN of the HBA connected to the Windows file server would be used to identify the file server on the fabric. There are some vendors that can implement LUN masking based on the port level; however, most vendors only implement port security based on the storage controller port and not the switch port, making the WWN of the HBA the only identifier that is used to recognize the file server. When a storage controller receives a request for LUN number 0001, 0002, or 0003, it will verify that the WWN of the HBA matches the WWN in the LUN masking table. If the LUN masking at the storage controller does not have an entry for the server's WWN, the request will be denied.

Thus far, LUN masking at the storage controller sounds fine and seems to provide an adequate level of control. The issue with LUN masking for security purposes falls back on the insecurities of a WWN. As mentioned previously in the Host Bus Adapter section, changing an HBA's WWN is a trivial process and is actually offered as a feature by many HBA device drivers. If another server connected to the SAN changed its WWN to one of the Windows file servers mentioned in our previous example and made the request to access LUN numbers 0001, 0002, 0003, the storage controller LUN masking table would grant access to the fake server. The issue is that LUN masking, whether it is implemented at the storage controller, Fibre Channel switch, the HBA, or application product, relies heavily on WWN for security, which is not good since WWNs can be changed, copied, spoofed, and enumerated easily with a trivial amount of effort from attackers.

A good example why LUN masking is a poor security tool is to compare it to using your phone number as the sole entity to grant or deny you access to your home. If an attacker could get access to a home based on knowing the phone number that is used at that home, there would be a great deal of security problems. The fact that an attacker could use a phone book, which has a listing of everyone's address and their correlating phone number (similar to a LUN masking table or a switch's name server table that correlate WWNs to LUNs), makes the process of finding the correct phone number that is used for a particular home a trivial process. Although a WWN is a unique number that is used to grant access to a LUN, the phone number is a unique number that is used to grant access to a home line. We can all agree that no one would use their own phone number—an entity that not only can be enumerated easily, but is also something that we give out freely to friends, family, credit card agencies, stores, and repair service personnel, and is not a strong security control. Similarly, while the use of WWN for LUN masking adequately partitions and segments data from different servers, it is not a strong security control to prevent access to certain LUNs from unauthorized servers. Furthermore, since

LUN masking is usually the sole entity provided by storage controllers for any type of security mechanism, the security risks with storage controllers implementing LUN masking as the sole security entity is high.

LUN MASKING ATTACKS

Logical Unit Numbers (LUNs) are used to categorize data blocks in storage controllers. It is an efficient method to divide and partition a large array of storage space into logical storage units. The idea behind LUN masking is hiding (masking) certain LUNs from a given storage node. Specifically, LUN masking is the process of hiding or revealing parts of a storage disk (specific LUNs) to a client node. LUN masking creates subsets of storage within the SAN virtual pool and allows only designated servers to access the storage subsets.

For example, server A is a database server running Oracle with production data, which uses storage LUNs of 1, 2, and 3. Server B is also a database server running Oracle, but with development data, and only needs access to its storage LUNs of 4, 5, and 6. LUN masking is a method that could be used to ensure that the production Oracle database and the development Oracle database do not accidentally access the incorrect storage units. See Figure 3.15 for an example of the Oracle architecture described previously.

Similar to our earlier discussion, LUN masking also has its weaknesses due to it reliance on WWN information. LUN masking was originally designed to be a segmentation tool and not a security tool, thus revealing many security weaknesses.

LUN masking relies on two types of WWNs: port WWN (WWPN) or node WWN (WWNN). In some cases, LUN masking uses a target's fabric address (24-bit fabric address). If LUN masking uses node WWNs, which uses WWNs that can be changed via software drivers, LUN masking can be subverted easily. If LUN masking uses port WWNs, which uses WWNs that cannot be changed via software drivers, LUN masking can be a stronger security tool. So why would anyone want to use node WWNs since port WWNs are more secure? The reason is that node WWNs are far more flexible and easier to use in dynamic environments. For example, a defunct or bad HBA can be replaced easily without major configuration changes using node WWNs. Additionally, if a SAN is using hot-swappable array controllers on its hosts, which is used in many SANs, using node WWNs is required.

So how do you know if WWPNs or WWNNs are being used? On a Windows environment using Emulex software, the information can be found in the registry. Under HKLM\System\CurrentControlSet\Servers\Emulex, you should see keys for the HBA. The mappings shown in Table 3.1 show if a WWPN, WWNN, or the target's 24-bit address is being used for LUN masking.

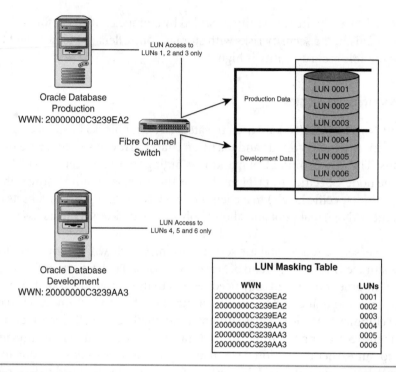

Figure 3.15   LUN masking.

Table 3.1   LUN Masking Usage for WWPN, WWNN, or 24-Bit Addresses

Setting	Registry Value
WWPN	HardAddress=0;MapNodeName=0;
WWNN	HardAddress=0;MapNodeName=1;
D_ID (24-bit address)	HardAddress=1; (MapNodeName=0)
	Or
	HardAddress=1; (MapNodeName=1)

If WWNNs are being used, several spoofing attacks can occur to subvert LUN masking. If WWPNs are being used, WWN spoofing is more difficult, but in some cases still possible (as described next).

LUN masking does have more control over LUN access than zoning, which is discussed in the next chapter. Additionally, LUN masking can occur at four different places: on the client node, the Fibre Channel switch, the storage-node, or a third-party masking application/device. We will now discuss the weakness of each implementation of LUN masking.

LUN Masking at the Client Node

If LUN masking is conducted at the client node and uses the more flexible node WWNs, which means that mapping would be conducted at the HBA level using HBA drivers, there are a couple of security issues. The first one we will discuss is the fact that access to the LUN masking software on the server is available without any authentication. For example, many HBA drivers provide the ability to conduct LUN masking using the HBA software. The ability to make changes to the LUN masking tables requires no authentication or authorization. Any user who has access to the server with the HBA software can access the LUN masking properties and make any change they desire. Furthermore, most LUN masking software also has the ability to find all available LUNs. If a malicious, unauthorized, or accidental user were to gain access to the operating system, he or she would not need to know the specific LUN information, but could use the LUN masking software to find and display all LUNs in the SAN and simply connect, which is especially dangerous on Windows operating systems since Windows like to own every LUN it can see. Again, should organizations be comfortable relying on the security of their Windows or Unix machines to protect their entire confidential SAN data? If not, they should not use LUN masking using node WWNs at the client node.

As shown in Figure 3.16, to disable LUN masking and gain access to view all accessible LUNs, a user can simply click on the Disable LUN Mapping button on the lower-right corner. Next, a user can use the LUN masking software to query the fabric for all available LUNs. Finally, after all available LUNs have been enumerated, a user can simply map all the LUNs (masking none of them) and subvert any prior LUN masking controls.

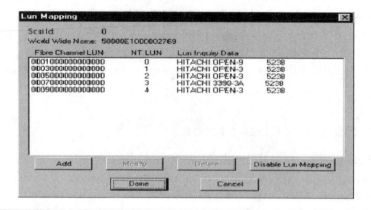

Figure 3.16   Disabling LUN masking.

ASSESSMENT EXERCISE

Complete the following steps to subvert LUN masking at the client node using the HBAnywhere software driver from Emulex. The architecture for the subversion is shown in Figure 3.17.

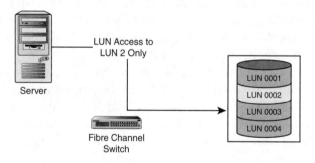

Figure 3.17   LUN masking architecture.

1. Log on to any Windows server connected to the SAN (use your favorite Windows attack, poor password, or insecure default configuration method to do so).

2. Open up the Emulex HBAnywhere Software:

   a. Start -> Programs -> HBAnywhere.

3. When the utility opens, the software will query the SAN fabric for all available adapters and show them in the left window of the software.

4. Highlight the local node's adapter on the left side in order to subvert the current LUN masking rules.

5. On the right side in the Category drop-down box, click on Persistent Bindings. Once selected, the available SCSI targets (LUNs) will appear in the window box (if zoning is not used, all LUNs available in the SAN will appear). See Figure 3.18.

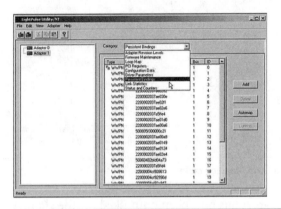

Figure 3.18 HBA software to unmask all LUNs.

6. Select the SCSI target to unmask for the node and then click the Lunmap button.

7. The LUN Mapping screen should appear. At this point, all LUNs masked and unmasked are displayed. See Figure 3.19.

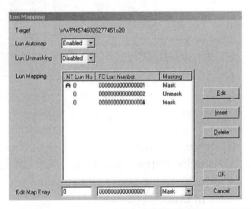

Figure 3.19 Masked LUN Mapping table.

8. To unmask a targeted LUN, select the LUN in the LUN Mapping window. In our example, we will choose LUN 0000000000000001.

9. In the Edit Map Entry row at the bottom, select Unmask from the drop-down menu in the last field and then click OK. See Figure 3.20.

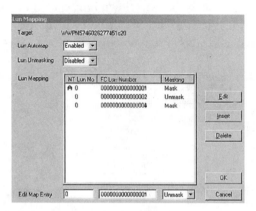

Figure 3.20   Unmasked LUN Mapping table.

10. Done! The SCSI target has now been unmasked for the client and is now available for access. See Figure 3.21.

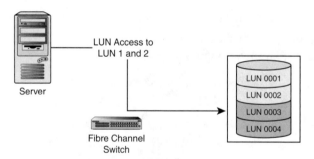

Figure 3.21   The SCSI target is now available.

Unmasking a specific LUN is a simple process with the use of client-based LUN masking; however, unmasking all LUNs in the entire SAN is not much harder. HBAnywhere software also has the ability to unmask all the LUNs globally on a certain HBA, allowing the node to see all LUNs available in the SAN (or zone).

ASSESSMENT EXERCISE

Complete the following steps to unmask all LUNs for an HBA:

1. Open the Emulex HBAnywhere software:
   a. Start -> Programs -> HBAnywhere.
2. Select the HBA in the left pane that you want to globally unmask all LUNs to.
3. On the right side in the Category drop-down box, click on Persistent Bindings. See Figure 3.22.

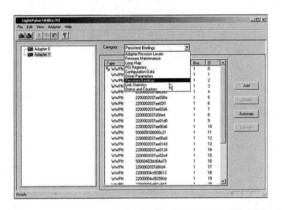

Figure 3.22   HBA software to unmask all LUNs.

4. The Global Automap textbox should appear. In the Unmask All Luns drop-down box, select Enabled.
5. Click OK.
6. Done! All LUN masking has now been disabled for the HBA. See Figure 3.23.

In addition to simply accessing the HBA driver software, changing the WWN method—using node WWNs instead of port WWNs—can be completed if LUN masking occurs at the client level. Again, no authentication or authorization is required to change LUN masking methods. All methods can be changed using existing software accessible on the server.

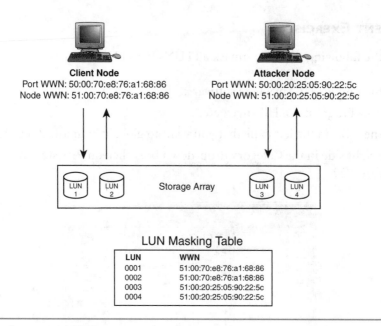

Figure 3.23   Automapping LUNs.

ASSESSMENT EXERCISE

In order to change the LUN masking methods using Emulex HBAs, complete the following steps:

1. Use the Iputilnt utility to change the mapping method to NodeName. Ensure the registry setting change to `HardAddress-0;MapNodeName=1`.
2. Ensure the WWN now being used for the target does not change (this will be the value that will be spoofed later on).
3. Reboot.
4. The new mapping should now be using Node WWN for SCSI targets.

Now that we understand that LUN masking at the client node offers no security whatsoever and can be subverted in a variety of ways, let's move on to LUN masking at other parts of the SAN fabric.

LUN MASKING AT THE SWITCH, STORAGE CONTROLLER, OR USING THIRD-PARTY SOFTWARE

LUN masking can be conducted on the storage controller, the switch, or a third-party software. Although subverting LUN masking rules configured at the client node is quite a trivial process, the act of subverting LUN masking when implemented at the storage controller, switch, or third-party software highly depends on the type of WWN in use (either port WWNs or node WWNs).

To recap, LUN masking relies on the WWN of the HBA for masking properties. If a switch or storage controller is enforcing LUN segmentation, then it would use the WWN of the HBA as the authorization entity to permit or deny access to a LUN or a set of LUNs. If the switch or storage controller uses a port WWN (pWWN) instead of the node WWN (nWWN), then LUN masking is more secure.

As you can probably guess by now, since the ability to change or spoof a HBA's node WWN is a trivial process, the ability to subvert a LUN masking entity is within grasp. The key question many of you might be asking is, "even if I could spoof my WWN and attempt to access a LUN I don't have authorization for, how do I gain access to the other WWNs and the LUNs that I want to access?" This is a very good question; however, they have been both answered already in an indirect fashion. The ability to enumerate WWNs and LUNs in the SAN can be done by the HBA device driver automatically. As mentioned previously, many HBA drivers had the ability to "learn" about its surrounding in the SAN, thus polling information from the fabric or switches' name server regarding information on all WWNs and LUNs in the fabric. Furthermore, most HBA device drivers also have a similar utility to find all LUNs, including their subsequent LUN IDs, and present the information to the client node. In order to subvert LUN masking properties, the user can simply change their node WWN to match the node WWNs enumerated from the switches' name server or fabric itself. This would allow the attacker to access any LUNs of the node WWN they have spoofed.

Because LUN masking on the switch, storage controller, or third-party application relies on WWNs for node identification, which is an entity that can easily be spoofed and enumerated in the fabric, LUN masking is a very high-risk item in terms of data exposure. The combination of a high-risk attack with low-level difficulty makes LUN masking a targeted attack type.

In order to defend against LUN mask subversion, several things can be done. The first one is the use of port WWNs instead of node WWNs for LUN masking. Since it is not possible to change an HBA's port WWN, it would be a lot harder for an attacker to spoof a port WWN under a node WWN and subvert LUN masking tables. However, there are attack methods to subvert LUN masking using port-based WWNs also. A malicious user can change their node WWN to be any HEX value they want, including the node WWN of another entity, which is the traditional spoofing attack, or the port WWN of another entity. The attacker can change their node WWN to match the port WWN of their target and bypass LUN masking tables using port WWN values for segmentation. While the attacker does not have the correct port WWN to spoof the LUN masking table, they would now have the correct node WWN to spoof the LUN masking table. The defense key would be to ensure the entity that is performing the LUN masking only checks for the correct port WWN of a client node and not the node WWN of a client node. If the LUN masking entities do check both WWNs (node and port) for a correct value, which some LUN masking software has done before, then LUN mask subversion with port WWNs would be successful since the node WWN of the attacker matches the port WWN of the target node. This attack tricks the LUN masking entity by showing the correct port WWN value even though it is in the node WWN field.

Assessment Exercise

Complete the following steps to subvert LUN masking at the storage array, switch, or third-party application using the elxcfg software driver from Emulex. The attack's architecture is shown in Figure 3.24.

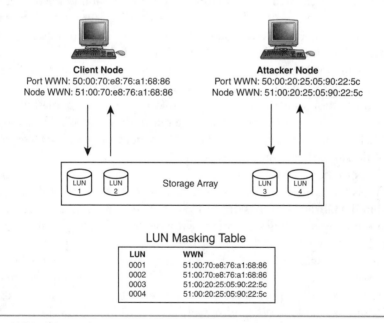

Figure 3.24   LUM masking subversion.

1. Find the WWN of a client node that has access to the LUN you want to compromise.

   a. Using any browser, type the IP address of the Fibre Channel switch that is used in the fabric.

   b. Click on the Name Server button.

   c. Select a WWN of a client node that appears on the name server table that you want to target. In this example, we target a node connected to port 1 with the WWN of 510070e876a16886. Our system is connected to port 15 with the WWN of 510020250590225c (see Figure 3.25).

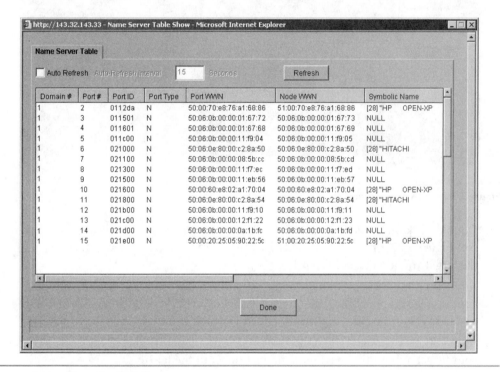

Figure 3.25 Name Server Table.

2. Open the Emulex configuration software (see Figure 3.26):

   a. Start -> Programs -> Emulex -> elxcfg.

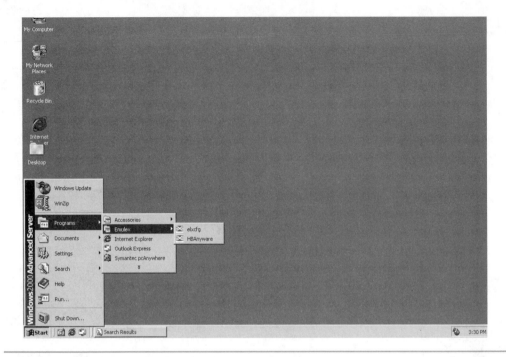

Figure 3.26   HBA configuration.

3. Double-click on the adapter in the Available Adapters section of the driver software (see Figure 3.27). This will be the HBA you want to change to match the WWN of the target you identified in step 1.

4. After you double-click on the adapter, the Adapter Information window should appear (see Figure 3.28). Click on the Change Node WWN button and enter in the node WWN of the HBA identified in step 1, which would be 510070e876a16886.

5. After you have changed the node WWN of your adapter to match the node WWN of your target, reboot the machines and reconnect to the fabric.

6. After the HBA driver connects to the fabric, the target LUN associated with the spoofed WWN should now appear.

7. Done! LUN masking has now been subverted via WWN spoofing.

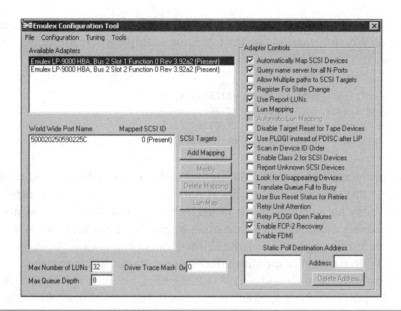

Figure 3.27   Emulex configuration tool.

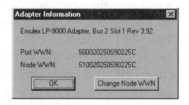

Figure 3.28   WWN spoofing.

If the storage array chooses to recognize a node by its port WWN and not its node WWN, an attacker could still successfully perform a WWN spoofing if the storage array searches both the node and port WWN when performing LUN masking. For example, if the LUN masking table in Figure 3.25 uses the port WWN and not the node WWN, it would use the value of 50:00:70:e8:76:a1:68:86 for LUN 0001. However, using step 4 in the preceding example, the attacker could change their node WWN to match the port WWN or their target instead of its node WWN. After the attacker changes their node WWN to the port WWN of their target, they would have the port WWN of 50:00:20:25:05:90:22:5c (existing non-changing WWN) and the node WWN of 50:00:70:e8:76:a1:68:86 (spoofed port WWN of target). When the storage array searches for the right node, if it checks the node WWN values as well as the port WWN values, the attacker would be allowed access to LUN 0001 since the node WWN matches the correct port WWN information. See the following example where the authorized user's port WWN is also the malicious user's node WWN:

```
Authorized user's port WWN: 50:00:70:e8:76:a1:68:86
Authorized user's node WWN: 51:00:70:e8:76:a1:68:86
Malicious user's port  WWN: 50:00:20:25:05:90:22:5c
Malicious user's node  WWN: 50:00:70:e8:76:a1:68:86
```

Despite the problems with WWN spoofing and LUN masking, there are other ways to protect against this attack besides the use of port WWNs. Many storage controllers now support the ability for a node to be identified by both its port WWN and its node WWN. Because identifying a node by one or the other opens the opportunity for WWN spoofing attacks (as described previously), the ability to identify a node by both port and node WWN would mitigate WWN spoofing attacks. For example, if the storage array recognized nodes by both the node and port WWN together, the node that the attacker spoofed in the previous example would be recognized as: 50:00:70:e8:76:a1:68:86:51:00:70:e8:76:a1:68:86. The attacker could change their node WWN to 51:00:70:38:76:a1:68:86 to match the node WWN of the target or 50:00:70:e8:76:a1:68:86 to match the port WWN of the target, but could not change their port WWN to match the target. This would leave the new WWN of the attacker to be 50:00:20:25:05:90:22:5c:51:00:70:38:76:a1:68:86 or 50:00:20:25:05:90:22:5c:50:00:70:e8:76:a1:68:86, neither of which would be recognized by the storage array as the correct WWNs. See the following example where the node WWNs match but the port WWNs do not match, thus mitigating WWN spoofing attacks by the use of both the node and port WWNs together as node identifiers.

```
Authorized node: 50:00:70:e8:76:a1:68:86:51:00:70:e8:76:a1:68:86
Malicious node:  50:00:20:25:05:90:22:5c:51:00:70:38:76:a1:68:86
```

ATTACK SUMMARY: LUN MASKING SUBVERSION

Attack description—Subverting LUN masking properties and gaining exposure to LUNs that should be masked-off to a particular storage node.

Risk level—High. An unauthorized entity could gain access to sensitive data with trivial attacks.

Difficulty—Low. Most HBA device drivers allow the ability to disable LUN masking when implemented at the storage node. If LUN masking is implemented at the storage controller, typical WWN spoofing would subvert the LUN masking rules also.

Best practice—Port binding should be used to lock a node's WWN to the physical switch port of the switch to prevent WWN spoofing attacks.

LUN masking subversion is also a very trivial attack that contains various methods to execute. Additionally, the reliance of LUN masking to protect data volume creates a significant security exposure for SAN architectures that depend on security. The LUN masking subversion attack has a high security threat and also is a high-risk item (see Figure 3.29).

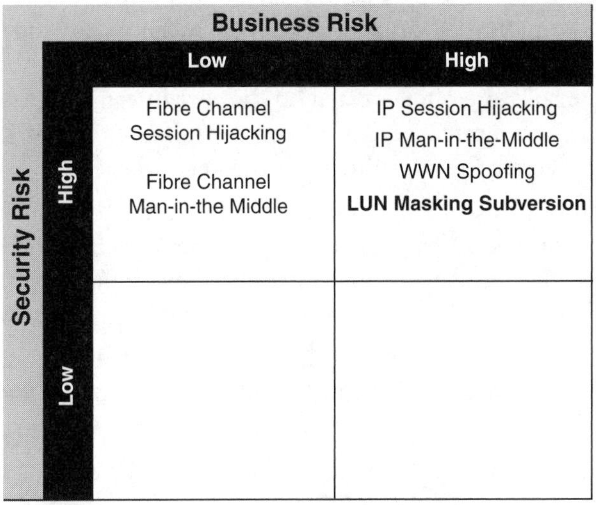

		Business Risk	
		Low	**High**
Security Risk	**High**	Fibre Channel Session Hijacking Fibre Channel Man-in-the Middle	IP Session Hijacking IP Man-in-the-Middle WWN Spoofing **LUN Masking Subversion**
	Low		

Figure 3.29   SBR chart—LUN masking subversion.

STORAGE MANAGEMENT CONSOLES

The last area of concern that we will discuss in terms of SAN risks is the management consoles that are used for SANs. Management consoles used to manage a SAN are often an ignored entity in terms of protection and risk management. As best practice, the entity that can control all the sensitive and critical data should be protected to a greater degree that the average desktop or server on the local area network (LAN). While this may seen to be an obvious point that should not need a lot of explanation, the amount of insecure management consoles in networks today far exceed any acceptable number. The key problem is that IT or operation groups do not always get the necessary support in order to secure their critical machines differently than their basic machines. As we all know, not all servers are equal—some hold critical data, such as source code, some have access to sensitive data, such as management consoles, and some don't have any sensitive data at all, like the MP3 server on the network. While the MP3 server is probably the most important server to most employees, it does not require a high level of security since all the data of the server can be open to the organization. On the other hand, management consoles should be limited only to key personnel with a high level of security. There are some key mistakes used by organizations where deployment management consoles not only have access to manage the SAN, but also house sensitive application such as Veritas SANPoint, EMC Control Center, or CA. The following lists the key areas:

- Management consoles are often located on the core internal network of an organization, which allows any employee, contractor, consultant, and possibly business partner to attempt to access this machine from the network.

- Management consoles are often configured by IT from a basic corporate image. Many of the insecure defaults, poor security settings, patches, and hotfix schedules are similar to the one basic operating system used by employee staff instead of ones that are used for critical servers such as mail, database, and file servers.

- Management consoles usually do not require two-factor authentication, but rather a simple username and password to authenticate. The ease of deploying key loggers makes the ability to gain a password from an internal trusted user a simple task.

- Many management applications are deployed on management consoles that are using default operating systems configurations. This includes running dangerous services, binaries, and applications by default that are not necessary for the management console and actually severely increase the security risk of the machines.

The fact that management consoles control access, and can delete all the data in a SAN is significant. This type of power for any type of machine should requite a higher level of security as it becomes a significant security risk for SAN architectures and a primary target for attackers.

SUMMARY

This chapter was able to identify some of the key risks in the Fibre Channel devices and how they affect the overall SAN architecture, such as WWNs and LUN masking. It focused on the major components of Fibre Channel SANs, including Host Bus Adapters, storage controllers, and storage management consoles. By reviewing each of these entities independently, the chapter was able to enumerate the risks associated with each and how they affect the overall security of the SAN. The chapter also discussed how many assumptions can undermine the SAN's security, such as spoofing and insecure LUN masking on management consoles.

SANs: Zone and Switch Security

A good defense is a strong offense. Translation: Test your SAN for security holes before malicious actions or accidental changes take place. Most of security is focused around attackers; however, security for SANs often translates into the assurance that employees or administrators do not accidentally perform actions (or have the ability to perform actions) that affect the SAN in a negative way (downtime or data loss). A SAN attack or configuration mistake is an interesting topic for many end users. For example, a storage administrator equipped with the right security information can implement protection in a more intelligent manner. On the other hand, an organization's legal council may need to understand the implications of SAN security for compliance reasons with government regulations.

This chapter is the last of three chapters on Fibre Channel SAN security, specifically focusing on zone and switch security, risks, and possible attacks. Each of the previous two chapters were very important in order to qualify storage security risks about severe SAN attacks that may compromise data or leave it unavailable.

Security risks in Fibre Channel switches vary depending on the type of exposures that are eminent, such as management exposures, data exposures, routing exposures, or configuration exposures. The following sections will describe several security risks in Fibre Channel switches regardless of the vendor, as they pertain to data protection and storage security. The areas that will be addressed are as follows:

- Zoning
- Zone hopping
- Switch attacks

ZONING

Security risks in Fibre Channel zoning are based on the pervious chapter concerning WWN spoofing. Although the ability to change a WWN, which happens to be the sole entity use for security (authorization) in most SANs, is a serious risk, the implementation methods of zoning make it a bigger security threat. The first idea is to discuss zoning and its security problems.

Zoning is the logical separation of nodes connected to a Fibre Channel switch. Zoning was originally intended to be used as a segmentation tool to logically separate data storage units. While zoning is an excellent segmentation tool, it has quickly turned into a security tool due to the lack of any other utility that can provide security. As SANs continue to connect to nodes with different trust levels (nodes in a DMZ or internal network as opposed to tape drives), zoning must be used for security as well as segmentation.

The following example will attempt to show why zoning is a good segmentation tool but not a good security tool. Let's say you have 10 files on a server, called A, B, C, D, E, F, G, H, I, and J. Files A through E are intended for computer 1, and files F through J are intended for computer 2. You want to segment the 10 files into two different folders, called folder 1 and folder 2. Computer 1 only has access to folder 1, and computer 2 only has access to folder 2. You place file A, B, C, D, and E into folder 1 and F, G, H, I, and J into folder 2. You have now logically segmented the data (files). Now if there was a real file server that contained sensitive information, you would probably place permissions on folder 1 and folder 2 so only computer 1 and computer 2 have access to the correct folders. The distinction with zoning is that it does not place added permissions. It only segments the block level data, but does not place any security on top of that segmentation. When applied to our example, zoning would be equivalent to restricting folder 1 to the name of "computer 1" and folder 2 to the name of "computer 2." Changing the host name of a computer is very easy on Windows, Unix, and Macintosh environments, similar to how WWN are easy to change with HBA drivers. The use of segmentation without proper security leaves data in either folder vulnerable to compromise.

At this point, you may be wondering why anyone would want to use the Fibre Channel SAN to access data instead of the regular IP network. After considering a sample attack path, you will see that the SAN can possibly be a better attack target than the IP networks. Consider the two paths to data based on IP and Fibre Channel described in Figure 4.1.

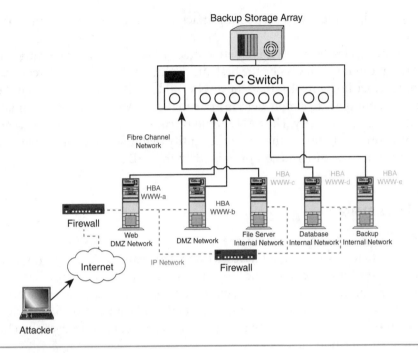

Figure 4.1 Data attack paths.

IP network:

1. Compromise the web server in the DMZ.
2. Via the web server, subvert the internal firewall.
3. Once the internal firewall is subverted, compromise the internal file server.
4. Once the file server is compromised, compromise the data on the storage array.

Fibre Channel network:

1. Compromise the web server.
2. Change the WWN and gain access to large volumes of data in the storage controller.

Based on the preceding attack vectors, which one seems more attractive for an external attacker looking for the path of least resistance? Also, which path will obtain more data with the least amount of work? Both attacks rely on an insecure operating system, which is more common than not for many enterprise networks. After the first-tier web servers are compromised, a simple WWN spoofing attack can cause data protection problems for the SAN.

In this example, clearly the SAN is a better attack target than the IP network; however, this does not mean it will always be the best attack path. If the SAN is only connected to the database server in Figure 4.1, then the SAN would still be inaccessible from the DMZ network. The example is to simply demonstrate that the SAN should not automatically be trusted due to its obscurity. The SAN should be considered as a valid attack route that needs to be addressed (along with every other entity that holds or controls data), which actually turns out to be easier to compromise than most IP devices.

ZONE HOPPING

Zone hopping is the act of an unauthorized node sending frames to another node in a zone that they do not or should not have access to. For example, let's say a node connected to the test environment in zone T should not have access to nodes that are in the production environment in zone P. By using zone hopping attacks, where the node in zone T can subvert the name server or the route table and gain access zone P, which allows frames from a test zone to reach the production zone. Figure 4.2 shows a high-level example of zone hopping.

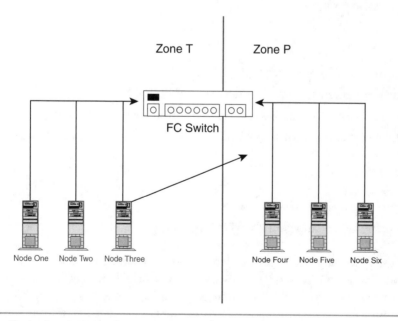

Figure 4.2   Zoning hopping example.

The idea behind zone hopping was first introduced many years ago in IP networking with the VLAN hopping attacks. VLANs (Virtual LANs) are logical segmentations of IP networks connected to a single switch. For example, if you have a Cisco 6500 series switch with 100 ports, you could divide the ports into 10 VLANs, each having 10 ports. While all devices are actually connected to one physical Cisco switch, there are virtually 10 separate switches connecting all the devices independently. VLAN hopping became a security issue when packets from a certain VLAN were able to reach nodes on other VLANs, subverting any security controls and keeping the two VLANs separate. The issue was a very big security concern because many networks were using VLANs to separate trusted networks from untrusted networks, such as DMZ networks from internal networks. VLAN hopping possibilities made the virtual gap between the two networks insecure and unstable. While Cisco has drastically improved their VLAN technology, zones on Fibre Channel switches have far to go. Similar to our discussion in Chapter 1, "Introduction to Storage Security," on how several attacks don't change, but get modified, the idea of VLAN hopping can be applied to SANs in the form of zone hopping.

Before we discuss zone hopping, we must first talk about Fibre Channel switch zoning.

DEFINING ZONING

Note that there different definitions from different vendors regarding zoning. Most of the similar definitions are listed here; however, since vendors can use the same terminology but add their own unique features, it would not be odd if a vendor had a slightly different definition than what is listed. For the most part, though, the following is a summarized look at zoning.

Soft and hard zoning are based on routing information, which uses the 24-bit fabric address of each SAN node (similar to an IP address in an IP network). The 24-bit address identifies a node in the fabric using Fibre Channel layer 2, the signaling/framing layer. The 24-bit fabric address, also referred to as the port ID, is used to route frames from one node to the other in a SAN fabric. There are two types of zoning: hard zoning and soft zoning. In additional to zoning, there are two additional methods to create members of a zone, including WWN-based zones and port-based zones. It is important to note that WWN-based zone membership is not the same as soft zoning, and port-based zone membership is not the same as hard zoning. There is a lot of documentation between vendors that might confuse the four items, but they are different things. The following is a definition for each item:

Types of zoning:

- **Hard zoning**—Enforcement-based zoning. Nodes must be authorized to communicate with each other in order to receive routing information as well as be actively permitted through routing filters. If two or more nodes are part of the same zone or are part of different zones that are allowed to communicate with each other, then they will receive routing information in order to access one another. If a node in one zone attempted to access a node in another zone that it does not have access to, hard zoning would restrict the traffic.

- **Soft zoning**—Information-based zoning. Nodes must be authorized to communicate with each other in order to receive routing information, but no active filtering is conducted to ensure the authorized routing. If two or more nodes are part of the same zone or are part of different zones that are allowed to communicate with each other, then they will receive route information to access one another. If a node in one zone knows how to route to another node in a different restricted zone, soft zoning would not restrict the traffic but only restrict the communication of route information to the unauthorized zone member.

The differences between soft and hard zoning can be better understood with an unlisted phone number example. If a person unlists their phone number from the public phone book to avoid all calls from unwanted callers, such as telemarketers, a potential caller would not be able to query the phonebook for their number and therefore would be unable to make the call. However, if the unwanted caller was able to find the person's phone number through other means, such as personal information that is often sold by certain credit card companies, the unwanted caller could place a call to the person's home and have their phone ring—thus, the unwanted caller would be able to call the person despite their unlisted phone number. This scenario closely corresponds to soft zoning on a Fibre Channel switch. In soft zoning, if a node in zone A wanted to communicate with a node in zone B but did not have permission to access zone B, they first would query the name server for the correct route information to the node in zone B. The name server would recognize that the node in zone A does not have permission to access the node in zone B and therefore would not divulge information on how to route to zone B from zone A. However, if the node in zone A already knew how to route to the node in zone B, soft zoning would not restrict the communication and would allow the unauthorized node in zone A to communicate with the node in zone B. Notice that there is no restriction of traffic in soft zoning, only restriction of route information.

Using the same unlisted phone number example and hard zoning, if the unwanted caller attempted to make a telephone call to the person with the unlisted number, the phone would not actually ring on the receiver's side because it is actively being filtered. The unwanted caller is actively restricted from calling the phone number (and so the phone never rings on the receiver side), even though he or she has identified the correct number. This scenario closely corresponds to hard zoning. In hard zoning, if a node in zone A wanted to communicate with a node in zone B but did not have permission to access zone B, it would query the name server for the correct route information. The name server would recognize that the node in zone A does not have permission to access the node and zone B and therefore would not divulge information. Unlike soft zoning, if the node in zone A already knew how to route to the node in zone B, hard zoning would actively restrict the communication and would not allow any traffic between the two zones. Notice that there is active restriction of traffic in hard zoning, as well as restriction of route information.

In addition to hard and soft zoning, there are two methods to identify zone members of a given zone. For example, a common method to identify what city you live in is your area code. The area codes of 510, 415, 612, and 605 correspond to Oakland, CA, San Francisco, CA, Minneapolis, MN, and Brookings, SD, respectively. The phone company can identify what city (or county) you belong to by your area code. This example correlates to WWN-based zone members, where zones members are identified by the 16-character (64-bit) WWN. Other methods used for zone membership allocation is the actual physical port number on the Fibre Channel switch. For example, a 16-port switch can have four zones where zone A is physical port 1 through 4, zone B is port 5 through 8, zone C is port 9 through 12, and zone D is port 13 through 16. The following descriptions explain the two types of zone membership allocation:

Types of zone membership:

- **WWN zoning**—A zone's membership based on the WWNs of the attached HBA of node.

  WWN-based zone membership can be based on a HBA's node WWN (nWWN) or port WWN (pWWN).

- **Port zoning**—A zone's membership is based on the physical port numbers on the FC switch that the HBA is connected to.

  Port-based zone membership is based on port numbers of each Fibre Channel switch, regardless of WWN values.

PORT AND NODE WWN

The distinction between a node WWN and port WWN is important to discuss. Earlier in the book, we briefly described how node WWN is the WWN of each Fibre Channel node, which is different from the port WWN that also distinguishes the node on the fabric, but from the port level, not the node level. The distinction is important because zone membership that is based on port WWN is harder to spoof. For example, when changing the WWN in your Emulex adapter (refer to Figure 3.28), notice that only the node WWN can be changed. If zone membership on the switch is using node WWNs to allocate members, then zone hopping attacks are possible (which is a very popular deployment in FC SANs). On the other hand, if port WWN were being used to allocate zone membership, the attacker would have to change their node WWN to match the correct port WWN value. After the attacker changes their node WWN to match their target's port WWN, any zones that are only accepting valid port WWNs from client nodes, versus valid port or node WWN from clients, would prevent the spoofing attack using WWNs. However, if a switch is querying either the port or node for a valid WWN, spoofing attacks would be possible despite the use of port WWNs. Since port WWNs cannot be changed with HBA drivers, the strict use of zone memberships based on port WWNs only (dropping any node WWN values and not querying the node WWN parameters on an HBA) dramatically increases security. See Figure 9.3 in Chapter 9, "Securing Fibre Channel SANs," for full details of port WWN usage.

Now that we fully understand what soft and hard zoning are and how WWN or ports can populate zones, let us proceed to zone hopping attacks. Since there are two types of zoning that can be used and two types of zone membership allocation methods, a zone hopping attack will be different based on the type of zoning that is being used and the type of zone membership that has been deployed. We will discuss how the attack can be completed depending on the following types of implementations:

- Soft zoning with WWN-based membership
- Soft zoning with port-based membership
- Hard zoning with WWN-based membership
- Hard zoning with port-based membership

SOFT ZONING WITH **WWN-BASED** MEMBERSHIP

The following sections describe all the methods to perform zone hopping attacks when soft zoning is used with WWN-based membership methods (node or port WWNs). It should be noted that an overwhelming majority of Fibre Channel SAN deployments use this type of zoning and zone allocation.

WWN-BASED MEMBERSHIP ATTACKS

WWN attacks target zones that have been set up with node WWN (nWWN) for zone memberships. Figure 4.3 shows an example architecture with nWWN for zone membership. The figure shows that six Fibre Channel nodes are connected to a Fibre Channel switch. Node one, three, and four are in zone A and nodes two, five, and six are in zone B. Zoning is based on each node's nWWN.

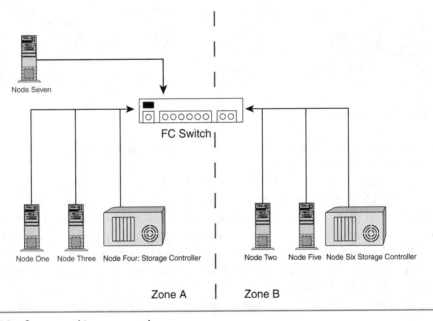

Figure 4.3 Storage architecture sample.

All switches have a name server that describes which nWWNs belong to which zones (see Figure 4.4).

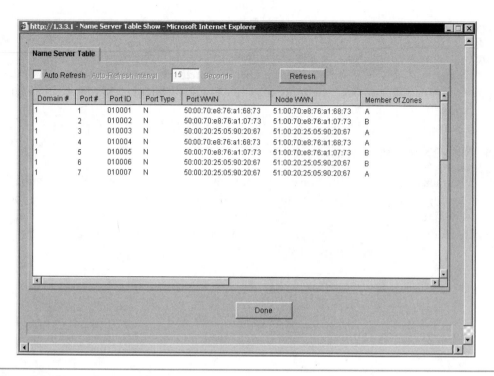

Figure 4.4   Name server sample.

Nodes in zone A are not authorized to access nodes in zone B. Additionally, the switch is using the node WWNs for zoning. If node five, which belong in zone B, wants to communicate with the storage controller in zone A, then node five would need to spoof or change its nWWN to be the nWWN of a node in that zone, such as node one. After node five changes their nWWN to match node one's nWWN, which will require re-initialization of the service on the operating system, then the switch will recognize two nodes with the same WWN trying to access the same LUNs in the storage controllers. Fibre Channel storage devices are not built to have two WWNs connecting to the same LUN at the same time. Unlike CIFS and NFS mounts, where multiple users/machines can access the same mount point, Fibre Channel SANs are built to have only one machine at a time. At this point, both nodes will be unable to access the LUN in the storage controller, confusing the original Fibre Channel node (node one). This equates into a successful denial-of-service attack. The legitimate WWN does not relinquish control of the LUN; however, it does not maintain full control either and cannot access its data anymore. The original WWN will have intermittent access to the remote LUN and possibly lose all real-time access to it altogether. Furthermore, the spoofed WWN doesn't have full access to the drive either, but only the ability to make it unavailable to the network. If this was an Oracle database, this would be a severe problem since all tables and columns will suddenly disappear from the server. It most situations, the actual SAN administrator will troubleshoot the machine and possibly reboot or reinitialize the service. Once the legitimate server reboots or reinitializes the service, it relinquishes control of the LUN. Once the original node (node one) relinquishes control (via reboot or restarts the service), the spoofing node (node five) captures full control of the LUN since there are not two requestors anymore but just one. While this may only last 5 or 10 minutes until the legitimate machines reboots or attempts to reconnect, the attacker is given full access to the data drive and can browse the LUN freely.

It should be noted that the attack is easier with certain switch implementations. Some switches will update name server information based on the most recent information received from the network. For example, if an attacker spoofs their WWN and the request is the most recent frame sent to the switch, the switch will dump the information it originally has and update it with the new information just received. Referencing the attack previously discussed, this would grant the spoofing entity full control of the data rather than a denial of service attack. The reason why many switches support this feature is for fault-tolerance. If one HBA fails on a node, it can automatically switch to the next HBA on the node, which means the Fibre Channel switch has to be willing to receive the new information and update its name server.

ASSESSMENT EXERCISE

Complete the following steps to perform a zone hopping attack on a switch using node WWN for zone memberships. This attack will also use the elxcfg software from Emulex. The attack's architecture is shown in Figure 4.5.

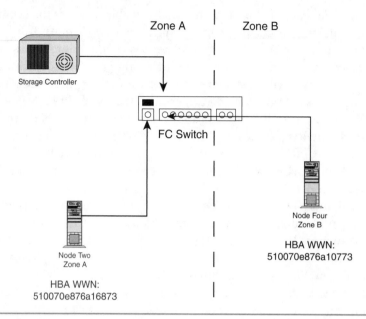

Figure 4.5   SAN architecture.

1. Find the zone you want to hop:

    a. Using any browser, type the IP address of the Fibre Channel switch that is used in the fabric.

    b. Click on the Name Server button.

    c. Select a WWN of a client node that appears on the name server table that belongs to the zone you want to access. In this example, our system (the attacker) is connected to port 2 with the WWN of 510070e876a10773 in zone B, and we want to access the storage controller connected to port 4 in zone A (see Figure 4.6). Our target node is connected to port 1, which is also in zone A, and has the WWN of 510070e876a16873.

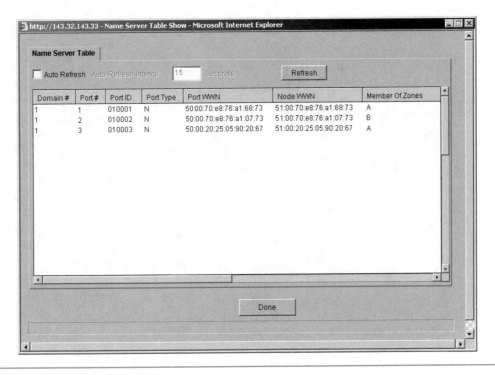

Figure 4.6 Name Server table.

2. Open the Emulex configuration software (see Figure 4.7):

   a. Start -> Programs -> Emulex -> elxcfg.

3. Double-click on the adapter in the Available Adapters section of the driver software (see Figure 4.8). This will be the HBA you want to change to match the WWN of the target you identified in step 1.

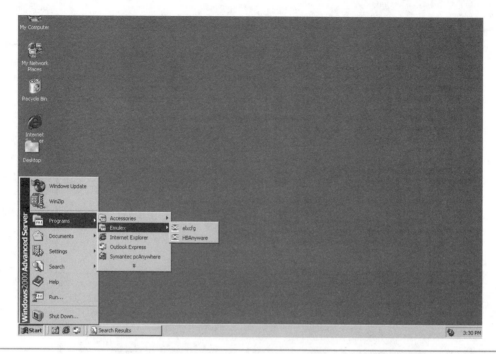

Figure 4.7   Emulex configuration.

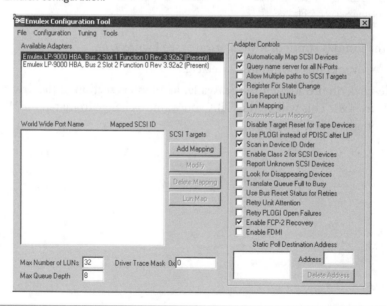

Figure 4.8   Emulex configuration Tool.

4. After you double-click on the adapter, the Adapter Information window should appear (see Figure 4.9). Click on the Change Node WWN button and enter in the node WWN of the HBA identified in step 1, which would be 510070e876a16873.

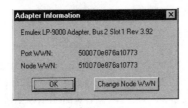

Figure 4.9 WWN spoofing.

5. After you have changed the node WWN of your adapter to match the node WWN of your target, reboot the machines and reconnect to the fabric.

6. After the HBA driver connects to the fabric, the target LUN associated with the spoofed WWN should now appear.

7. Done! Zone hopping has now completed on the Fibre Channel switch.

8. As described previously, at this point both nodes will be unable to access the LUN in the storage controller, confusing the original Fibre Channel node (node one). This equates into a successful denial-of-service attack. The legitimate WWN does not relinquish control of the LUN; however, it doesn't maintain full control either. The original WWN will have intermittent access to the remote LUN and possibly lose all real-time access to it altogether. If the actual SAN administrator reboots or reinitializes the service, node two (the attacker) will capture full control of the LUN since there are not two requestors anymore but just one. This allows the attacker to gain full access to the data.

pWWN-BASED MEMBERSHIP ATTACKS

WWN attacks with the use of port WWNs is more difficult than the use of node WWN, but still possible in certain environments. When switches use port WWN of client nodes, they still identify each entity connected by a WWN, but with a WWN that is static in nature (versus node WWNs that are dynamic since they can be changed). As we all know, WWNs can be spoofed, but only node WWNs, not port WWNs. As mentioned previously, each HBA has two types of WWN: port WWN and node WWNs. A HBA's node WWN can be changed to any value, but a HBA's port WWN cannot be changed.

If zone memberships are based on the port WWN of a client's HBA and zone membership lookups only query a client's port WWN, then port WWN is a secure method for client identification. However, if zone memberships are based on the port WWN of a client's HBA but zone membership lookups query both the port WWN and the node WWN values of a client's HBA for the correct WWN value, then WWN attacks are still possible despite the use of port WWWs. So how does one spoof a port WWN if it cannot be changed? Although an attacker cannot change their port WWN to match their target's port WWN, they can change their node WWN to match their target's port WWN. Because zone membership is based on the correct port WWN value, instead of changing a node WWN to match a target's node WWN, which would be of little value since zone membership is based on the port WWN, the attacker can change their node WWN to the target's port WWN, which is the same port WWN that is being used for zone membership. Figure 4.10 demonstrates this attack vector.

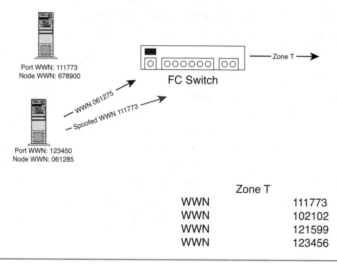

Port WWN: 111773
Node WWN: 678900

FC Switch

— Zone T ⟶

— WWN 061275
— Spoofed WWN 111773

Port WWN: 123450
Node WWN: 061285

Zone T	
WWN	111773
WWN	102102
WWN	121599
WWN	123456

Figure 4.10   Change the node WWN to the target's port WWN.

ASSESSMENT EXERCISE

Complete the following steps to perform a zone hopping attack on a switch using port WWN for zone memberships. This attack will also use the elxcfg software from Emulex. The attack's architecture is shown in Figure 4.11.

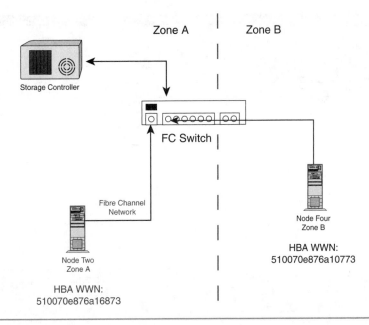

Figure 4.11 SAN architecture.

1. Find the zone you want to hop:

   a. Using any browser, type the IP address of the Fibre Channel switch that is used in the fabric.

   b. Click on the Name Server button.

   c. Select a port WWN of a client node that appears on the name server table that belongs to the zone you want to access. In this example, our system (the attacker) is connected to port 2 with the port WWN of 500070e876a10773 in zone B, and we want to access the storage controller connected to port 3 in zone A. Our target node is connected to port 1, which is also in zone A, and has the WWN of 510070e876a16873.

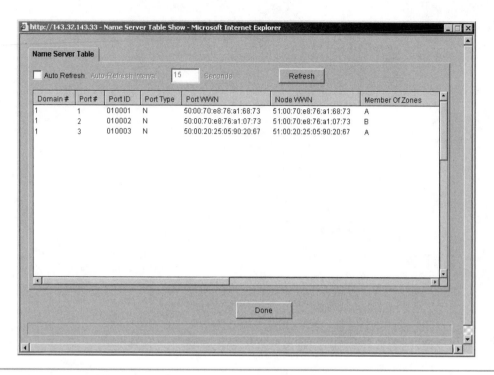

Figure 4.12   Name Server table.

2. Open the Emulex configuration software (see Figure 4.13):

   a. Start -> Programs -> Emulex -> elxcfg.

3. Double-click on the adapter in the Available Adapters section of the driver software (see Figure 4.14). This will be the HBA you want to change to match the port WWN of the target you identified in step 1.

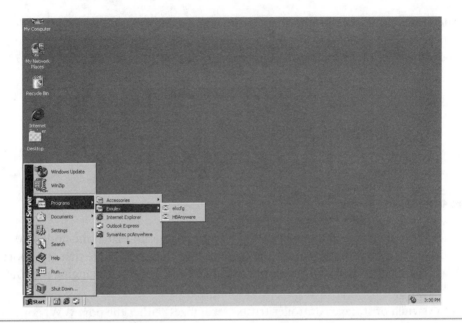

Figure 4.13 Emulex Configuration.

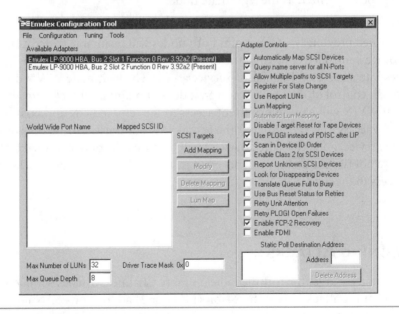

Figure 4.14 Emulex Configuration Tool.

4. After you double-click on the adapter, the Adapter Information window should appear (see Figure 4.15). Click on the Change Node WWN button and enter in the node WWN of the HBA identified in step 1, which would be 500070e876a16873.

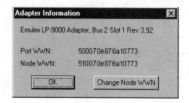

Figure 4.15   WWN spoofing.

5. After you have changed the port WWN of your adapter to match the node WWN of your target, reboot the machines and reconnect to the fabric. Note that even port WWNs are being used; nothing is preventing an attacker from changing their node WWN to match the port WWN of their target system.

6. If the switch or storage controller trusts (recognizes) either the port WWN or node WWN of a client node, then the valid port WWN entry in the attacker's node WWN field will be recognized as the legitimate node.

7. Done! Zone hopping has now completed on the Fibre Channel switch.

8. As described previously, at this point both nodes will be unable to access the LUN in the storage controller, confusing the original Fibre Channel node (node one). This equates into a successful denial-of-service attack. The legitimate WWN does not relinquish control of the LUN; however, it doesn't maintain full control either. The original WWN will have intermittent access to the remote LUN and possibly lose all real-time access to it altogether. If the actual SAN administrator reboots or reinitializes the service, node two (the attacker) will capture full control of the LUN because there are not two requestors anymore but just one. This allows the attacker to gain full access to the data.

SOFT ZONING ATTACKS

Soft zoning attacks target the routing table on Fibre Channel switches. Unlike WWN attacks, soft zoning attacks target the 24-bit (FC layer 2) address of a SAN node. Soft zoning sends route information to nodes in the same zone or nodes in different zones that are authorized to communicate with each other. For example, in Figure 4.3, if node two wanted to communicate with node five, it would be given route information because they both belong in the same zone. Furthermore, if node five wanted to communicate to node one and did not have authorization to zone A, then soft zoning rules would not distribute the routing information to node five. The issue with soft zoning is that if node five knew how to route to node one in zone A, despite the fact that it is in a zone that is restricted to access zone A, node five would be allowed to send frames to zone A because soft zoning does not restrict any frames; it relies on the fact that route information was not given. This would allow any client node with route information the ability to communicate with any and all storage arrays connected to the SAN. For example, let's say an EMC storage array has the 24-bit address of 0x10004 and belonged to zone A, while a client with the 24-bit address of 0x10001 belonged zone B. Despite the fact that zone B is not authorized to access zone A, if the client in zone B knew the route information from 0x10001 to 0x10004 in the fabric, it would have the ability send any frames to it, including frames with SCSI commands such as read, write, seek, and erase.

Denial of service is good example in order to understand how risky the issue really is. Referring back to Figure 4.3, if node five were able to route frames to node one, without authorized access to zone A, then the potential for malicious frames—frames attempting to take a node offline or make it inaccessible to legitimate nodes—can be sent to node one. Furthermore, if node four was the target, which is the storage controller, a denial-of-service attack from an unauthorized node in zone B becomes quite devastating because parts of the SAN may become unavailable and inaccessible for long periods of time. While a denial-of-service attack with VLAN hopping in an IP network would not necessarily equate to network devastation, denial of service with zone hopping attacks would have horrendous results, with large amounts of data becoming unreachable. Next are some high-level steps to perform this attack. In the following example, node five, which is connected to port 5 and belonging to zone B, wants to access node one, connected to port 1 and belonging to zone A. Refer to Figure 4.3 for architectural details:

1. After gaining access to a server connected to the SAN, locate the 24-bit address of node one, also known as the port ID (do not confuse port ID with port number on a switch). This is located in the port ID column on the name server of the Fibre Channel switch, which can be accessed via the web interface. In our example, the port ID of our target is 010001 in hex and 02711 in decimal format.

2. Verify that soft zoning is being used (no real way to verify this besides sending frames to zones that you don't have access to).

3. Using a traffic analyzer, such as Finisar, or software sniffer, such as Ethereal with an IP to Fibre Channel connector, create a frame with the destination ID (D_ID) of 010001 in hex or 02711 in decimal.

4. Ensure the domain ID field (similar to default route) of your frame is set to the Fibre Channel switch's domain ID, which can be found under the "Fabric Topology" button on Brocade switch's web management interface. The value under "Destination Domain ID" on the "Fabric Topology" page is the one you want. If there are multiple Destination Domain IDs, which means there are multiple switches connected to the fabric, go back to the "Name Server" table and verify what Domain your target node belong to. In our example, our targeted node belongs to domain 1. Note: The source address (S_ID) is not important since soft zoning is not doing a restriction based on S_ID, and there is no need to return any frames back to your device.

5. Now that the destination ID and the domain ID fields of the frame have been sent, begin abusing soft zoning methods by sending large amounts of garbage frames to the address of 010001.

6. Done! Despite the restriction of zone B to zone A, node four is now able to send frames to zone two.

SOFT ZONING WITH PORT-BASED MEMBERSHIP

Unlike the use of nWWN for zone membership, using physical port numbers on the FC switch for zone membership has several security advantages; however, it also includes more operational overhead. For example, instead of using nWWNs at a trusted entity, which can be changed quite easily by end users, using physical port numbers as a security control makes the possibility to perform zone hopping virtually impossible. For example, referring back to Figure 4.3, let's say node two, which belongs in zone B, wants to hop across to zone A and communicate with node four, which is the storage controller. The zone membership table on the switch could read that ports 1, 3, 4, and 7 belong to zone A and port 2, 5, and 6 belong to zone B. See Figure 4.16 for an example on how this would look using a Brocade switch.

Notice in Figure 4.16 that any physical switch ports from the left side can be selected and added to the zone b on the right side. By expanding the SwitchPorts folder in the left pane and select the appropriate physical port number, the user can simply select the Add Member button and add the physical port to zone b, which already has ports 2, 5, and 6 in the group. If port-based zoning was being used, any type of spoofing attack would be useless since each time node five attempts to access node four, the zone table would see that node five is connected to physical port 5 and node four is connected to physical port 4, each of which belong to different zones. Port zoning prevents node 5 from hopping across zones by the use of port-based zone memberships.

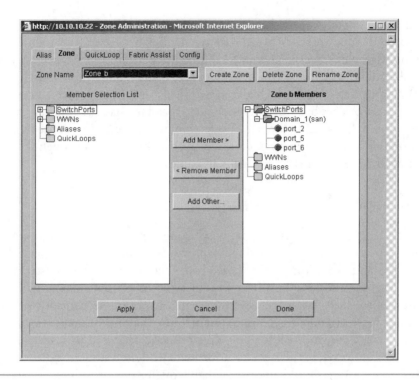

Figure 4.16 Port-based zone membership on a Brocade switch.

You might be asking yourself, if port-based zone membership is significantly harder to subvert, why don't more people use it. There are two reasons: one is the potential for malicious or accidental changes and the other is management overhead.

Many switch vendors actually do not promote the use of port-based zoning because of its security weaknesses. "What weaknesses," you ask? Well, if you had an employee who had access to your internal storage data center, he or she could maliciously or accidentally move cables from one physical switch port to another. For example, let's say node five was physically disconnected from the physical switch port 5 and the reconnected to the physical switch port 1, which belong to zone A. Node five would now have the ability to access zone A. Furthermore, this might not be a malicious employee, but rather it could be an employee who carelessly disconnects and reconnects ports with little to no concern about the security implications. In this aspect, port-based zone membership can be subverted, but physical access to the switch is required. Although that may be a big issue in certain data centers, the weaknesses of WWN overshadow the weaknesses of physical security.

The next criticism about port-based zone membership is the management overhead that it requires. If your SAN is between 4 to 6 switches, port-based zone membership is probably manageable; however, as your SAN grows to be 12 to 14 switches, port-based zone membership can be a very cumbersome process and a management nightmare. Also, WWNs are often over shared between two HBA cards in one server, just in case one goes bad. If an HBA goes bad, the operational overhead to change zoning can be considered burdensome. At the same time, the protection of data and compliance to regulations rely on this cumbersome process; hence, the benefits might outweigh the negatives. This is where the process of risk management comes into play.

SOFT ZONING ATTACKS

Soft zoning attacks under the use of port-based zone membership would be vulnerable to the same type of attacks mentioned in the previous section for soft zoning. The key issue to understand here is that if port-based zone membership is being used, route-based zone hopping attacks with soft zoning rules are still possible. Often many organizations secure one entity, but forget about the other. For example, consider the root or administrator password on an operating system. More than likely, the root or administrator password is a very difficult to guess alphanumeric password with special characters and spaces. However, users in the root (or users who have suid or sudo access) or in the administrator group should also have equally tough passwords due to the fact that a suid, sudo, root, or the administrators group accounts are just as powerful as the real root or administrator account. The idea here is to protect passwords that belong to powerful accounts, not just the root or administrator account. If you are using port-based zone membership with soft zoning, be aware that zone hopping attacks are still possible with routing techniques, though the ability to perform the attack is reduced considerably.

HARD ZONING WITH WWN-BASED MEMBERSHIP

The following sections describe hard zoning security options.

HARD ZONING

Unlike soft zoning, hard zoning is very difficult to subvert. Similar to soft zoning, hard zoning distributes route information to all authorized nodes in a single zone or all nodes that have authorization to access nodes in other zones. Unlike soft zoning, hard zoning also enforces the zones by permitting or denying each frame that is submitted from one zone to the other. Unlike soft zoning, where there is no restriction of frames between zones, hard zoning will also verify that a frame has the permission to access another node in a different zone. If the node has permission, access is granted, if the node does not have permission and is possibly attempting a zone hopping attack, the frame is denied.

With the security benefits of hard zoning, you might be asking yourself why soft zoning is used so predominantly. The first reason is there is a lot of misunderstanding about what hard and soft zoning really is and what it really does. Furthermore, a lot of end users are not aware of the fact that soft zoning has some security limitations. The major reason is probably because a variety of management applications do not work well with switches that have deployed hard zoning in their switches. Many SAN management applications only support switches that are using soft zoning, thus making it very difficult for the SAN administrator to use one management tool for the SAN and yet another tool for only the switches.

nWWN- or pWWN-Based Membership Attacks

Similar to our discussion of using soft zoning with port-based zone memberships, the same idea applies to this section. If you are using hard zoning for the security benefits and are still deploying zones based on nWWNs or pWWNs, then the ability to hop across zones is still possible. Furthermore, the ability to hop across zones using WWN attacks is easier than switch attacks.

Hard Zoning with Port-Based Membership

Hard zoning using physical switch ports for zone membership is the most secure alternative to Fibre Channel switch zoning. Not only would any nWWN spoofing attack be useless, but route-based subversion attacks would also be useless. Hard zoning with port-based zone membership is clearly the more secure method to deploy a Fibre Channel switch. A close second to hard zoning with physical port numbers would be the ability to deploy hard zoning with port WWN, which is one step away from using a physical port number on the switch versus the port WWN assigned to the switch port.

While this is the most secure alternative, as mentioned previously, the process of risk management needs to take place to properly take the statement in context. For example, if your data center has poor physical security and your SAN administrators are very careless when it comes to switch deployment, the fact that WWN-based zone membership protects against these attacks might be more secure than port-based zone membership.

The idea behind risk management is to properly assess the SAN's risk and match it up with the correct functionality that supports security guidelines. Figure 4.17 is a high-level thought process that could be used to determine the type of zoning that can be used.

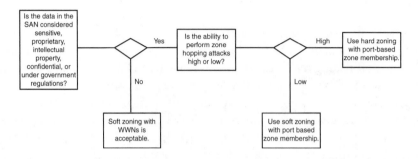

Figure 4.17 Zone alternatives.

Zone hopping is a very trivial attack that contains various methods to execute. Additionally, since zoning is the primary tool used for security, attacks on zoning can compromise, damage, or just make data unavailable for a significant period of time. The zone hopping attack has a high security threat and also is a high-risk item (see Figure 4.18).

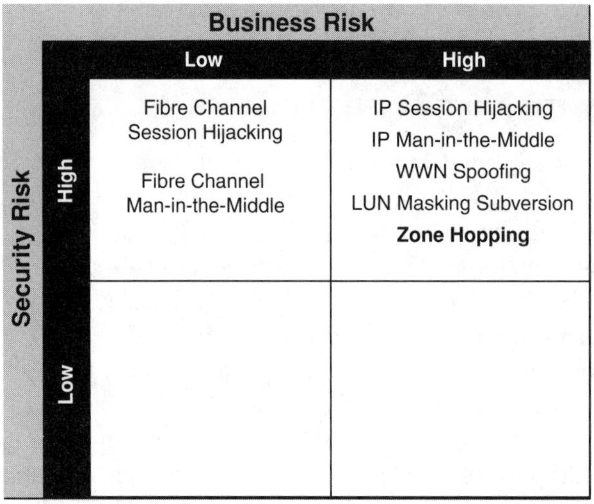

| Business Risk | |
Low	High
Fibre Channel Session Hijacking Fibre Channel Man-in-the-Middle	IP Session Hijacking IP Man-in-the-Middle WWN Spoofing LUN Masking Subversion **Zone Hopping**

Security Risk — High / Low

Figure 4.18 SBR chart—zone hopping.

ATTACK SUMMARY: ZONE HOPPING (WWN)

Attack description—A storage node accessing a zone on a switch when the node is not authorized for that zone.

Risk level—High. An unauthorized entity could gain access to sensitive data with trivial attacks.

Difficulty—Moderate. Zone hopping requires the ability to change a WWN, which is easy to do, and the zones to be set up using nWWN.

Best practice—Fibre Channel zone-sets should be allocated based on physical port numbers on zones to prevent WWN spoofing attacks. However, if physical port numbers cannot be used, ensure that zone memberships based on WWNs are using pWWN and not nWWN for zone membership allocation.

ATTACK SUMMARY: ZONE HOPPING (ROUTING)

Attack description—A storage node accessing a zone on a switch when the node is not authorized for that zone.

Risk level—High. An unauthorized entity could gain access to sensitive data with trivial attacks.

Difficulty—High. Creating routes to nodes on a Fibre Channel switch requires third-party traffic analyzer hardware and software.

Best practice—Fibre Channel zone should use hard zoning if possible to enforce zoning tables, which only publishes routes to authorize nodes, and to ensure that nodes do not attempt to access nodes that they are not authorized for.

SWITCH ATTACKS

Circumventing security controls managed by Fibre Channel switches are key targets. There are also attacks that target poor switch configurations, including the following attacks:

- Switch enumeration
- E-port replication
- Cut-through switching
- Switch management

SWITCH ENUMERATION

Switch enumeration simply involves the process of gaining a significant amount of information about the fabric from the switch's management IP interface. Unfortunately, no authentication is required to gain this information from most Brocade Silkworm switches. The only thing that is required is a web browser, such Internet Explorer or Firefox, and the IP address of the Ethernet interface of the FC switch. A Fibre Channel switch can identify on a SAN by doing a simple port scan on port 80 on the IP network. The result that returns a header with Brocade or McData is the IP management interface of the Fibre Channel switch. Port scanners such as nmap are an easy method to get this information. Once the items have been identified, simply type the IP address of the switch into the URL field in the web browser, download the Java component if your web browser does not already contain it, and then enumerate information from the fabric, including the following items:

- WWNs for spoofing attacks
- Zones names and allocation for zone hopping
- Fabric events for errors
- Fabric topology for fabric enumeration
- Complete name server information

You should notice several tabs that are available to you, including information about the fabric events, fabric topology, name server, zone administration (the only area that requires a password), and a summary view. See Figures 4.19 and 4.20.

With this information, several other attacks, including spoofing and zone hopping, become a lot easier for the unauthorized user.

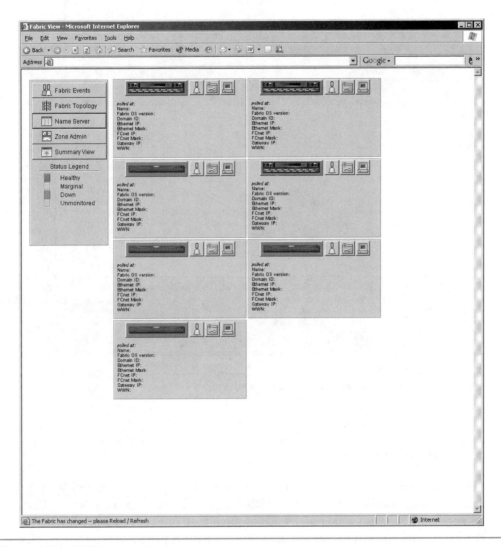

Figure 4.19 SAN Topology view.

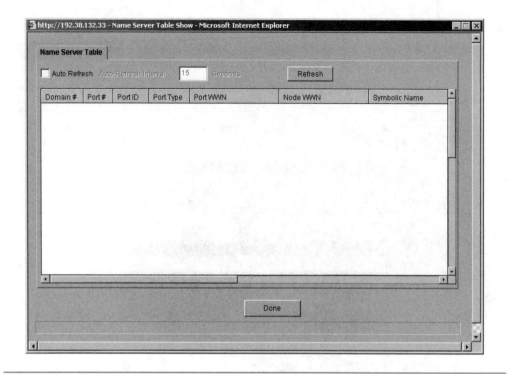

Figure 4.20   Name server view (including zones and WWNs).

E-PORT REPLICATION

Each port on a Fibre Channel fabric, including all ports on a switch, has a distinct type, such as E_Port (expansion port), F_Port (fabric port), G_Port (generic port), L_Port (loop port), and N_Port (node port). Each of them have different uses in a SAN. The E_Port on a switch is used to connect other Fibre Channel switches for an interswitch link. E_Ports are used to link switches for a multi-switch fabric. E-port replication is a feature available on most, if not all, Fibre Channel switches. E-ports are similar to an uplink port on an Ethernet switch. If a port on a Fibre Channel switch is configured as an E_Port and is then connected to another port on a Fibre Channel switch that is also an E_Port, then various types of information is automatically transferred between the switches, such as name server information, route information, and zoning information. This allows motile switches on a single fabric to contain the same information that is always up to date.

There are two main risks with E-port replication. The first one is the ability for unauthorized and untrusted switches to gain access to sensitive fabric information in the SAN. This risk is highlighted in shared infrastructures where all switches and data stores do not belong to the same organization or same trust levels. For example, since there is no authentication or authorization required to transmit sensitive fabric information via E_Ports, the only thing that is required is a single port to be configured as an E_Port. The risk escalates with the fact that all ports on a switch are usually configured as G_Ports, where the port can automatically change to an F_Port if it is connected to a N_Port on the other side, or an E_Port if it recognizes another E_Port on the other side. In a shared environment where a Storage Service Provider (SSP) is granting access to storage nodes, the SSP could accidentally relinquish zone and name server information of the entire fabric that contains sensitive information belonging to other customers of the SSP. Furthermore, your own information could now be exposed to other parties that are also using the same SSP, creating issues with security and several government regulations such as HIPAA, Sarbanes-Oxley, and GLBA.

The second risk with E-port replication is only theoretical at this point; however, there are many methods to making the theoretical practical. When a port on a switch is initialized, it attempts a port initialization and then link initialization in order to see if it should be an F_Port or an E_Port (remember, it is by default a G_Port that can switch to either automatically). If the initialization completes with Internal Link Service (ILS), then it has identified an E_Port on the connecting side so it also becomes an E_Port, assuming the connecting side is a switch. If the switch port receives a FLOGI, then it determines that it is connected to an N_Port and changes itself to an F_Port. The theoretical attack would be a malicious node with an HBA to send ILS frames and not a FLOGI. If the HBA could send ILS frames, a switch may recognize it as an E_Port switch port (since it did not receive a FLOGI) and send fabric information to the port. Because authentication or authorization is not required, the malicious node could receive all types of information about the SAN by only sending ILS communication and mimicking an E_Port and not sending FLOGI information to switches.

The fact that no authentication and authorization is required by default to send and receive information to and from E_Ports is a major risk of a SAN. Furthermore, many Fibre Channel switch ports are configured to automatically become an E-Port if it recognized that another E-Port is connected to it, making the attack as easy as plug and play. Maybe the attack should be renamed the "Plug-and-Play" attack instead of E-port replication!

E-PORT REPLICATION ATTACKS

E-Port (Expansion Port) is a port type available on all FC switches that have the ability to join several switches to become part of a single fabric (similar to an uplink port on an Ethernet switch). Each port on an FC switch has a particular type, including an E-port, F-port, and G-port; however, many switches allow all ports on switches to be E-ports or F-ports, depending on the type of node connected to it. For example, if another switch is connected to the port, it will automatically turn into an E-port; however, if a HBA is connected to a port, it will turn into an F-port. Each different port type provides a different function. For example, F-port types allow the port to connect to client nodes for communication. Additionally, an E-port type would allow the port to connect to other switches for communication. E-port connections between switches enable one switch to exchange information with another switch. The type of information that is exchanged is usually fabric information such as routing, zoning, and fabric name server topologies. The issue with E-port replication is that there is also no authentication required to exchange information from one E-port on one switch to another E-port on another switch. In the case of a storage service provider (SSP) extending its fabric to a client using E-port replication, the trivial act of plugging the SSP's E-port to the client's E-port would exchange all the routing, zoning, and name server information for the entire SSP fabric, not the portion limited to the client itself. This action would allow an unauthorized switch to access information that the switch may not be authorized to have. In addition to SSP issues, default E-port replication without authentication can cause various issues in closed networks or internal SANs also, but the core issue remains that sensitive name server information is given away without any real authentication or validation. Figures 4.21 and 4.22 show an example.

To protect against E-port replication, many Fibre Channel switches provide port-type locking, port binding, and key-based authentication. Port-type locking actually locks the specific port on the Fibre Channel switch to only function as the specific port type, such as F-port only or E-port only. Since any port on a Fibre Channel switch can be an E-port, disabling E-port functionally from all ports except where needed should be set. Additionally, port binding can be used to lock in a particular WWN to a specific port. This not only helps against E-port attacks, but also prevents against spoofing attacks since only a single WWN can belong to a single port, eliminating the ability to connect another switch to a port that already is assigned to a server or spoof a WWN that belongs to another port on the switch.

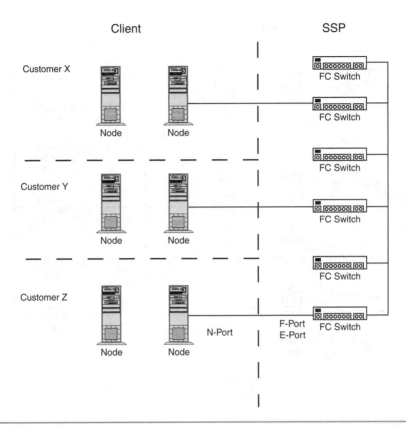

Figure 4.21 SSP architecture example.

In addition to port type locking and port binding, some switch vendors support or will be supporting key-based authentication between the switches. This will prevent unauthorized E-ports from gaining access to fabric information by requiring each switch to authentication before being added to the fabric. Since each authorized switch would be registered, as well as its public key, to the fabric, any not-registered switch without a valid public key would not be allowed to join the fabric. This will disable any type of communication from any two switches until valid keys or certificates have been exchanged. See Chapter 9 for more information on securing SANs.

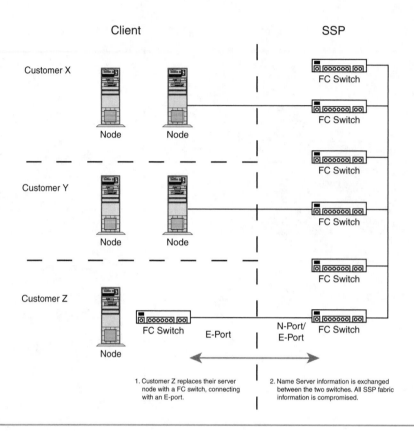

Figure 4.22   E-port attack against an SSP architecture.

E-port replication is a very simple attack since it just requires two E-ports to plug in to each other, but requires physical access to the switch. This attack affects SSP more since shared infrastructures are being used, unlike an organization's own data center storage system. The E-port replication attack has a low security threat and also is a low-risk item (see Figure 4.23).

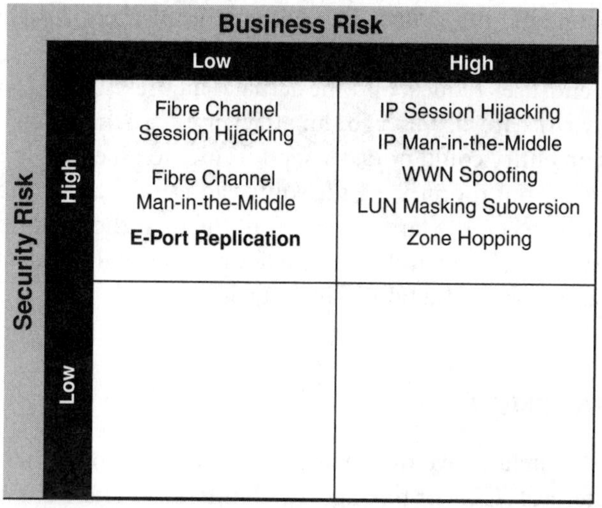

Business Risk		
	Low	**High**
Security Risk — High	Fibre Channel Session Hijacking Fibre Channel Man-in-the-Middle **E-Port Replication**	IP Session Hijacking IP Man-in-the-Middle WWN Spoofing LUN Masking Subversion Zone Hopping
Security Risk — Low		

Figure 4.23 SBR chart—E-port replication.

ATTACK SUMMARY: E-PORT REPLICATION

Attack description—Replicating name server information, fabric information, and sensitive fabric and management information from an authorized switch to an unauthorized switch.

Risk level—High. An unauthorized switch could gain access to an entire fabric.

Difficulty—Moderate. Physical access to a trusted switch as well as improper configuration is required.

Best practice—Lock each port on a Fibre Channel switch to its specific function, such as an F-port or E-port.

CUT-THROUGH SWITCHING

Cut-through switching is another feature on Fibre Channel switches that poses a security risk. *Cut-through switching* is the ability for a switch to start routing frames from one entity to another once the destination ID of the frame has arrived and not waiting until the source ID has arrived to the switch. The ability to implement cut-through switching can drastically increase performance on many Fibre Channel switches, thus reducing the latency between an end-user request and the actual data presentation. While the benefits are nice, the security risks are also nice for an attacker. If cut-through switching has been implemented, then an entity could possibly send frames to an entity in any restricted zone. Since the switch is not monitoring the source address but only the destination, the frame could potentially reach the target node from the unauthorized node without any blocking from the switch. This would open the door for several attack classes, but most notably denial-of-service and data tampering attacks.

SWITCH MANAGEMENT

Most Fibre Channel switches have two methods of management, either through a Command-Line Interface (CLI) or through a web interface. There are two security risks with Fibre Channel switches that pertain to management. One is the use of clear-text protocols, such as Telnet for the CLI and HTTP for web management. Both HTTP and Telnet are clear-text protocols, meaning that anyone with a network IP sniffer could capture the username and password that is used over the wire. The use of Ethernet switches instead of hubs does not prevent attacker from sniffing either, since Man-in-the-Middle attacks are quite trivial to perform on IP networks. See Figure 4.24 more details.

Using any network sniffer, such as Ethereal, we are able to retrieve the user's username and password and compromise the switch. Notice in Figure 4.24 that the username for the connection is in clear-text: admin. Additionally, notice the admin's password is also clear-text, which is password. While some Fibre Channel switches have the ability to implement SSH, most come only with telnet access enabled by default. The username and password, admin and password, traverse the wire in clear text for any malicious user to grab and attack. Considering the amount of data that can be managed by the switch, why would anyone want to use something so insecure to control terabytes of information?

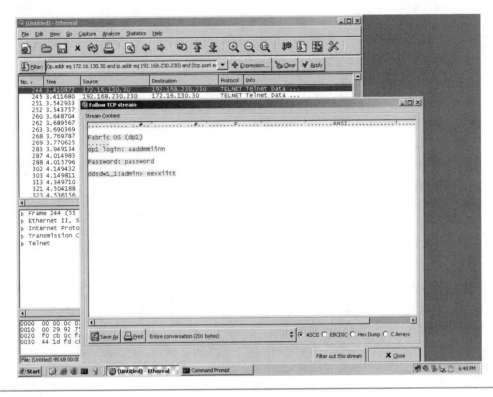

Figure 4.24 Captured username and password from a telnet session.

Similar to telnet session, management can also be conducted via a web (HTTP) interface. It should be noted that many Fibre Channel switches use HTTP for web management but also allow end users to initiate a telnet session from a Java applet on the web browser. Either way, both protocols are still using clear-text communication. Figure 4.25 shows a web management session.

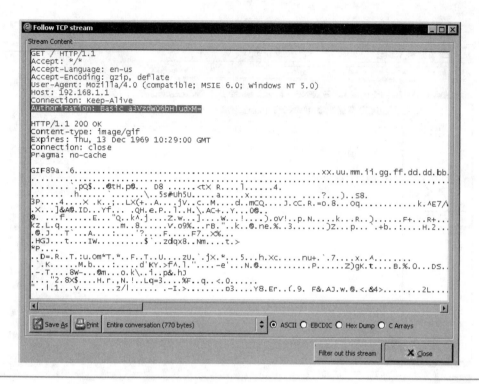

Figure 4.25 Web Authenication Session (Basic Auth).

Notice in Figure 4.25 that the HTTP connection is also in clear-text. All of the data is clear-text HTML. While reading the HTML is much easier in a browser, all information traverses the network in the clear. You may be wondering where the username and password information is. While many devices use HTTP for management, they do require basic authentication from the end user to protect the password. Basic authentication uses the following procedures:

1. The client's web browser display a login box where the end user can enter his or her username and password.

2. The web browser establishes a connection to the device with the username and password entered by the end user.

3. The username/password combination is Base64-encoded before being sent over the network.

4. The device verifies the username and password combination and accepts the connection.

Although using basic authentication, which uses Base64 encoding, helps obfuscate the password, it does not really do much to protect the password. An attacker can easily get the username and password combination from the sniffed HTTP connection. For example, you'll notice that in Figure 4.25, the Authorization row is highlighted because that is where the username and password has been protected. The Base64 encoding has changed the username/password to `a3VzdW06bH1udXM=`. Using any Base64 decoder (Cain and Abel has a Base64 decoder), the Base64 translation of `a3VzdW06bH1udXM=` can be changed to the username kusum and password lynus. See Figure 4.26 for details.

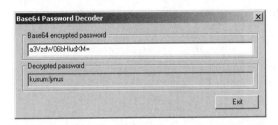

Figure 4.26   Decodes Base64 to clear-text from an HTTP connection.

The use of clear-text protocols for management make all the sensitive and critical data storage in using SANs reduced to a simple attack that has been identified for over 20 years. Nevertheless, the issue of clear-text protocols is not exclusive to Fibre Channel switches. Many other storage devices, including storage controllers, tape devices, and management software, are still using clear-text protocols for access.

While the use of clear-text protocols applies to many network devices, the other issues concerning management are even more interesting. If web management is enabled on many Fibre Channel switches, including Brocade Silkworm series, an abundant amount of information is displayed to the end user without any authentication required at all! Simply connecting to the switch via the management interface (as described earlier)—which means typing the IP address of the Fibre Channel switch into your web browser—is all that is required to gain a significant amount of information, which includes information on the entire fabric. The information includes all WWN names that are used on the fabric, which can be used for spoofing attacks, all zone information (including zone names and allocation of WWN into zones), which can be used for zoning hopping attacks, fabric events, and fabric topology. Basically, all information of the fabric, the SAN, and any connected devices can be gained from just pointing to the web management console, without any username or password required. However, to actually make changes to the switch, a username and password is required, but is usually offered up by telnet, a clear-text protocol. The ability to enumerate a significant amount of information in fabric that is needed to perform a successful attack makes attackers very happy. Additionally, it makes their attacks a lot easier and faster. For example, if a malicious entity wanted to spoof a WWN to hop across a zone, they could start the attack by eventually guessing the right WWN or could just connect to the Fibre Channel switch and view all the WWNs in the fabric and select the one of their choice. Remembering back to the enumeration dialog from Chapter 1 (Figure 1.1), the more information that can be enumerated about a SAN, the more chances of data compromised by an attacker significantly increases.

Switch management attacks are very simple attacks since either no authentication is required or authentication is conducted over insecure protocols such as telnet or HTTP. Since management access to switches would lead to data compromise, insecure switch management is a severe problem for SAN architectures. The switch management attacks have a high security threat and also is a high business risk item (see Figure 4.27).

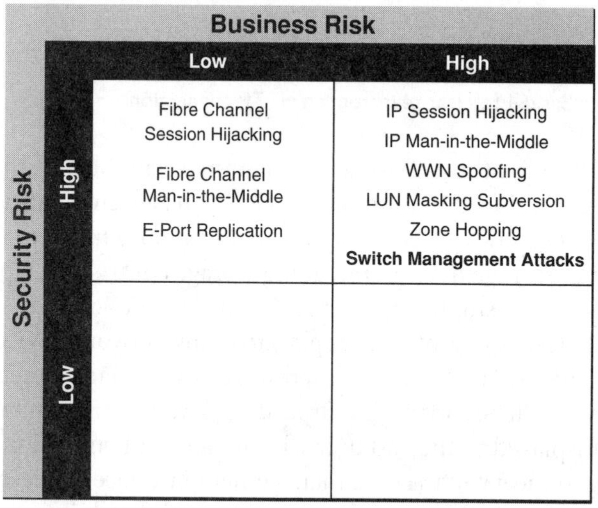

		Business Risk	
		Low	High
Security Risk	High	Fibre Channel Session Hijacking Fibre Channel Man-in-the-Middle E-Port Replication	IP Session Hijacking IP Man-in-the-Middle WWN Spoofing LUN Masking Subversion Zone Hopping **Switch Management Attacks**
	Low		

Figure 4.27   SBR chart—Switch management attacks.

ATTACK SUMMARY: SWITCH MANAGEMENT

Attack description—Compromising a storage device's HTTP or telnet interface, both of which are clear-text, and managing the device. Additionally, HTTP management on switches does not require a username/password to enumerate a significant amount of information, information that can be used to escalate a storage attack.

Risk level—Moderate. An unauthorized entity could gain access to fabric information.

Difficulty—Low. An attacker only needs a web browser to gain fabric information from an FC switch.

Best practice—Ensure that management interfaces on storage devices and SAN management applications are protected from unauthorized users.

SUMMARY

In this chapter, we discussed the core attacks with switch zoning and overall switch security, from the theory to the actual demonstration. The purpose of this chapter was to give you enough knowledge to understand if specific zone and switch attacks affect your environment and to make strong judgments on the risks that these attacks will have on your storage. Key issues about any vulnerability is the ability to perform the attack, the ease of the attack, the risk the attack offers, the likelihood of the attack, and to understand the possible mitigation(s) of the attack. This chapter has presented all these items to prepare you to understand what SAN attacks are, how to perform them, and finally, how to mitigate the issue.

The next chapter shifts away from SAN weaknesses and attacks to NAS weaknesses and attacks.

PART II
NAS SECURITY

NAS Security 5

Security risks in Network Attached Storage (NAS) do not differ greatly from the risks in SANs. Sensitive data in both environments are vulnerable to security attacks or accidental configuration mistakes. NAS storage devices contain weak protocols/communication mediums, insecure configurations, and poor security practices. When comparing NAS environments to the security basics discussed in Chapter 1, "Introduction to Storage Security," NAS has poor authentication, weak authorization, and absent encryption. These measures do not scale well when trying to protect large amounts of data.

Although SANs and NAS have similar security problems, NAS environments can be more susceptible due to their use of IP and Ethernet, equating to more accessibility to unauthorized users. Furthermore, the reliance of protocols such as Common Internet File System (CIFS) and Network File System (NFS), which includes an enormous amount of security issues, makes these environments vulnerable to basic security attacks. Because NFS and CIFS were designed many years ago when the security of IP networks was not a major concern, the tremendous reliance of the weak protocols make any device supporting NFS and CIFS equally as weak and insecure, which includes storage devices.

Although the security issues in NAS architectures are quite alarming, there are existing solutions that can mitigate the security issues to provide a more secure NAS environment. Many NAS storage organizations provide a great deal of security for their products; however, most of the time they are disabled by default and are not communicated to an administrator effectively.

This chapter is one of three chapters where we discuss the security risks and weaknesses associated with NAS architectures. The primary discussion for this chapter is a brief introduction of NAS security risks, which are the basis for the next two chapters. If you are well versed on NFS and CIFS, you may want to proceed to the next two chapters. Those chapters dive deep into CIFS and NFS security weaknesses. The focus of this chapter includes the following topics:

- NAS architectures
- NAS communication
- NAS security
- CIFS basics
- NFS basics
- Command syntax

NAS ARCHITECTURES

NAS storage networks are quite similar to a typical three-tier architectural model, where a client connects to a server and the server is connected to the NAS storage device. The server is connected to the storage device via CIFS or NFS, which is seamless to the client, as if the server and the storage device are one entity. Figure 5.1 shows an example of a storage architecture, and Figure 5.2 shows the virtual representation of the storage architecture to a client.

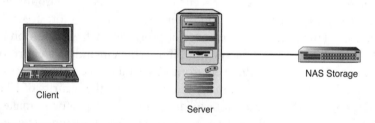

Client

Server

NAS Storage

Figure 5.1   NAS architecture.

Figure 5.2 shows how storage may look to a client connecting to a server, as if the storage volumes are on the server operating system locally.

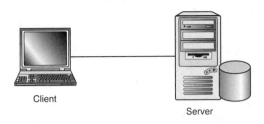

Figure 5.2 NAS virtual architecture.

An important aspect of NAS devices is their seamless connection to other network nodes, allowing storage to be presented as if it is actually local on the machine itself and not over the network. This allows for obvious benefits such as centralized backup, easy data expansion, and storage consolidation. For example, the mail server (e.g. Exchange) that is always running out of storage space due to the fact that users do not delete their email is no longer a significant issue. If the Exchange server has a back-end NAS device connected to it, the storage capacities can be increased as needed in a virtualized manner, requiring very little interaction with the Exchange server itself.

NAS architectures can also include a NAS gateway, also referred to as a NAS head. A NAS head does not have any storage, but is a gateway device that sits in-between a server and the back-end in storage devices running IP or Fibre Channel. It is a true gateway for large amounts of storage using a variety of vendors and communication mediums to front-end servers. Figure 5.3 shows an example architecture with NAS gateways.

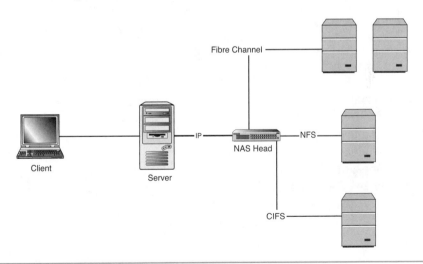

Figure 5.3 NAS head architecture.

NAS COMMUNICATION

NAS products primarily support IP communication over Ethernet. Unlike SANs, which work with block layers, NAS products use file/record layers. NAS uses the upper layers in the OSI model, such as layers 4 through 7, where application protocols such as CIFS and NFS provide file/record services via the network. Unlike block data, NAS relies on TCP/IP, ports, and application services. For example, CIFS relies on Ethernet and IP for layer 2 and layer 3, and then uses layers 4 through 7 for file and port services, such as SMB communication over port 445. Figure 5.4 shows the communication architecture for NAS products.

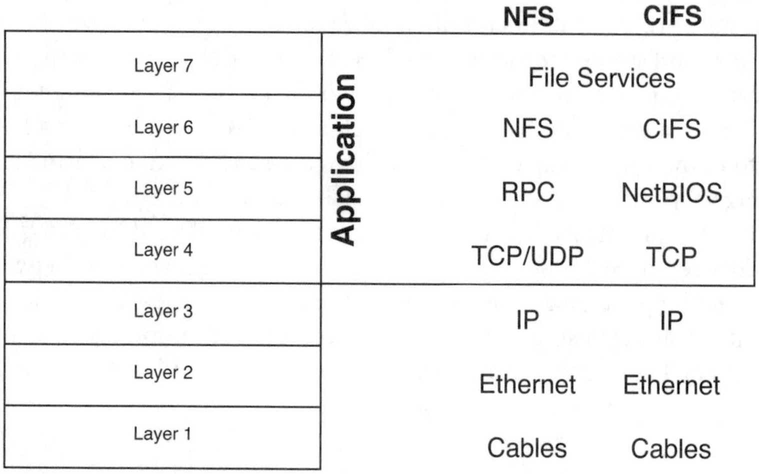

		NFS	CIFS
Layer 7	**Application**	File Services	
Layer 6		NFS	CIFS
Layer 5		RPC	NetBIOS
Layer 4		TCP/UDP	TCP
Layer 3		IP	IP
Layer 2		Ethernet	Ethernet
Layer 1		Cables	Cables

Figure 5.4   NAS communication architecture.

One of the strongest aspects of NAS devices is that they plug right into traditional networks. The devices support IP, use NFS and CIFS, and are transparent to the end user. All these aspects allow organization to purchase NAS products and deploy them easily. Because NAS products work well with existing operating systems and network architectures, there is not a lot of re-design, architecture, or implementation changes that need to be in place before deploying a NAS device. NAS storage vendors want to blend in transparently to existing networks that require large volumes of storage.

NAS SECURITY

NAS products use Ethernet, IP, TCP, and UDP to provide application services such as CIFS and NFS. While CIFS and NFS provide the services at the upper-layer protocols, they depend on the lower-level protocols for networking. This also means they inherit all the security problems that the lower levels have. For example, Ethernet and IP are not secure. Attackers can execute network attacks targeted at the security gaps in layer 2 and layer 3. Furthermore, upper-layer protocols such as CIFS and NFS have a wide range of security problems, too. Any NAS device supporting both the lower and upper layers will also inherit their security problems. Although this may seem obvious, it is often ignored. Many organizations deploy NAS devices and think they are secure because they are two- or four-unit appliances that plug right into a rack in a data center. Because it is a net-work device and not a Solaris, Linux, or Windows operating system, many organizations think they don't need to worry about it. Unfortunately, this is not true. Network devices are no more secure than the average operating system. In fact, many network devices are running some form of Linux with default services enabled and using vulnerable versions of applications, such as Apache, Sendmail, Syslog, or SNMP. The administrator does not have the ability to update any of the embedded operating systems or applications, which is a security issue itself, but rather wait for the vendor to release an update based on the vendor's release cycles. Furthermore, NAS storage devices supporting CIFS and NFS are not immune to the security problems with SMB on Windows operating systems or NFS on Unix (e.g. Solaris) operating systems. Often, the security problems are greater because a security problem with a NAS device that supports NFS or CIFS will directly grant access to large amounts of data when compared to an operating system that may or may not have access to large volumes of data.

NAS SECURITY STANDARDS

As mentioned previously, NAS protocols and products often struggle to provide the basic security requirements. Many organizations apply a tremendous amount of security around a Windows or Solaris operating system running SMB (CIFS) or NFS; however, due to the fact that both the protocols are running on a network device and not a tradi-tional operation system, organizations feel that the protocols are somehow already inherently secured. This would be equivalent to putting a 1970s engine from a very old car into a brand new Lexus. While the car looks nice, shiny, and great from the outside, inside it has the same problems that any old car would have, such as overheating, oil leakage, and poor gas mileage. While it is unfair to compare storage protocols to an old car engine, it is certainly fair to compare the act of taking something broken, such as the security of CIFS and NFS, wrapping something new around it, such as a two-unit appliance, and thinking it is okay to put into a data center without any hesitation.

NAS security standards usually fall back to the false sense of security of a perimeter firewall, or the idea that no one knows that the data is residing on a NAS device and not on a operating system, or even that products in appliances are somehow more secure than software products. NAS storage products do not usually secure themselves, but rely vainly on network filtering, such as firewalls and router ACLs, to protect data. The fact is that a firewall or router will not protect any storage device from the flaws of NFS and CIFS, unless an organization puts a firewall in front of every NAS device in the internal network. If firewalls actually protected the perimeter, a network would never be infected by a virus, worm, or Trojan. Even if firewalls could do anything to protect storage, providing access to CIFS and NFS through firewalls will still make it available to the network. If an attacker would like to get more bang for their buck, attacking a NAS device rather than an operating system would render more data. For example, the following is an attack timeline for an unauthorized user attacking an operating system for data access:

1. Attack an operating system's low-level account.
2. Gain access to a low-level account. Gain access to 10 megs of data.
3. Attempt to gain access to an administrator account.
4. Gain access to an administrator account. Gain access to 3 gigabytes of data.
5. Attempt to gain access to other machines or the domain itself.
6. Gain access to other machines or the domain itself. Gain access to 10 gigabytes of data.
7. Attempt to gain domain admins rights on the domain.
8. Gain access to domain admin rights on the domain.
9. Attempt to crack the primary domain administrator account's password.
10. Gain access to the primary domain administrator account's password. Gain access to 100 gigabytes of data.

Notice that it would take an attacker approximately ten steps to get access to large amounts of data, but what if that data was kept centrally on the NAS device and not on several local operating systems? The attacker could skip quite a few steps and simply try to gain privileges on the NAS device itself. Following is an attack timeline for an unauthorized user attacking a NAS device for data access:

1. Attack the NAS device low-level account.
2. Gain access to a low-level account; get 3 gigabytes of data.
3. Attempt to gain access to an administrator account.
4. Gain access to an administrator account; gain access to 100 gigabytes of data.

Notice how the same steps were used from our first example, but the attacker was able to have immediate access to data, skipping quite a few steps from before. Also, we did not consider the one-step attack where any compromised domain administrator account equates into the full access of the NAS device and its data.

Because all the data is centralized on the NAS device and both scenarios are using weak transports and protocols, such as IP or CIFS/NFS, the ability to attack and gain control of a NAS device becomes easier. Furthermore, since both examples use default installations of NFS or CIFS, attacking either system is equal from an exposure perspective. For example, a Windows or Solaris operating system is not harder or easier to attack than a NAS storage device running NFS or CIFS (both with the default settings enabled). Since all things are equal from an attacker's perspective, attacking a storage device offers a lot more access to data than the operating system attack. Organizations have overlooked this key fact for many years; thankfully, attackers have also. However, it usually does take much time for attackers to find shortcuts that make their process quicker. See Table 5.1 for an attack target comparison between a Windows/Unix file server and a NAS appliance.

As shown in Table 5.1, a NAS appliance is very similar to an operating system, including the security vulnerabilities. It is true that an operating system usually has more services enabled by default than a dedicated appliance; however, since many of the most dangerous services (e.g. CIFS and NFS) are enabled on NAS devices, the more vulnerable points of entry have been included on both (including clear-text management protocols like Telnet, RSH, FTP, and HTTP). Furthermore, since appliances are often ignored by security groups, but often contain more data, the risk can be greater. In general, the top security weaknesses of network appliances, including storage appliances, are as follows:

- They are often built off of commercial/open source operating systems.
- Organizations cannot easily perform security updates.
- Organizations treat them as if they are secure (by default).

Table 5.1   Data Target Comparison from an Attack Perspective

	Windows/ UNIXServer	NAS Appliance
Communication method	TCP/IP	TCP/IP
Access methods	Direct—Over the LAN	Direct—Over the LAN
Protocol	CIFS/SMB or NFS	CIFS/SMB or NFS
Authentication	Local username/password or UID/GID AD domain or NIS	Local username/password or UID/GID AD domain or NIS
Stored data type	Local data storage	Corporate-wide centralized storage
Operating systems' data	One	Several
Average data size (approx)	30 to 80 Gigabytes	300 Gigabytes to 1 Terabyte of data

COMMON INTERNET FILE SYSTEM (CIFS)

CIFS is a client server protocol that was developed as an extension to Server Message Block (SMB), which was first defined in 1984. CIFS servers listen on port 445 or 139, as well as other RPC ports. It can listen on port 445 or 139 to support Windows 2000 and later (port 445) or older version of Windows (port 139). CIFS and SMB are primarily used by NAS devices to support Windows operating systems. (Note. Microsoft first supported SMB to support IBM OS/2 environments back in the 80s.) Other implementations of CIFS exist outside of Microsoft environments, such as Samba under Unix environments. Samba provides interoperability for CIFS environments when using Unix-based systems.

The premise behind CIFS is to offer a service that allows the sharing of files, directories, and folders (e.g. file system) across a network. Similar to a network share on a Windows operating systems, such as C$, NAS devices provide the same purpose, which is a basic share to a directory. In the case of NAS devices, the directory is remote and can be used by multiple nodes on the network. Additionally, NAS devices do not contain a high amount of operating system overhead because they are specifically designed to provide storage.

While NAS devices using CIFS support other operating systems, they do not need any other system to exist. NAS devices can be plugged into the network and directly communicate with any client node without any servers required or agent software on the client. Many NAS devices often look like operating systems on the network by their TCP/IP traces, discussed in Chapter 6, "NAS: CIFS Security," but are actually just a NAS device offering storage. They are often used as file servers, even though they are not really a server, or as dedicated storage for large applications such as Exchange, SQL Server, PeopleSoft, Oracle, or SAP. The basic aspect of NAS devices using CIFS is that it is just another drive letter on your system. The Windows operating system won't care if the drive is local, like the c:\ drive, or if it is remote, like a n:\, as long as the connection is always available and the storage space is large enough. A key note about CIFS-based drives is that the operating system knows that it is over the network rather than local. When we talk about iSCSI later, the operating system is actually tricked a bit when identifying local versus network storage.

NFS BASICS

Network File System (NFS) is a client server protocol that was developed in 1984. It listens on port 2049, as well as several other RPC ports. It was introduced by Sun Microsystems to be the standard method to transfer files on Solaris operating systems. Since then, it has been adopted by all flavors of Unix and Linux operating systems and even has been ported to Windows systems, too.

The basic idea behind NFS is to offer a simple and easy method to export (share) parts of the file system to remote users and computers. Similar to CIFS, NFS offers seamless access to other network systems. A client connecting to an NFS export could mount the remote export to any local file path, such as /mount. NFS servers can export parts of their file systems, such as /home, or the entire file system itself, such as /. NAS devices that support NFS are able to emulate a Unix system running NFS because all that it needs are exports (shares) and clients. NFS exports can include which hostnames or IP addresses should have the ability to connect to a network export for mounting; however, in many NAS devices, this is exported to the entire network by default, denoted by the asterisk variable (*).

Similar to CIFS, NFS plays a crucial role for enterprise applications requiring large amounts of data or easy access for the expansion of data. NFS is often used for email applications, home directories for Unix clients, Oracle databases, or just a general purpose file server. Additionally, NFS exports can be mounted by several operating systems at the same time, allowing multiple nodes to connect to a single mount point.

Another major advantage of NAS devices is that they can easily support NFS and

CIFS together. This allows a NAS device to offer NFS exports for Unix clients and CIFS shares for Windows clients on the same directory on the NAS device. All types of operating systems, applications, and servers gain access to a single directory, files, or folders.

COMMAND SYNTAX

In the next two chapters, we will be using several commands to connect to NAS devices running CIFS or NFS. The next section covers a sampling of the commands with a brief description of the syntax.

CIFS

Using common commands on Windows and Unix CIFS/SMB clients will allow nodes to connect to CIFS servers and often NAS devices. Figures 5.5 through 5.7 show some of the methods to connect to a NAS device running CIFS from a Windows or Unix operating system.

Figure 5.5   Windows client syntax connecting to a NAS device running CIFS.

The following is a description of the syntax used in Figure 5.5:

- `net use`—Network connection command in Windows operating systems.
- `*`—Variable telling the operating system to mount the drive as the next available drive letter, such as F:\.
- `\\172.16.1.100`—IP address of the NAS device running CIFS.
- `\share`—Share name for the CIFS directory.
- `*`—Variable to tell the binary to prompt the user for a password when enter is selected.
- `/user`—Signals the local or domain username.

- `Aum.com`—Domain that the NAS device is connected to. If the NAS device is not connected to a domain, then the domain name is not necessary.
- `kusum`—Username attempting to connect to the NAS device.

Once enter is selected on the command line, the drive will appear on the local operating system. This allows applications such as Exchange, Oracle, SQL Server, or PeopleSoft to contain and expand large amounts of storage simply over the network. Additionally, no client-side agent software or operating system updates are required to talk to third-party CIFS servers such as NAS devices.

Another method to connect to NAS devices running CIFS is by simply using a web browser, as shown in Figure 5.6.

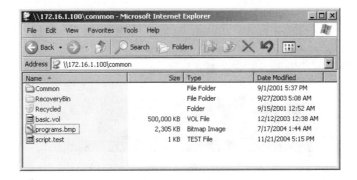

Figure 5.6   Web client connected to a NAS device running CIFS.

Notice how `\\ip.address.\ShareName` is the only thing required when using a web browser. After the user selects enter, he or she will be prompted for a username and password and then allowed into the NAS device.

Unix clients using `smbclient` can also connect to NAS devices running CIFS. Figure 5.7 shows the syntax of the command.

The following is a description of the syntax used in Figure 5.7:

- `smbclient`—Network connection command in Unix operating systems.
- `\\\\ip.address`—IP address of the NAS device running CIFS.
- `\\Share`—Share name for the CIFS directory.
- `-U`—Username attempting to connect to the NAS device.
- `-p 445`—Port that the NAS device is using, usually 445 or 139.

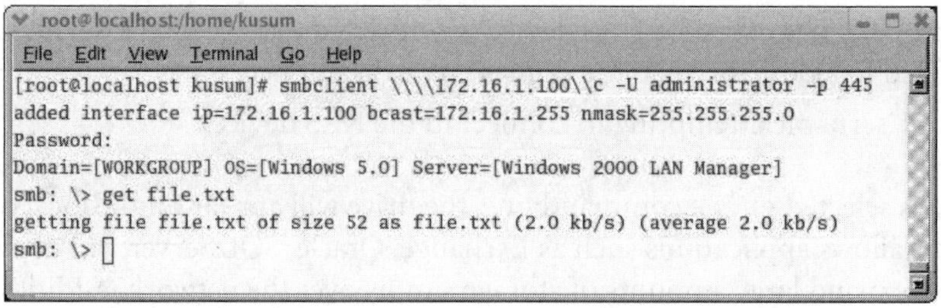
root@localhost:/home/kusum
File Edit View Terminal Go Help
[root@localhost kusum]# smbclient \\\\172.16.1.100\\c -U administrator -p 445
added interface ip=172.16.1.100 bcast=172.16.1.255 nmask=255.255.255.0
Password:
Domain=[WORKGROUP] OS=[Windows 5.0] Server=[Windows 2000 LAN Manager]
smb: \> get file.txt
getting file file.txt of size 52 as file.txt (2.0 kb/s) (average 2.0 kb/s)
smb: \>

Figure 5.7 Unix client connecting to a NAS device running CIFS.

NFS

The use of common commands on Unix will allow nodes to connect to NFS servers, and often NAS devices. Figure 5.8 shows an example method to connect to a NAS device running NFS from a Unix operating system.

Command Prompt
c:\>mount 172.16.1.100:/home /mount

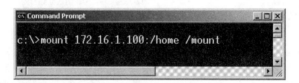

Figure 5.8 Unix client connecting to a NAS device running NFS.

The following is a description of the syntax used in Figure 5.8:

- `mount`—Network connection command in Unix operating systems.
- `172.16.1.100`—IP address of NAS devices running NFS.
- `/home`—Remote NFS export on NAS device.
- `/mount`—Local file location to mount the remote NFS directory.

SUMMARY

This chapter briefly introduced NAS storage environments and devices. We covered typical NAS architectures, NAS communications, and the basics about NAS security. We also discussed the primary protocols that NAS devices use, including NFS and CIFS. We concluded with a review of some basic syntax to connect to NAS devices running NFS and CIFS from both Windows and Unix systems, which is used often in the next two chapters.

In those chapters, we will dig deep into CIFS and NFS security, respectively. Now that we understand the basics of NAS storage environments from this chapter, we can also understand the security problems associated with each NAS environment, including security flaws with both NFS and CIFS.

NAS: CIFS Security

NAS devices supporting Common Internet File System (CIFS) are growing rapidly in all types of organizations. CIFS has become the de facto standard for many NAS devices. The use of CIFS allows organizations to improve storage and backup solutions with ease and efficiency. With the spread of Windows-based operating systems that rely on Server Message Block (SMB), which is what CIFS is based on, along with the consistent problem of users, applications, and servers running short of storage space, NAS devices supporting CIFS are offering significant solutions to organizations. NAS devices using CIFS allow organizations to expand storage capacities by simply plugging a device on the network, as opposed to opening a server machine, replacing or adding more hard drives, and using partitioning software to increase the logical partition size. Furthermore, NAS devices using CIFS can support multiple servers at once, including Exchange servers (although there might be I/O issues with Exchange and NAS devices), databases, share user directories, or simply just a community file server. The limitation on a NAS device is small for storage solutions.

The security of NAS devices using CIFS has been overlooked. A major goal for most NAS CIFS vendors is to appear as a Window server on the network; hence supporting every Windows client in a seamless (invisible) manner. The issue with this is that many of the security vulnerabilities that exist in the SMB/CIFS implementation of a Windows operating system also exist in SMB/CIFS implementation of a NAS device. Furthermore, there can actually be more security issues with the SMB/CIFS implementation on a NAS device than a SMB/CIFS implementation on a Windows server. This situation can leave a default NAS device using CIFS equal to or worse than the security of CIFS on a Windows machine. Furthermore, because a NAS device holds a lot more data than a single Windows operating system, the attack damage is greater.

Many organizations overlook these issues due to a NAS appliance being a network device on the LAN rather that a Compaq or Dell machine. Would you consolidate all your sensitive data on a single Windows server with default settings? I should hope not. Therefore, NAS devices running CIFS need to be secured also.

This chapter discusses the following topic concerning NAS CIFS devices:

- CIFS security basics
- Enumeration
- Authentication
- Authorization (spoofing IP and hostname)
- Encryption (clear-text Telnet, HTTP, and RSH)

CIFS SECURITY BASICS

CIFS (or SMB) is a client server protocol where a CIFS-enabled client, which is every Windows machine and every Unix machine with smbclient, connects to a CIFS server for file and share services. Most CIFS implementations use TCP port 139 or TCP port 445. See Figure 6.1 for a typical CIFS architecture.

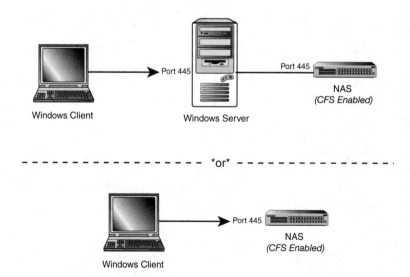

Figure 6.1   NAS devices using CIFS.

All NAS devices are stand-alone appliances on the network. Figure 6.1 shows two architectural examples for data access. The top diagram in Figure 6.1 shows a Windows client accessing data via a Windows server that has connected to the NAS appliance via CIFS. Additionally, since the NAS appliance is connected to the LAN using IP, the Windows client can connect directly to the NAS appliance over the network, without the need of a Windows server (as shown in the bottom example in Figure 6.1). If a client were to directly access the file server for data, it could authenticate directly (locally or via a domain) to the NAS appliance. This situation makes NAS appliances accessible to any system connected to the LAN and also makes it a viable stand-alone target.

In addition to being a direct target, CIFS is a clear-text protocol that can be enumerated over the network quite easily. Critical details on the CIFS connection can be sniffed over the wire, such as CIFS server information, shares, authentication method, and CIFS client information. Figure 6.2 shows a sample connection between a Windows client and a NAS appliance with CIFS enabled.

Protocol	Info
TCP	2520 > microsoft-ds [SYN] Seq=0 Ack=0 Win=65535 Len=0 MSS=1460
TCP	microsoft-ds > 2520 [SYN, ACK] Seq=0 Ack=1 Win=8760 Len=0 MSS=1460
TCP	2520 > microsoft-ds [ACK] Seq=1 Ack=1 Win=65535 [CHECKSUM INCORRECT] Len=
SMB	Negotiate Protocol Request
SMB	Negotiate Protocol Response
SMB	Session Setup AndX Request, NTLMSSP_NEGOTIATE
SMB	Session Setup AndX Response, NTLMSSP_CHALLENGE, NTLMSSP_CHALLENGE, Error:
SMB	Session Setup AndX Request, NTLMSSP_AUTH
SMB	Session Setup AndX Response
SMB	Tree Connect AndX Request, Path: \\10.60.60.10\IPC$
SMB	Tree Connect AndX Response
SMB	Trans2 Request, GET_DFS_REFERRAL, File: \10.60.60.10\web
SMB	Trans2 Response, GET_DFS_REFERRAL, Error: STATUS_NO_SUCH_DEVICE
SMB	Session Setup AndX Request, NTLMSSP_NEGOTIATE
SMB	Session Setup AndX Response, NTLMSSP_CHALLENGE, NTLMSSP_CHALLENGE, Error:
SMB	Session Setup AndX Request, NTLMSSP_AUTH
SMB	Session Setup AndX Response
SMB	Tree Connect AndX Request, Path: \\10.60.60.10\WEB
SMB	Tree Connect AndX Response
TCP	2520 > microsoft-ds [ACK] Seq=1514 Ack=1169 Win=64367 [CHECKSUM INCORRECT]

Figure 6.2 CIFS communication.

As you can see from Figure 6.2, the server name, the share name, and the username (not directly shown but in the body of one of the IP packets) of the connection are all captured over the network in clear-text. As mentioned in Chapter 1, "Introduction to Storage Security," enumeration is a big part of an attack timeline and NAS devices using CIFS leak a tremendous amount of useful information.

CIFS security primarily relies on authentication parameters, discussed in the next section. Although there are options to enable other security items, such as authorization, encryption, and integrity, the core component to access a NAS appliance using CIFS is a local username/password or domain (Active Directory or NIS) authentication.

In addition to authentication, CIFS supports authorization at the IP address/hostname level or the file/folder level. For example, a particular IP address or hostname can be given rights to a NAS appliance. Furthermore, NAS appliances use system access control lists. Windows system permissions, such as NTFS (NT File System), or Unix-style permissions, such as read-write-execute for root, owner, and world access, can be applied to NAS devices. Later in the authorization section, we discuss how many file/folder security permissions can be subverted on NAS appliances that use both CIFS and NFS.

Encrypting CIFS communication may occur during the authentication process, discussed in the next section, or at the IP layer using IPSec. Most NAS appliances that support IPSec can be used as an IPSec end-point to a CIFS client. While this is not a standard deployment for NAS devices, CIFS clients with an IPSec client, which is included in most Windows and Unix operating systems, can use IPSec between the client and the NAS device. The IPSec tunnel would fully encrypt all communication from the CIFS client to the CIFS server, especially the clear-text communication.

CIFS servers are based on the premise of shares or mount points. For example, a CIFS-enabled file system can have a variety of folders and directories, but only the ones that have been shared will be accessible to the network. For example, a NAS device can have a directory of /volume0 and five subdirectories of HR, Finance, Engineering, IT, and Executives. The NAS device can have a main share or mount point at the core of the file system called volume0, or can have five individual shares called HR, Finance, Eng, IT, and Execs that correlate to the individual departments. For any CIFS share, such as "Execs," the NAS device is able to verify the authentication of a CIFS client to that share, either by a local account on the NAS appliance or an account on third-party authentication server. If users are authenticating via a third-party authentication server/domain, such as an Active Directory domain, then the NAS appliance would need to join and be part of the domain, which is possible with all major NAS appliances. After the authentication process of the Execs share, the NAS device could verify authorization, assuming the IP address or hostname restriction was set. In most cases, there are no authorization controls set on a NAS device. Finally, file system security can be applied to the folder called Executives, allowing only authorized accounts, using the local NAS device or Active Directory, to access the folder. At this point, the security of files and folders on NAS appliances can be secure using multiple controls, without requiring encryption. However, while the high-level model for CIFS security seems good, there are a lot of flaws and issues in its implementation, including issues on the NAS device and in the CIFS protocol.

Because CIFS is the evolution of SMB, all tools, utilities, and attacks against SMB work on CIFS. You might hear people say that there are no tools or attacks against storage devices; therefore, it is okay that the security on them is weak. Not only is this premise completely false (fix something only when people find out about it), but the fact is that many security tools and attacks that targets SMB on Windows operating systems also work on NAS appliances running CIFS. As you may have guessed, there are a significant number of tools and attacks to target Windows operating systems, equating into a large number of readily available tools and attacks to target NAS appliances running CIFS. While most, if not all, of the current tools were written to target Microsoft environments, since most NAS vendors implement CIFS to seamlessly mirror SMB on Windows, all the attacks, vulnerabilities, and security weaknesses are also mirrored. Hopefully, you can now imagine how many attacks exist for NAS appliances running CIFS and how this will continue to grow as long as Microsoft is the favorite target to many attackers. The following sections describe the high-level approach to CIFS security in detail, as well as its security weaknesses and exposures.

ENUMERATION

As stated in Chapter 1, enumeration is a very big part of any attack process, whether it is against storage devices or application servers. Unfortunately, common implementation of the CIFS/SMB protocol allows users to enumerate a great deal of information from a storage device. Since NAS devices implement CIFS to mirror a typical Windows implementation, a great deal of information can be gathered from a NAS device running CIFS as a prelude to an attack.

In this section, we learn how to enumerate several types of information from a NAS device. All of the enumeration steps in this section helps an attacker start, escalate, or complete an attack to compromise data in the storage network. The following entities can be enumerated from a NAS device running CIFS without any authentication:

- NAS device version
- Open ports and services
- Usernames and groups
- NAS device administrators
- Shares

NAS DEVICE VERSION

Enumerating the version of a target is an important step for an unauthorized user. Attackers use the information to narrow down the scope of attacks for a potential target. For example, if an attacker is targeting a web server and finds out that the target is running IIS 6.0, he/she can remove or eliminate all of the IIS 5.0 attacks and not waste any time on that attack surface or attack tree. However, if they cannot enumerate the type and version of the web server, he/she will have to use all their Apache, IBM WebSphere, iPlanet, and IIS 3.0/4.0/5.0 attacks, creating a significant amount of extra effort for the attacker.

By retrieving the type and version of the NAS device, the unauthorized user will know that he/she is attacking a storage device. This information is usually obtained by banners on open ports. For example, if a NAS device has a web server for web management, a simple connection to port 80 will usually dump information about the NAS device, including type (vendor) and version. Complete the following exercise to enumerate the type and version of the NAS device.

ASSESSMENT EXERCISE

1. Open a command prompt (Start -> Programs -> cmd.exe).
2. Telnet to port 80 on the NAS device:
   a. telnet <IP address of NAS device> 80.
3. telnet 172.16.1.100.
4. Done! You should now see the type of NAS device that has been deployed. Some common banners you may see are Cellera Web Manager (EMC), EMC Control Center, NetApp (na_admin), and Storage Management (IBM). Some banners may also tell you the version number of the device.

OPEN PORTS AND SERVICES

A NAS device can be scanned similar to any other device on the network. Using any port scanner, information can be gathered on the enabled services and open ports on the NAS device. The results from a port scan will allow an attacker to determine what services are running for file access—CIFS, NFS, or both—and what management methods are being used—Telnet, RSH, SSH, HTTP, and/or HTTPS. The port scan is the first step for an attacker as he or she begins to profile the environment. The following exercises demonstrate scans on storage devices using two tools, StorScan and nmap. StorScan is a storage only port scanner that includes checks focused for NAS and iSCSI storage devices and services. Nmap is an all-purpose port scanner and is definitely the standard for port scanning tools. Complete the following exercise to scan the NAS device using either tool.

ASSESSMENT EXERCISE

1. Download StorScan from http://www.isecpartners.com/tools.html.
2. Unzip the file to a folder on your system, such as c:\tools.
3. Open up a command prompt (Start -> Program -> cmd.exe) and change directories to the location where you unzipped StorScan (cd c:\tools).
4. Type **StorScan.exe** for the help and syntax information.
5. Type **StorScan.exe -h <IP address of NAS device>** to port scan the NAS device for all open ports and running services:

   StorScan.exe -h 172.16.1.100

6. After StorScan completes the scan, all running services and open ports are displayed.

ASSESSMENT EXERCISE

1. Download nmap from http://www.insecure.org/nmap/nmap_download.html, written by Fyodor.
2. Unzip the file to a folder on your system, such as c:\tools.
3. Open up a command prompt (Start -> Program -> cmd.exe) and change directories to the location where you unzipped nmap (cd c:\tools).
4. Type **nmap.exe** for the help information.
5. Type **nmap.exe <IP address of NAS device>** to port scan the NAS device for all open ports and running services:

   nmap.exe 172.16.1.100

6. As shown in Figure 6.3, after nmap completes the port scan, all running services and open ports are displayed.

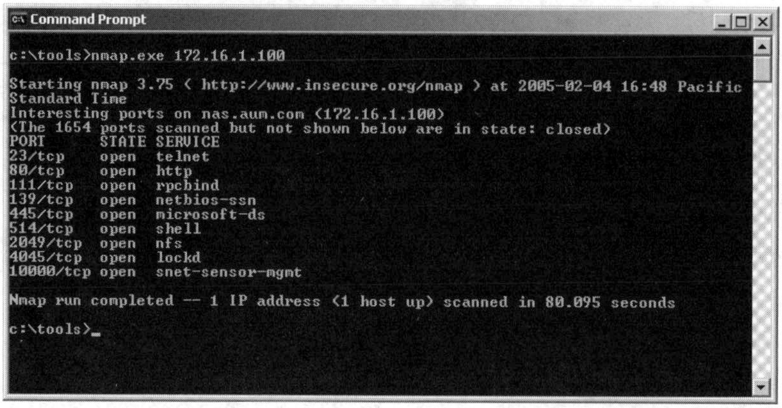

Figure 6.3   Port scan of NAS device.

From the results of the port scan, the attacker can deduce that the NAS device is running both CIFS and NFS by the fact that ports 139 and 445 are open, which are used for CIFS, and ports 2049 and 4045 are open, which are used for NFS. This allows an attacker to target the NAS device based on CIFS attacks, NFS attacks, and attacks that target both NFS and CIFS in mixed environments. The next thing we can conclude is that the NAS device is being managed using insecure clear-text protocols where usernames and passwords traverse the network in the clear. Port 23 is open, which is used for Telnet, port 80 is open, which is HTTP web management, and port 514 is open, with is used for Remote Shell (RSH). All three of these protocols are clear-text and can be very insecure. Furthermore, any attacker who sniffs the username and password with a network sniffer, from a Telnet, Web (HTTP), or RSH session, will have complete control of the NAS device and all of the data on the device. While this is the same if root was sniffed from a Unix machine, the amount of data that is accessible from a single NAS device versus a Unix operating system are significantly different, yet this has not equated into stronger management security for NAS devices.

At this point, the avenue for attacking the NAS device is quite large. Based on the information that was retrieved by the port scan only, the attacker has five different methods to penetrate the NAS device, including CIFS, NFS, Telnet, HTTP, and RSH. Every open port is an attack surface for the unauthorized user. The more open ports or services, the greater likelihood that one of the services enabled is insecure. For example, protecting five different doorways in a home is more difficult than protecting two. Every night you ensure that the door is locked and chain is on. However, if you had to do this for five different entry methods to your house, chances are at least one of them will be forgotten, overlooked, or just ignored (for example, you might lock the front door and back door every night, but is the kitchen window or the exterior garage door locked, too?). In our NAS device, one could argue that NFS and CIFS need to be enabled, but having three different insecure methods for managing the NAS device is not good from a security perspective. This is a classic example of how port scans are used to formulate an attack for an unauthorized user.

USERNAMES AND GROUPS

The next entity that can be enumerated on NAS devices running CIFS are usernames (or UserIDs) and authorized groups. The usernames and authorized groups that can be enumerated are either local accounts on the NAS device or accounts on the domain that the NAS device belongs to. Because most NAS devices running CIFS are part of a Windows domain, it is easier to grant usernames or groups from a domain rather than set up several hundred (or even thousand) user accounts locally on the NAS device. Not only does this help with management, but authentication is now handled via the domain itself and passed through to the NAS device. Since most NAS devices are able to be domain joined, stating that any user from the domain "Aum.com" is allowed to connect to the NAS device is a simple process.

The problem with CIFS is that it leaks a tremendous amount of information, including information on the administrative usernames and groups that are allowed to connect to the NAS device. This information gives a malicious user a list of possible targets for attack, which can use a variety of methods, including brute force, sniffing, or password retrieval. During an attack, if an unauthorized user is not able to determine actual usernames or groups of a target, the process of compromising someone's account becomes extremely difficult. For example, if a burglar knew that the code to enter your home was 4374, but there was absolutely no public or private method for the attacker to gain your home address, then his or her attack would be significantly more difficult. Part of the process to break into your home would be the actual ability to know where you live. If the burglar did not know or could not find out where you lived, the fact that he or she has your code is of little value. The same idea applies to usernames and groups. Once an attacker can enumerate valid usernames and groups that are allowed access to the stored data on the NAS device, a popular and largely successful attack surface opens up that allows attackers to compromise powerful and authorized accounts.

One issue with CIFS is a default share that is often used, called the Interprocess Communication Share (IPC$). The IPC$ is found on all Windows operating systems and most NAS devices running CIFS that attempt to mirror a Windows system. The purpose of the IPC$ is to allow the communication between several CIFS-enabled systems, including Windows servers and NAS devices. The IPC$ is often used to transfer information about username accounts and login information from one server to the other. The problem with the IPC$ share is that it does not require any authentication by default. Any anonymous user with no username or password can connect to the IPC$ share on a NAS device or on a Windows system and dump sensitive information from the entity, including username information. In the following exercise, we will enumerate usernames from the IPC$ that are allowed to connect to the NAS storage device. The same tools that are used to target SMB services on Windows operating systems can also be used to target CIFS services on NAS devices. The tools will allow an attacker to leak username information from the CIFS services running on the NAS device.

ASSESSMENT EXERCISE

1. Download DumpSec from http://www.systemtools.com/somarsoft/.
2. Install DumpSec using its default installation steps.
3. Once you have installed Dumpsec, open a command prompt (Start -> Run -> cmd.exe).
4. Connect to the IPC$ on the NAS device anonymously, using no username or password, with the following syntax: **net use \\< IP address of NAS Device>\IPC$ ""** **/user:""**

    a. **net use \\172.16.1.100\IPC$ "" /user:""**

    Now we have connected to the NAS device anonymously. See Figure 6.4.

Figure 6.4   Anonymous connection to the NAS device.

Now that we are connected to the NAS device, open DumpSEC:

b. Start -> Programs -> SystemTools -> DumpSec.

c. From the menu bar, select Report -> Select Computer....

d. In the Select Computer window, type the IP address of the NAS device, such as 172.16.1.100, and select OK. See Figure 6.5.

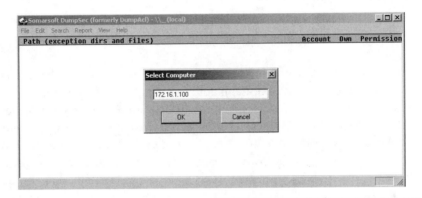

Figure 6.5 DumpSec connection to the NAS device.

5. From the menu bar, select Report -> Dump Users as Table.

6. Done! You have now enumerated the usernames and domain groups that are allowed to connect to the NAS device. See Figure 6.6.

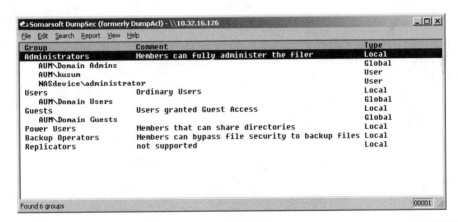

Figure 6.6 DumpSec enumeration of the NAS device.

We have now enumerated the following users who are allowed to connect to the NAS device:

- All domain admins from the domain AUM.
- User ID called kusum from the domain called AUM.
- User ID called administrator locally on the NAS device.
- All domain users from the domain called AUM.
- All domain guests from the domain called AUM.

The username kusum is actually a domain admin on the AUM domain that can connect to the NAS device. Additionally, all domain admins users from the domain called AUM is allowed to connect to the NAS device. You might be thinking that the categories of users that can connect to the NAS device are nice, but what about the specific names of these users. While we were able to enumerate the user called kusum, what about the other several hundred users in the domain users group that are allowed to make a connection? In order to complete this, you must also connect to the IPC$ share on the Windows domain called AUM and dump the specific users. This will allow you to identify all users in the group called Domain Admins and Domain Users, which can be targeted to get access to the NAS device itself. Complete the following exercise to get access to the specific user names:

1. Start -> Run -> cmd.exe.
2. Type `ipconfig /all`.
3. Locate the IP address of the DHCP server or any Windows domain controller (often DHCP servers in a Windows domain are also domain controllers). We will use this IP address to leak the username information. See Figure 6.7 where it shows the DHCP server as 172.16.1.115.
4. Connect to the IPC$ share on the domain controllers for the AUM domain.
   a. `net use \\172.16.1.115\IPC$ "" /user:""`
5. Now we have connected to the domain controller anonymous.
6. Now that we are connected to the domain, open DumpSEC.
   a. Start -> Programs -> SystemTools -> DumpSec.
   b. From the menu bar, select Report -> Select Computer….
   c. In the Select Computer windows, type the IP address of the NAS device, such as 172.16.1.115, and select OK.

Figure 6.7 Domain controller.

7. From the menu bar, select Report -> Dump Users as Table.

8. Done! You have now enumerated the usernames and domain groups on the domain. Every specific user under the category called Domain Admins or Domain Users is a legitimate user who can connect to the NAS device for data access. See Figure 6.8.

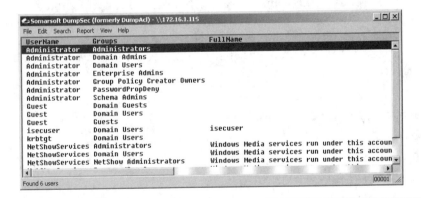

Figure 6.8 Specific username information.

At this point, the attacker knows all the usernames and groups that are allowed to connect to NAS devices for data access. All of the usernames are potential targets to compromise data. The username information can now be used in a very popular and successful attack target that endlessly uses bruteforce, sniffing, or password-retrieval attacks to gain access.

NAS DEVICE ADMINISTRATORS

Enumeration of local system administrators can also occur on NAS devices running CIFS. Similar to the previous section where valid end-user usernames can be enumerated, the local system accounts on the NAS device can be enumerated also. Compromising a valid end-user account can allow attackers to have access to all data that a user has access to; however, compromising a local system administrator account allows an attacker to have access to potentially all the data on the NAS device. Administrator accounts have the ability to manage the NAS device, but what is often overlooked is that it also has full control of the data. If sensitive data were stored on the NAS device, such as customer credit card numbers, financial spreadsheets, or medical information, the local system account has full control of the data. Furthermore, the ability to enumerate all administrator accounts on the local NAS device opens the door for brute-force, sniffing, and password-retrieval attacks (explain further in the NTLM section). Additionally, many NAS devices are managed using clear-text protocols, allowing the username to be enumerated and the passwords to be sniffed in clear-text, leaving all data sitting on the NAS device extremely vulnerable. Essentially, the data residing on the NAS device is one weak password or one Telnet, RSH, or web connection away from being fully compromised. While many organizations spend countless hours and resources securing operating systems and putting up network firewalls, the ability to attack the NAS device directly is an easier attack vector that is simply overlooked. The following exercise will demonstrate the ability to enumerate local systems accounts on NAS devices running CIFS.

ASSESSMENT EXERCISE

1. Download enum.exe, written by Jordan Ritter, from www.bindview.com/razor/utilities.
2. Unzip the file to a directory on your local system, such as c:\tools\.
3. Open a command prompt (Start -> Run -> cmd.exe) and change directories to the location of the tool (such as cd c:\tools).
4. Type `enum -U <IP address of NAS device>` to enumerate all the local administrator accounts on the NAS device itself (see Figure 6.9):
   a. `enum -U 172.16.1.100`
5. Done! Local admin accounts have been enumerated.

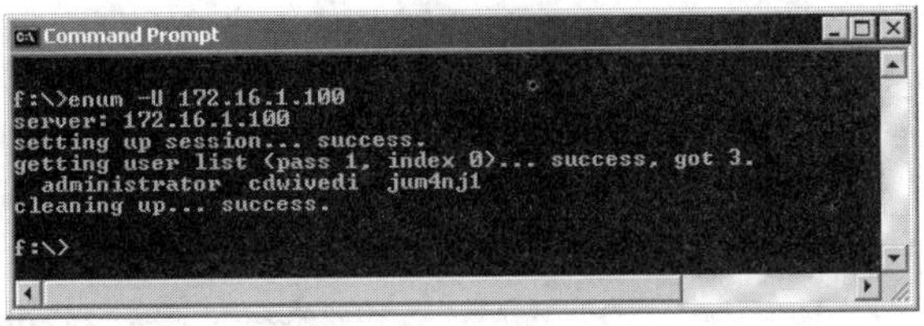

```
Command Prompt                                      _|□|X|
f:\>enum -U 172.16.1.100
server: 172.16.1.100
setting up session... success.
getting user list (pass 1, index 0)... success, got 3.
    administrator  cdwivedi  jum4nj1
cleaning up... success.

f:\>
```

Figure 6.9 Enumeration of local admin accounts.

Notice in Figure 6.9 that three different local admin accounts were enumerated, including administrator, cdwivedi, and jum4nj1. Each of these accounts can now be targeted by attackers for several other attack vectors. If any one of these accounts were to be compromised, which will be demonstrated in the authentication section, then all the data on the NAS device would be under the control of an unauthorized user.

SHARES

We have learned how to enumerate services, end-user accounts, domain groups, and local admin accounts; however, all that information won't be of any use to an attacker unless they actually know what shares are open on the NAS device. What good are the keys to the kingdom of you can't ever find the gate to get in? The shares on CIFS-enabled NAS devices are actually the entry point to the systems. The shares are mount points that allow external network hosts to map a directory locally from a remote NAS device. For example, the mount point of /volume0 on a NAS device might be shared as "root" and the mount point of /volume0/finance might be shared as "finance" to a remote host. See Figure 6.10 for a description.

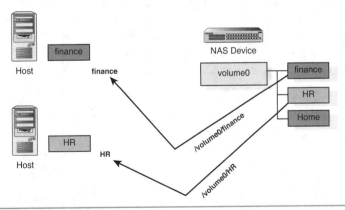

Figure 6.10 NAS CIFS shares point to host.

Unfortunately, the shares that are the entry points for NAS devices running CIFS can also be enumerated anonymously in a default installation of the CIFS protocol. In additional to easy enumeration of all the CIFS shares, most administrative directories on a NAS device are also shared. While this may seem obvious (why would an organization purchase a NAS device if they did not want it shared to the network), there are security issues with sharing the administrative directories as well as the operational (functional) directories. It is perfectly normal to share operational directories such as finance, HR, and user home directories; however, it is less secure to share directories that contain configuration information of the NAS device. For example, most NAS devices have directories that contain configuration files that hold the details of the settings/services that are enabled or disabled. A CLI management tool, such as Telnet, or a GUI management tool, such as web management, may be used to manage a NAS device, but many times these tools are just providing a front-end GUI to modify lines in a flat-text file on the NAS device. Several settings in the configuration files hold sensitive security information, such as the IP addresses that are allowed to connect to the NAS device or the users that are allowed to manage the NAS device. If an unauthorized user were able to view or even edit this information, they could potentially modify the security settings on the NAS device using a network share point rather than the usual management tools such as Telnet, SSH, or other web management tools. Although the management tools may have some level of security, the share may not. Furthermore, if editing is not possible, unauthorized users could read the setting in the files and potentially find out that the host with the IP address of 172.16.1.5 and hostname of Win2003_backup has admin access to the NAS device. The attacker could then spoof his/her IP address or hostname and attempt to gain admin access to the NAS device. While the directories that hold administrative information are shared out to the network, they often contain access controls based on IP addresses or hostnames. Although this is a great start to ensure anonymous or unauthorized users do not get access to these directories, some older versions of NAS devices have shared the critical directories to everyone on the network, with no access control whatsoever. A better method to secure sensitive directories with configuration information on a NAS device would be to disable (remove) the shares on these directories and use secure management methods such as SSH or web management using HTTPS. The following section demonstrates how to enumerate all shares from a NAS device, including administrative and operational shares.

ASSESSMENT EXERCISE

1. Download winfo.exe, written by Arne Vindstrom, from www.ntsecurity.nu and download it to a folder on your system (for example, c:\tools).

2. Open a command prompt (Start -> Programs -> cmd.exe).

3. Change directories to the location of the tool (**cd c:\tools**).

4. Type **winfo.exe** on the command line to get the help information. Notice the tool is written for a Windows environment; however, the product that has implemented CIFS can be enumerated by this tool. See Figure 6.11.

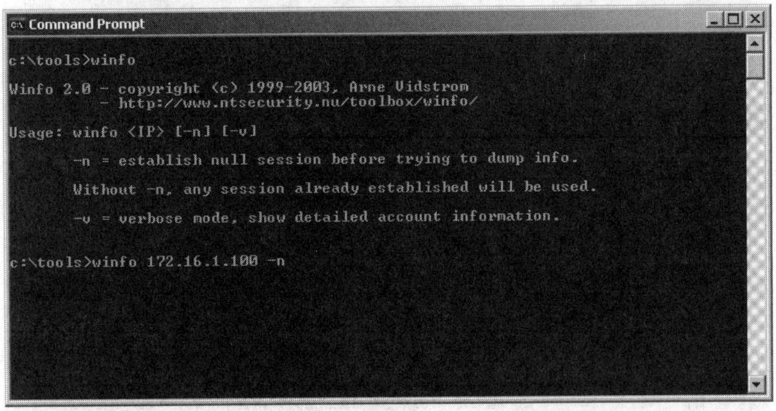

Figure 6.11   Winfo usage.

5. Type **winfo.exe <IP address of NAS device> -n** to enumerate the shares on the remote NAS device (The -n flag is used to connect anonymous to the IPC$ share mentioned above). See Figures 6.12 and Figure 6.13.

   winfo.exe 172.16.1.100 -n

   The bottom half of the results are shown in Figure 6.13.

6. Done. You now have enumerated all the shares (entry points) on the NAS device running CIFS.

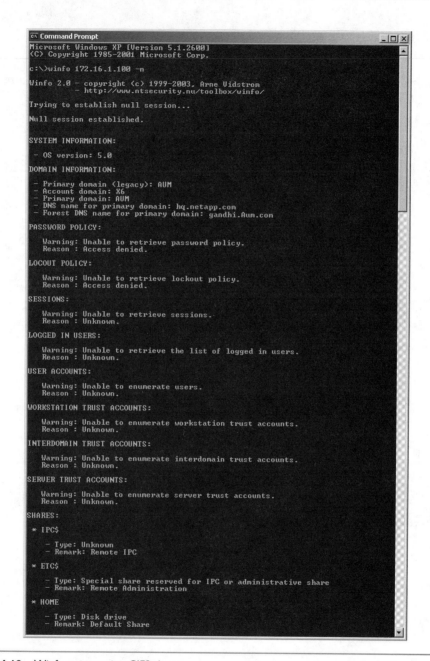

Figure 6.12   Winfo enumeration CIFS shares.

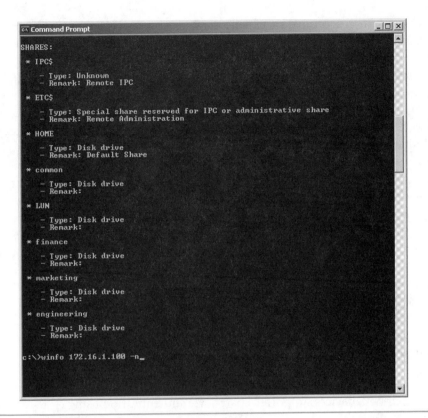

Figure 6.13   Winfo enumerations of CIFS shares.

Notice from Figure 6.12 that no policy or system information was enumerated from the NAS device, such as password policy, logout policy, sessions, logged in users, and user accounts. The information is usually enumerated from Windows systems using winfo. However, we were able to get that information using other tools shown previously. Since NAS devices use CIFS and enable the IPC$ share, winfo can be used to enumerate all the share information. Furthermore, notice there are many operational shares on our NAS devices, such as common, LUN, finance, marketing, and engineering, as well as many administrative shares, such as ETC$. While the operational shares are required, the ETC$ should be removed in favor of other CLI or GUI management tools. Furthermore, the IPC$ should be secured to prevent the anonymous enumeration of the information from the NAS device (see Chapter 10, "Securing NAS").

We have now been able to anonymously enumerate the version of the NAS device, what open ports and services are being used, the end-user accounts and groups, the local administrator system accounts, and finally the shares on the NAS device. This information is used by unauthorized users to profile their target and begin an attack. All this information was retrieved anonymously (without any authentication).

The information that can be enumerated on NAS devices using CIFS is significant. Any device or host on a network, especially a device that holds gigabytes of sensitive data, should not be so easily enumerated or attacked. For example, think of the expensive jewelry you have in your home. Most likely it is not sitting on the kitchen counter but rather hidden somewhere in the house. The location of where you hide your jewelry is not openly shared by you to any guests in your home. You do not allow anonymous guests to find out what room the jewelry is located, what dresser is used, what drawer in the dresser is used, whose underwear it is under, or even what color the box is where the jewelry is contained. These same ideas are not met in a NAS storage device. Most of the information to compromise a NAS device is enumerated anonymous by the CIFS protocol. The only thing that is not retrieved anonymously is user and admin passwords, which will be discussed next in the Authentication section. We will see how attackers can take the enumerated information and start targeting authentication process that is used on NAS devices.

AUTHENTICATION

Implementing CIFS security on NAS devices can occur in many forms. Earlier implementations of NAS devices supported share-level authentication using clear-text protocols and a common (shared) password. For example, any share on a NAS device could be password protected. While this many seem nice and easy, using shared passwords is a security problem, which happens to traverse the network in clear-text. More recent versions of CIFS authentication usually involves LM, NTLM, NTLMv2, or Kerberos. All the authentication methods operate well with existing Windows NT domains or Active Directory domain controllers. In this section, we will discuss the following authentication methods available on most CIFS NAS devices, the security weaknesses with each of them, and the short- and long-term solutions:

- Share-level authentication
- Plain-text passwords
- LANMAN (LAN Manager) and NTLM (NT LAN Manager)
- Kerberos (Active Directory)

SHARE-LEVEL AUTHENTICATION

Share-level authentication should not be confused with user-level authentication. User-level authentication is what most environments use, where users enters their username/userID and password to get access to a directory. Share-level authentication controls access to a share based only on a single password that has been assigned to that share. The share does not require any username, but only the correct password for authentication. Users would share the password among each other, but would not ever need to identify themselves with a username or userID. Since it does not ask for a username, there is no identity management in place with share-level authentication. Figure 6.14 shows an example of share-level authentication.

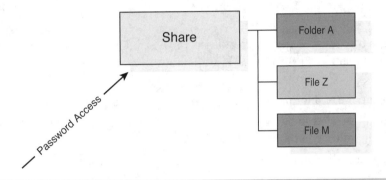

Figure 6.14   Share-level authentication.

Share-level authentication has a few security issues. The first is the sole use of a password. No username is required, just a common shared password. If an employee leaves the organization, the password would have to be changed. More than likely, the password will not get changed very often unless it is shared with several people, negating the whole purpose of the password in the first place since all users, authorized or not authorized, might know of the passwords. Share-level passwords also prevent user accountability. There is no ability to understand which user authenticated to the share since username information is not required. Lastly, the password could be brute forced by unauthorized users also using a simple SMB/CIFS brute-force utility.

The second issue with share-level authentication, which is much bigger, is that it is clear-text. The password that is protecting the share is sent across the network in the clear, allowing any person on the LAN the ability to sniff the password and gain access to the share. Because usernames are not required, it would be hard to detect an unauthorized user who has sniffed the password and is accessing the share, since there is no way to identify the user who is accessing the share.

Share-level passwords are by far the weakest security control on a NAS device running CIFS. In fact, many current implementation of NAS devices running CIFS do not support share-level authentication anymore. The following exercise will demonstrate a self-assessment step that shows how easy it would be to brute force a share-level CIFS share.

ASSESSMENT EXERCISE

1. This exercise will use the CIFS/SMB brute-forcer tool called smbbf.exe (SMB Brute forcer), written by Patrik Karlsson from http://www.cqure.net/tools.jsp?id=1. In our example, the target NAS device running CIFS has an IP address of 172.16.1.100, the network name of "NASdevice," a share called "finance," and is using share-level authentication to protect the share.

2. Browse to http://www.cqure.net/tools.jsp?id=1 and download "SMB Auditing Tools Windows Binary Ver 1.0.4 (~1MB)" at the bottom of the page (second to the last link).

3. Save the zip file to a folder on your system, such as c:\tools\.

4. Unzip the file called smbat-win32bin-1.0.4.zip to your system. Ensure that smbbf.exe and cygwin1.dll are in the same directory.

5. Download any dictionary file to use with the brute-force tool. A popular dictionary file can be downloaded with the CPT tool located at www.isecpartners.com/tools.html. Make sure this file is in the same folder of the smbbf.exe tool, such as c:\tools\.

6. Open a command prompt and change directories (cd c:\tools) to the location of the tools.

7. Type **smbbf.exe** on the command line to see the options.

8. Since SMB Brute Forcer was written for Windows operating systems, it is expecting a username to attempt a password. Because we are brute forcing a share-level password, we can create a blank file with no contents for the usernames. When you create this file, ensure that you hit the spacebar once for a blank username. Save this file as blankuser.txt on the same directory as the tool (e.g. c:\tools\).

9. Enter the following syntax to brute force the NAS device called "finance" on the NAS device:

```
Smbbf.exe -i 172.16.1.100 -u blankuser.txt -p words-english.dic -r results.txt
-P 1 -v -s NASdevice
```

10. Hit Enter and you will see the tool brute force every password from the words-english.dic file against the NAS device. See Figure 6.15 for more details.

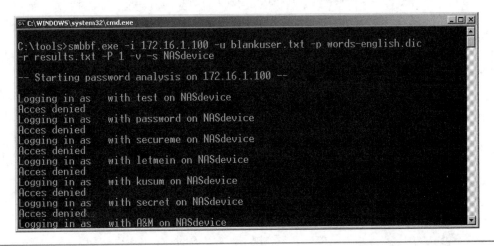

Figure 6.15 Brute forcing share-level CIFS shares.

11. If the password used to protect the share is a dictionary password, the SMB Brute forcer tool will eventually identify it. See Figure 6.16.

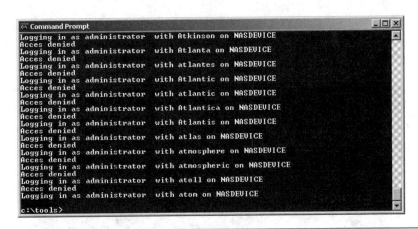

Figure 6.16 Successful brute force of share-level CIFS shares.

12. Done! The NAS device's share-level CIFS password has just been cracked.

Because there were no tools that specifically target NAS devices using share-level pass-words, I wrote one for the purposes of this self-assessment exercise. You can complete the following steps to conduct a brute-force attack specifically at CIFS share-level shares on NAS devices. In our example, the environment is the same as the previous exercise, where the NAS device running CIFS has an IP address of 172.16.1.100, the network name of "NASdevice," a share called "finance," and is using share-level authentication to protect the share.

1. To request the CIFS share-level password brute forcer, send an email request to securingstorage@gmail.com and put CIFShareBF in the title. The tool can also be found at www.isecpartners.com/securingstorage. Unzip the zip file to a directory on your machine (such as c:\tools).

2. Open a command prompt and change directories (cd c:\tools) to the location of the tool.

3. The syntax of the tool is

   a. CIFShareBF.exe <IP Address of the Target> <Share Name>

4. Where <IP Address of the Target> is the NAS device's IP address and <Share Name> is the password-protected share on the NAS device.

5. To execute the tool, type the following:

   a. **CIFShareBF.exe 172.16.1.100 finance**

6. The tool will take a lot longer than smbbf.exe. However, once the share password is cracked, a network drive from your machine will be mapped to the NAS device. See Figure 6.17.

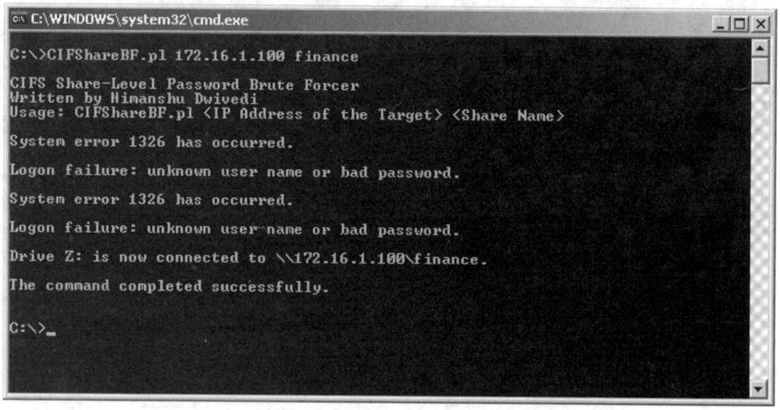

Figure 6.17   Successful brute force of share-level CIFS share using CIFShareBF.exe.

7. Done! Once the tool finds the correct password for the share, it will map a drive to the NAS device and display "The command completed successfully." As you can see, for each incorrect password attempted, the display will be "Logon failure: unknown user name or bad password." If logging has been enabled on the NAS device, each failed attempted will be recorded.

The best way to defend share-level password attacks is to disable share-level authentication. However, if it is a requirement, consider using a strong password, creating an IPSec tunnel from the NAS device and the client machines, and rotating the password every 90 days. In most cases, it is probably easier to move away from share-level authentication and move toward user-level authentication. See Figure 6.18.

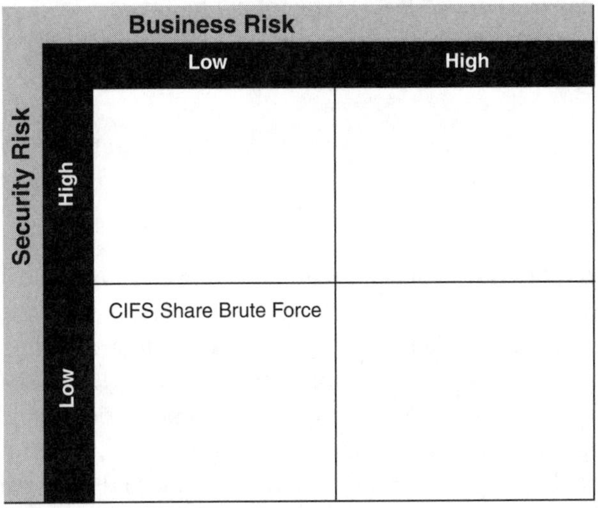

Figure 6.18   SBR chart—Share-level passwords.

ATTACK SUMMARY: SHARE-LEVEL PASSWORDS

Attack description—An unauthorized user can sniff the password in clear-text or simply brute force a password without any username required.

Risk level—Difficulty: Low.

Best practice—Disable share-level passwords.

PLAIN-TEXT PASSWORDS

NAS appliances using CIFS encrypt passwords by default as they traverse the network, discussed later in this chapter. In some cases, the password is sent over the network in clear-text due to a NAS device communicating with a third-party SMB server that does not support password encryption. For example, earlier versions of SAMBA, which provide SMB/CIFS services on Unix, and pre-SP3 NT 4.0 servers did not support SMB username/password encryption. In order for NAS appliances to have backward compatibility to these types of servers, NAS devices are able to support plain-text passwords.

There are simple fixes to this issue in order prevent CIFS clients from using plain-text passwords. Recent versions of Samba and all post-sp3 NT 4.0 and Windows 2000/2003/XP support hashed passwords, even though many of those hashed passwords have turned out to be weak (LM and NTLM). The following registry key can be added to any Windows operating system to ensure plain-text passwords are disabled:

```
HKEY_LOCAL_MACHINE\
System\CurrentControlSet\Services\Rdr\Parameters\EnablePlaintextPassword

Reg_Dword = 0
```

Another key vulnerability is the forced downgrade between a NAS device and a third-party server. For example, during a Man-in-the-Middle attack, as discussed in Chapter 2, "SANs: Fibre Channel Security," a malicious third party that was running NT 4.0 with no service pack could force the communication between a NAS device and another server to be plain-text, tricking the NAS device that CIFS/SMB encryption could not be used and thus should drop down to the least common denominator, which would be plain-text. Once the two entities begin to communicate, the malicious attacker performing the Man-in-the-Middle attack would be able to sniff the plain-text password going over the wire. The issue becomes apparent when NAS devices are forced to use plain-text passwords when they are told (or tricked) rather than the standard methods of CIFS/SMB communication. See Figure 6.19 for the details.

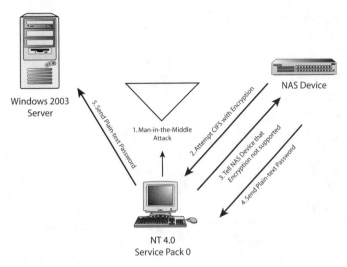

Figure 6.19 Plain-text password downgrade attacks.

LANMAN (LM) AND NT LANMAN (NTLM)

Most NAS devices support LM or NTLM authentication to/from any CIFS client. LM authentication was developed for OS/2 environments by IBM. Microsoft supports LM to have interoperability with OS/2. Consequently, NAS vendors support LM for interoperability with Microsoft environments, specifically Windows 95/98; however, most modern Microsoft environments will attempt NTLM first before attempting LM. There are many security issues with LM and NTLM. Let's discuss each of them individually.

LM

LANMAN performs the following actions after a user has selected a password:

1. Converts the password to uppercase.
2. If the password is less than 14 characters, it is filled with spaces to reach 14 characters. If it is more than 14 characters, it is shortened to 14 characters only.
3. The 14-character password is split into two separate seven character password halves.
4. Using DES, the seven-character password halves create two 16-byte hashes.
5. The 16-byte hashes are combined to create a single 32-byte hash.

For example, using the preceding steps, the password of Shreya would be as follows:

1. SHREYA
2. SHREYA00000000
3. SHREYA0 and 0000000
4. 4C1052981C7EF7F3 and AAD3B435B51404EE
5. 4C1052981C7EF7F3AAD3B435B51404EE

Because the password is less than eight characters, the second hash turns out to be AAD3B435B51404EE, which is the same for every password less than eight characters. When any password hash contains AAD3B435B51404EE, attackers will know that the password is eight characters or less, which reduces the amount time spent on it for cracking. What is left in the password hash is from a single seven-character password that is all uppercase, which is easy for most brute-forcing tools. Furthermore, if the password was actually 14 characters to begin with, it would only require the brute force of two separate seven character passwords that are all one case, which is a lot easier than brute forcing one 14-character password with upper- and lowercase.

As you can probably guess, LANMAN has several security issues associated with it. First, LM is not case sensitive. No matter what letters are used, upper- or lowercase, LM changes everything to uppercase when using an LM password hash. The other major issue is that the password is split in two separate seven-byte halves and hashed separately. It is always easier to brute force two smaller passwords/hashes than a single big one. The last item is that the hashing algorithm than LM uses is not very strong and it does not using password salting. Most cryptographers have concluded the LM hash to be very weak.

So why are we talking endlessly about LM? LM is supported by many NAS devices for authentication and is also used in NTLMv1, which will discussed in the next section. The issue here is that since NAS devices are based on TCP/IP, network sniffing, including sniffing on a switched network, is a trivial process. Since sniffing the communication from a NAS device and a CIFS client is possible, the security of the password is quite important. While the CIFS protocol is not encrypted, the password is at least hashed; however, if the password hash uses LM, the LM hash can be sniffed over the network and easily brute forced due to the security weaknesses of LM mentioned previously. This situation makes an CIFS client using LM authentication to access a NAS device severely vulnerable to password compromise. If a user's password is compromised, all files and folders that the user has access to, which is probably most files unless strong ACLs have been implemented, are vulnerable. Furthermore, if an administrator is using LM hashes across the network, the entire volume of data on the NAS device can be compromised.

NTLM

Microsoft tried to improve on the security issues with LM with the creation of NTLM (NT LAN Manager). The following are the steps that it took to produce the NTLM hash:

1. Password is hashed using a MD4 hash, which creates the 128-bit (16 bytes) "NTLM hash."
2. The 128-bit hash (NTLM hash) is broken up into three keys:
   a. Key 1 is the first 56-bits (7 bytes)
   b. Key 2 is the second 56-bits (7 bytes)
   c. Key 3 is the left over 32 bits (2 bytes) with 0s added to end to make it 56-bits (7 bytes)
3. Password is now three 56-bit keys.
4. An 8-byte challenge is received from the server.
5. The challenge and keys are now DES (Data Encryption Standard) encrypted
   a. DES encrypt the challenge and Key 1 (DES (Challenge + Key 1))
   b. DES encrypt the challenge and Key 2 (DES (Challenge + Key 2))
   c. DES encrypt the challenge and Key 3 (DES (Challenge + Key 3))
6. The three resulting DES values are concatenated together to produce the "NTLM Response."
   a. DES (Challenge, Key 1) + DES (Challenge, Key 2) + DES (Challenge, Key 3)

For example, using the preceding steps, the password of Shreya would be as follows:

1. MD4 (Shreya) = 3CE2EE14F48FFD47E61FB247B292A2A6
2. The 128-bit hash (NTLM hash), is broken up into three keys:
   a. Key 1 is 3CE2EE14F48FFD
   b. Key 2 is 47E61FB247B292
   c. Key 3 is A2A60000000000
3. Password is now three 56-bit keys.
4. An 8-byte challenge is sent from a CIFS server, such as 2FF8ADC9A71E9918.

5. The challenge and keys are now DES encrypted: DES(Challenge + Key).

   a. DES (2FF8ADC9A71E9918 + 3CE2EE14F48FFD)

   b. DES (2FF8ADC9A71E9918 + 47E61FB247B292)

   c. DES (2FF8ADC9A71E9918 + A2A60000000000)

6. NTLM Response is the concatenation of DES (Challenge, Key 1) + DES (Challenge, Key 2) + DES (Challenge, Key 3).

Certain security improvements were made with NTLM; however, there are still significant security issues. The core problem with NTLM (version 1) is that it uses password equivalent values for the NTLM hash (step 1 above). The MD4 (NTLM hash) of a password is a password equivalent value since there is no salting involved. Therefore, an attacker who gains access to the NTLM hash can compare it to a list of precomputed MD4 hashes from a large password file. If the NTLM hash and the precomputed hash match of a password, then the password has been cracked. It is very easy to perform a brute-force attack against the NTLM hashes by tools like Cain and L0pthCrack; however, the NTLM hash must be gained in the MD4 format. Another issue with NTLM connections is the use of LM and NTLM hashes in parallel during the authentication process, which allows attackers to deduce the NT hash from the LM hash. Lastly, another big issue with NTLM is that it is vulnerable to a known challenge (step 4 above) reflection attack with active attackers. For more security information on LM or NTLM hashes, refer to http://www.isecpartners.com/documents/NTLM_Unsafe.pdf or http://pintday.org/advisories/l0pht/l0phtcrack.html. We will discuss each of these weaknesses in the following sections.

Using LM or NTLM for authentication with NAS devices supporting CIFS is very close to using plain-text passwords. While the usage of LM has been reduced significantly in NAS devices, an alarming majority of current NAS devices still use NTLM by default. Since NTLM is considered to be a very poor hashing algorithm, the use of NTLM for password protection is not much better than using clear-text passwords across the network. It some cases, it could be considered worse since it could create a false sense of security for many storage administrators using NTLM on NAS devices running CIFS. This situation places a significant number of NAS devices that rely on NTLM in jeopardy to attack. Furthermore, this situation places sensitive, critical, and confidential data residing on NAS devices open to easy attacks.

To show the severity of using LM and NTLM for authentication on NAS devices running CIFS, including the impact on data on a NAS device as well as the simplicity of the attack, perform the following assessment exercise.

Figure 6.20 shows the architecture for the assessment exercise. We will first have to sniff the network using a Man-in-the-Middle attack and sniff the LM and NTLM authentication from two of our targets. The attacker can perform the attack at two places. The attacker could target the segment between the CIFS clients and the NAS device to target a particular end user. However, since the NAS device authenticates all CIFS clients via a NT PDC/Active Directory server, the attacker could also target the segment between the NAS device and the NT PDC/Active Directory server. In fact, if the attacker wanted to capture as many LM and NTLM hashes as possible, it would be better to attack the segment between the NAS device and the NT PDC/Active Directory, since all requests on the network would always traverse that network segment, allowing the attacker to receive every request from an end user via the NAS device rather than one request of a targeted end user.

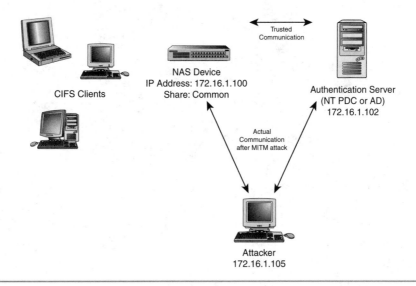

Figure 6.20 Assessment exercise architecture.

ASSESSMENT EXERCISE

1. Download Cain from http://www.oxid.it/cain.html.
2. Install the program using its defaults.
3. Install the WinPCap packet driver also, if you don't already have one installed.

4. Reboot.

5. Launch Cain and Abel (Start -> Programs -> Cain).

6. Select Configure from the menu bar and select the correct adapter for the machine (for example, 172.16.1.105). See Figure 6.21.

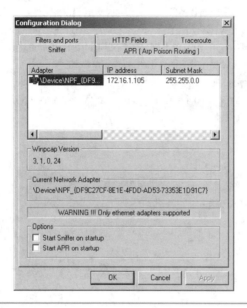

Figure 6.21   Adapter information.

7. Select the icon in the upper-left corner that looks like a network interface card.

8. Select the Sniffer tab.

9. Select the + symbol in the toolbar.

10. Ensure the subnet or range information is correct and select OK.

   a. This will enumerate all the MAC addresses on the local subnet. See Figure 6.22 for the results.

11. Select the APR tab on the bottom of the tool to switch to the ARP Pollution Routing tab.

12. Select the + symbol on the toolbar to show all the IP addresses and their MACs. See Figure 6.23.

13. On the left side of Figure 6.23, choose the target for your MITM attack, with our NAS device at 172.16.1.100.

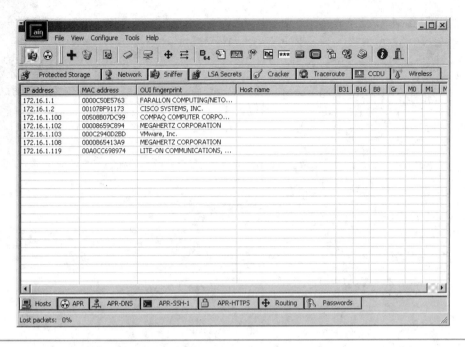

Figure 6.22 MAC address scanner results.

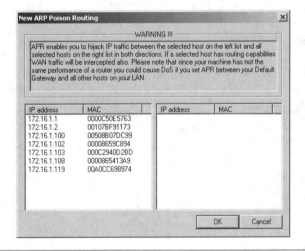

Figure 6.23 IP addresses and their MACs.

14. Once you select your target, select the hosts on the right side that you want to inter-cept traffic, which is the NT PDC/Active Directory server at 172.16.1.102. If we wanted to intercept all the communication from any CIFS client to any NAS device, we could select every IP address on the right side. However, since we know that the NAS device will send all authentication requests to the NT PDC/Active Directory server, we can target that segment and gain access to all the hashes Choose the tar-geted NT PDC/AD server, which is 172.16.1.102. Select OK. See Figure 6.24.

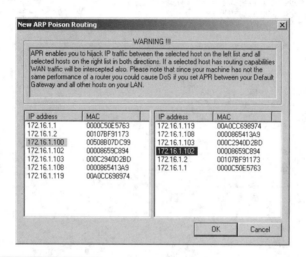

Figure 6.24   Man-in-the-Middle targets.

15. Now select the yellow and black icon (second one from the left) to officially start the MITM attack. This will allow an attacker's machine to start sending out ARP responses on the network subnet, telling 172.16.1.102 that the MAC address of 172.16.1.100 has been updated; therefore, sending all traffic to the attacker machine first before the NAS device. See Figure 6.25.

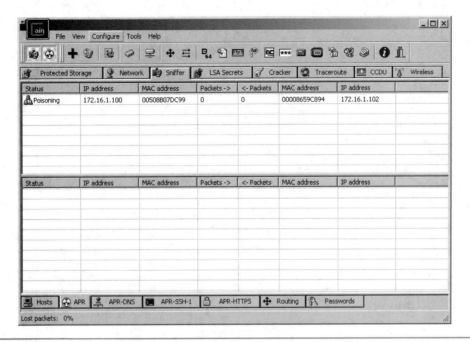

Figure 6.25 Man-in-the-Middle attack in process with ARP poisoning.

16. At this point, all traffic from the NT PDC/AD server to the NAS device is going to the attacker's machine first. The attacker can open up a network sniffer to view all the LM or NTLM authentication over the network. Additionally, Cain has a Passwords tab at the bottom that will capture the LM and/or NTLM hashes for us. Select the Passwords tab (see Figure 6.26).

17. Once the NAS devices send authentication information on behalf of the client to the NT PDC/AD server, the LM or NTLM hash will be captured. Click on SMB in the left column on the Passwords tab to view the LM and/or NTLM information. See Figure 6.27.

18. Highlight the row with the captured LM/NTLM hashes and right-click.

19. Select Send to Crack and then select the Cracker tab at the top of the panel.

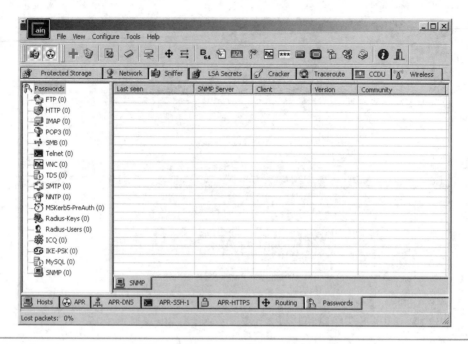

Figure 6.26   Capture password due to the Man-in-the-Middle attack.

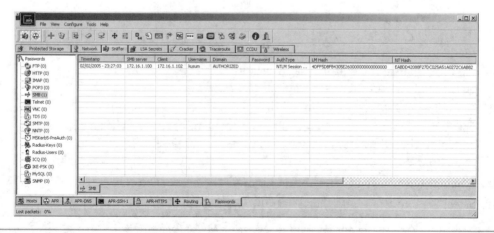

Figure 6.27   Captured LM/NTLM hashes.

20. Notice in Figure 6.28 that both the LM and NTLM hashes appear and are ready to be cracked or brute forced.

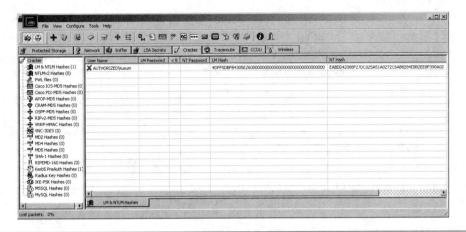

Figure 6.28   LM and NTLM hashes.

21. Highlight the row with the hashes and right-click. You now have a choice to do a dictionary attack, brute-force attack, cryptanalysis attack, test a password manually, or even export the hashes to another program called L0pthcrack (version 2.5). Select brute-force attack (NTLM Session Security).

22. Select Start on the Brute-Force Attack window.

23. After Cain has cracked LM or NTLM, it will display the results. See Figure 6.29 where the cracked password of the user kusum is Varanasi!.

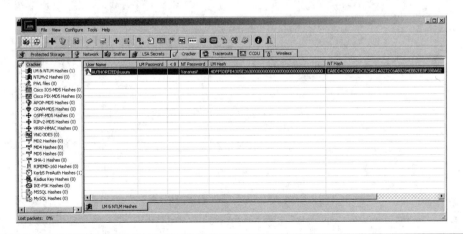

Figure 6.29   Cracked LM and NTLM password.

24. Using Cain to brute force the passwords might take a bit of time for NTLM since the NTLM response uses a challenge, but a very short amount of time for LM since no challenge is used. L0pthcrack 2.5 is also a good tool that solely focuses on cracking LM and NTLM hashes. Right-click on the row with the hashes and select Export.

25. Save the file as hashes. It will automatically be saved in L0pthcrack 2.5 format.

26. Download L0phtcrack 3.0 from http://www.packetstormsecurity.org/NT/lc3setup.exe (for the most recent version of L0pthcrack, visit http://www.atstake.com/products/lc/ for LC5).

27. Install L0pthcrack 3.0 on your system. After the install and reboot, open LC3 (Start -> Programs -> LC3 -> LC3).

28. Select Cancel to remove the wizard.

29. From the menu bar, Select File -> New Session.

30. From the menu bar, Select View -> Password Hashes.

31. From the menu bar, Select Import -> Import from .LC file....

32. From the menu bar in L0pthcrack 2.5, open File and Open Password File....

33. Browse to the location of your hashes.lc file from Cain (by default, Cain stores the file in c:\Program Files\Cain\Wordlists\hashes.lc).

34. From the menu bar, select Session -> Begin Audit. LC3 will now try dictionary, brute-force, and hybrid attacks. See Figure 6.30.

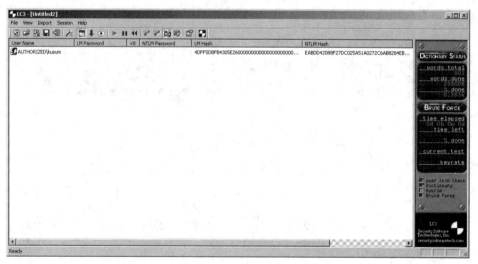

Figure 6.30   LC3 cracking LM and NTLM hashes.

35. Done! You have now compromised the NAS device (and its data) without an author-ized user and password because of its implementation of CIFS.

If you want to perform the same attack but do not want to perform a Man-in-the-Middle attack, which means that you are on a hub or you are on a network segment where you can sniff communication already, then you might want to use the ScoopLM tool from SecurityFriday that will sniff LM and NTLM hashes over the network. After we sniff the hashes from the NAS device, we will insert them into L0phtcrack 2.5 and crack the passwords. Complete the following steps to complete this attack on the NAS device running CIFS:

1. Download ScoopLM from SecurityFriday (http://www.securityfriday.com/tools/ScoopLM.html).

2. Unzip the file to a location on your system (such as c:\tools).

3. Double-click on ScoopLM.exe.

4. Select the correct interface (IP address) in the drop-down menu (e.g. 172.16.1.5). See Figure 6.31.

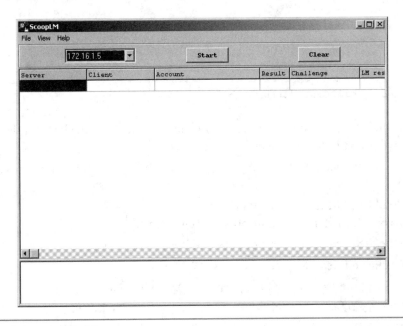

Figure 6.31   ScoopLM IP address.

5. Select Start. As the NAS device attempts to authenticate CIFS clients, their LM and NTLM hashes will be capture by ScoopLM. See Figure 6.32.

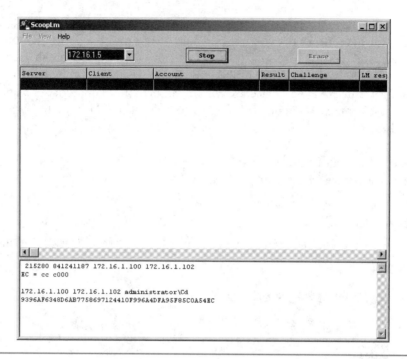

Figure 6.32   Captured LM and NTLM hashes with ScoopLM.

6. Done! You have now captured the authentication of the NAS device. Now let's crack the password with BeatLM, also from SecurityFriday.

7. From the menu bar, select File -> SaveAs -> Sniffed Session (it will save it as a cvs file).

8. Download BeatLM from SecurityFriday (http://www.securityfriday.com/tools/BeatLM.html).

9. Unzip the file to a location on your system (such as c:\tools).

10. Double-click on BeatLM.exe.

11. From the option drop-down box, select NTLM: 7 characters log A-z 0-9.

12. From the menu bar, select File -> Open and browse to the location of SniffedSession.csv. Hit OK when it tells you that import is complete.

13. From the menu bar, select Run -> Run.

14. Done! Now BeatLM will begin brute forcing the password similar to LC3. See Figure 6.33.

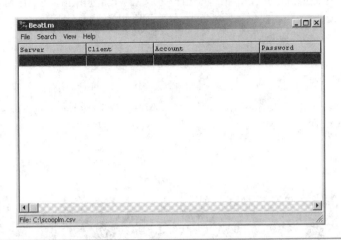

Figure 6.33 BeatLM brute forcing NTLM hashes.

You now understand how CIFS authentication using LM and NTLM is very bad, but you may be wondering if there are any ways to speed up the cracking process. The answer is yes. Precomputed LM and NTLM hashes can be generated and used to gain a user's passwords. For example, if someone took all the words in the English language and created LM or NTLM (MD4) hashes for it, these precomputed hashes could be used to match LM hashes or the NTLM hashes (not the NTLM Response) you obtained from Cain or ScoopLM. Instead of crack or brute forcing a LM hash with LC3 or BeatLM, you could take a large list of hashes you already have from English words and simply see which ones match the ones you captured with Cain or ScoopLM. For more technical details on how this is done, refer to Philippe Oechslin's web site (http://lasecwww.epfl.ch/philippe.shtml). The are several tools to perform precomputed attacks including RainbowCrack (http://www.antsight.com/zsl/rainbowcrack/) and LC5 (http://www.atstake.com/products/lc/).

An additional method to speed up the process of password retrieval is to forget about the password itself and use an attack technique called "passing the hash." In many CIFS servers, including NAS devices, the LM or NTLM hashes are password-equivalent values. This means that if the correct LM or NTLM hash is presented to the NAS device, it will accept that in the authentication process and allow the user to login. This allows an attacker to dump an LM or NTLM hash using Cain or L0pthcrack, bypass cracking and actually present that hash value to the NAS device and become authenticated. This now allows an unauthorized user to compromise all the data in a NAS device supporting CIFS without a password! There are two tools to allow end users to present the LM or NTLM hash to the NAS device instead of the password, including SMBproxy, available at http://www.cqure.net/tools.jsp?id=2, and SmbShell, written by Jesse Burns of iSEC Partners (www.isecpartners.com).

DEMONSTRATION

Jesse Burns presented his tool at the SyScan Conference in 2004. The following is a demonstration of the tool.

1. From the command line, type **Java -jar SmbShell.jar** (see Figure 6.34).

Figure 6.34 SmbShell.

2. Type **cd <IP address of the NAS device>** and press Enter. For example, type **cd 172.16.1.100** (see Figure 6.35).

3. Type **cd <name of CIFS share>** and press Enter. For example, type **cd common** (see Figure 6.36).

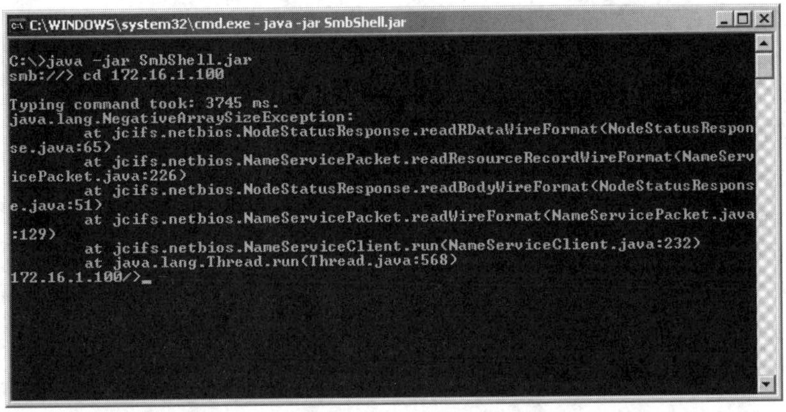

Figure 6.35 SmbShell connection.

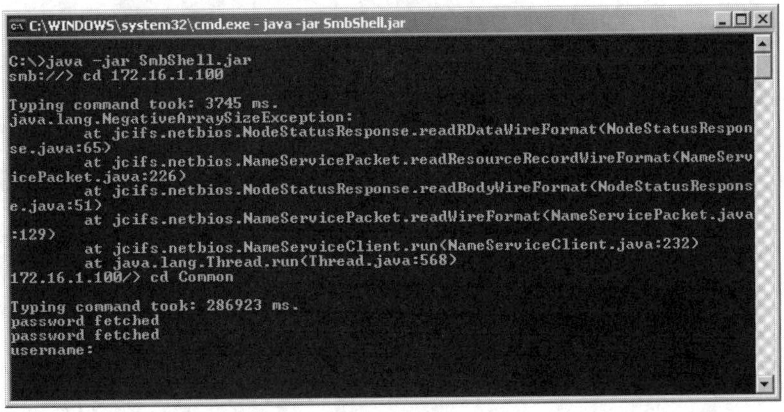

Figure 6.36 CIFS share connection.

4. Type the username and press Enter. For example, type **kusum** (see Figure 6.37).

5. Finally, type the NTLM hash and press Enter. For example, type **44516496E97719ACE03386BAFD7FDFE4** (see Figure 6.38).

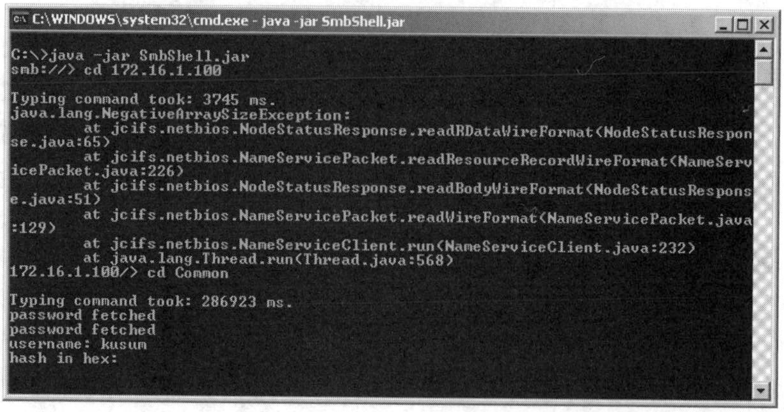

Figure 6.37 CIFS username connection.

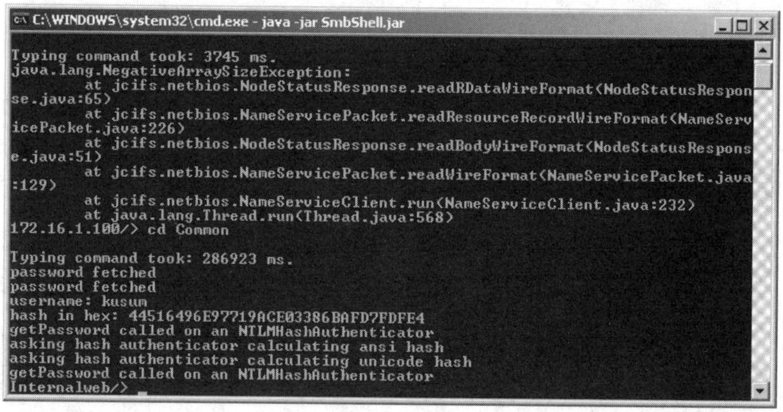

Figure 6.38 CIFS login.

6. Done! The NAS device is now compromised without a password and using only the NTLM hash! We can type **ls** to list the directories, **put** to place a file on the device, or more importantly **get** to pull any file from the NAS device. For example, on our NAS device, the file called MedicalRecords.xls can now be retrieved. (see Figure 6.39 and notice the Fetched result).

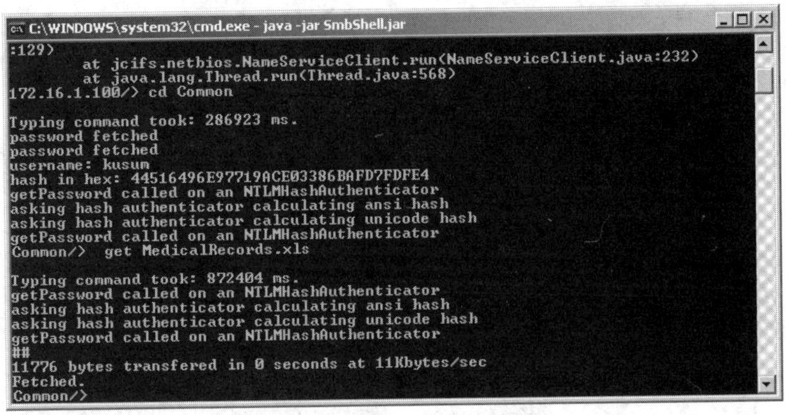

Figure 6.39 CIFS file retrieval.

Another attack on NTLM allows an attacker to get into a NAS device running CIFS (using NTLM) without knowing any password, but also requires a little more effort from an attacker. The attack is a message reflection attack of a known and reflected challenge. As stated above, the NT hash is an MD4 hash. The NT hash can be brute-forced very quickly since it uses the MD4 hash of the password; however, what about the NTLM Response hash that actually authenticates the end user to the NAS device? A correct NTLM response can be used by an attacker without knowing a valid password using the challenge reflection attack across multiple connections. The challenge is the key entity in the NTLM response that makes it unique from the NT hash (the MD4 hash value). As stated previously, a client would take its NTLM hash and the challenge from the NAS device and make an NTLM response hash value. The NTLM response hash is sent to the NAS device over the network. A challenge reflection attack would first begin with the attacker starting a new authentication process. The attacker will receive a challenge from the NAS device. Because the attacker does not know the any valid password, it cannot formulate the correct NTLM response. However, the attacker can open a completely separate second connection to the NAS device (connection number 2) and get the NAS device to authenticate to it (NAS device authenticating to the client). The client (the attacker) would send the same challenge it received from the NAS device on connection number 1 to the NAS device on the second connection. The NAS device would receive the challenge on the second connection (the same challenge that was sent to the attacker in the first connection), combine it with a valid password, and make a NTLM response value of it and send it to the attacker. The attacker now has the correct NTLM response value that is made from the same challenge that from the original connection and the correct password. The attacker can now present the NTLM response value from the second connection to the NAS device on the first connection. The NAS device would see the correct NTLM response value on the first connection and authenticate the attacker without the attacker not knowing the password. The following steps show how to complete this attack using two connections to/from an attacker and a NAS device using CIFS (NTLM).

1. Connection 1: The attacker attempts to authenticate to the NAS device.

2. Connection 1: The NAS device sends the attacker challenge in order to receive a NTLM response.

3. Connection 2: The attacker does not know the correct password, so it cannot create a valid NTLM response to get authenticated. Therefore, the attacker opens up a second connection and forces the NAS device to authenticate to itself (the attacker), which can be done in several ways, including ARP poisoning (Man-in-the-Middle attack) targeting the NAS device. The same challenge that was sent in step 2 from the NAS device will be used, which will ensure the ensuing NTLM response is the correct one for the original connection.

4. Connection 2: The NAS device receives the challenge on the second connection and thinks it must respond with a NTLM response. The NAS device creates a valid NTLM response using the given challenge and the valid password (the NAS device knows the real password). The valid NTLM response is then sent to the attacker.

5. Connection 1: The attacker receives the valid NTLM response and will go back to the first connection and send the response to the NAS device.

6. Connection 1: The attacker is now authenticated by the NAS device since it sent a valid NTLM response that was created with the correct password, using the valid challenge from the original connection.

Jesse Burns of iSEC Partners (jesse@isecpartners.com) has written a tool called SMBMeow that performs this attack on CIFS devices using NTLM.

Hopefully by now you are convinced that the use of LM and NTLM hashes on NAS devices supporting CIFS is a bad idea. While many devices support Kerberos, discussed in the next section, most NAS devices can use NTLM by default or can be forced to use NTLM quite easily (even if Kerberos is enabled).

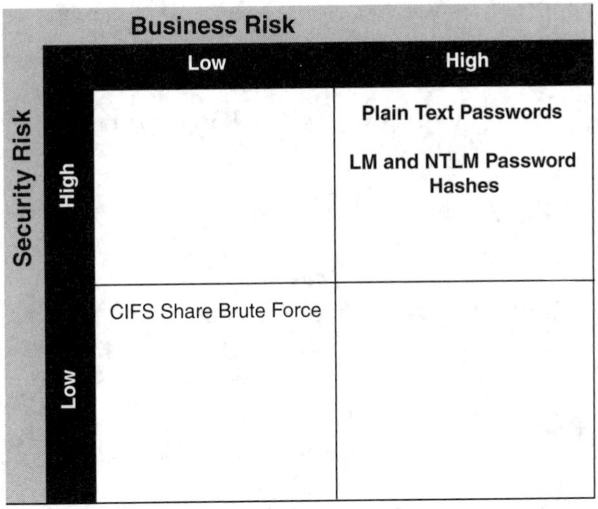

Figure 6.40 SBR chart—CIFS authentication.

ATTACK SUMMARY: CIFS AUTHENTICATION

Attack description—A unauthorized user can sniff the password in clear-text or crack the LM or NTLM password hashes and gain unauthorized access to the NAS device running CIFS.

Risk level—Difficulty: Low.

Best practice—Disable plain-text, LM, and NTLM passwords and support Kerberos only.

SOLUTIONS

So what are the solutions? That is easy—don't use LM or NTLM and only use NTLMv2 or Kerberos. Currently, most NAS vendors support NTLMv2 and Kerberos; however, all of them can be downgraded to LM or NTLM, which is a very trivial process. It would be nice if storage vendors had a "Kerberos-only mode" or a "Kerberos/NTLMv2-0nly mode" that proactively disables LM and NTLM communication on the NAS device.

Additionally, the ability to disable LM or NTLM on Windows 2000/XP machine is quite easy. Complete the following to disable LM or NTLM on Windows CIFS clients:

1. Start -> Programs -> Administrative Tools -> Local Security Policy.
2. Expand Local Policies –> Security Options.
   a. Under Security Options, browse to Network security: LAN Manager authentication level. See Figure 6.41.

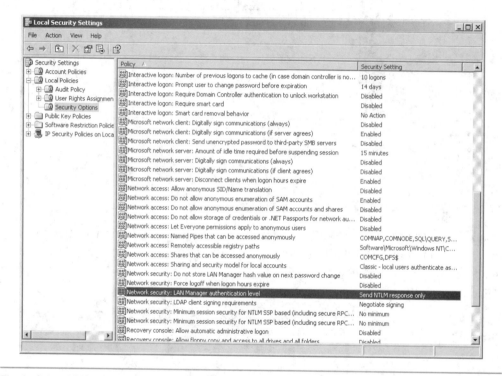

Figure 6.41   LM/NTLM on options Windows.

3. Double-click on Network security: LAN Manager authentication level.
4. From the drop-down box, choose one of the following options (see Figure 6.42):
   a. Most Secure: Send NTLMv2 responses only/refuse LM and NTLM.
   b. Moderate Secure: Send NTLMv2 responses only/refuse LM.
   c. Secure: Send NTLMv2 responses only.

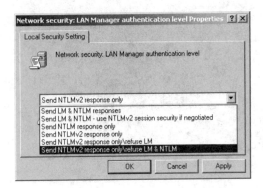

Figure 6.42   Disabling LM/NTLM on Windows.

KERBEROS

Due to the enormous security issues with LM and NTLM, Kerberos has been supported on most NAS devices. Before we discuss how NAS devices use Kerberos, let's explain a bit about the technology. The word Kerberos comes from Greek mythology, where Kerberos was the three-headed hound that guarded the entrance of Hades. The technology came out of the Project Athena from MIT. The technology involves three parts: a Kerberos client, a Kerberos Distribution Center (KDC), and the Ticket Granting Server, as specified in RFC 1510. The premise of Kerberos is to use service tickets for authentication rather than passwords. The service tickets do not contain the user's password, cannot be used to deduce the user's password, and are time stamped to work only for a limited period of time. The idea is to prevent actual passwords from traversing the network and instead use service tickets that identify and authenticate the user. Kerberos will never reveal any information of the actual password of the user. The following steps describe the Kerberos process according to Figure 6.43:

1. Client authenticates to KDC with their password.
2. KDC issues a Ticket Granting Ticket (TGT).
3. Client sends TGT to the Ticket Granting Server.
4. TGS issues a Service Ticket to client.
5. Client uses the Service Ticket to authenticate to devices, servers, and applications.

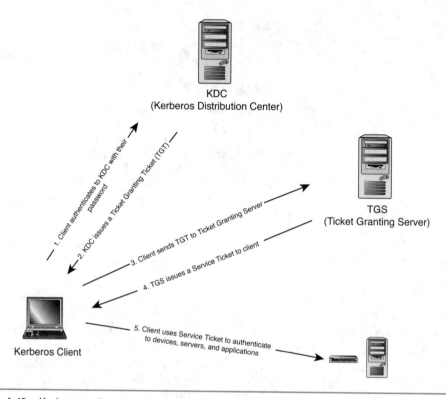

Figure 6.43 Kerberos authentication process.

The implementation of Kerberos often has the KDC and the TGS as the same physical server. For example, Active Directory domain controllers in a Windows environment are all Kerberos enabled (Kerberos version 5). The Active Directory server acts as the KDC and the TGT on the network, and every Windows 2000 machines (or later) are Kerberos clients by default. While all the Kerberos steps still take place, it only involves the Windows client (Kerberos client) and the Active Directory server (the KDS and TGS), as shown in Figure 6.44.

While Kerberos may seem like a complicated process, all the steps are invisible to the end user. Hence, the user would log in to a domain, server, application, or device the same as a non-Kerberized environment, without requiring any additional steps for the end user.

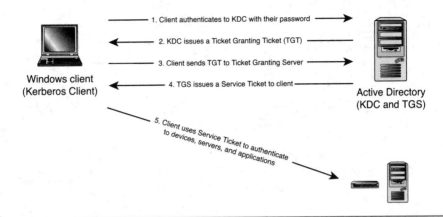

Figure 6.44 Kerberos authentication with Active Directory.

As you can guess, the use of Kerberos and its ability to rarely send the user's password across the network is a strong security feature. Both LM and NTLM exposures are increased due to the fact that the hashes are constantly going across the network in the clear. Kerberos does not use passwords for authentication but rather the service tickets, which are only valid for a limited period of time and cannot be used to eventually reveal the end user's password. NAS devices supporting Kerberos have a strong advantage for authentication. Instead of relying on LM or NTLM, Kerberos adds an industry standard authentication process that has not had as many serious security issues associated with it as other authentication protocols. Furthermore, many NAS devices supporting Kerberos can use it for CIFS as well as NFS (discussed in Chapter 7), Telnet, and FTP.

In order to deploy a NAS device with Kerberos authentication, an existing Kerberized environment must exist with a KDC and a TGS. Since Windows 2000/2003 and Active Directory environments support Kerberos, the implementation with NAS devices can be quite easy. During the initial setup process, many NAS devices will search for the local domain and check to see if Active Directory domain is in place. If so, the device will attempt to join the domain (administrator privileges are required). Note: If the NAS device cannot find an Active Directory domain, it will be installed in basic or NT4.0 mode, which uses NTLM. Once a NAS device joins the domain, it is able to support Kerberos authentication automatically. In fact, a NAS device that is added to a Windows 2000/2003 domain will use Kerberos by default for authentication and only drop down to LM or NTLM if needed. Figure 6.45 shows this example

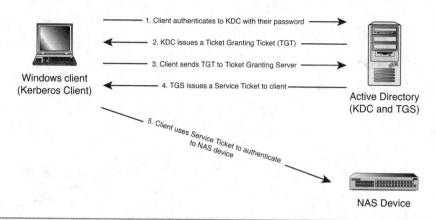

1. Client authenticates to KDC with their password →
← 2. KDC issues a Ticket Granting Ticket (TGT)
3. Client sends TGT to Ticket Granting Server →
← 4. TGS issues a Service Ticket to client
5. Client uses Service Ticket to authenticate to NAS device

Windows client
(Kerberos Client)

Active Directory
(KDC and TGS)

NAS Device

Figure 6.45 Kerberos and NAS devices.

While the security advantages to use Kerberos are overwhelming, there are a few security issues and attack classes with it also. For example, during the authentication procedure, the first step in the entire process requires a client to send his/her password to the KDC (Active Directory server) in Figures 6.43 and 6.44. This is also known as the pre-authentication process of Kerberos because the user is not technically authenticated at step 1 but actually attempting to authenticate. This is the only time in the process that the end user's password is sent over the wire; however, a hash of the password is sent over the network. If an attacker were able to sniff that part of the Kerberos session, they would be able to brute force the Kerberos hash. While brute forcing a captured Kerberos hash is not an easy task and definitely a lot harder than brute forcing an LM or NTLM hash, if an end user had poor passwords, it can be a trivial process. This is another good reason why administrators and end users should have strong passwords when deploying NAS devices that are Kerberos enabled. Although Kerberos is a strong authentication method, it is not a free ride to have poor passwords. The following exercise shows the pre-authentication attack against Kerberos, as outlined in Figure 6.46.

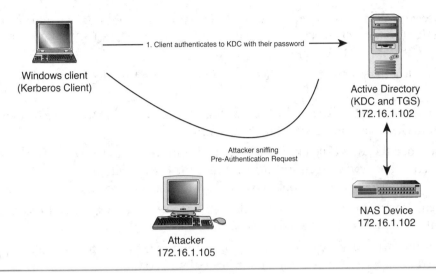

Figure 6.46 Kerberos pre-authentication sniffing.

1. Conduct a Man-in-the-Middle attack (you can skip to step 14 if you are feel familiar enough with Cain and Abel to do the Man-in-the-Middle attack) between the CIFS client, 172.16.1.108, and the AD Server, 172.16.1.102, and NAD device, 172.16.1.100.

2. Launch Cain and Abel (Start -> Programs -> Cain).

3. Select Configure from the menu bar and select the correct adapter for the machine (such as 172.16.1.105).

4. Select the icon in the upper-left corner that looks like a network interface card.

5. Select the Sniffer tab.

6. Select the + symbol in the toolbar.

7. Ensure the subnet or range information is correct and select OK.

   a. This will enumerate all the MAC addresses on the local subnet.

8. Select the APR tab on the bottom of the tool to switch to the ARP Pollution Routing tab.

9. Select the + symbol on the toolbar to show all the IP addresses and their MACs.

10. On the left side, choose the target for your MITM attack, which for our CIFS client is 172.16.1.108.

11. Once you select your target, then select the hosts on the right side that you want to intercept traffic, which is the Active Directory server at 172.16.1.102 and the NAS device at 172.16.1.100.

12. Now select the yellow and black icon (second one from the left) to officially start the MITM attack.

13. At this point, all traffic from the Active Directory server and NAS device is going to the attacker's machine first before the CIFS client.

14. Download the tools called kerbcrack and kerbsniff from www.ntsecurity.nu/ kerbcrack and www.ntsecurity.nu/kerbsniff, which were written by Arne Vindstrom. Download the tools to your system, such as c:\tools.

15. Open a command prompt (Start -> Run -> cmd.exe) and change directories to the location of the tool (such as cd c:\tools\).

16. Copy the dictionary file from Cain to the location of the tools (for example, copy "c:\Program Files\Cain\Wordlists\Wordlist.txt" c:\tools\).

17. Type **kerbsniff.exe** on the command line to see the help information.

18. Type **kerbsniff.exe preauthenication.txt** to capture the Kerberos pre-authentication sessions. See Figure 6.47.

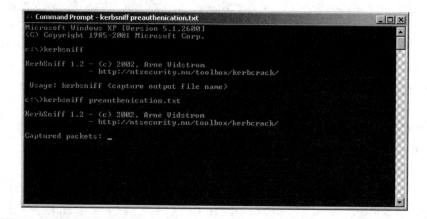

Figure 6.47 Kerbsniff execution.

19. Notice the "Captured Packets" line. Once CIFS clients begin their Kerberos process with the pre-authentication session, an asterisk (*) will be displayed by kerbsniff denoting that it has captured a Kerberos pre-authentication session from the client to the NAS device/AD server. See Figure 6.48 for a captured session.

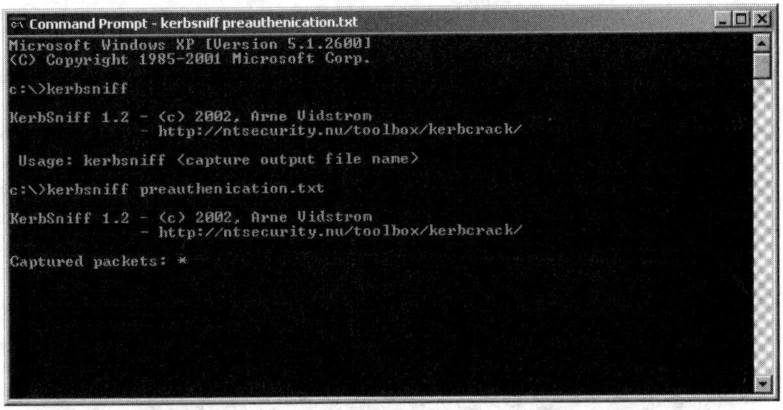

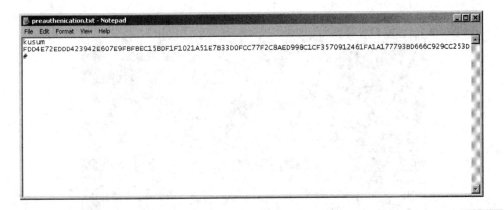

Figure 6.48 Captured Kerberos session.

20. You can keep the sniffer running to capture more authentication sessions between the CIFS clients and NAS devices; however, to stop sniffing, press Ctrl-C in the command prompt window.

21. Type **notepad preauthenication.txt** on the command line to view the Kerberos pre-authentication hash. See Figure 6.49.

Figure 6.49 Display of captured Kerberos hash.

22. Close the notepad file (File -> Exit).

23. Now type **kerbcrack.exe** on the command line to see the help menu and start brute forcing the Kerberos pre-authentication session.

24. As you can see, there are several methods to brute force the Kerberos session, including a typical brute-force attack or even a dictionary attack.

25. Type the following text on the command line to attempt a dictionary attack: `kerbcrack.exe preauthenication.txt -d Wordlists.txt`, shown in Figure 6.50.

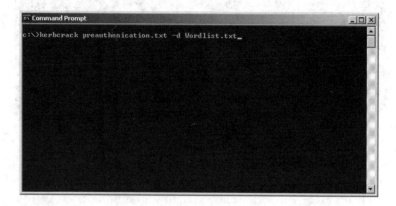

Figure 6.50 Kerbcrack syntax.

26. If the password is a dictionary word that is held in the dictionary file, kerbcrack will reveal the password, as shown in Figure 6.51.

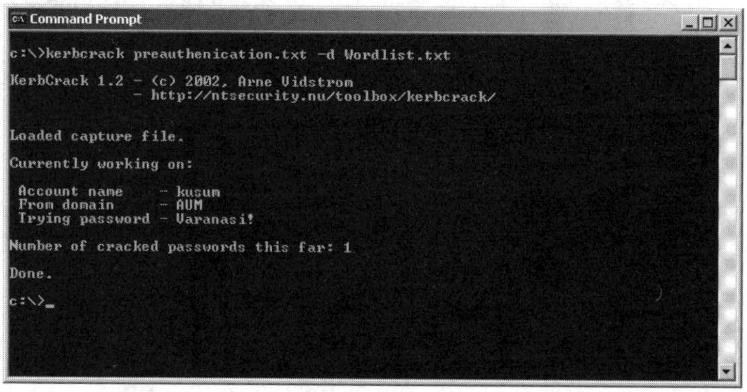

```
c:\>kerbcrack preauthenication.txt -d Wordlist.txt

KerbCrack 1.2 - (c) 2002, Arne Vidstrom
            - http://ntsecurity.nu/toolbox/kerbcrack/

Loaded capture file.

Currently working on:

 Account name     - kusum
 From domain      - AUM
 Trying password - Varanasi!

Number of cracked passwords this far: 1

Done.

c:\>_
```

Figure 6.51 Revealed pre-authentication Kerberos session.

27. In addition to a dictionary attack, a brute-force attack can also be conducted. However, it requires the knowledge of the password length, which might be anywhere from 1 to 14 characters (the next section with Cain and Abel will not need the actual password size). Type **kerbcrack.exe -b3 9** to perform a brute-force attack, as shown in Figure 6.52.

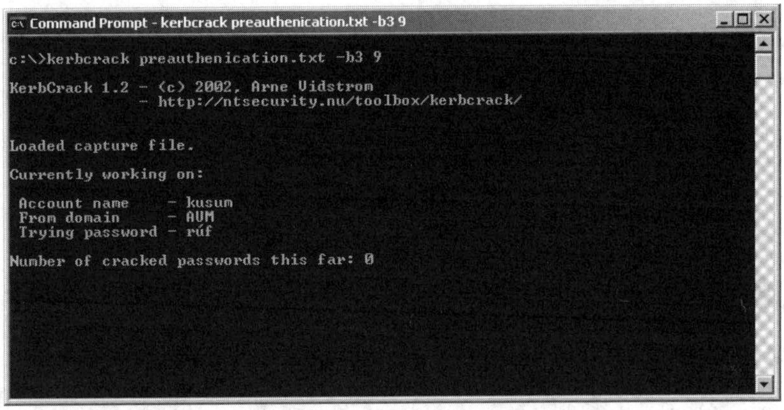

Figure 6.52 Brute forcing of the pre-authentication Kerberos session.

28. Once the Kerberos session ticket is captured, it can also be inserted into Cain and Abel for a dictionary attack or a brute-force attack.

    a. Type **notepad preauthenication.txt** to open the file with the Kerberos hash.

29. Copy the Kerberos hash section (A976B6F6C73F4A4CC46101BF1F0C281DEAE0EE6E11AD0AC3985899F517BF7C 7A6A70C6CCD93E69F8B1DA2528861BEA05C91043E5), as shown in Figure 6.53.

30. Open Cain and Abel (Start -> Programs -> Cain -> Cain 2.5).

31. Select the Cracker tab from the top portion of the tool.

32. In the left panel, highlight Kerb5 PreAuth Hashes.

33. In the right pane, right-click and select Add to List, as shown in Figure 6.54.

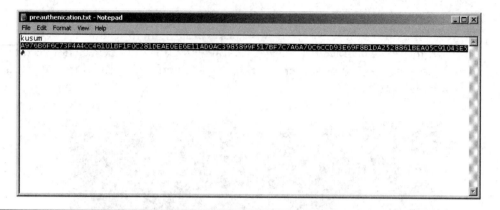

Figure 6.53   Copying Kerberos hash.

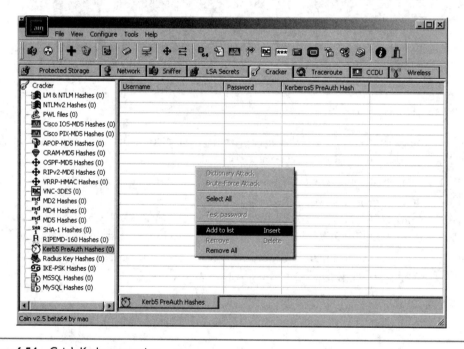

Figure 6.54   Cain's Kerberos section.

34. In the Add to List window, paste the copied Kerberos hash from step 29 and select OK. See Figures 6.55 and 6.56.

Figure 6.55   Kerberos Insert window.

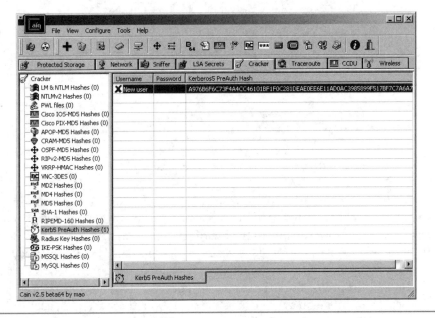

Figure 6.56   Kerberos hash in Cain Cracker.

35. Once the hashes are inside Cain's Cracker tab, highlight the row and right-click.

36. You will see the options to attempt a dictionary attack, a brute-force attack, or to test the password manually. Select Brute-Force Attack.

37. The Brute-Force Attack window should appear. Select Start.

38. Once Cain has brute forced the password, which may be a short or long amount of time depending on the strength of the password, it will be displayed in this window, as shown in Figure 6.57.

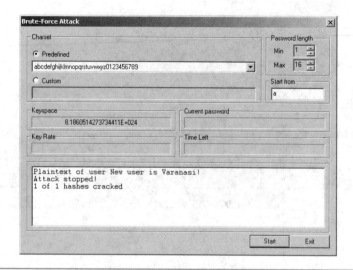

Figure 6.57   Brute forced Kerberos pre-authentication hash in Cain.

While we were still able to brute force a weak password with Kerberos, it is far more secure than LM or NTLM hashes. If a user has a strong password, Cain or Kerbcrack will take a very long time. However, due to the use of CIFS by NAS devices and the insecurities of IP, the ability to take control of a NAS device and its data is not necessarily a difficult task. Some storage vendors may say that these issues are not unrelated to storage devices but rather the protocols (CIFS) and transports (IP) that they use. However, a storage device, or any node on a network, is the collection of the services, protocols, and transport is uses. For example, if Honda, Toyota, or Chevrolet had a problem with its keyless entry system (the remote keychain) that allowed unauthorized people to enter the car, would you accept the answer that this is not a problem with the car but rather a problem with the key system that it uses? I think not. When you purchase a car, you purchase everything that it uses, from the keyless entry system to the type of tires that come with the car. The same ideas apply to the storage devices. When you deploy a storage device, you are deploying all of its third-party services also, including CIFS, LM, NTLM, Kerberos, or IP. Just like any other device that supports these protocols and transports, it needs to ensure that it is securing itself and also securing the data that resides in it. Figure 6.58 shows the SBR chart for Kerberos.

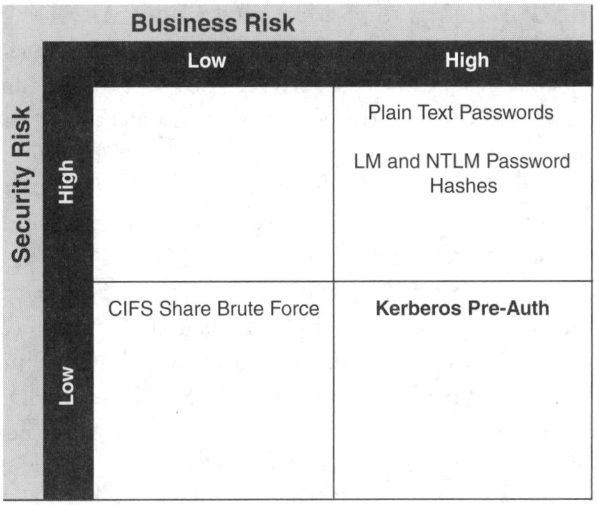

Figure 6.58   SBR chart—Kerberos authentication.

ATTACK SUMMARY: KERBEROS AUTHENTICATION

Attack description—An unauthorized user can capture the first packet in the Kerberos authentication process and attempt to brute-force the password from the pre-authentication information.

Risk Llvel—Difficulty: Moderate.

Best practice—Continue to enable Kerberos; however, ensure that the pre-authentication packets cannot be sniffed by using IPSec.

AUTHORIZATION

Authorization is a method to ensure that a potential entity is allowed to access another entity. Unlike authentication, which is meant to ensure that an entity is actually who they say they are, authorization is solely meant to ensure that the entity is allowed to access the machine or not. A good example of authorization is an ATM card. If you possess an ATM card, you are authorized to attempt to withdraw money out of an ATM machine; however, holding an ATM card does not authenticate you. The pin number that you type in on the ATM machine actually authenticates you, but possessing an ATM card means that you are authorized to attempt to perform transactions. An ATM card is merely authorization for attempted communication, but no other trust is place until you have authenticated. If you were not granted an ATM card by your bank, it means you have not been authorized to perform transactions with the ATM machine.

Common attributes for authorization in NAS devices are IP addresses and hostnames. IP addresses can be used as stand-alone addresses, such as 172.16.1.102, which would only allow the IP address of 172.16.1.102 to access the NAS device, or a subnet, such as 172.16.1.0/24, which would allow all addresses from 172.16.1.1 to 172.16.1.254 to access the NAS device. Additionally, IP addresses can be used to access a particular share on a NAS device. For example, the IP address of the management station can be the only host authorized to access an administrative share, such as ETC$. Furthermore, if the finance department on your network belongs to the subnet of 172.16.1.0/24, the finance share on the NAS device can be restricted to 172.16.1.0/24. In both examples, users are still required to authenticate to the NAS device; however, unless users are accessing the NAS device or share from the correct source IP, the possibility to even attempt authentication will be denied, which adds an additional layer of security.

Similar to IP addresses, hostnames of nodes can also be used for authorization. For example, the hostname of gandhi.Aum.com can set as the only host that can connect to the NAS device or even just the management share on the NAS device. In addition to hostnames, variables can be set as part of hostnames. For example, *.Aum.com can set as the filter, which are only allowed to connect to the NAS device or the finance share of the NAS device. Hostnames are useful since an IP address is more cumbersome to configure and may change periodically. Additionally, if your domain is Aum.com, you could set an authorization filter that states that hostnames from *.Aum.com can only connect to the NAS device and gandhi.Aum.com can only connect to the administrative share. This is a nice way to ensure that only computers that have joined your domain, which requires a domain administrator to configure, are allowed to connect to the NAS device. (Note: Most NAS devices using CIFS actually do not use authorization but solely rely on authentication.) For example, if a remote attacker or just an unauthorized user plugs into your network, they will not be able to connect to the NAS device since their hostname will not end with Aum.com.

Unfortunately, IP addresses and hostnames are also easy to spoof. An unauthorized user could change their IP address and/or hostname and get access to the NAS device and bypass any authorization parameter. However, while spoofing an IP address or hostname is a trivial process, it does not necessarily equate to full access. For example, if an unauthorized user is able to enumerate that the IP address of 172.16.1.102 is able to access the NAS device, the attacker can spoof their IP address to be 172.16.1.102 and send packets to the device. However, when the NAS device receives the packet, they will send their response to 172.16.1.102 since that is the IP address they received the initial packet from (the NAS device does not know the address has been spoofed and sends packets as normal). This situation allows any attacker spoofing IP addresses to bypass filters to send packets, but not be able to receive packets. The attacker could perform a Man-in-the-Middle attack in combination with IP address spoofing to fully complete an attack. For example, if an unauthorized user spoofed their IP address to be 172.16.1.102 and also performed a Man-in-the-Middle attack that made any packets intended for the real 172.16.1.102 to go to the attacker instead, when the attacker spoofs the packets, they would then also be able to receive the packets from the NAS device—thus bypassing authorization filters entirely that are based on IP addresses (the same attack applies to hostnames also). The problem here is that NAS devices rely on entities that can be changed (spoofed) for security purposes. This would be like using a person's name as the sole entity to authorize them to get access to their bank account. While a name is a good way to identify someone, anyone can go to the courthouse and have their name changed legally to anything they want. If attackers had the correct name, the bankers would allow them to access your bank account. For the right amount of money, many people would change their name to anything (just ask Hollywood stars). This is why banks use picture IDs, ATM cards, and ATM codes, in addition to having the correct name, to grant customers access to their accounts. The following exercises show the method to spoof an IP address and/or a hostname.

ASSESSMENT EXERCISE

1. Download winrelay, written by Arne Vinstrom, from http://www.ntsecurity.nu/toolbox/winrelay/ to a directory on your systems, such as c:\tools.

2. cd (change directory) to the directory where the tool is located (cd c:\tools).

3. Type **winrelay.exe** for the help menu.

4. We will spoof the IP address of 172.16.1.102, which is an authorized administrator workstation, to 172.16.1.100, which is the NAS device, from the IP address of 172.16.1.105, which is the attacker. See Figure 6.59.

5. Type the following on the command line:

   a. **winrelay -lip 172.16.1.105 -lp 80 -sip 172.16.1.102 -sp 80 -dip 172.16.1.100 -dp 80 -proto tcp**

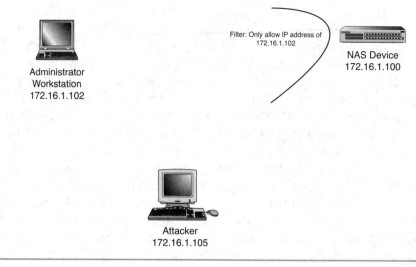

Figure 6.59   Sample architecture for authorization.

6. Open up a browser and type the IP address of **172.16.1.105**. After the connection is made, winrelay will relay the connection from itself (172.16.1.105) to the target (172.16.1.100), using the spoofed source IP address with 172.16.1.102.

7. Done! You are now able to subvert the authorization parameters on the NAS device by sending packets to it that appear from the source IP of 172.16.1.102.

Now that we understand how to spoof an IP address and/or a hostname, the attacker could perform a Man-in-the-Middle attack first and then perform the previous exercise to entirely subvert the authorization parameters of the NAS device.

ENCRYPTION

Encrypting communications from a NAS device to any host on the network is not an out-of-the-box function. Unfortunately, many protocols that are used by NAS devices are clear-text, such as CIFS, NFS, Telnet, HTTP, RSH, and FTP. As described earlier, CIFS is a clear-text protocol where all information traverses the network in the clear. This allows attackers to sniff authentication protocols such as LM and NTLM. Refer back to Figure 6.2 for CIFS communication. Hashing passwords over the clear-text CIFS protocol is not a bad idea if the hashing method is strong, which is not the case for LM or NTLM. This amplifies the issues that CIFS is clear-text protocol. Furthermore, using clear-text usernames and passwords across unencrypted protocols such as Telnet and

RSH adds a great deal of insecurity to these devices since admin accounts can be sniffed over the network, which happen to have full control over the NAS device and its data. It is somewhat amusing that Kerberos is supported on many NAS devices for end-user authentication; however, Telnet and RSH are often enabled for administrative/ management authentication. The former may have access to a percentage of data on the NAS device, while the latter has access to all the data on the NAS device.

Although NAS devices seem to have deployed many clear-text protocols, most of them now support encrypted protocols also. For example, IPsec can be enabled by most NAS devices. A NAS device can create an IPSec tunnel between itself and any host on the network, including all types of servers or clients. If IPSec is enabled between the NAS device and a host, all communication is encrypted, negating any sniffing attacks, which also negates many attacks we have discussed in this chapter. The implementation of IPSec may be cumbersome in some architectures due to the fact that it needs to be configured between the NAS device and every host on the network that you want to secure communications. If you want to only encrypt communication from server class machines and administrative workstations, the process is manageable.

Another use of encryption on most NAS devices is SSH (Secure Shell). Implementing SSH is a great method for secure remote management. SSH has been supported on a few NAS devices for secure CLI management. It can be used to replace Telnet and RSH entirely, both of which are insecure clear-text protocols. SSH (version 2) is a very strong and standard method to connect to remote devices. It supplies the same interface that Telnet or RSH have, but in an encrypted fashion. It also supports public and private key authentication as well as a username and password. Environments that use SSH on NAS devices should disable Telnet and RSH. The only thing that is required for SSH is an SSH client on administrative workstations.

The last major method of encryption that can be used on NAS devices is the use of SSL with HTTPS, which is used for secure web management. Most NAS devices have web management capabilities that use HTTP by default, another clear-text protocol where usernames and passwords can be captured and stolen. Similar to SSH, HTTPS can used to replace HTTP entirely, ensuring that management functions and authentication methods are secure from remote attackers. Enabling HTTPS is a very simple task on a NAS device and does not require any changes on administrative workstations since all browsers can support the use of HTTPS.

The list of encryption protocols on NAS devices include IPSec, SSH, and SSL, which is a pretty good list for encryption. By enabling the encrypted protocols, many vulnerabilities and attack classes are not possible for unauthorized users. For example, if SSH is enabled, Telnet and RSH can be disabled. Furthermore, if HTTPS is enabled, HTTP can be disabled. Additionally, since only one method of management is more secure, either using SSH or SSL is probably a better idea. Finally, if IPSec, is enabled, it will not only secure data protocols such as CIFS and NFS, but will actually secure any protocols being used from the client to the NAS device, such as Telnet or HTTP. It should be noted that SSH and SSL can only be used to help secure the management/administrative connections and cannot help secure the data protocols such as CIFS and NFS. However, IPSec can be used to secure the data protocols, such as CIFS and NFS, of the NAS device, as well as Telnet, RSH, and HTTP.

The following overview will briefly highlight the lack of security of clear-text protocols, such as Telnet, RSH, and HTTP. Additionally, it will show the strengths of using secure communication such as SSH, SSL, and IPSec. Figure 6.60 shows the architecture that is being used for the demonstration.

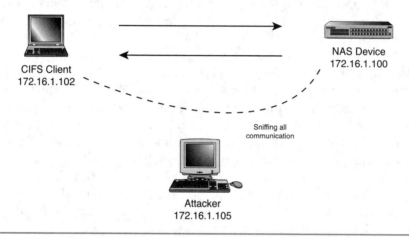

Figure 6.60   Protocols and NAS devices.

The first demonstration we will cover is the use of Telnet to manage NAS devices. This is similar to the Telnet session capture in Chapter 2 with the Fibre Channel switch. When the administrative host connects to the NAS device, the unauthorized user can capture their username and password over the network. See Figure 6.61.

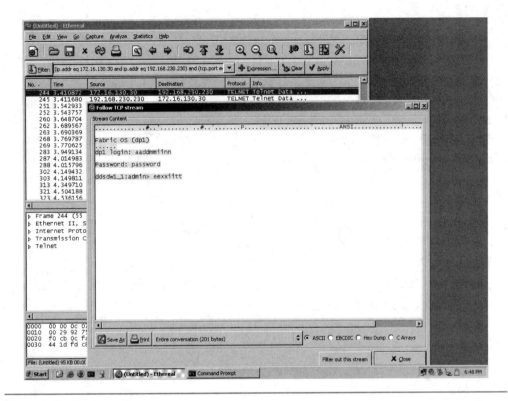

Figure 6.61   Telnet session.

Notice the account username and password traverses the network in clear-text (admin and password). Similar to Telnet, RSH also traverses the network in clear-text. Unlike Telnet, RSH can also be configured to work with a password but with simple hostname authorization. Figure 6.62 shows an RSH session with the account username and password also in clear-text (root and root).

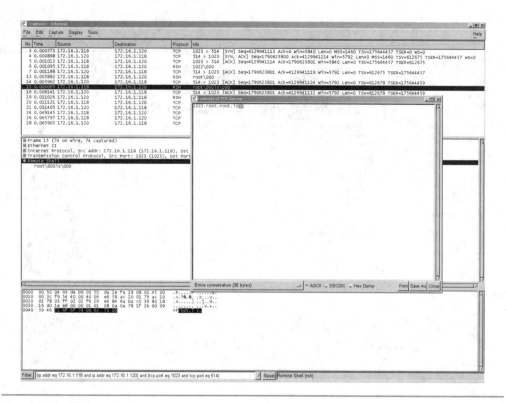

Figure 6.62 RSH session.

Notice the same username and password also appear in the clear. So far, the two most popular methods to administer an NAS device are very poor. The next method that will be shown is SSH. Implementing SSH on the NAS device, which is described in Chapter 10, "Securing NAS," can be used with any SSH client. W will now see that the information is encrypted and no longer in the clear. See Figure 6.63.

Notice how SSH encrypts all the communication so that no username or password can be sniffed over the network. Also, SSH give the same access that a Telnet or RSH connection would deliver, requiring virtually no trade-off in the functionality.

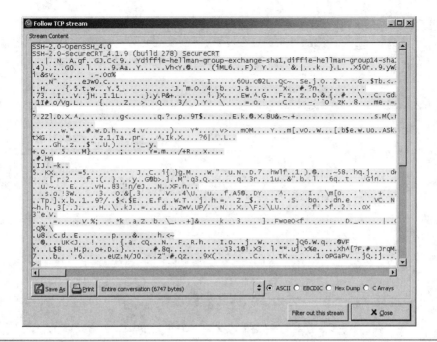

Figure 6.63 SSH session.

Next we will see how HTTP also traverses the network in the clear. While the use of web management is easy for administration, if it solely uses HTTP or HTTP Basic Auth, the username and password is vulnerable to sniffing also. See Figure 6.64 for HTTP communication traversing the network in clear-text using Basic Auth. Figure 6.65 shows the authorization parameter being decrypted with Cain (username is kusum and password is 1ynus).

Figure 6.64   HTTP session with Basic Auth.

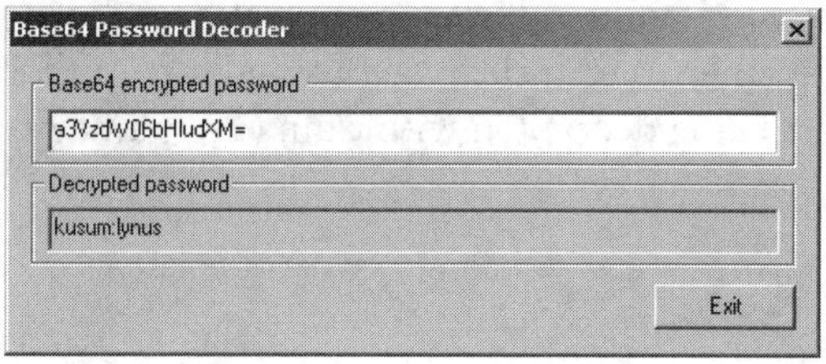

Figure 6.65   Basic Auth decryption.

Any type of web management should never occur over HTTP. For example, you would never perform online banking without an encrypted session protecting your financial information, so you should follow the same standards when managing giga-bytes of sensitive data. Enabling SSL (HTTPS) on most NAS devices is also a simple task, described further in Chapter 10. After SSL support is enabled, open a web browser using

Https:// before the IP address and hostname to manage the machine. See Figure 6.66 for an SSL session between the management workstation and the NAS devices using HTTPS.

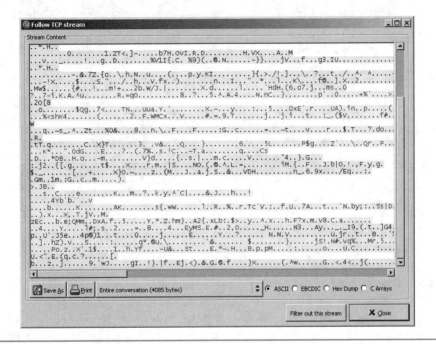

Figure 6.66 HTTPS communication.

The last method we will demonstrate is IPSec. IPSec can be used to encrypt the entire communication channel from a host to a NAS device. Unlike SSH or SSL, which are encrypting particular TCP services, IPSec works much lower on the OSI model to encrypt all communication to and from both entities. Furthermore, since IPSec works lower on the OSI model, common insecure protocols such as Telnet can be used since it would be wrapped inside an IPSec packet, remaining unreadable to any attacker sniffing the network. See Figure 6.67 for the IPSec session. Notice how all information shows up as ESP and is unreadable to the anonymous sniffer.

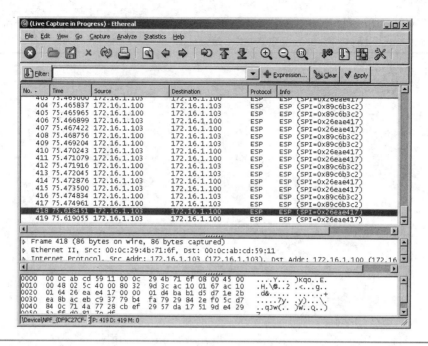

Figure 6.67 IPSec session.

Encryption plays an important role in communication security between a NAS device and hosts. While many insecure and clear-text protocols are enabled by default, most NAS devices offer the ability to replace older protocols for more secure ones that can be used for administration and data access.

SUMMARY

In this chapter, we learned about the problems with NAS devices running CIFS. We began by discussing the security basics with CIFS as it applies to NAS devices. We then were able to enumerate several entities from the NAS device anonymously, just by having an IP address on the network. We enumerated the type of NAS device, the version, its open ports and services, all end-user accounts, end-user groups, end-user administrator accounts, and all CIFS shares. The only entitles we were not able to enumerate was an account's password. However, in the authentication section, we covered the last piece of the puzzle and obtained valid passwords from weak hash methods used by CIFS such as LM and NTLM. We showed the benefits of Kerberos while showing a pre-authentication Kerberos attack also. Next, we discussed how authorization is used on NAS devices using

CIFS and some of the simple spoofing methods for IP addresses and hostnames. Finally, we saw the abundance of clear-text protocols enabled by default on NAS devices, and also the availability of encryption to replace most, if not all, of the clear-text protocols.

The key idea from this chapter is that CIFS is not a natively secure protocol. It has an abundance of enumeration issues, it uses poor hash methods for passwords, it uses spoofable entities for authorization, and it does not have a lot of native encryption. All the facts combined together do not paint a pretty picture for secure data transfer. However, although the default state of CIFS in a NAS device is not strong, there are a variety of methods to make it more secure, such as disabling anonymous access, using Kerberos, and enabling encrypted protocols like SSH, SSL, and IPSec.

In the next chapter, we continue our discussion on NAS devices, but focus on NFS security.

NAS: NFS Security

Network File System (NFS) is a remotely accessible file system that was developed for Unix-style workstations and servers in 1984 by Sun Microsystems. NAS devices have supported NFS as a standard for remote file access. In fact, many early versions of NAS devices solely support NFS with CIFS supported later on in the product lifecycle. The use of NFS allows organizations to seamlessly provide near-line and primary storage solutions to any Unix or Linux hosts (NFS clients). Many systems offering web services or database services are often Unix-based systems. NFS allows hundreds of web servers to provide the same content from a single NFS directory on a NAS device. The storage resources are off-loaded from the Unix server to the NAS devices, where the files are located. Similarly, database applications, such as Oracle, are often running out of space. Oracle databases running on a Unix platform can use NFS to expand data storage, which is much easier than a local file system. NAS devices using NFS support multiple servers at once, including email servers, databases (such as Oracle), and home directories. In fact, home directories in organizations are usually a NFS mount from a remote NAS device. Because home directories are always filling up, a NAS device running NFS is a great method to ensure that capacity is never an issue and that the local systems are not being bogged down for space due to local home directories.

The security of NAS devices running NFS is a significant issue. Similar to CIFS, the security of a NAS device has little to do with the problem, but the fact that the NAS devices support an insecure protocol with a long history of significant security issues is the problem. For example, let's say your car has a state-of-the-art security system with an alarm, a security chip on your key, and a direct connection to a roadside assistance organization. However, the car you purchased was a convertible, which means that any valuables sitting on the seat can be taken by anyone who is walking by your car. Although the ability to steal the car may be difficult, any valuables residing inside the car can be stolen at any time.

NFS security has been overlooked by many organizations. NFS has greatly improved its security with version 3 and version 4, especially with its support for Kerberos, but many organizations fail to capitalize on those advances and just run the system in its default state. The security issues and vulnerabilities that exist in a NFS implementation on a Unix system also exist in NFS implementation of a NAS device. Furthermore, since many NAS devices are deployed with CIFS and NFS enabled, there can be more security issues with NAS devices since it would be susceptible to both sets of vulnerabilities. Many organizations overlook these issues due to a NAS device being a network device on the LAN rather than a Solaris or Linux operating system. Would you consolidate all your sensitive data on a single Solaris or Linux server with default settings?

This chapter will discuss the following topics concerning NAS NFS devices:

- NFS security basics
- Enumeration
- Authentication
- Authorization
- Encryption

NFS SECURITY BASICS

NFS is a client server protocol where a NFS client, which is every Unix/Linux machine and Windows machine that has installed some form of NFS compatibility (such as Unix services for Windows), connects to a NFS server for a remote file system. Most NFS implementations use TCP port 2049, as well as some RPC ports. See Figure 7.1 for a typical NFS architecture.

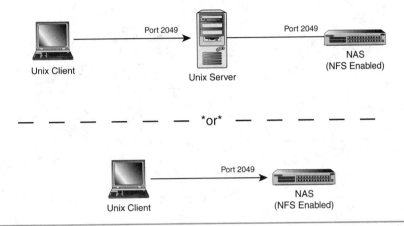

Figure 7.1 NAS devices using NFS.

Similar to CIFS-enabled NAS devices, all NFS clients can connect directly to NAS devices without the need for any intermediary server. Direct connections are often used for user home directories or server machines, which is used for application data. NAS devices running NFS share the file system as remote exports. For example, a NFS-enabled file system can have a variety of folders and directories, but only the ones that have been exported will be accessible to the network. For example, the file path of /volume0/finance and /volume0/home can be exported. These NFS exports can be mounted by remote clients on their local systems by mounting the NFS export called /volume0/finance to their local directory such as /nfsmount. After they have mounted the remote NFS export locally to /nfsmount, they can browse directly to /nfsmount and see on the contents of the remote file system. See Figures 7.2a and 7.2b for details.

Because all NAS devices are stand-alone appliances, a client or server host can make direct connections via the IP network, as shown in Figure 7.1. Many times, a single NAS device will be performing NFS services for both Unix clients and Unix servers. This not only makes any NAS device running NFS a potential target for attackers, but most likely a high-profile target since a tremendous amount of data is held on the NAS NFS device.

In addition to being a direct target, NFS is a clear-text protocol (no encryption and freely viewable to all anonymous listeners) that can be enumerated over the network easily. In additional to being clear-text, NFS fails to meet basic security standards in the areas of authentication, authorization, and encryption. In fact, online documentation from a major NAS vendor states that the NFS protocol can be compromised "relatively easy," which goes to show you that even NAS device vendors know that NFS should not be used with sensitive data; however, it already is by Fortune 500 companies.

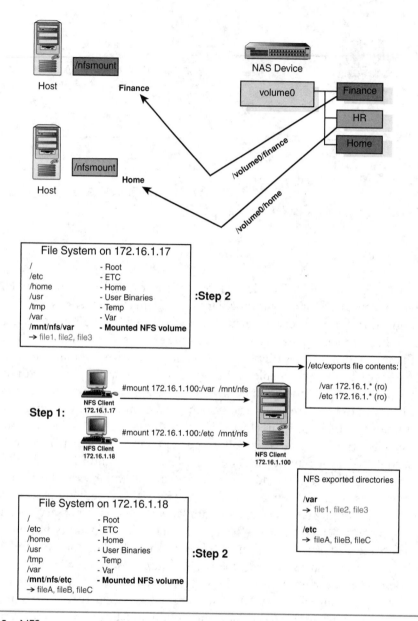

Figure 7.2 NFS exports.

Because NFS is clear-text, sensitive information can be sniffed over the wire, such as NFS exports information and authorization parameters. Figure 7.3 shows a sample connection between a Unix client and a NAS appliance with NFS enabled.

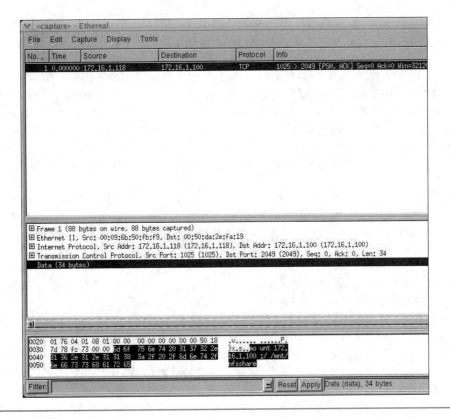

Figure 7.3 NFS communication.

As you can see from Figure 7.3, the NFS exports and the UID/GID information (not directly shown but in the body of one of the IP packets) of the connection is all captured over the network in clear-text. As mentioned in Chapter 1, "Introduction to Storage Security," enumeration is a big part of an attack timeline. Unfortunately, NAS devices using NFS leak a tremendous amount of useful information.

Authentication in NAS devices can be implemented with Kerberos, but only if NFS version 3 or 4 has been implemented and if the NFS client supports Kerberos, which is definitely not the majority installation base. Unlike CIFS, where individual users are authenticated, most NFS security implementations do not rely on authentication of individual users but rather authorization with individual hosts. NFS assumes individual user authentication takes place at the host, so if a particular host is trusted by a NAS device running NFS, every user account on the client is allowed to mount a NFS directory. For example, if the IP address of 172.16.1.102 is authorized to connect to the /volume0/finance export, then every user account on 172.16.1.102 is allowed to access files in /volume0/finance. Determining which host should be able to connect to NFS exports and which hosts should not have any access is not an easy process. In fact, most NFS exports are often deployed to the entire network. This creates significant security problems since any host on the network can connect to the NAS device and gain access to all files and folders. In order to mitigate this concern, file and folder permissions are often used to protect file systems; however, the entities used for file permissions can be easily subverted by an attacker (changing or spoofing UID/GIDs), leaving all files on an NFS system exposed to attackers.

Encryption for NFS communication does not occur natively, but can be implemented at the IP layer with the implementation of IPSec. Most NAS appliances support IPSec and can be an IPSec end-point to a NFS client. Although this is not a standard in most deployments of NAS devices, NFS clients with an IPSec client, which is included in most Windows and Unix operating systems, would be able to set up an IPSec tunnel between the client and the NAS device. This would fully encrypt all communication from the NFS client to the NFS server, including clear-text communication.

Since NFS NAS devices support the same protocol used on Unix operating systems, all tools, utilities, and attacks against NFS on Unix also work on NFS services on NAS devices. Similar to CIFS, you might hear people say that there are no tools or attacks against storage devices; therefore, it is okay that the security on them is weak. In reality, any security tool or attack that targets NFS on Unix operating systems also works on NAS appliances running NFS. As you may have guessed, there are a significant number of tools and attacks that target Unix operating systems. While most, if not all, of the current tools were written to target Unix environments, most NAS vendors that have implemented NFS to mirror NFS on Unix machines are exposed to all the attacks, vulnerabilities, and security weaknesses also. You probably can now imagine the number of existing attacks for NAS appliances running NFS and how this number will continue to grow. The following sections describe the major security concerns of NFS services on NAS devices, as well as their security weakness and exposures.

ENUMERATION

As stated in Chapter 1, enumeration is a very big part of any attack process, whether it is against storage devices or application servers. In this section, we learn how to enumerate several types of information from a NAS device running NFS. All of the information enumerated in this section will play a critical role to help an attacker to start, escalate, or complete an attack and compromise data in the storage network. In this section, we learn how to enumerate the following information from a NAS device running NFS:

- NAS device version
- Open ports and services
- Exports

> **NOTE:** The "NAS Device Version" and "Open Ports and Services" sections use the same methods described in Chapter 6, "NAS: CIFS Security." Please skip to the "Export" section if you already have covered Chapter 6.

NAS Device Version

Being aware of the type (vendor) and running version of any target is an important step for an unauthorized user. Attackers use this information to narrow down the scope of attacks for a potential target. For example, if an attacker is targeting a web server and finds out that the target is running IIS 6.0, he/she can remove or eliminate all of the IIS 5.0 attacks and not waste any time on that attack surface. However, if he/she cannot enumerate the type and version of the web server, he/she will have to use all their Apache, IBM WebSphere, iPlanet, and IIS 3.0/4.0/5.0 attacks, creating a significant amount of extra effort for the attacker.

By retrieving the type and version of the NAS device, the unauthorized user will know that he/she is attacking a storage device. This information is usually obtained by banners on open ports. For example, if a NAS device has a web server for web management, a simple connection to port 80 will usually dump information about the NAS device, including type (vendor) and version. Complete the following exercise to enumerate the type and version of the NAS device.

Assessment Exercise

1. Open a command prompt (Start -> Programs -> cmd.exe).
2. Telnet to port 80 on the NAS device:
   a. `telnet <IP address of NAS device> 80`
3. `telnet 172.16.1.100`

4. Done! You should now see the type of NAS device that has been deployed. Some common banners you may see are Cellera Web Manager (EMC), EMC Control Center, NetApp (na_admin), and Storage Management (IBM). Some banners may also tell you the version number of the device.

OPEN PORTS AND SERVICES

A NAS device can be scanned similar to any other device on the network. Using any port scanner, information can be gathered on the enabled services and open ports on the NAS device. The results from a port scan will allow an attacker to determine what services are running for file access—CIFS, NFS, or both—and what management methods are being used—Telnet, RSH, SSH, HTTP, and/or HTTPS. The port scan is the first step for an attacker as they begin to profile the environment. The following exercises demonstrate scans on storage devices using two tools, StorScan and nmap. StorScan is a storage only port scanner that includes checks focused for NAS and iSCSI storage devices and services. Nmap is an all-purpose port scanner and is definitely the standard for port scanning tools. Complete the following exercise to scan the NAS device using either tool.

ASSESSMENT EXERCISE

1. Download StorScan from http://www.isecpartners.com/tools.html.
2. Unzip the file to a folder on your system, such as c:\tools.
3. Open up a command prompt (Start -> Program -> cmd.exe) and change directories to the location where you unzipped StorScan (cd c:\tools).
4. Type **StorScan.exe** for the help and syntax information.
5. Type **StorScan.exe –h <IP address of NAS device>** to port scan the NAS device for all open ports and running services:

   StorScan.exe -h 172.16.1.100
6. After StorScan completes the scan, all running services and open ports are displayed.

ASSESSMENT EXERCISE

1. Download nmap from http://www.insecure.org/nmap/nmap_download.html, written by Fyodor.

2. Unzip the file to a folder on your system, such as c:\tools.

3. Open up a command prompt (Start -> Program -> cmd.exe) and change directories to the location where you unzipped nmap (cd c:\tools).

4. Type **nmap.exe** for the help information.

5. Type **nmap.exe <IP address of NAS device>** to port scan the NAS device for all open ports and running services:

   nmap.exe 172.16.1.100

6. As shown in Figure 7.4, after nmap completes the port scan, all running services and open ports are displayed.

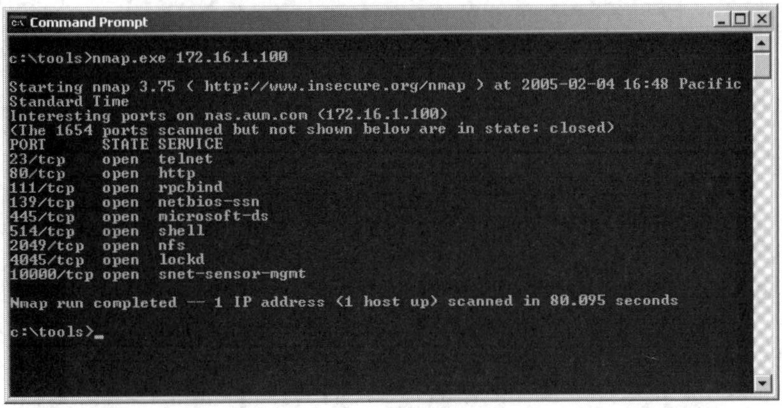

```
Command Prompt                                                    _ □ ×

c:\tools>nmap.exe 172.16.1.100

Starting nmap 3.75 ( http://www.insecure.org/nmap ) at 2005-02-04 16:48 Pacific
Standard Time
Interesting ports on nas.aum.com (172.16.1.100)
(The 1654 ports scanned but not shown below are in state: closed)
PORT        STATE SERVICE
23/tcp      open  telnet
80/tcp      open  http
111/tcp     open  rpcbind
139/tcp     open  netbios-ssn
445/tcp     open  microsoft-ds
514/tcp     open  shell
2049/tcp    open  nfs
4045/tcp    open  lockd
10000/tcp   open  snet-sensor-mgmt

Nmap run completed -- 1 IP address (1 host up) scanned in 80.095 seconds

c:\tools>_
```

Figure 7.4 Port scan of NAS device.

From the results of our port scan, we can now conclude that the NAS device is running both CIFS and NFS by the fact that ports 139 and 445 are open, which are used for CIFS, and ports 2049 and 4045 are open, which are used for NFS. This allows an attacker to target the NAS device based on CIFS attacks, NFS attacks, and attacks that target both NFS and CIFS in mixed environments. The next thing we can conclude is that the NAS device is being managed using insecure clear-text protocols where usernames and password traverse the network in the clear. Port 23 is open, which is used for Telnet, port 80 is open, which is HTTP web management, and port 514 is open, which is used for Remote Shell (RSH). All three of these protocols are clear-text and very insecure. Furthermore, any attacker who sniffs the username and password with any network sniffer from a Telnet, web (HTTP), or RSH session will have complete control of the NAS device and all of the data on the device.

At this point, the avenues for attacking the NAS device are quite large. Based on the information that was retrieved by the port scan only, the attacker has five different methods to penetrate the NAS device, including CIFS, NFS, Telnet, HTTP, and RSH. Every open port is an attack vector for the unauthorized user. The more open ports or services, the greater likelihood that one of the services enabled is insecure. For example, protecting five different doorways in a home is more difficult than protecting two. Every night you ensure the door is locked and chain is on. If you had to do this for five different entry methods to the house, however, chances are at least one of them will be forgotten, overlooked, or just ignored (for example, you might lock the front door and back door every night, but what about the kitchen window or the exterior garage door?). In our NAS device, one could argue that NFS and CIFS need to be enabled, but having three different insecure methods for managing the NAS device is not good from a security perspective. This is a classic example of how port scans are used to formulate an attack for an unauthorized user.

EXPORTS

NAS devices running NFS can have their exports enumerated easily. In fact, enumeration of NFS exports is considered more of a feature rather than information leakage. Before we discuss how to enumerate NFS exports, let's fully understand how they work. A file system on a NFS server has many folders. Any of these folders can be exported to a remote NFS client. Once the remote NFS client mounts the NFS export, the remote folder appears on the local NFS client, as if the file system was local to that machine. For example, the exported folder on a NAS device can be /volume0/finance and also can be locally mounted from an NFS client at /nfsmount. When the user on the local NFS client changes directories to /nfsmount, it will actually be /volume0/finance on the remote file system. See Figure 7.5.

In additional to easy enumeration of all the NFS exports, many NAS devices export their administrative directories also. Similar to CIFS shares, there are some significant issues with exporting the administrative directories as well as the operational directories. Although it is perfectly normal to export operational directories on the NAS devices, such as user home directories, it is very insecure to export directories that contain configuration information about the NAS device, including password files and services information. For example, most NAS devices have directories that contain configuration files that have all the details of the settings that are enabled or disabled. An example directory would be /etc. /etc is a configuration folder on most Unix operating systems, but also is a configuration folder on many NAS devices. The /etc directory may contain password files, exports files, and host authorization files. If the /etc directory is exported, a remote user could mount this directory and browse all readable files on the NAS devices, hence giving them more information to perform a potential attack and compromise. A strong method to secure sensitive directories with configuration information on a NAS device would be to disable (remove) exports on these directories. The following section will demonstrate how to enumerate all exports from a NAS device, including administrative and operational exports.

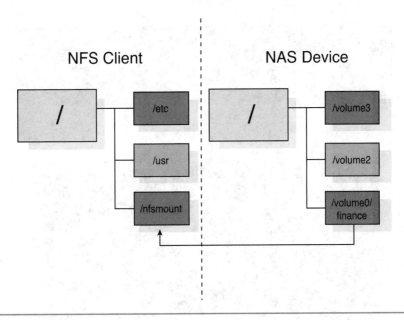

Figure 7.5   NAS NFS exports to host.

ASSESSMENT EXERCISE

1. The utility we will be using is showmount, which is a native NFS client binary on Unix systems. Because enumeration of NFS exports is considered a feature, there is no special tool you need to download if you are using a Unix or Linux machine. If you are using a Windows machine, I recommend using showmount.exe from Windows Services for Unix, provided by Microsoft (http://www.microsoft.com/windows/sfu/).

2. Type **showmount -e <IP address of the NAS device>** to enumerate the NFS exports on the remote machine:

   a. showmount -e 172.16.1.100

3. Notice the NFS exports on the left side and the machines that are allowed to mount the exports on the right side. See Figure 7.6 for the results on Unix clients and the Figure 7.7 for the results on a Windows client.

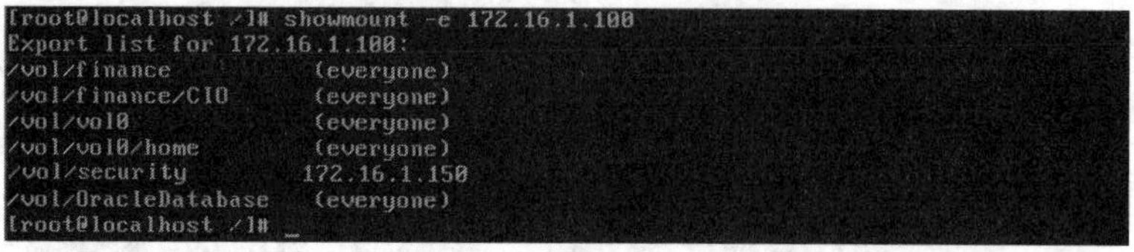

Figure 7.6   Showmount enumeration of NFS exports (Unix).

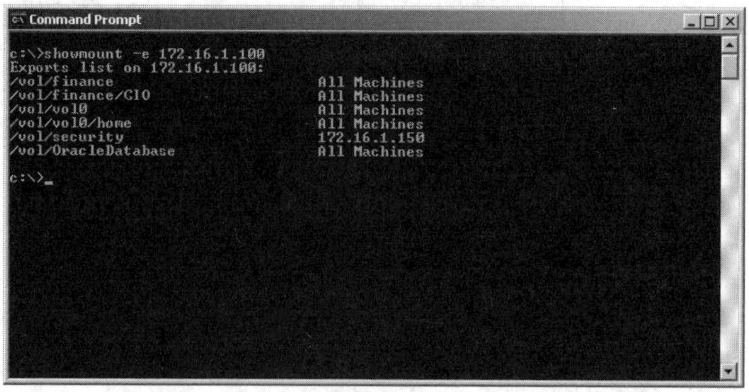

Figure 7.7   Showmount enumeration of NFS exports (Windows).

4. Done! You have now enumerated all the NFS exports from the NAS device. You have also enumerated the authorized IP address and/or hostnames that are allowed to connect to the NFS exports.

Notice that all machines (everyone) are allowed to connect to all exports except for the /vol/security export, which only can be accessed by the IP address of 172.16.1.150. This gives an unauthorized user two key pieces of information: the entry points to the NAS device for file/folder access and the restrictions (if any) that are placed on the entry points. Because all of the exports have no restrictions, any unauthorized user can mount the remote file system and get access to data. At this point, the file system permissions that are used on the NAS device would be the only form of security protection; however, we will demonstrate how that can also be subverted later in this chapter, leaving all files and folders exported on a NAS device using NFS fully accessible to any unauthorized user or attacker. Additionally, the attacker now knows that the IP address of 172.16.1.150 has access to the /vol/security export. If they choose to do so, they can attempt IP spoofing attacks with Man-in-the-Middle attacks and get access to the restricted export because using IP addresses or hostnames do not really secure an export, but just make it a bit more difficult for an attacker to get access.

Unlike CIFS, where we were able to enumerate user accounts, groups, and admin accounts, all user authentication entities are not needed in most installations of NFS (unless Kerberos has been enabled with NFS). The only item required to get access is the export name, which we have retrieved using the showmount command. You might now be wondering that if a machine is able to access an NFS export, can it simply connect without any type of authentication or further authorization. The quick answer is yes; this is described in the next section about authentication mechanisms that are available.

AUTHENTICATION

NFS authentication is simply an afterthought. While some organization have implemented kerberized NFS, which is an excellent security option, most installations of NAS devices running NFS only enable the default settings, which uses no authentication. As stated previously, NFS assumes that a proper authentication process has taken place at the NFS client before it attempts to mount a directory. If an IP address or hostname has access to a NFS export, all user accounts have access to it. Furthermore, if a NFS export is open to the entire network (All Machines), then all users on the network are able to mount the exported directory.

The problem becomes more amplified with the fact that an anonymous user can access export NFS directories. Unlike CIFS, where we were able to anonymously enumerate a significant amount of information, anonymous NFS clients cannot only enumerate NFS exports; however, they can also connect to an NFS export and mount the remote directory anonymously, which is not possible with CIFS. The anonymous mount is only read-only access; however, it still gives an unauthorized user the ability to read all the information on the NAS device, including sensitive files, spreadsheets, database information, and whatever else is held on the device. A proper defense to this is to use file permission and limit access to sensitive folders; however, file permissions can also be subverted on NAS devices running NFS.

In this section, we discuss the following authentication methods available on most NFS NAS devices, the security weaknesses with each of them, and the short- and long-term solutions:

- Default authentication
- Kerberos

DEFAULT AUTHENTICATION

Authentication methods on an NFS client rely on user identifications (UID) and group identifications (GID). A remote user can use Telnet, SSH, Kerberos, or even NIS to authenticate to a Unix machine. The user's account on the Unix machine is assigned a UID and GID. The UID and GID for the root account is 0 and 0. This is the identifying value that is assigned to root. The passwd file in the `/etc` directory has the information regarding each account's UID and GID. See Figure 7.8 for details.

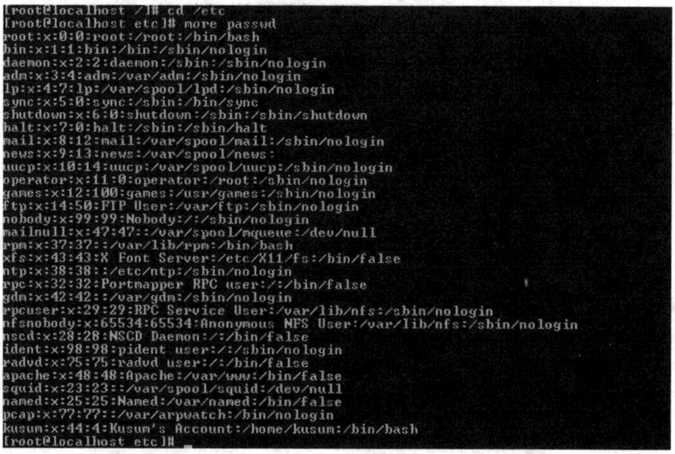

```
[root@localhost /]# cd /etc
[root@localhost etc]# more passwd
root:x:0:0:root:/root:/bin/bash
bin:x:1:1:bin:/bin:/sbin/nologin
daemon:x:2:2:daemon:/sbin:/sbin/nologin
adm:x:3:4:adm:/var/adm:/sbin/nologin
lp:x:4:7:lp:/var/spool/lpd:/sbin/nologin
sync:x:5:0:sync:/sbin:/bin/sync
shutdown:x:6:0:shutdown:/sbin:/sbin/shutdown
halt:x:7:0:halt:/sbin:/sbin/halt
mail:x:8:12:mail:/var/spool/mail:/sbin/nologin
news:x:9:13:news:/var/spool/news:
uucp:x:10:14:uucp:/var/spool/uucp:/sbin/nologin
operator:x:11:0:operator:/root:/sbin/nologin
games:x:12:100:games:/usr/games:/sbin/nologin
ftp:x:14:50:FTP User:/var/ftp:/sbin/nologin
nobody:x:99:99:Nobody:/:/sbin/nologin
mailnull:x:47:47::/var/spool/mqueue:/dev/null
rpm:x:37:37::/var/lib/rpm:/bin/bash
xfs:x:43:43:X Font Server:/etc/X11/fs:/bin/false
ntp:x:38:38::/etc/ntp:/sbin/nologin
rpc:x:32:32:Portmapper RPC user:/:/bin/false
gdm:x:42:42::/var/gdm:/sbin/nologin
rpcuser:x:29:29:RPC Service User:/var/lib/nfs:/sbin/nologin
nfsnobody:x:65534:65534:Anonymous NFS User:/var/lib/nfs:/sbin/nologin
nscd:x:28:28:NSCD Daemon:/:/bin/false
ident:x:98:98:pident user:/:/sbin/nologin
radvd:x:75:75:radvd user:/:/bin/false
apache:x:48:48:Apache:/var/www:/bin/false
squid:x:23:23::/var/spool/squid:/dev/null
named:x:25:25:Named:/var/named:/bin/false
pcap:x:77:77::/var/arpwatch:/bin/nologin
kusum:x:44:4:Kusum's Account:/home/kusum:/bin/bash
[root@localhost etc]# _
```

Figure 7.8 Contents of /etc/passwd.

For each account in the passwd directory, the row specifies their username, the password hash (or X if the hash is stored in /etc/shadow), the UID, the GID, the description of the account, the user's home directory, and the user's shell. For example, let's break down the last account in Figure 7.8:

```
kusum:x:44:4:Kusum's Account:/home/kusum:/bin/bash
```

- Username: kusum
- Password hash: x (which means the hash is kept in the /etc/shadow file)
- User ID (UID): 44
- Group ID (GID): 4
- Description: Kusum's Account
- Account's home directory: /home/kusum
- Accounts shell type: /bin/bash

When the user called Kusum authenticates to the Unix client, her UID and GID will determine what folder access she should have access to and what files should be accessible. When a user from a Unix client connects to a NAS device running NFS, the UID and GID is sent from the client to the NAS device so the NAS device also knows what files and folders the user should access. For example, if the user called Kusum mounts a NFS volume from the NAS device, the UID 44 and the GID 4 will determine what folder she will be able to access. Note that a user's UID or GID does not authenticate them to the NAS device, but it just tells the NAS device which files and folders that may access, which is actually an authorization parameter. By default, any export open to the network (such as All Machines) will be available to any user, no matter what UID and GID they have. This process means that there is virtually no authentication taking place from the NFS client user to the NAS device, but rather authorization of files/folders based on UID/GID values.

In addition to mounting a NFS export as an end user, it can also be mounted anonymously. This means that any user can access the NFS export without a username or a password. In fact, every file or folder that is world readable (for example, drwxr-r-) on the NAS device is open to the anonymous user. This is a major problem for NFS and why many storage devices can be more insecure than a Windows or Solaris operating system not running NFS. For example, any Windows and Unix operating system would require an end-user to authenticate to get access to the file systems. A NAS device running NFS (or any device running NFS) requires no authentication whatsoever by default. To demonstrate this problem, complete the following exercise.

ASSESSMENT EXERCISE

1. The utility we will be using is called mount, which is a native NFS client binary on Unix systems. Since mounting NFS exports is not really an attack but a functional entity, there is no special tool you need to download if you are using a Unix or Linux machine. If you are using a Windows machine, I recommend using mount.exe from Windows Services for Unix, provided by Microsoft (http://www.microsoft.com/windows/sfu/).

2. Type **mount -h** to get the help information.

3. On the Windows client, you can mount the NFS export anonymously (no username and no password) with the –o anon flag. This tells the NAS device running NFS that an anonymous connection is being attempted. To complete the command, type **mount –o anon <ip address of NAS device>:<export> <drive letter>** to access the NFS export on the NAS device anonymously. See Figure 7.9.

   a. `mount –o anon 172.16.1.100:/vol/vol0 w`

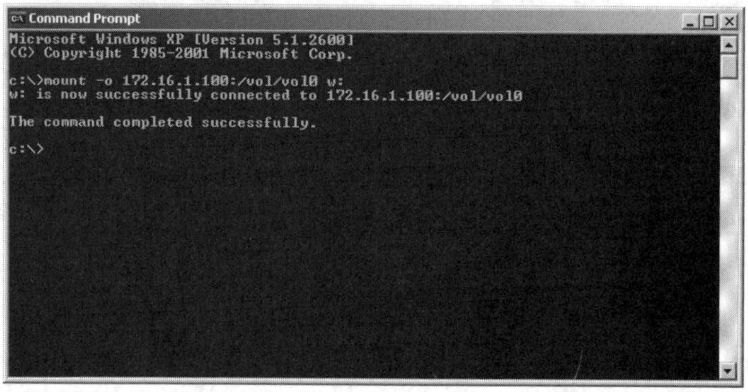

Figure 7.9   NFS mount on Windows.

4. On the Unix client, type **mount <ip address of NAS device>:<export> <local file path>** to access the NFS export on the NAS device anonymously. See Figure 7.10.

   a. `mount 172.16.1.100:/vol/vol0 /nfsmount`

5. Done! You have now mounted the NFS export on the NAS device anonymously.

Figure 7.10   NFS mount on Unix.

6. You can now change directories to the mounted file system and browse any
   file/folder that is readable, including the /etc/exports file on the NAS device, which is
   the file that lists the authorized IP addresses and hostnames. See Figure 7.11 for
   Windows and Figure 7.12 for Unix.

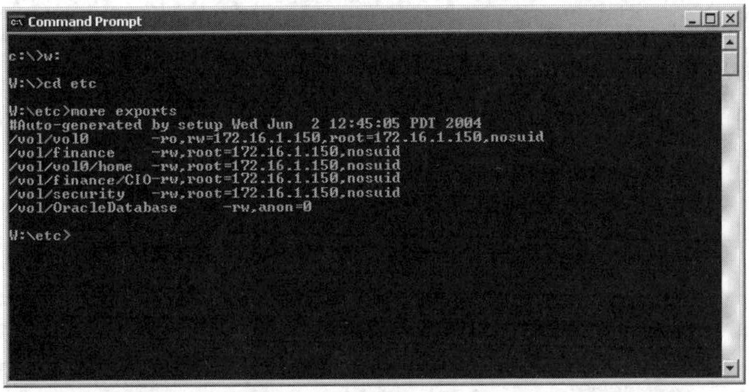

Figure 7.11   /etc/exports using Windows mount client.

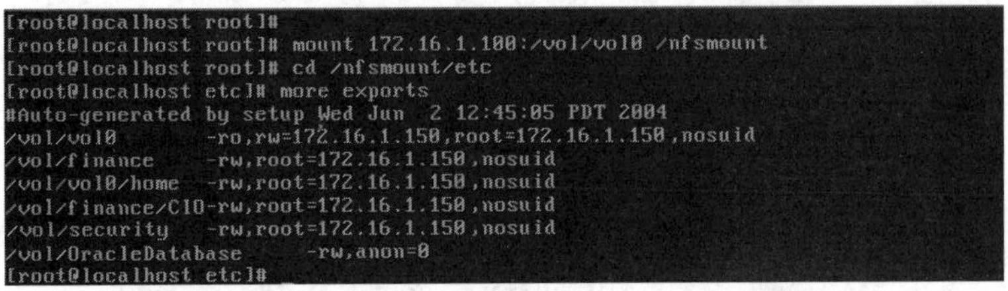

Figure 7.12   /etc/exports using Unix mount client.

Let's discuss the security settings in the /etc/exports files:

- **-ro**—Permits read-only mount access.
- **-rw**—Permits read/write mount access.
- **Root=host**—Gives root access to the root user on the listed host.
- **anon=o**— Allows any user to access files with root privileges.

All machines have read-only (ro) access to the vol/vol0 export except for 172.16.1.150, which has read/write access (rw). While it is good to give users read-only access, attackers only need to read certain files, such as the exports file or the passwd file, to get sensitive information. Additionally, notice that all other NFS exports on the NAS device give everyone read/write access to all files and give 172.16.1.150 root (administrator) access, which means the only layer of security is the file permissions on the directory that may have been set. Finally, notice the /vol/OracleDatabase export gives everyone read/write access and allows any user to access files and folders at a root level user (anon=0), which means the export is wide open to everyone on the network.

1. On the Windows machine, the mount drive shows up as a browseable directory. See Figure 7.13.

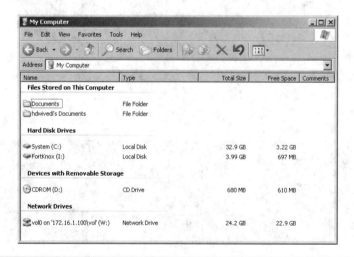

Figure 7.13   Mount NFS directory on Windows.

2. Double-click on the directory and browse to the `etc` directory. See Figure 7.14.

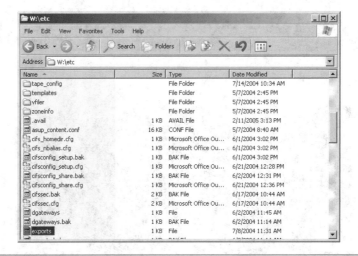

Figure 7.14 Browsing NFS exports anonymously.

3. Although we are able to view any world-readable file on the NAS device anonymously, notice from Figures 7.15 (Windows) and 7.16 (Unix) that any attempt to add a file (write) would be denied. This would not be the case on any other NFS export on this NAS device since those exports can be mounted as read/write, as shown in Figure 7.17.

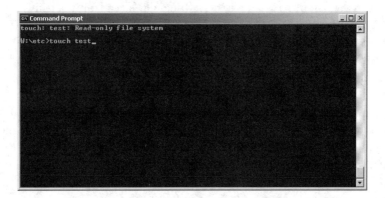

Figure 7.15 Writing files on read-only (Windows).

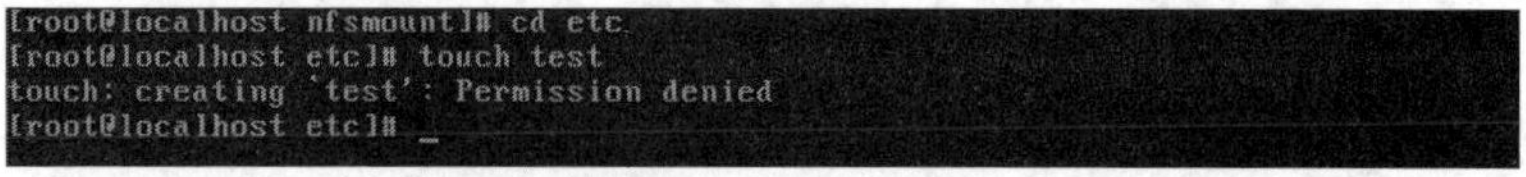

[root@localhost nfsmount]# cd etc
[root@localhost etc]# touch test
touch: creating `test': Permission denied
[root@localhost etc]# _

Figure 7.16 Writing files on read-only (Unix).

Command Prompt
W:\>cd Finance
W:\Finance>echo "Shreya" >> Shreya.txt
W:\Finance>_

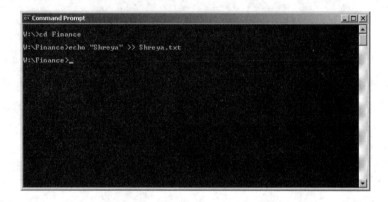

Figure 7.17 Writing files on read/write (Windows).

Now that you have successfully mounted the NFS export from a NAS device, you might be wondering why this is possible and what is going on. Well, what is happening is that the anonymous user is given a UID of –2 or 65534 when he/she attempts to mount the directory. Because each of these exports have the default read-only settings on the management of export and read/write permissions on every other export, the UID –2 or 65534 is treated like any other UID, authenticated or not. Refer back to Figure 7.8, where the UID of the user called "nfsnobody" is 65534 from our Unix machine, and our Windows machine takes the UID of –2, as shown in Figure 7.18, which also has the value of anonymous.

The issue here is that if a user is anonymous, he/she are not treated any differently. An anonymous account is given a UID and held to the same access controls on files and folders like any other UID. If the file system is exported as read-only or read/write, the anonymous user has as much access as any other UID. Furthermore, if the files and folders are world-readable, the anonymous user also has as much access as any other legitimate user.

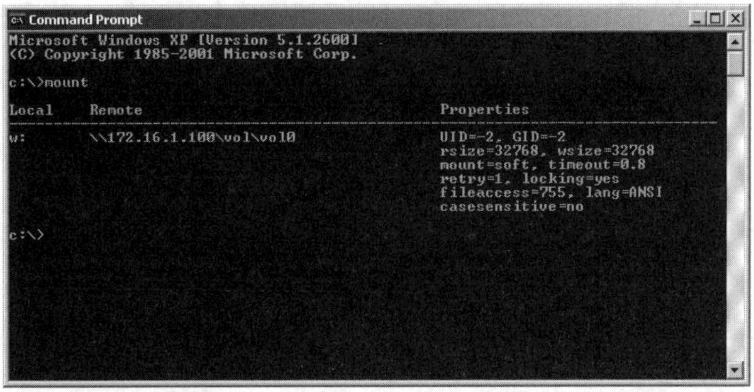

Figure 7.18   Anonymous UID value.

KERBEROS AUTHENTICATION

NFS has supported Kerberos authentication due to the security problems described in the previous section. In order to understand and implement NFS authentication with Kerberos, refer to Chapter 10, "Securing NAS," in the "NFS Security" section.

AUTHORIZATION

Authorization is a method to ensure that a potential entity is allowed to access another entity. Unlike authentication, which is meant to ensure that an entity is actually who they say they are, authorization is solely meant to ensure whether the entity is allowed to access the machine or not. As we have just seen in the authentication section, authorization is a big part of security in NAS devices running NFS. NFS security relies on authorization parameters such as IP address and UID/GID values.

Similar to CIFS, common attributes for authorization in NAS devices running NFS are IP addresses and hostnames. Unlike CIFS, NFS does not have a proper authentication model to mitigate security issues with NFS authorization.

Authorization in NFS can come at the device level, as we saw in the previous section where IP addresses can be authorized to access certain NFS exports, or the file/folder level. Because NFS allows anonymous users to have read and read/write access, the security of files and folder are heavily dependent on Unix-style directory permissions. For example, since anyone can mount the exported file system of /vol/finance, it is very important that files and folders in the file system are protected. NFS uses Unix-style permissions, which uses the owner, the group, and the world format. See Figure 7.19 for the Unix-style format.

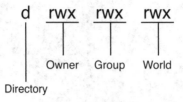

Figure 7.19   Unix-style permissions.

Let's say a file called test was located in the /etc directory. A user called Shreya, who had a UID of 10 and a GID of 12, is the owner of a file where she can read, write, and execute the file. Also, no one else could access the file. The permission on the file would look like rwx---. Furthermore, if the permission were changed on the file to allow everyone to read it, the permissions would change to rwxr-r-. In addition to the permission placed on the folder, the owner's UID and GID would be listed when the ls -al (list directory and show all details) command was executed. A description of the results from the ls -al command is shown in Figure 7.20.

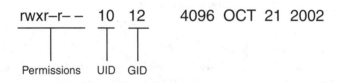

Figure 7.20   ls -al results.

Notice that the permissions are displayed for the file as well as the file's owner (UID) and group (GID). This is true for any directory listings.

The security issue with authorization and NFS lies within the Unix-style permissions. Each file and folder has its permissions, including owner, group, and world access. The ability to access a folder/file depends on the requesting entity's UID and GID. For example, each time a file is accessed, the NAS device will check the requestor's UID and GID. If the UID and GID are correct, the user is allowed to read, write, or execute the file depending on its request. The same idea applies to folder access. The UID and GID value that a user is assigned to is set up when the user account is created. The information is stored in the /etc/passwd directory on the Unix machine. Referring back to Figure 7.8, each user account on the system has a UID and GID assigned to them. This is the value that is checked each time a user attempts to access a file or folder. This may seem perfectly fine on the surface, but since the file/folder permissions depend on the UID and GID values, the ability for a user to change their UID and GID should be restricted; however, this turns out to be a significant problem for NAS devices running NFS. If a low-rights user wanted to access a file on a Solaris machine that they did not have access to, the user could attempt to change their UID and GID values in the /etc/passwd or /etc/shadow files. However, low-rights users only have the ability to read the /etc/passwd file; therefore, any attempt to change their UID or GID value would be denied, which also denies them the ability to view the desired file on the local operating system.

What if a user is accessing a file system from a NFS export, where there is no local /etc/passwd file to look up UIDs and GIDs? NFS clients pass their UID and GID values from the connecting machine (the user's NFS client machine) to the NFS server (the NAS device). The vulnerability that opens up here is that the user (the connecting machine) can change the UID and GID values of their own machine to equal the values required to access any file or folder on the NAS device running NFS. This subverts the file-level security permissions that have been placed on the device and allows anyone that had changed his or her UID/GID values to the correct parameter to access any requested file. For example, while unauthorized users may not have the ability to modify the /etc/passwd or /etc/shadow file on a server operating system, they would have the ability to modify both files on their own operating system. Similar to how you may have control of your own laptop/desktop on your Windows XP operating system, users can also install a Unix or Linux operating system on their desktop/laptop (or virtual machine) and have root access to their own operating system. An attacker could use his or her own Unix or Linux operating system to connect to the NFS export, which is accessible anonymously. After they have enumerated the UID and GID values that are required to access sensitive files and folders, they could then change the UID and GID values in their own /etc/passwd file and attempt to access the protected files and folders. NFS would pass the changed UID and GID values from the client's /etc/passwd file, which are the UID and GID that were just modified by the attacker, and allow the unauthorized user to gain access to the sensitive information. To fully understand this authorization attack, we will walk-though the following demonstration. The architecture for the demonstration is shown in Figure 7.21.

Figure 7.21 shows five folders on the NAS device, including Internal Medicine, Patient Information, Pharmacology, Genetic Research, and IT Support. All folders are open to the public, except for the folder called Patient Information, which is restricted to authorized users only since it holds personal health information (PHI) of individuals. Additionally, the NAS device is accessible to the network using CIFS (for Windows) or NFS (for Unix/Linux). Because this folder holds medical records from individual patients, it is imperative that it is limited to authorized users only or be in violation of HIPAA (discussed in Chapter 12, "Compliance, Regulation, and Storage"). The Patient Information folder should only be accessible to the authorized user called Kusum and should not be accessible to anyone else.

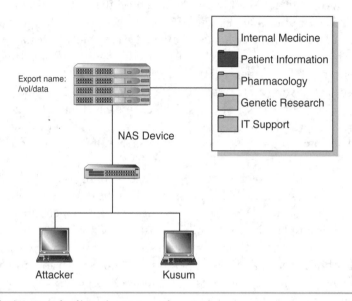

Figure 7.21   Architecture for file authorization subversion.

The following demonstration secures the folder called Patient Information to the authorized user called Kusum. The permission will be set with Windows (CIFS) file permission options. We will see how the permissions that are set to control the data in the NAS device can be subverted by the weaknesses in NFS. The demonstration will reveal the false sense of file system security for any NAS devices running CIFS and NFS together (or simply NFS only).

DEMONSTRATION

1. The authorized user Kusum connects to the NAS device under CIFS. See Figure 7.22.
2. The authorized user Kusum opens up the permission window under CIFS by right-clicking on Patient Information and selecting Properties. After the Patient Information Properties menu is displayed, Kusum will click on the Security tab to see the current security permissions. See Figure 7.23.

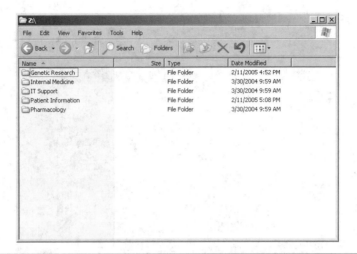

Figure 7.22 Directories under CIFS.

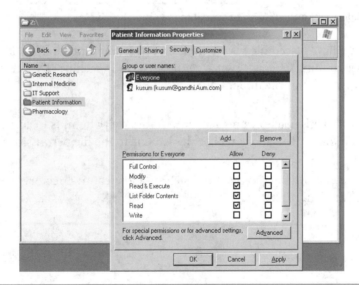

Figure 7.23 Windows permissions for Patient Information folder.

3. The authorized user Kusum now removes the Everyone group from the folder and allows only the user ID of Kusum from the Active Directory Aum.com domain to have any access to the directory. This eliminates the possibility for any unauthorized user from accessing the directory and complying with HIPAA (so it appears). See Figure 7.24.

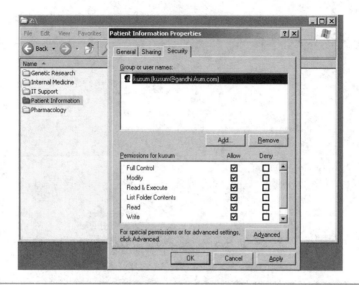

Figure 7.24 Patient Information folder restricted to the user ID of Kusum.

Now that we have placed file permissions on our Patient Information folder on the NAS device running CIFS, we switch to the attacker's machine. The attacker attempts to access this file under CIFS and NFS.

4. Using the attacker's machine and account, the attacker attempts to access the Patient Information folder. The attack will be denied due to the file permissions. See Figure 7.25.

5. The attacker next switches to a Linux machine and create a directory called nfsmount. See Figure 7.26.

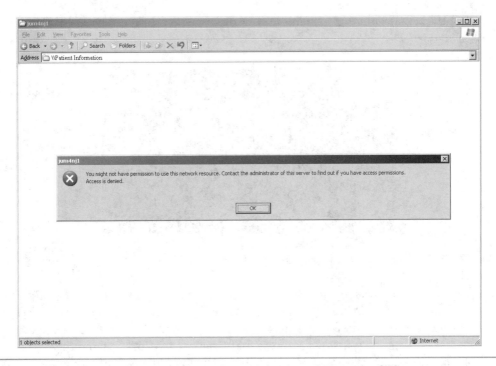

Figure 7.25 Attacker being denied to access Patient Information folder under CIFS.

Figure 7.26 Making /nfsmount directory.

The attacker also mounts the remote NAS file system to the local nfsmount directory. See Figure 7.27.

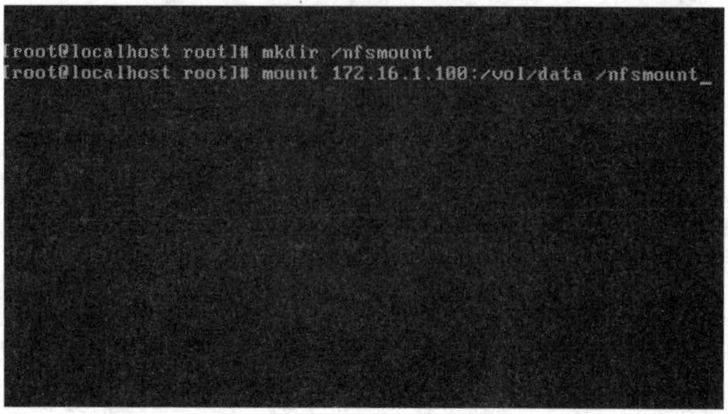

```
[root@localhost root]# mkdir /nfsmount
[root@localhost root]# mount 172.16.1.100:/vol/data /nfsmount_
```

Figure 7.27   Mounting the NFS file system from the NAS device.

6. The attacker now lists the permissions on the file system using the command ls -al. See Figure 7.28. Notice that all folders are available to everyone (drwxrwxrwx); except the Patient Information folder, which is restricted to only the owner of that folder (drwx---). Notice that the owner of the folder has the UID of 6161 and the GID of 30. This tells the attacker that only the UID of 6161 and the GID of 30 can access the folder.

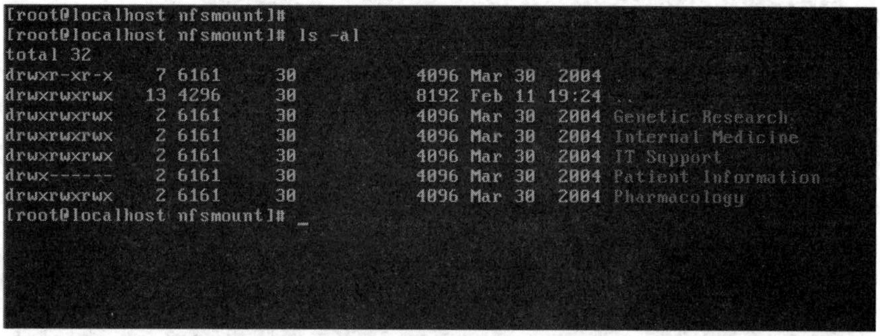

```
[root@localhost nfsmount]#
[root@localhost nfsmount]# ls -al
total 32
drwxr-xr-x    7 6161     30        4096 Mar 30  2004 .
drwxrwxrwx   13 4296     30        8192 Feb 11 19:24 ..
drwxrwxrwx    2 6161     30        4096 Mar 30  2004 Genetic Research
drwxrwxrwx    2 6161     30        4096 Mar 30  2004 Internal Medicine
drwxrwxrwx    2 6161     30        4096 Mar 30  2004 IT Support
drwx------    2 6161     30        4096 Mar 30  2004 Patient Information
drwxrwxrwx    2 6161     30        4096 Mar 30  2004 Pharmacology
[root@localhost nfsmount]#
```

Figure 7.28   Patient Information permissions under Unix.

7. When the attacker attempts to access the Genetic Research folder, he/she is allowed to do so since the permission allows everyone to access that directory. When the attacker accesses the Patient Information folder, however, he/she is denied. See Figure 7.29.

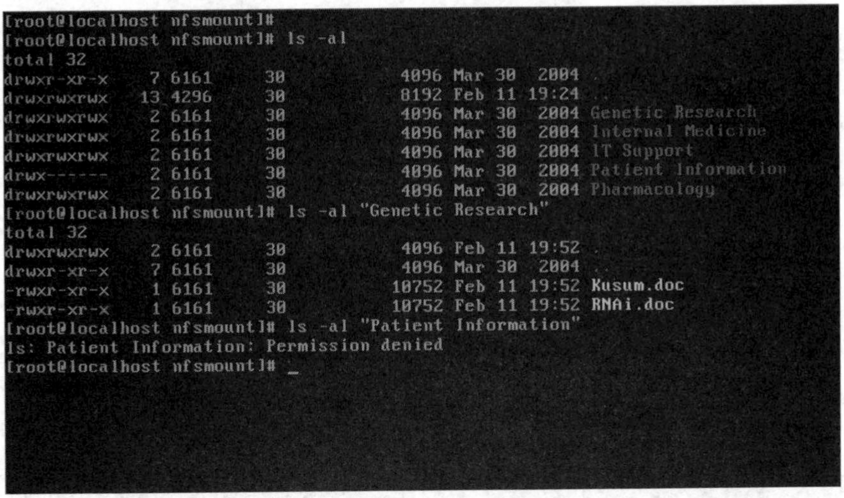

Figure 7.29 Access denied to unauthorized user.

8. At this point, everything is good in terms of security. The attacker has been rejected on both the Windows side (Figure 7.25) and on the Unix side (Figure 7.29). However, the attacker was able to enumerate the entities on the directory without needing to authenticate, which is the UID of 6161 and GID of 30.

9. In order to subvert the security permissions, the attacker needs to trick the NAS device by making it think that a user on their machine has the UID of 6161 and a GID of 30. The attacker can perform this by creating a new user on his/her Linux machine with the UID of 6161 and the GID of 30. See Figure 7.30, which shows the attacker adding the account called nfsuser to his/her own Linux machine with the UID of 6161 and GID of 30.

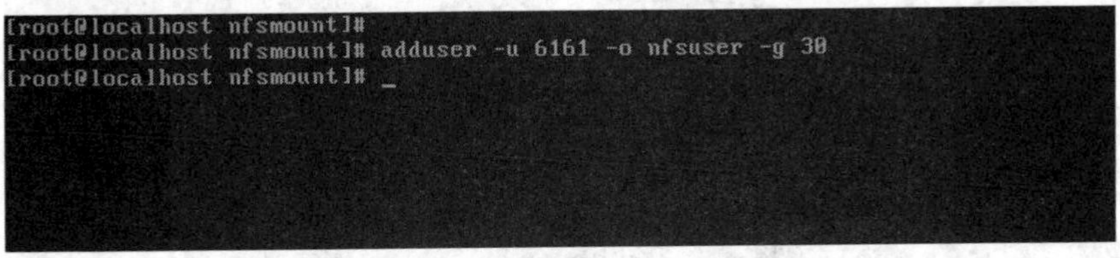

Figure 7.30 Adding a user called nfsuser with the UID of 6161 and GID of 30.

10. Additionally, the attacker can also change the UID and GID of an existing account on his/her Linux machine instead of creating a new account. Because the attacker has root access on his/her own machine, this is also a simple process. See Figure 7.31 to see the /etc/passwd directory before the attacker changes the UID and GID, and see Figure 7.32 to see the /etc/passwd directory after the attacker changes the UID and GID.

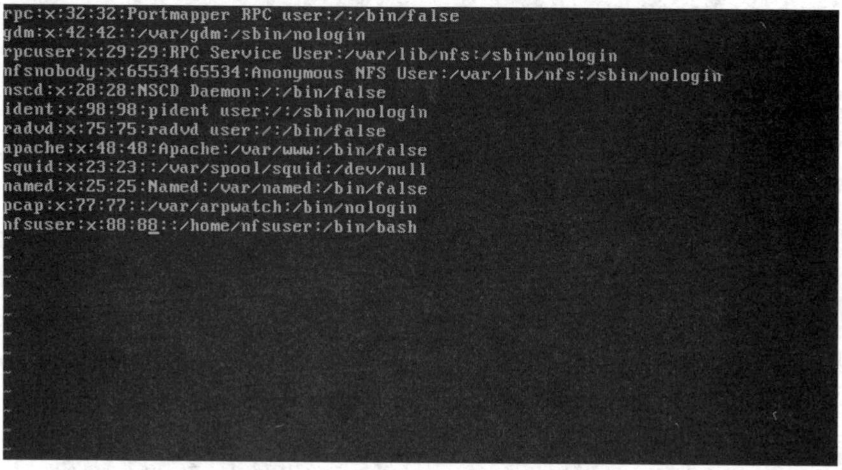

```
rpc:x:32:32:Portmapper RPC user:/:/bin/false
gdm:x:42:42::/var/gdm:/sbin/nologin
rpcuser:x:29:29:RPC Service User:/var/lib/nfs:/sbin/nologin
nfsnobody:x:65534:65534:Anonymous NFS User:/var/lib/nfs:/sbin/nologin
nscd:x:28:28:NSCD Daemon:/:/bin/false
ident:x:98:98:pident user:/:/sbin/nologin
radvd:x:75:75:radvd user:/:/bin/false
apache:x:48:48:Apache:/var/www:/bin/false
squid:x:23:23::/var/spool/squid:/dev/null
named:x:25:25:Named:/var/named:/bin/false
pcap:x:77:77::/var/arpwatch:/bin/nologin
nfsuser:x:88:88::/home/nfsuser:/bin/bash
```

Figure 7.31 /etc/passwd before the UID and GID is changed.

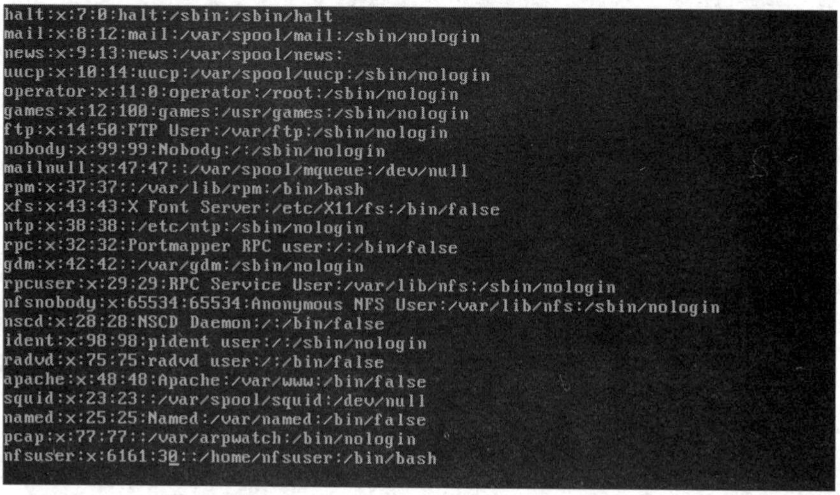

```
halt:x:7:0:halt:/sbin:/sbin/halt
mail:x:8:12:mail:/var/spool/mail:/sbin/nologin
news:x:9:13:news:/var/spool/news:
uucp:x:10:14:uucp:/var/spool/uucp:/sbin/nologin
operator:x:11:0:operator:/root:/sbin/nologin
games:x:12:100:games:/usr/games:/sbin/nologin
ftp:x:14:50:FTP User:/var/ftp:/sbin/nologin
nobody:x:99:99:Nobody:/:/sbin/nologin
mailnull:x:47:47::/var/spool/mqueue:/dev/null
rpm:x:37:37::/var/lib/rpm:/bin/bash
xfs:x:43:43:X Font Server:/etc/X11/fs:/bin/false
ntp:x:38:38::/etc/ntp:/sbin/nologin
rpc:x:32:32:Portmapper RPC user:/:/bin/false
gdm:x:42:42::/var/gdm:/sbin/nologin
rpcuser:x:29:29:RPC Service User:/var/lib/nfs:/sbin/nologin
nfsnobody:x:65534:65534:Anonymous NFS User:/var/lib/nfs:/sbin/nologin
nscd:x:28:28:NSCD Daemon:/:/bin/false
ident:x:98:98:pident user:/:/sbin/nologin
radvd:x:75:75:radvd user:/:/bin/false
apache:x:48:48:Apache:/var/www:/bin/false
squid:x:23:23::/var/spool/squid:/dev/null
named:x:25:25:Named:/var/named:/bin/false
pcap:x:77:77::/var/arpwatch:/bin/nologin
nfsuser:x:6161:30::/home/nfsuser:/bin/bash
```

Figure 7.32 /etc/passwd after the UID and GID is changed.

11. The attacker now lists the permissions on the directory using the `ls -al` command. Notice the permissions are the same, but the owner of the file shows up as nfsuser and gopher. The reason why it does not show up as 6161 anymore is because it is looking at the client's `/etc/passwd` file and showing that username value. It displayed 6161 previously because there were no usernames in the `/etc/passwd` directory that correlated to 6161; however, now the nfsuser has the UID 6161. See Figure 7.33.

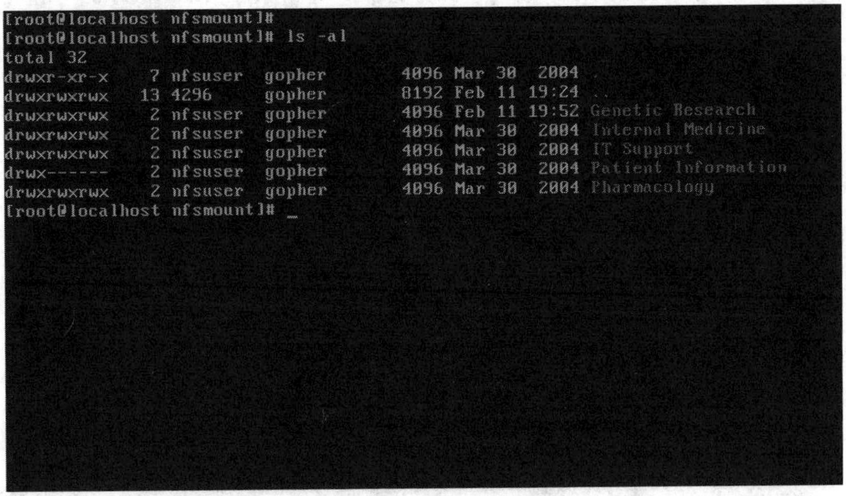

```
[root@localhost nfsmount]#
[root@localhost nfsmount]# ls -al
total 32
drwxr-xr-x    7 nfsuser  gopher    4096 Mar 30  2004 .
drwxrwxrwx   13 4296     gopher    8192 Feb 11 19:24 ..
drwxrwxrwx    2 nfsuser  gopher    4096 Feb 11 19:52 Genetic Research
drwxrwxrwx    2 nfsuser  gopher    4096 Mar 30  2004 Internal Medicine
drwxrwxrwx    2 nfsuser  gopher    4096 Mar 30  2004 IT Support
drwx------    2 nfsuser  gopher    4096 Mar 30  2004 Patient Information
drwxrwxrwx    2 nfsuser  gopher    4096 Mar 30  2004 Pharmacology
[root@localhost nfsmount]# _
```

Figure 7.33 Directory listings with an nfsuser.

12. The attacker next attempts to login into the Genetic Research folder and succeeds; however, when the attacker attempts to access the highly confidential Patient Information folder, he/she is still denied. See Figure 7.34. The reason why this happens is the current user the attacker is utilizing is the root and not the nfsuser.

13. The good part about this is that the NAS device does not trust any UID or GID that comes up as root; hence, the UID of 0 and the GID of 0 will not be assumed as the root user by the NAS device. The problem is that it does allow every other UID and GID; hence, any other UID or GID can be passed by the attacker to get access to the directory. The attacker now switches user (su) to the nfsuser account, which has the UID of 6161 and GID of 30. See Figure 7.35.

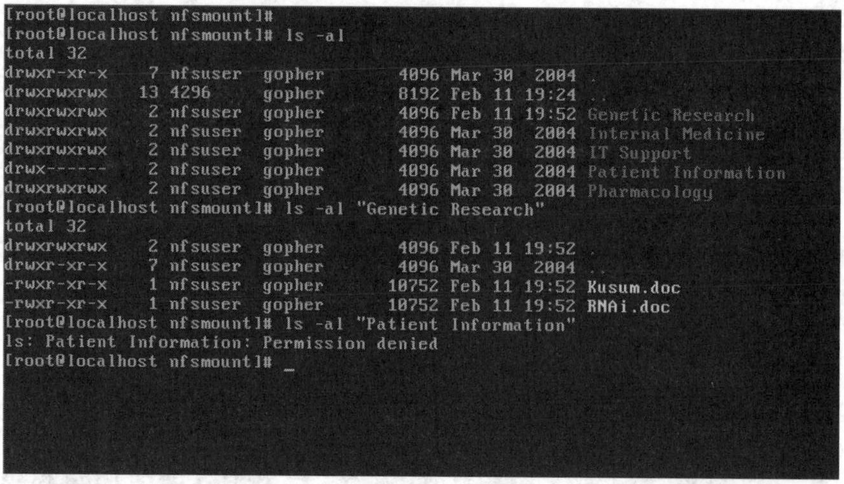

```
[root@localhost nfsmount]#
[root@localhost nfsmount]# ls -al
total 32
drwxr-xr-x    7 nfsuser  gopher       4096 Mar 30  2004 .
drwxrwxrwx   13 4296     gopher       8192 Feb 11 19:24 ..
drwxrwxrwx    2 nfsuser  gopher       4096 Feb 11 19:52 Genetic Research
drwxrwxrwx    2 nfsuser  gopher       4096 Mar 30  2004 Internal Medicine
drwxrwxrwx    2 nfsuser  gopher       4096 Mar 30  2004 IT Support
drwx------    2 nfsuser  gopher       4096 Mar 30  2004 Patient Information
drwxrwxrwx    2 nfsuser  gopher       4096 Mar 30  2004 Pharmacology
[root@localhost nfsmount]# ls -al "Genetic Research"
total 32
drwxrwxrwx    2 nfsuser  gopher       4096 Feb 11 19:52 .
drwxr-xr-x    7 nfsuser  gopher       4096 Mar 30  2004 ..
-rwxr-xr-x    1 nfsuser  gopher      10752 Feb 11 19:52 Kusum.doc
-rwxr-xr-x    1 nfsuser  gopher      10752 Feb 11 19:52 RNAi.doc
[root@localhost nfsmount]# ls -al "Patient Information"
ls: Patient Information: Permission denied
[root@localhost nfsmount]# _
```

Figure 7.34   Attacker still rejected as root.

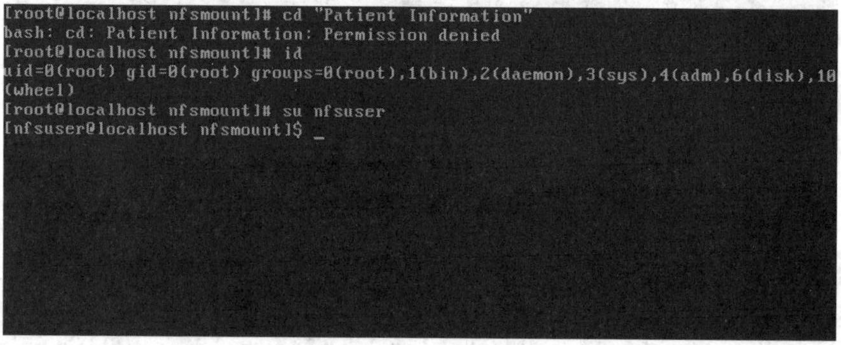

```
[root@localhost nfsmount]# cd "Patient Information"
bash: cd: Patient Information: Permission denied
[root@localhost nfsmount]# id
uid=0(root) gid=0(root) groups=0(root),1(bin),2(daemon),3(sys),4(adm),6(disk),10
(wheel)
[root@localhost nfsmount]# su nfsuser
[nfsuser@localhost nfsmount]$ _
```

Figure 7.35   Root account switching to the nfsuser account.

14. The attacker now has the username of nfsuser, which has the UID of 6161 and GID of 30, as noted by the ID command. See Figure 7.36.

15. Now the attacker can subvert the file permissions on the directory by accessing the patient information folder with the cd Patient Information command. See Figure 7.37.

```
[root@localhost root]# su nfsuser
[nfsuser@localhost root]$ id
uid=6161(nfsuser) gid=30(gopher) groups=30(gopher)
[nfsuser@localhost root]$ _
```

Figure 7.36   User ID for the nfsuser account.

```
[nfsuser@localhost nfsmount]$
[nfsuser@localhost nfsmount]$ ls -al
total 32
drwxr-xr-x   7 nfsuser  gopher    4096 Mar 30  2004 .
drwxrwxrwx  13 4296     gopher    8192 Feb 11 19:24 ..
drwxrwxrwx   2 nfsuser  gopher    4096 Feb 11 19:52 Genetic Research
drwxrwxrwx   2 nfsuser  gopher    4096 Mar 30  2004 Internal Medicine
drwxrwxrwx   2 nfsuser  gopher    4096 Mar 30  2004 IT Support
drwx------   2 nfsuser  gopher    4096 Feb 11 20:08 Patient Information
drwxrwxrwx   2 nfsuser  gopher    4096 Mar 30  2004 Pharmacology
[nfsuser@localhost nfsmount]$ cd "Patient Information"
[nfsuser@localhost Patient Information]$ ls
Aisha-PatientHistory.doc  Rohan-PatientHistory.doc   Sunith-PatientHistory.doc
Delia-PatientHistory.doc  Rohini-MediicalRecord.doc
Jai-PatientHistory.doc    Shreya-MedicalRecord.doc
[nfsuser@localhost Patient Information]$ _
```

Figure 7.37   Subverting file permissions.

16. Done! The attacker is not denied anymore but is allowed to enter the restricted directory and get access to information. See Figure 7.38.

```
[nfsuser@localhost Patient Information]$ ls -al
total 32
drwx------   2 nfsuser  gopher    4096 Feb 11 20:08 .
drwxr-xr-x   7 nfsuser  gopher    4096 Mar 30  2004 ..
-rwx------   1 nfsuser  gopher       0 Mar 30  2004 Aisha-PatientHistory.doc
-rwx------   1 nfsuser  gopher   10752 Feb 11 20:07 Delia-PatientHistory.doc
-rwx------   1 nfsuser  gopher       0 Mar 30  2004 Jai-PatientHistory.doc
-rwx------   1 nfsuser  gopher       0 Mar 30  2004 Rohan-PatientHistory.doc
-rwx------   1 nfsuser  gopher       0 Mar 30  2004 Rohini-MediicalRecord.do
c
-rwx------   1 nfsuser  gopher       0 Mar 30  2004 Shreya-MedicalRecord.doc
-rwx------   1 nfsuser  gopher   10752 Feb 11 20:07 Sunith-PatientHistory.do
c
[nfsuser@localhost Patient Information]$ _
```

Figure 7.38   Accessing the sensitive files.

Despite the fact that the Windows user set permissions on the folder via CIFS (Figure 7.24), the attacker was able to subvert those file permissions under NFS. Note that this also gives a false sense of security to Windows users since they may think that their folder is actually protected from the general public, when instead any user who can mount that directory from NFS is able to gain full control.

The problem gets worse when the user figures out the UID and GID values of all the administrators on the Windows domain. While the administrator account is probably mapped to the root account, which is UID=0, all the other accounts in the administrator group have a unique UID and GID value. If the attacker finds out the UID/GID of one of those accounts, he or she can perform the previous attack and completely own the NAS device from administrator perspective. Ensure that the usermap.cfg file is only accessible to the root user (UID=0) because this file is equivalent of having control of the /etc/shadow or sam database file in Unix and Windows, respectively.

The best way to defend against this attack is to enable Kerberos authentication under NFS, which is supported in NFS version 3 and version 4. Most of the major NAS vendors that deploy NFS support Kerberos authentication. This should be enabled in your environment in order to protect the information residing on the NAS device. Kerberos authentication is described in detail in the Chapter 10.

Encryption

Similar to CIFS, NFS is also a clear-text protocol that sends sensitive information over the network, such as NFS mount information, IP addresses, UIDs, and GIDs. As discussed in Chapter 6, many protocols that are used by NAS devices are clear-text, such as CIFS, NFS, Telnet, HTTP, RSH, and FTP. Refer to the "Encryption" section in Chapter 6 to review how each of these protocols can be sniffed. In this section, we limit our focus to NFS because Telnet, HTTP, and RSH has already been covered.

NFS is a clear-text protocol where all information traverses the network in the clear. Any unauthorized user can sniff the communication easily, despite network subnetting and switched environments. A communication protocol that is responsible for the transfer of sensitive data, user credentials, and access to data should not be clear-text. Most end users would not tolerate banks transferring their own financial information over poor security protocols, so the fact that it is used for large amounts of confidential information doesn't make it any better. See Figure 7.39 for NFS communication.

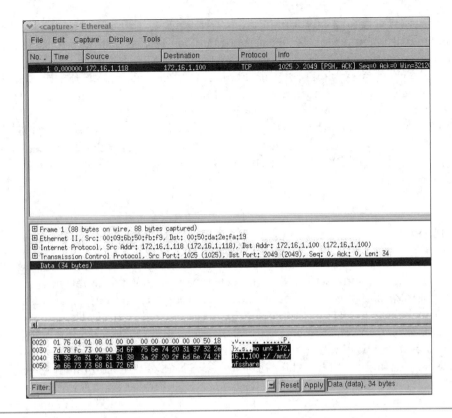

Figure 7.39 NFS communication.

Notice that the following entities have been enumerated from a passive sniffing attack:

- Mounts
- Authorized IP addresses
- Remote NFS directories
- Read and read/write directories

While NAS devices seem to have deployed many clear-text protocols, the use of NFS can be used with IPSec. An IPSec tunnel can be created to protect NFS communication from an unauthorized user who is sniffing the network. If IPSec is enabled between the NAS device and a host, all communication is encrypted, negating any sniffing-based attacks as well as many attacks discussed in this chapter.

Similar to IPSec for data communication, SSH and SSL can be used to replace insecure management protocols such as Telnet and HTTP. See Chapter 6 to review the benefits of implementing SSH over Telnet and using SSL over HTTP.

The support of encryption protocols on many NAS devices include IPSec, SSH, and SSL. Enabling encrypted protocols will prevent many vulnerabilities and attack classes on NAS devices. SSH removes weaknesses in Telnet and RSH; SSL removes weaknesses in HTTP. Finally, IPSec removes the significant security issues with CIFS and NFS. Although we have covered many issues in these two protocols, much of it can be protected immediately with IPSec options on NAS devices; refer to Chapter 10 on enabled IPSec on NAS devices.

SUMMARY

In this chapter, we learned about the problem with NAS devices running NFS. The basics told us that NFS has some serious security issues by default. We were able to enumerate all types of information from the NAS device, including NFS mounts, IP addresses, world-readable exports, and legitimate hostnames (all can be retrieved by anonymous connections). This information allowed us to connect to NAS devices running NFS without any authentication and barely any authorization.

We were able to show the need for Kerberos with NAS devices running NFS version 3 or 4. Also, IPSec would have the ability to secure NFS protocols from several security attacks. We were also able to see the abundance of clear-text protocols enabled by default on NAS devices, but also see the availability of encryption to replace most, if not all, of the clear-text protocols.

The key idea from this chapter and Chapter 6 is that NFS and CIFS are not natively secure protocols. Both have an abundance of enumeration issues, use poor authentication methods (or no authentication methods), use spoofable entities for authorization, and do not have a lot of native encryption. All of these facts combined together do not paint a pretty picture for NAS devices. However, while the default state of NFS and CIFS is not strong, there are a variety of methods to make it more secure, such as disabling anonymous access, using Kerberos, and enabling encrypted protocols like SSH, SSL, and IPSec.

In the next chapter, we continue our discussion on IP networks, but focus on iSCSI security.

PART III
iSCSI SECURITY

SANs: iSCSI Security

iSCSI (Internet Small Computer Systems Interface) is an exciting technology that allows block data to be available over traditional IP networks. SCSI blocks traditionally have been used with Fibre Channel SANs, where a Fibre Channel infrastructure is required such as HBAs, FC switches, and FC storage arrays. Unlike NAS storage devices using IP at the file level, SCSI blocks do not operate at higher levels using CIFS or NFS, but rather at the lower block level by offering entire data stores (LUNs) to iSCSI clients. For example, NAS solutions offer remote CIFS and NFS file systems over a network connection, where SANs offer up the actual drive (not the file system) over a network connection (Fibre Channel or iSCSI).

iSCSI offers the availability of SCSI block data with the convenience and interoperability of IP networks, which does not require any specialized hardware. An iSCSI packet uses IP, but with additional iSCSI aspects. See Figure 8.1 for an example iSCSI packet.

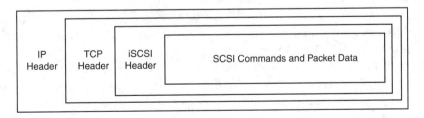

Figure 8.1 iSCSI packet.

Other methods to offer block data over IP can also be performed with FCIP or iFCP, but iSCSI seems to be the most prominent. There are negatives to iSCSI also, such as possible performance penalties, quality of service, or efficiency loss. A Fibre Channel frame is very efficient when compared to an IP packet. Security can be considered both a positive or negative for iSCSI. Overall, iSCSI and Fibre Channel SANs have very similar security issues that are equally significant and scary. iSCSI does offer authentication with CHAP, which has security issues, but Fibre Channel is beginning to support DH-CHAP also. iSCSI is connected to the IP network, making it more accessible to unauthorized users. However, the fact is that an unauthorized user or attacker also can access a Fibre Channel SAN pretty easily. All it takes is one management station connected to the IP network, one Exchange server, one Oracle database, or even one Storage Admin's desktop machine, and access is there.

iSCSI SANs and Fibre Channel SANs use a similar security model, where there are significant issues with authentication and authorization. iSCSI also has to address the situation that it is insecure in terms of standard security practices, but also available to IP networks, which includes hostile internal networks, partner networks, VPNs, and of course, the Internet. These facts, combined with the growing popularity and promise of iSCSI, make it a very high-profile target to attackers and unauthorized users, which becomes a significant issue for the storage administrator.

iSCSI storage networks are excellent for high I/O applications such as a Microsoft Exchange Server. Applications like Exchange need to communicate to hard drives quickly; hence, using a physical six-inch SCSI ribbon inside your machine has always been quick enough. However, IP connection over NFS or CIFS has had too much I/O latency to be truly successful with these types of applications. iSCSI allows all the effectiveness of the six-inch SCSI ribbon with all the capacity of a SAN.

The security of iSCSI storage devices is a significant issue. iSCSI has made the false assumption that security is taken care of elsewhere on the IP network; hence, it does not have to be a primary focus. This is a similar argument that application vendors, such as Microsoft, made in the 1990s and wireless device vendors made in the 2000s. The key difference here is that there is a lot less data on an operating system or a wireless network than iSCSI storage drives. Take a home, for example. If a person has two cars, the garage might be filled up with several things, so they may want to purchase a shed for the backyard. In the shed, they store their bikes, lawnmower, weed trimmer, and other big equipment. Because the bikes and lawn equipment are expensive, they purchase a lock for the side gate that leads to the backyard. The person spends a lot of money on the lock to ensure it could not be broken. However, the mistake the person made is that they assumed an intruder would use the gate to break into the backyard, not securing the shed itself. The problem increases with the fact that the backyard does not have any fences between it and the backyard of any neighbors. Even worse, the neighbors do not lock their gates nor do they have a gate to lock the entrance to the backyard area. In this scenario, an intruder could just walk into the backyard of a neighbor and then casually walk onto the person's property (because of the lack of a fence between properties) and take all the expensive items in the shed. If we apply the example to iSCSI, administrators might have hardened the operating system that is connected to the iSCSI device, but the fact is that IP allows connectivity to the iSCSI device directly without the need to touch any operating system. Any person on the IP network can attempt to connect to the iSCSI device and get into the system and its data. Because the security methods in use are weak, the process to compromise large volumes of data can be quite simple.

iSCSI security does not affect one vendor or one company, but any device that supports iSCSI as data communication method. While iSCSI does offer some out-of-the box security, many of the security methods are poor or disabled by default. Many organizations overlook these issues due to an iSCSI device being an obscure technology, however, security by obscurity, especially an IP network, will never last. This chapter will discuss the following topic concerning iSCSI devices:

- iSCSI security basics
- Enumeration
- Authentication
- Authorization
- Encryption

iSCSI Security Basics

The key parts to an iSCSI network are iSCSI clients (referred to as iSCSI Initiators), iSCSI devices (referred to as iSCSI Targets), and iSNS servers (iSCSI Name Services). The core aspects of iSCSI security are

- Enumeration
  iSNS registration
  iSNS Man-in-the-Middle attacks
  iSCSI sniffing
- Authentication
  CHAP

- Authorization

    iSCSI node names

    iSCSI LUN groups

    Domain hopping attacks

- Encryption

    IPSec

The best way to discuss iSCSI security is to walk through an example. The following steps demonstrate the process of connecting to an iSCSI storage device, according to Figure 8.2.

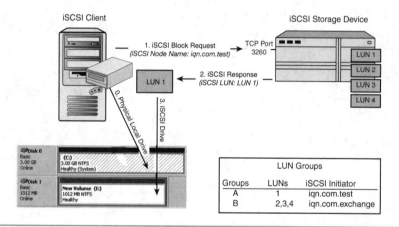

Figure 8.2   iSCSI storage architecture.

0. The client machine has a physical hard drive locally inside the machine itself.

1. The client makes an iSCSI request to the iSCSI storage device. The client sends its iSCSI node name (iQN) to the device to get access to the correct storage block (LUN).

2. The iSCSI storage device receives the request and looks up the iSCSI node name in its LUN group/zone/domain. Once the correct LUN is identified, the iSCSI storage device responds to the client with the appropriate LUN.

3. The iSCSI drive shows up as a local drive on the iSCSI client.

An iSCSI client is granted access to data blocks (LUNs) from the storage controller rather than individual file shares or exports (CIFS/NFS NAS environments). iSCSI storage devices listen on TCP port 3260 and can be accessed by any iSCSI client driver over the IP network. Often times, an Internet Storage Name Service (iSNS), which listens on port 3205, can be used to facilitate the discovery, management, and configuration of iSCSI storage devices. Similar to a Simple Name Server (SNS) in a Fibre Channel SAN, an iSNS is used to discover and manage iSCSI storage devices on the network. The iSNS allows the dynamic discovery of all available storage targets and initiators on the network. After a target is discovered, it can be accessed by any authorized iSCSI client (based on the iSCSI node name).

iSCSI security involves authentication, authorization, integrity, and encryption. On the surface, iSCSI security looks pretty decent, where many key security aspects discussed in Chapter 1, "Introduction to Storage Security," are included in the security architecture. Unlike Fibre Channel security, which lacked authentication, until DH-CHAP becomes enabled by default, and encryption, iSCSI includes the three core areas of security. However, as we take a closer look, we will see the iSCSI security is not necessarily as great as it looks in terms of security.

One of the first issues is that iSCSI is a clear-text protocol that can be sniffed over the network quite easily. Critical details from an iSCSI connection can be captured over the wire such as iSCSI node names, CHAP usernames/ID/challenges, LUN targets, and available iSCSI Targets. As mentioned in Chapter 1, enumeration is a big part of an attack timeline, and iSCSI devices leak a tremendous amount of useful information to any unauthorized user. Figure 8.3 shows a sample clear-text connection between an iSCSI client and an iSCSI storage device.

```
82 19.748356 1C 10 TCP      1152 > 3260 [SYN] Seq=0 Ack=0 Win=64240 Len=0 M!
83 19.748540 1C 10 TCP      3260 > 1152 [SYN, ACK] Seq=0 Ack=1 Win=65535 Ler
84 19.748651 1C 10 TCP      1152 > 3260 [ACK] Seq=1 Ack=1 Win=64260 Len=0
85 19.749106 1C 10 iSCSI    Login Command
86 19.751357 1C 10 iSCSI    Login Response (Success)
87 19.751360 1C 10 iSCSI    Login Command
88 19.751816 1C 10 iSCSI    Login Response (Success)
89 19.751819 1C 10 iSCSI    Login Command
90 19.752520 1C 10 iSCSI    Login Response (Success)
91 19.752523 1C 10 iSCSI    Login Command
92 19.753288 1C 10 iSCSI    Login Response (Success)
93 19.775362 1C 10 iSCSI    SCSI: Report LUNS
94 19.776289 1C 10 iSCSI    SCSI Data In (Good)
```

Figure 8.3   iSCSI communication.

The first method to secure iSCSI architecture is the use of authentication, which uses Challenge Handshake Authentication Protocol (CHAP). CHAP is an authentication protocol that uses random challenges from a server to hash a user's password for authentication. A goal of CHAP is to never send the password of the user in clear-text and/or not make standard MD5 hashes of passwords that could be replayed.

CHAP is not the best method of authentication since it is vulnerable to username sniffing, offline brute force attacks, and possible message challenge attacks; however, some form of authentication is better that none. The main issue with CHAP authentication is that it is disabled by default, which means that it will rarely get enabled unless storage vendors educate their customers about the importance of authentication. Even if CHAP is used, it is vulnerable to many attacks and security weaknesses. The next item is authorization, which is the only required entity for iSCSI security. The problem with the authorization values for iSCSI is that it can be completely sniffed over the network and then spoofed, allowing one iSCSI client to become another. iSCSI authorization values traverse the network in clear-text. In fact, the entire iSCSI protocol is clear-text, with all of the information, including authorization information, vulnerable to any network sniffer. Many people will say this is the reason why IPSec is available for iSCSI communications, to ensure the clear-text traffic is protected from unauthorized sniffers. However, the fact that IPSec is disabled by default and probably has performance penalties will deter several organizations from enabling it. These aspects and many more will be described in detail in the chapter as we take a closer look at iSCSI security—it strengths, weaknesses, and flaws.

In order to fully understand the security issues with iSCSI and complete the assessment exercises, an iSCSI client (initiator), an iSNS server, and an iSCSI Target will be used in most examples. To follow along with the exercises in this chapter, download the following iSCSI components respective to Figure 8.4. For a perfect lab to coincide with this chapter, install the iSCSI Initiator on one machine; install the iSNS server on a second machine, and the iSCSI Target software on a third machine (if you don't already have an iSCSI Target device).

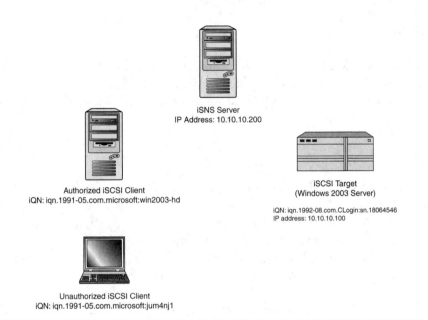

Figure 8.4 LAB iSCSI architecture.

iSCSI Initiator (Client)

- Download any iSCSI Initiator software, such as the Cisco, IBM, HP, or Microsoft software. All the examples in this book use the Microsoft iSCSI Initiator, which can be downloaded from http://www.microsoft.com/downloads/details.aspx?FamilyID= 12cb3c1a-15d6-4585-b385-befd1319f825&DisplayLang=en.

To configure the iSCSI Initiator software according to the exercises in this book, complete the following steps:

1. Install the software with all defaults on both the authorized and unauthorized iSCSI clients.
   a. The authorized iSCSI client will be called win2003-hd. Change the initiator node name iqn.1991-05.com.microsoft:win2003-hd (shown later in this chapter if you are not sure how to do it yourself).
   b. The unauthorized iSCSI client will be called jum4nj1. Change the initiator node name iqn.1991-05.com.microsoft:jum4nj1(shown later in this chapter if you are not sure how to do it yourself).

iSCSI iSNS Server

- Download any iSCSI iSNS server software. All the examples in this book use the Microsoft iSNS Server software, which can be downloaded from http://www.microsoft.com/downloads/details.aspx?FamilyID=0dbc4af5-9410-4080-a545-f90b45650e20&DisplayLang=en.

iSCSI Target

- If you have access to a lab environment with an iSCSI storage device (LeftHand, EqualLogic, EMC, NetApp, or Cisco), you can use that iSCSI storage device. If this type of hardware is not accessible to you in a lab environment, then download the WinTarget software (software-based iSCSI Target) that will turn a Windows operating system into an iSCSI storage device (iSCSI Target). The evaluation software can be downloaded from http://www.stringbeansoftware.com.

To configure the iSCSI Target software according to the exercise in this book, complete the following steps:

1. Install the String Bean Software with all the installation defaults. If you choose to use this software after its review period, ensure that you contact the vendor for a license.
2. Start -> Programs -> String Bean Software -> WinTarget -> WinTarget Console.
3. Highlight WinTarget and select Action -> Properties from the menu bar.
4. Set the Target Name (IQN) value to iqn.1992-08.com.CLogin:sn.18064546. (Note: The Target name can be anything you want; however, if you want to mirror your lab environment with the book's examples, you can change it to the previous setting.)
5. Select OK.
6. Highlight WinTarget and select Action -> Properties from the menu bar and select the Security tab.
7. Select Add to enable authentication for an iSCSI Target.
   a. In the Initiator name field, type the Initiator name from your iSCSI driver software.
   b. In the secret fields, type your secret, such as iscsisecurity.
   c. Select OK and OK again.
8. Highlight the Devices icon in the left pane.

9. Right-click on the disk on the right side and select Create WinTarget Disk -> New File Base WinTarget Disk.

   a. Select Next.

   b. Next to the c:\, type **iSCSI.DATA** for the name of the file for the WinTarget Disk and select Next.

   c. Select the size of your new disk, which is labeled iSCSI.DATA, to 100MB.

   d. In the descriptive name filed, type **iSCSI.DATA**.

   e. In the iQN Assign window, type the following iQN, which will be the only iQN that should have access to the data block: **iqn.1991-05.com.microsoft:win2003-hd**

   f. Select Next.

   g. Select Finish.

10. You have now created an iSCSI LUN (data block) called iSCSI.DATA that should only be accessible to the node of iqn.1991-05.com.microsoft:win2003-hd. This is how most iSCSI Targets are set up and will be used for our exercises in this chapter.

11. Repeat step 9 to create another iSCSI LUN called iSCSI.DATA.Secure.

12. Highlight WinTarget and from the menu bar, select Action -> Properties.

13. Select the iSNS tab.

14. Select Add and type the IP address of the iSNS server from your previous setup. In our examples, we are using the Microsoft iSNS server with the IP address of 10.10.10.200, but it will be a different IP address in your lab environment.

15. Select OK.

iSCSI Security Tools

- www.isecpartners.com/tools.html
- www.isecpartners.com/securingstorage.html

ENUMERATION

Similar to Fibre Channel SANs and CIFS/NFS NAS, iSCSI networks reveal sensitive information that can be used to gain access to data. The two key aspects that an unauthorized user can utilize to enumerate iSCSI storage devices are iSCSI Name Servers (iSNS) and clear-text iSCSI communication. As we have shown with Fibre Channel, NFS, and CIFS, preventing enumeration is a key aspect for data defense; however, it is often overlooked. In this section, we learn how to enumerate several types of information from an iSCSI network. All of the information enumerated in this section will provide critical information for unauthorized users to start, escalate, or complete attacks against an iSCSI network. The following entities will be enumerated:

- iSNS servers
  iSCSI targets/devices
  iSCSI LUNs
  iSNS Man-in-the-Middle attacks
- iSCSI sniffing
  iSCSI Initiator node names
  iSCSI CHAP usernames
  iSCSI CHAP password hashes
  iSCSI Target Node Names

iSNS SERVERS

An iSNS server is similar to a DNS (Domain Name Service) for name lookups. Similar to how DNS servers will tell a DNS client what hostname a particular IP address has or what IP addresses a particular hostname has, an iSNS server will tell an iSCSI client what iSCSI Targets (iSCSI devices) are available on the network for respective iSCSI client (iSCSI Initiators).

An iSNS server can be identified on a network rather easily. iSNS servers listen on port TCP 3205. A network port scan on port 3205 will reveal the network's iSNS server. If a Windows-based iSNS server is used, it is very likely the iSNS server will be running on the same machine as the DHCP server. The DHCP server can be identified with the `ipconfi/all` command. A port scan on that IP address that shows port 3205 is open verifies that the iSNS server is located on the DHCP server. If the iSNS server is not located on the DHCP server, then a general network port scan on port 3205 should be conducted. On a Class B network (65534 network nodes); it would take about 15 minutes with a good port scanner.

ASSESSMENT EXERCISE

1. Download a copy of Storage Scanner written by the author from www.isecpartners.com/tools.html or request it from securingstorage@gmail.com.

2. Type **StorScan.exe** to retrieve the syntax of the tool.

3. Type **StorScan.exe** and the ip address of the storage devices to determine what storage protocols have been enabled. See Figure 8.5.

   a. StorScan.exe –h 10.10.10.100

4. Done!

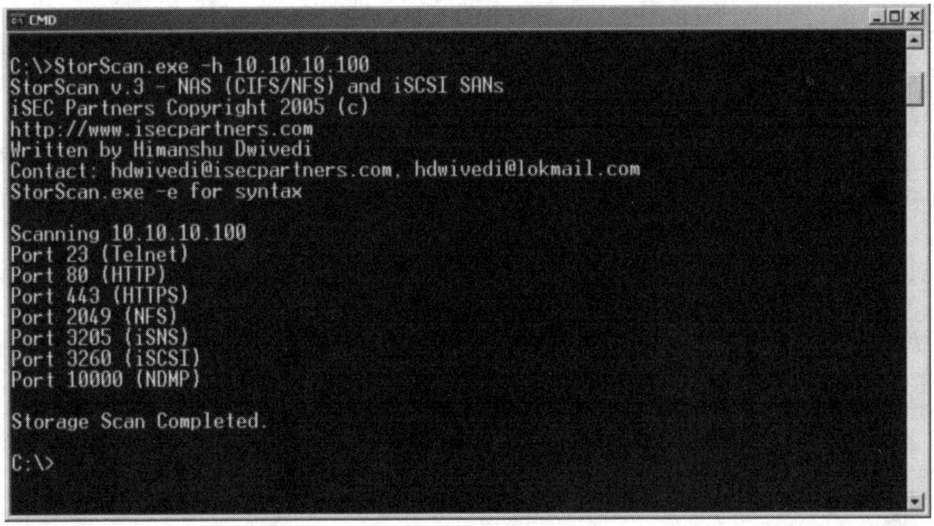

```
 CMD                                                          _|□|x|
C:\>StorScan.exe -h 10.10.10.100
StorScan v.3 - NAS (CIFS/NFS) and iSCSI SANs
iSEC Partners Copyright 2005 (c)
http://www.isecpartners.com
Written by Himanshu Dwivedi
Contact: hdwivedi@isecpartners.com, hdwivedi@lokmail.com
StorScan.exe -e for syntax

Scanning 10.10.10.100
Port 23 (Telnet)
Port 80 (HTTP)
Port 443 (HTTPS)
Port 2049 (NFS)
Port 3205 (iSNS)
Port 3260 (iSCSI)
Port 10000 (NDMP)

Storage Scan Completed.

C:\>
```

Figure 8.5 StorScan—Storage Port Scanner.

Although StorScan is a great tool to target storage devices to see what services are enabled (NFS, CIFS, iSCSI, iSNS, or management services), nmap is a better tool that gives a deeper analysis of general network devices.

Once the iSNS server has been identified on the network, an iSCSI client can register with the iSNS server. There is no restriction for registration. Any iSCSI client can register to any iSNS server. Once an iSCSI client registers to an iSNS server, the iSNS server will tell the client of all available iSCSI devices (iSCSI Targets) on the network that are available (unless unique Domain Sets are used). Just like a DNS server will tell any client on the network the correct IP address for the requested hostname, the iSNS server will tell any client all the available iSCSI Targets on the network. This allows any anonymous unauthorized user to find all iSCSI devices on the network, including their iSCSI node names. Complete the following exercises to enumerate iSCSI Targets.

ASSESSMENT EXERCISE

1. Download the iSCSI Software Initiator from Microsoft (http://www.microsoft.com/downloads/details.aspx?FamilyID=12cb3c1a-15d6-4585-b385-befd1319f825&DisplayLang=en).
2. Install the software accepting all the defaults.
3. Once installed, open the iSCSI Initiator (Start -> Programs -> Microsoft iSCSI Initiator -> Configure Initiator).
4. Click on the iSNS Servers tab (see Figure 8.6).

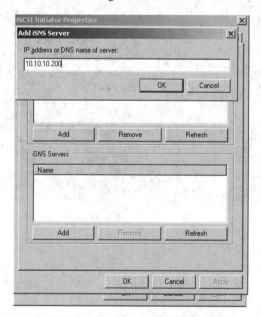

Figure 8.6   iSNS Servers tab.

5. Click the Add button.
6. Type the IP address or DNS name of the iSNS server in the pop-up box. (Note: If you downloaded the iSNS software previously, type the IP address of the server you downloaded it to.) See Figure 8.7.

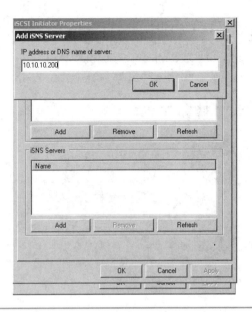

Figure 8.7   iSNS IP address.

7. The iSCSI Initiator is now registered with the iSNS server. See Figure 8.8.

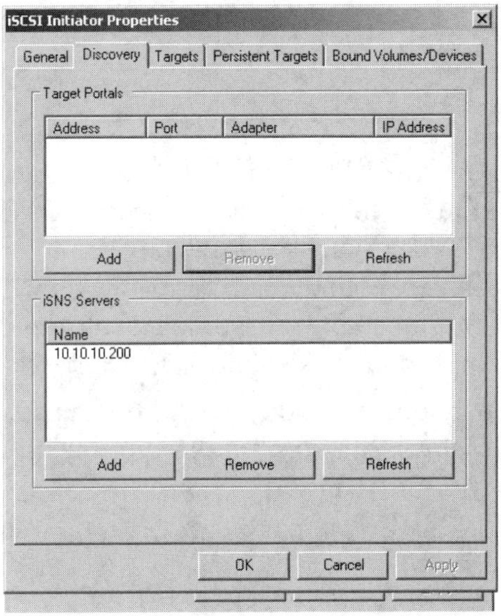

Figure 8.8   iSNS registration.

8. Once the iSCSI Initiator is registered, its discovery methods will update the iSNS server automatically. The iSCSI Initiator will query the iSNS server immediately for the list of iSCSI Targets (iSCSI devices) available on the network in the default domain, as shown on the Available Targets tab on the iSCSI Initiator. See Figure 8.9.

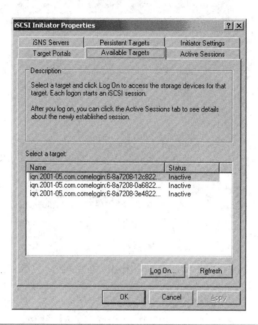

Figure 8.9   iSCSI Targets.

The default domain is the virtual domain that is used for all newly registered initiators and targets. You can think of it as a zone or VLAN for iSCSI Targets and Initiators. If an actual domain is not set up, all targets and initiators will reside in the default domain and will view each other. If a separate domain is set up, then only the Targets and Initiators that are in the same domain will appear to each other. See Figure 8.10 for an example domain setup for iSCSI Targets and Initiators.

However, just like zone hopping and old VLAN hopping attacks, domain hopping attacks are possible to subvert this control, allowing any Initiator to view any target, which is discussed in the Authorization section.

9. Done! We have just enumerated all the iSCSI Targets from the iSNS server without any authentication.

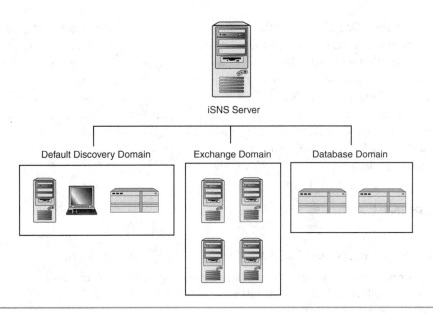

Figure 8.10 iSNS domains.

You may be wondering, now that we have enumerated all iSCSI Targets, why don't we hit the Log On button and attempt to log in? The reason is that in order to successfully mount a LUN from an iSCSI device, an iSCSI Initiator will need the correct iSCSI Node Name (iqn value), which we will enumerate in the next section.

iSNS Man-in-the-Middle Attack

Since iSNS servers do not require authentication for established connections, an attacker can trick an iSCSI client in connecting to a malicious iSCSI Target (iSCSI device) instead of the intended target by masquerading as the iSNS server. Using Man-in-the-Middle attacks, the attacker can claim to be the real iSNS server. Additionally, the attacker's fake iSNS server can send spoofed heartbeat messages to an iSCSI client, tricking the client into connecting to the incorrect iSNS server. When queries from iSCSI clients arrive, the attacker's fake iSNS server can direct the legitimate iSCSI clients to a malicious iSCSI Target. The malicious iSCSI Target can contain hostile data, such as viruses, worms, and Trojan horses, which can completely damage the client or steal information from the client. It would also allow attackers to capture critical authentication information, such as CHAP usernames and CHAP challenges/IDs.

A Man-in-the-Middle attack with an iSNS server could also downgrade the security for connections. For example, a hostile iSNS server controlled by an attacker could tell an iSCSI client that was expecting to use IPSec with an iSCSI Target to actually downgrade to clear-text protocols. Similar to the downgrade attacks we discussed in Chapter 6, "NAS: CIFS Security," with NTLM and Kerberos, an attacker emulating the iSNS server could claim that no IPSec traffic is supported; therefore, all clients should use clear-text protocols. This allows sensitive authentication information to traverse the network for the attacker to compromise. Complete the following exercise for the iSNS Man-in-the-Middle attack.

ASSESSMENT EXERCISE

1. From the attacker's machine, locate the iSNS server on the network.
   a. Use nmap port scanner or StorScan storage scanner to find the iSNS server listening on TCP port 3205. In our lab architecture in Figure 8.4, the IP address of the iSNS server is 10.10.10.200.
2. Conduct a Man-in-the-Middle attack using Cain and Abel by targeting the IP address of 10.10.10.200 (iSNS server). Make all the hosts on the network communicate to your machine first before contacting the real iSNS server.
3. Open up a sniffer, such as Ethereal, and sniff/capture all packets on port 3205 (iSNS packets).
4. Once an iSCSI client attempts to contact the iSNS server, the packet will come to the attacker's machine first and then on to the real host. Figure 8.11 shows a captured iSNS packets with iqn values.

Figure 8.11   iSNS MITM packet capture.

iSCSI SNIFFING

Now that we have enumerated the IP addresses and names for iSCSI devices and targets, we can continue to enumerate the other essential entities to connect and map an iSCSI LUN, which includes iSCSI node names, CHAP usernames, CHAP challenges, CHAP IDs, and CHAP hashes.

Sniffing iSCSI communication does not require anything special since iSCSI is a cleartext protocol. Using any network sniffer, iSCSI communication can be captured over the wire, similar to any Telnet or HTTP session. Unlike a Telnet or HTTP session, which can give an attacker access to a network device or a particular web application, the capture of the iSCSI node name can give an attacker access to gigs of data. Most iSCSI communication takes place over TCP port 3260 (iSCSI) or TCP 3205 (iSNS). Since iSCSI node names are the only entities required for LUN access, the ability to capture them over the network in clear-text is a crippling blow to iSCSI security. Furthermore, if authentication is used, which is disabled by default, the usernames used during the authentication process can be captured over the wire in the clear. Both of these issues are discussed later in this chapter. For now, let's study the process of capturing these two entities.

Sniffing iSCSI communication can be completed using two methods. The first is to simply open up a network sniffer and capture iSCSI traffic on port 3260 and port 3205. While this can be completed from a local machine, many times attackers don't actually attack from their own machines, but from another machine they have already compromised. These compromised machines are usually server class machines, such as any server that has not been hardened but belongs to the domain or an email, DHCP, or DNS server with poor security. Attacking from another compromised machine is a key aspect that storage administrators often overlook and a fact that security professionals already know. It is surprisingly scary how many administrators underestimate the security issues with the use of clear-text protocols for sensitive information, mainly due to that fact that they think it is not likely for an attacker to sniff from that segment. Most attackers perform hopping attacks, where they hop around from one machine to the next in order to capture (sniff) and compromise as many machines as possible. If any of your machines were affected by the SQL Slammer worm, you know that infrastructure class machines inside your network can get compromised by attackers. Also, internal users are often the worst attackers. They have access to any location inside the network.

The second method to sniff iSCSI communication is to first perform a Man-in-the-Middle attack and then sniff the network. Since an attacker is already able to enumerate the iSCSI devices, they can perform a targeted Man-in-the-Middle attack by capturing all the traffic between the iSCSI device and the rest of the network. Once any node connects to the iSCSI device, the attacker will be able to capture the communication since they are performing a Man-in-the-Middle attack. If iSCSI Initiators or CHAP authentication is being used, sensitive information can be captured by the attacker that will allow them to access the data LUNs on iSCSI Targets. Once an iSCSI CHAP communication process is sniffed, the following fields and values can be enumerated:

- CHAP_A: Authentication (authentication type)
- CHAP_C: Challenge (message challenge)
- CHAP_N: Name (CHAP username)
- CHAP_R: Responses (hash of CHAP password)

The fields will help us attack CHAP authentication later in this chapter. Complete the following exercises to enumerate iSCSI node names and CHAP usernames.

ASSESSMENT EXERCISE

1. In order to capture iSCSI node names and CHAP usernames, we will perform a Man-in-the-Middle attack against our iSCSI device. This will allow us to capture all communication to and from the iSCSI Target. For more information on Man-in-the-Middle attackers, refer to Chapter 2, "SANs: Fibre Channel Security."

2. Download Cain from http://www.oxid.it/cain.html.

3. Install the program using its defaults.

4. Install the WinPCap packet driver also, if you already don't have one installed.

5. Reboot.

6. Launch Cain and Abel (Start -> Programs -> Cain).

7. Select the icon in the upper-left corner that looks like a network interface card.

8. Ensure your NIC card has been identified and enabled correctly by Cain.

9. Select the Sniffer tab.

10. Select the + symbol in the toolbar.

11. The MAC Address Scanner window will appear. This will enumerate all the MAC addresses on the local subnet. Hit OK. See Figure 8.12 for the results.

12. The iSCSI storage device in our example is 10.10.10.100. We will perform a Man-in-the-Middle attack from any machine communicating to and from 10.10.10.100.

13. Select the APR tab on the bottom of the tool to switch to the ARP Pollution Routing tab.

14. Select the + symbol on the toolbar to show all the IP addresses and their MACs. See Figure 8.13.

15. On the left side of Figure 8.13, choose the iSCSI storage device, which is 10.10.10.100.

16. Once you have selected 10.10.10.100, select all the hosts on the right side. This will allow you to capture all communication from or to 10.10.10.100 and the rest of the network. Select OK.

17. Now select the yellow and black icon (second one from the left) to officially start the MITM attack.

18. At this point, all traffic from the network to the iSCSI storage device is going to the attacker first.

19. Now we will open a network sniffer (for example, Ethereal) to capture the traffic over ports 3205 and 3260.

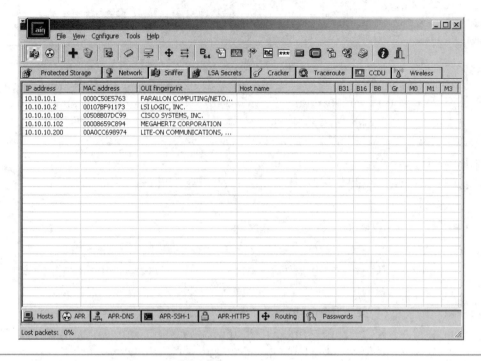

Figure 8.12 MAC Address Scanner results.

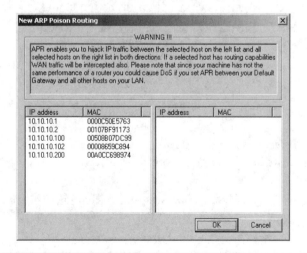

Figure 8.13 IP addresses and their MACs.

20. Download and install Ethereal from www.ethereal.com.

21. Open Ethereal (Start -> Programs -> Ethereal -> Ethereal).

22. From the menu bar, select Capture -> Start.

23. Select the correct network card from the Interface drop-down box.

24. Under the Display Options, check Update list of packets in real time and Automatic scrolling in live capture. Select OK.

25. You are now sniffing all communications to/from the iSCSI device and the network. Once any iSCSI communication occurs over port 3205 or 3260, Ethereal will display the packet. In the Protocol column, you will see iSCSI for all communication over port 3205 and iSNS for all communication for port 3260. See Figure 8.14 for our captured iSCSI communication.

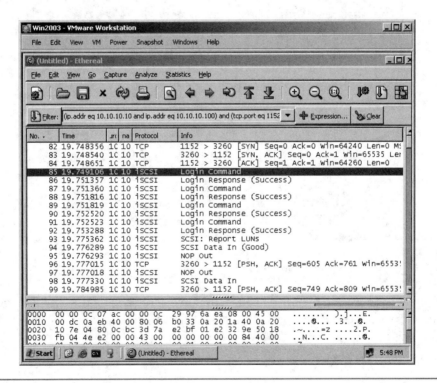

Figure 8.14 iSCSI communication.

26. Now that we have sniffed and captured the iSCSI communication, we can double-click on the packet in Ethereal to view the contents. Because all the communication is in clear-text, all the contents of the communication will be readable to us.

27. Figure 8.15 shows the iSCSI Node Name from an iSCSI packet, which is `iqn.1991-05.com.microsoft:win2003-hd`. The iSCSI Node Name is the only required value needed to access the iSCSI Target. If authentication is disabled, which is the default setting, the attacker now has the equivalent of a password to connect to large amounts of data from the storage device. This attack will be described further next.

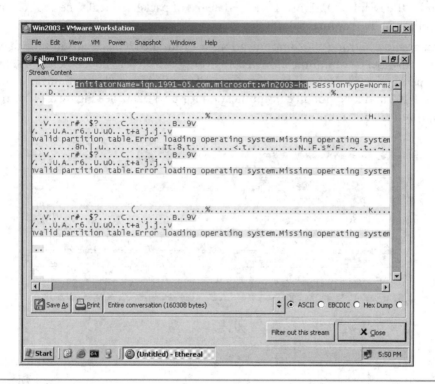

Figure 8.15 iSCSI Initiator Node Name.

28. Figure 8.16 shows another iSCSI connection that shows where the CHAP authentication method is used. This lets the attacker know to look for the CHAP username, which also traverses the network in clear-text.

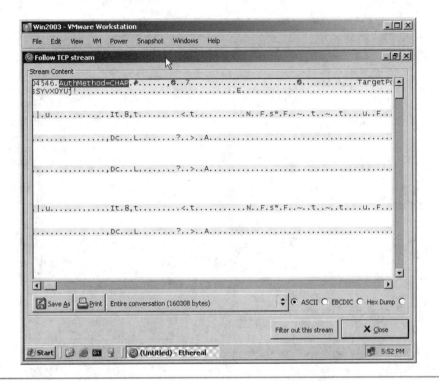

Figure 8.16 iSCSI CHAP method used.

29. Figure 8.17 shows the iSCSI CHAP username that was being used for the session, which is `iscsisecurity`. If authentication is enabled, this value can now be used by the attacker in a brute-forcing attack.

Figure 8.17   iSCSI CHAP username.

30. Figure 8.18 shows the iSCSI CHAP password (value after CHAP_R) in encrypted format, which is AC3576F6AA95A0438BA08A60D5AF99E6. CHAP has had numerous security issues associated with it, including message reflection attacks and offline brute-forcing attacks.

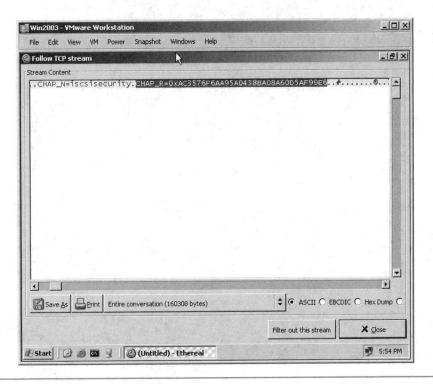

Figure 8.18 iSCSI CHAP password hash.

Other items that can be captured from the iSCSI packet is the iSCSI device itself. We were able to gain the iSCSI Target node name from our iSNS server; however, if an attacker was simply sniffing the network without any targets, they would be able to capture the target information also, which is iqn.1992-08.com.CLogin:sn.18064546, as shown in Figure 8.19.

You can also download a tool called iSCSIgrab from www.isecpartners.com/tools.html that will search the contents of a Ethereal log file (e.g. sniff.log) and display all the important iSCSI security entities, such as initiator node names, CHAP IDs, CHAP message challenges, CHAP usernames, and CHAP hashes.

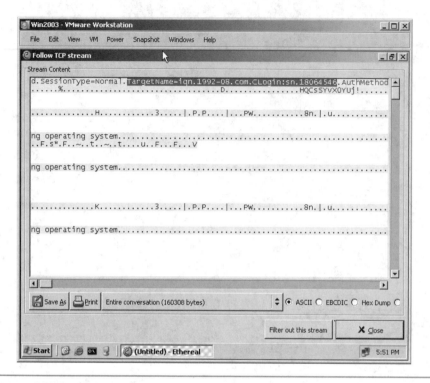

Figure 8.19   iSCSI Target Node Name.

We have now enumerated an iSCSI Initiator Node Name and an iSCSI CHAP username, two of the primary entities required to connect to large volumes of data for an iSCSI storage device. Notice that we have not done anything special except simply sniff the network and look at clear-text packets. From a security perspective, this is a very trivial task and would not even be considered a security exploit. Additionally, we were able to capture the iSCSI CHAP password hash and the iSCSI Target Node Name. These two items simply show that any item in iSCSI communication can be captured.

The use of clear-text communication for large amounts of sensitive data allows attacker to enumerate an abundance of information, including iSCSI Targets/devices, iSCSI LUNs, iSCSI Initiator Node Names, iSCSI CHAP usernames, iSCSI CHAP password hashes, and iSCSI Target Node Names. All this information enables attackers to initiate, continue, and successfully complete iSCSI attacks.

AUTHENTICATION

Give credit where credit is due. Fibre Channel SANs did not support authentication for several years and have now recently supported DH-CHAP due to the security issues and the market pressures. iSCSI SANs do support CHAP authentication natively, allowing for iSCSI SAN to authenticate entities as well as authorize them. Some form of authentication is always better than none, despite the fact that CHAP has its security problems also. RFC 3723, section 3.1, states that iSCSI login provides a weak security solution and continues to push iSCSI to be used with IPSec, which is discussed later in this chapter.

The first problem with iSCSI authentication is the fact that it is disabled by default. The fact that authentication is disabled by default on an entity that stores gigabytes of data is amazing. No one would ever dream of not putting a password on their online bank account, but an entire store of data without a password is somehow overlooked. The second issue is if authentication is disabled by default, the only real security left on the iSCSI Target is the authorization value using the initiator node name (iQN). The iQN can be sniffed over the network and spoofed easily, which pretty much always gives access to the storage device. I am sure there is a lot of ease-of-use or back-end storage reasons why people felt it would be okay to make authentication optional, but to the author this is a big issue. It also states in RFC 3723, section 2.4.1, that compliant iSCSI implementation must enable CHAP, which has not been done by many vendors. Not only should authentication be enabled for obvious security reasons, but the fact that it is disabled means that most organizations will leave it disabled. Some of the more security conscious organizations will make the effort to learn about it and enable it, but most of the organizations will probably not be exposed to this fact and unknowing leave it disabled, creating an open door to attackers. The fact is, authentication is very important for a strong security model. NFS ignored authentication and was vulnerable to many security issues. iSCSI did a great thing by providing authentication, but it will be better if each vendor enables it by default. Enabling authentication by default will make deployments less easy, but when you're storing sensitive, confidential, and regulated data, a bit of work to secure the data should not be a tough decision.

Hopefully by knowing the iQN authorization values offer little to no security, you should be convinced to enable authentication in your iSCSI device. As stated previously, if authentication is enabled, it uses CHAP. CHAP was defined by RFC (Request For Comment) 1994. It uses a three-way handshake to authentication. The following is the process used by CHAP:

1. The CHAP client makes a connection and requests authentication.
2. The CHAP authenticator sends a challenge message and the CHAP ID to the client.

3. The client takes the challenge message, ID, and concatenates it with the locally stored secret and creates a one-way MD5 hash value. This hash value is sent to the authenticator.

4. The authenticator calculates the hash also based on the challenge message and ID that was sent to the client and the locally stored secret. This is independent of the client to ensure that the hash sent by the client is correct. If the hashes match, the authenticator accepts the connection and authenticates the client. At no point is the password sent over the network but only the hash value of the username and challenge message.

5. During the connection, the authenticator will randomly send the client a new challenge, which will be used to re-authenticate (seamlessly to the end user) the client. See Figure 8.20.

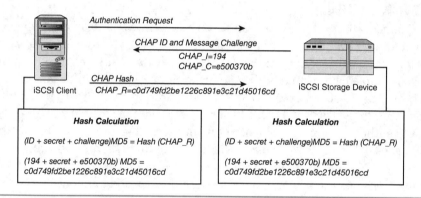

Figure 8.20   iSCSI CHAP authentication.

Let's walk through a real example of an iSCSI client using CHAP to authenticate to an iSCSI storage device. Figure 8.21 is the example architecture we will be using.

1. Open the iSCSI Initiator (Start -> Programs -> Microsoft iSCSI Initiator -> Configure Initiator).

2. Under the Target Portals tab, click on the Add button.

3. Type the IP address of the iSCSI Target, which is **10.10.10.100** in our example, and select the Advanced button.

4. Check the CHAP logon information checkbox.

5. Type the username for the iSCSI client set on the iSCSI device, which can be `iscsisecurity` or the iQN value of the machine, such `as iqn.1991-05.com.` `microsoft:win2003-hd`.

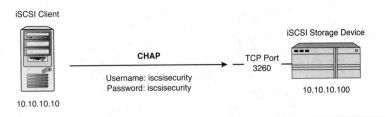

Figure 8.21 iSCSI architecture.

6. Type the secret for the iSCSI Target, which is **iscsisecurity** See Figure 8.22.

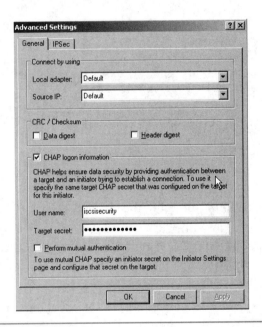

Figure 8.22 CHAP authentication settings.

7. Select OK on the Advance Settings window.
8. Select OK on the Target Portal menu. At this point, the iSCSI client will attempt to login to the iSCSI storage device using CHAP authentication.
9. After authentication has taken place successfully, the Target Portals tab will show the available portals. See Figure 8.23.

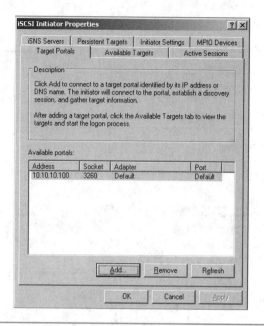

Figure 8.23   Target portals.

10. Click on the Available Targets tab to see the available targets.

11. Click the Log On button to connect to the target. See Figure 8.24.

12. Click on the Advanced tab. Notice it is the same tab where we enter our username and secret information from steps 5 and 6. You can re-enter that information or leave it as is if the information is correct.

13. Select OK in the Log On to Target window.

14. At this point, you will see a "Connected" in the Status column in the Available Targets tab. See Figure 8.25.

15. Done! You have now logged into the iSCSI storage device (iSCSI Target) using CHAP authentication.

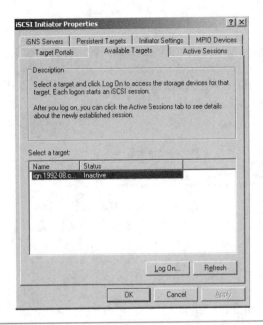

Figure 8.24   Available targets.

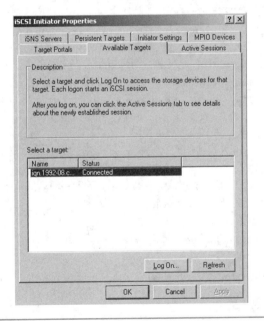

Figure 8.25   Connected status.

MUTUAL AUTHENTICATION

In addition to client-side authentication, there are other ways to further secure iSCSI CHAP. One feature is mutual authentication. Mutual authentication allows the ability for the server to authenticate to the client; however, it also allows the client to authenticate the server. See Figure 8.26.

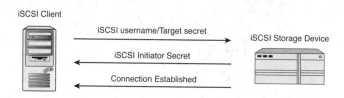

Figure 8.26   iSCSI mutual authentication.

For more information on mutual authentication, refer to Chapter 11, "Securing iSCSI."

Now that you understand iSCSI authentication with CHAP, let's discuss the third major issue with iSCSI authentication, CHAP security weaknesses. First, CHAP is vulnerable to an offline dictionary attack. An attacker can sniff the network and capture the challenge message (CHAP_C), the ID (CHAP_I), and also the hash value (CHAP_R). The ID, message challenge, and password are concatenated and hashed to make the hash value send to the iSCSI Target. After an attacker captures the ID, message challenge, and the hash, they will have three of four values needed to compromise the password. The values that are used to create the hash can be captured over any clear-text iSCSI session. All the user needs is the password. The attacker can get a long list of passwords, concatenate each one with the message challenge and ID, and get a whole bunch of hashes. Once the attacker gets a hash that matches the hash they also captured over the network, they will know that they have guessed the correct password. This all happens offline (not online against the target but offline on the attacker's own machine); therefore, the attack can continue indefinitely until a password is found. The following is an equation that is used when iSCSI authentication is enabled:

```
(ID + Password + Message Challenge)MD5 = Hash
```

If you insert the known values that can be sniffed over network into the previous equation, the only unknown is the password, as shown in the new equation:

```
(194 +  ?   +   e500370b  )MD5 = c0d749fd2be1226c891e3c21d45016cd
```

The attacker can now attempt passwords until they receive the correct hash that was sniffed over the network. For example, if you know that $2 + x = 5$ and you need to know what x is, you can start from the number 1 and guess the answers as many times as you want until the answer equals 5. In this simple example, after three attempts (for example, $2 + 1$ does not equal 5, $2 + 2$ does not equal 5, $2 + 3$ equals 5), you will have brute forced your answer offline. However, an attacker can try three times or 300,000 times if they choose, with absolutely no timeouts and no other restrictions.

The following demonstration shows the offline brute-forcing attack from a sniffed iSCSI session using CHAP authentication. The first column shows the sniffed ID (CHAP_I), the second column is the variable that uses a big list of dictionary words, the third column shows the sniffed message challenge from the session (value after CHAP_C in the sniffer), and the last column shows resulting hash value (CHAP_R) that was also sniffed. Once the hash value matches the one sniffed over the network (highlighted in bold), the attacker knows they have guessed the correct password used for iSCSI CHAP authentication.

```
Sniffed (Captured) Entities:
- ID (CHAP_I): 194
- Message Challenge (CHAP_C): e500370b
- Hash (CHAP_R): c0d749fd2be1226c891e3c21d45016cd


ID  +  Dictionary Word  +  Message Challenge  =  Hash


194        Hello            e500370b              ea8c9e0f236082fc810042cec874b71c
194        My               e500370b              2db5f956905e85e6fd242a54d9213e9a
194        Name             e500370b              08dd57f2fcb535ae6c3d32716d54c97c
194        Is               e500370b              bc7329be2a9fa99fa596802b6a00424d
194        Kusum            e500370b              13ec91aeb5ea120e971a29ad0e2d0e86
194        And              e500370b              0708568450c40b67fc885e6685579cc4
194        My               e500370b              2db5f956905e85e6fd242a54d9213e9a
194        Voice            e500370b              28b255f4e1ecbe44e8c7827d039b523e
194        Is               e500370b              bc7329be2a9fa99fa596802b6a00424d
194        My               e500370b              2db5f956905e85e6fd242a54d9213e9a
194        Passport         e500370b              4983811b661e3d1dfda16a1c39f2b201
194        Verify           e500370b              629c2a938740d0332042b486db58b8dd
194        Me               e500370b              efb2712166bfafe7fcf6b3c0f0cf60d3
194        iscsisecurity    e500370b              c0d749fd2be1226c891e3c21d45016cd


Actual Password: iscsisecurity
```

All the attempts fail except when the hash that was created matches the hash that was sniffed over the network (noted with bold). This attack shows how vulnerable the use of iSCSI CHAP authentication can be, especially over clear-text protocols, as seen in Figure 8.27.

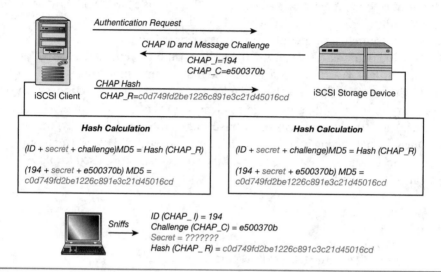

Figure 8.27   Capture of CHAP information for offline brute-force attacks.

The author has created an example tool that can perform this previous exercise automatically. The tool will take a dictionary file of passwords that the end user would like to test, concatenate it with the ID and challenge message sniffed over the network (user supplied), and determine whether the resulting MD5 hash matches the hash value that was also sniffed over the network. For a copy of the tool, called CFP.exe, visit www.isecpartners.com/tools.html or email the author at securingstorage@gmail.com. A screenshot of the tool is in Figure 8.28.

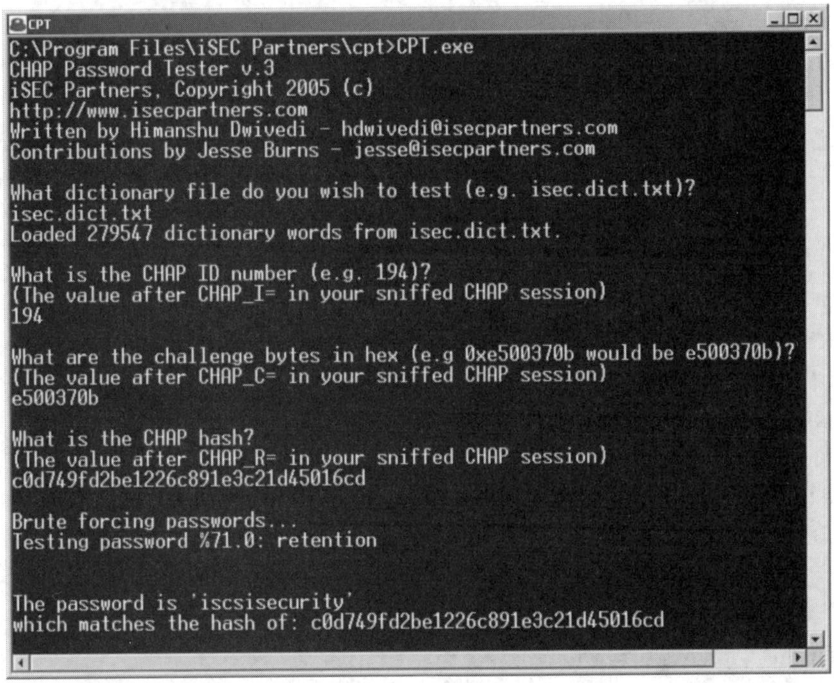

```
C:\Program Files\iSEC Partners\cpt>CPT.exe
CHAP Password Tester v.3
iSEC Partners, Copyright 2005 (c)
http://www.isecpartners.com
Written by Himanshu Dwivedi - hdwivedi@isecpartners.com
Contributions by Jesse Burns - jesse@isecpartners.com

What dictionary file do you wish to test (e.g. isec.dict.txt)?
isec.dict.txt
Loaded 279547 dictionary words from isec.dict.txt.

What is the CHAP ID number (e.g. 194)?
(The value after CHAP_I= in your sniffed CHAP session)
194

What are the challenge bytes in hex (e.g 0xe500370b would be e500370b)?
(The value after CHAP_C= in your sniffed CHAP session)
e500370b

What is the CHAP hash?
(The value after CHAP_R= in your sniffed CHAP session)
c0d749fd2be1226c891e3c21d45016cd

Brute forcing passwords...
Testing password %71.0: retention


The password is 'iscsisecurity'
which matches the hash of: c0d749fd2be1226c891e3c21d45016cd
```

Figure 8.28 CHAP password testing.

ASSESSMENT EXERCISE

Using the lab scenario in Figure 8.4, complete the following attack to perform an offline brute-forcing attack against iSCSI CHAP:

1. On the attacker's machine:

   a. Initiate a Man-in-the-Middle attack using Cain (see prior assessment exercise for step-by-step details).

   b. Sniff the network using Ethereal (see prior assessment exercise for step-by-step details).

   c. You are now sniffing the network for iSCSI communication. Once any iSCSI communication occurs over port 3205 or 3260, Ethereal will capture the packet. In the Protocol column, you will see iSCSI for all communication over port 3205.

2. On the trusted machine:

   a. Open the iSCSI Initiator (Start -> Programs -> Microsoft iSCSI Initiator -> Configure Initiator).

   b. Under the Target Portals tab, click on the Add button.

   c. Type the IP address of the iSCSI Target, which is **10.10.10.100** in our example, and select the Advanced button.

   d. Check the CHAP logon information checkbox.

   e. Type the username for the iSCSI client set on the iSCSI device, which is **iqn.1991-05.com.microsoft:win2003-hd** from our WinTarget Target.

   f. Type the secret for the iSCSI Target, which is **iscsisecurity**.

   g. Select OK on the Advance Settings window.

   h. Select OK on the Target Portal menu. At this point, the iSCSI client will attempt to login to the iSCSI storage device using CHAP authentication.

   i. After authentication has taken place successfully, the Target Portals tab will show the Available portals.

   j. Click on the Available Targets tab to see the available targets.

   k. Hit the Log On button to connect to the target.

   l. Click on the Advanced tab. Notice it is the same tab where we entered our username and secret information from steps e and f. You can re-enter that information or leave it as is if the information is correct.

   m. Select OK in the Log On to Target window.

   n. At this point, the authorized client will see a "Connected" in the Status column in the Available Targets tab.

   o. The authorized client has logged into the iSCSI storage device (iSCSI Target) using CHAP authentication. The attacker has sniffed the entire communication.

3. The attacker's machine should have sniffed and captured all iSCSI packets, including the ID (CHAP_I), the message challenge (CHAP_C), and the resulting hash (CHAP_R), as shown in Figure 8.27.

4. Download CPT.exe from www.isecpartners.com/tools.html or request it from securingstorage@gmail.com.

   a. Type **CPT.exe** to start the program.

   b. Type **isec.dict.txt** for the dictionary file with a large list of passwords.

   c. Type the value after CHAP_C when asked for the CHAP ID number (for example, **194**).

    d. Type the value after CHAP_C when prompted for the challenge (for example, **e500370b**).

    e. Type the value after CHAP_R when prompted for the hash (for example, **c0d749fd2be1226c891e3c21d45016cd**).

5. The tool will now show if you have brute forced the correct password.

6. Done! If the hashes match, you have brute forced the password. If not, continue to try another password.

Another issue with CHAP is that CHAP usernames pass the network in the clear, as shown previously in Figure 8.17. If client-side authentication is the only entity enabled for iSCSI communication, then half of the authentication parameter is given away freely. The other half, which is the password, can now be brute forced with a dictionary list of shared secrets. Also, since most iSCSI storage environments will set up iSCSI secrets as an entity that can easily be remembered, it probably isn't very unique. In order to capture iSCSI usernames, complete the following steps.

ASSESSMENT EXERCISE

1. Open Ethereal (Start -> Programs -> Ethereal -> Ethereal).

2. From the menu bar, select Capture -> Start.

3. Select the correct network card from the Interface drop-down box.

4. Under the Display Options, check Update list of packets in real time and Automatic scrolling in live capture. Select OK.

5. You are now sniffing the network for iSCSI communication. Once any iSCSI communication occurs over port 3205 or 3260, Ethereal will display the packet. In the Protocol column, you will see iSCSI for all communication over port 3205.

6. Once you have sniffed and captured an iSCSI packet, double-click on the packet in Ethereal to view the contents. Since all the communication is in clear-text, all the contents of the communication will be readable to us.

7. Figure 8.29 shows the section of the iSCSI connection that shows where the CHAP authentication method is used. The value displays the CHAP username in clear-text (the value immediately after the CHAP_N field).

8. Done! CHAP usernames have just been captured over the network.

Figure 8.29   iSCSI CHAP username.

Another possible weakness of certain CHAP implementations are replay attacks. A replay attack could occur only if the intervals where a new challenge message is not sent often enough by the iSCSI authenticator (iSCSI Target). For example, if a challenge message is sent once every 30 minutes, an attacker that captures the hash value from the client can simply replay that value to the authenticator to log in. The authenticator would accept it since it contains the correct hash value. If the authenticator has sent out a new challenge message to the client, the old hash value obtained by the attacker would be incorrect; hence defeating the replay attack by the unauthorized user. The interval time where a new challenge is sent to the client is key to defeating replay attacks with CHAP.

The second weakness is the reflection of the CHAP message challenges across multiple connections. The message challenge is the key entity in the hash. As stated previously, a client would take its secret (password), the CHAP ID/message challenge from the responder and make an MD5 hash value. The value is sent to the authenticator over the network. A message challenge reflection attack would first begin with the attacker starting a new authentication process. The attacker will receive an ID and challenge from the iSCSI Target. Because the attacker does not know the secret (password), it cannot formulate the correct MD5 hash. However, the attacker can open a completely separate second connection to the target (connection number 2) and attempt to authenticate the target (instead of the target authenticating the client). The attacker would then send the same ID and challenge it received from the first connect back to the target in the second connection. The target would receive the ID/challenge on the second connection (the same ID/challenge it just sent to the attacker in the first connection), combine it with the secret (password), and make a hash value of it and send it to the attacker. The attacker now has the correct hash value for authentication, which used the same ID/challenge by the target in the first connection and the real secret. The attacker can now present the hash value from the second connection to the target on the first connection. The target would see the correct hash value and authenticate the attacker without the attacker ever knowing the secret (password). The following steps and Figure 8.30 walks through this example with six steps.

1. Connection 1: The attacker attempts to authenticate to the iSCSI target.
2. Connection 1: The iSCSI target sends the attacker a CHAP ID and message challenge in order to receive a MD5 response.
3. Connection 2: The attacker does not know the correct secret (password), so it cannot create a valid MD5 response to get authenticated. Therefore, the attacker opens up a second connection and forces the iSCSI target to authenticate to itself (the attacker) by sending the iSCSI target a CHAP ID and CHAP challenge. This will be the same CHAP ID and message challenge that was sent in step 2 from the iSCSI target, which will ensure the ensuing MD5 hash is the correct one for the original connection.
4. Connection 2: The iSCSI target receives the CHAP ID and message challenge on the second connection and thinks it must respond with a MD5 response. The target creates a valid MD5 hash using the given CHAP ID/message challenge and the valid password (the target knows the real password). The valid MD5 hash is then sent to the attacker.
5. Connection 1: The attacker receives the valid MD5 hash and will go back to the first connection and send the hash to the target.
6. Connection 1: The attacker is now authenticated by the target since it sent a valid MD5 hash that was created with the correct password, using the valid CHAP ID/message challenge for the original connection.

iSCI targets that comply with Section 8.2 of RFC 3720 are not vulnerable to this attack; however, if protections stated in Section 8.2 are not implemented, the iSCSI targets would be vulnerable.

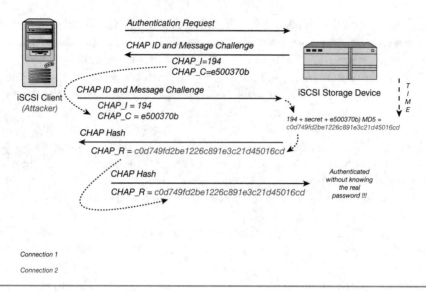

Figure 8.30 iSCSI challenge attack.

AUTHORIZATION

iSCSI authorization is usually the only required security control enabled on iSCSI Targets, which uses initiator node names (iQN) for identification. Authorization of iQNs in storage networks can also involve domain sets and iSCSI LUN groups. The first section we will discuss is iSCSI node names.

ISCSI NODE NAMES

iSCSI uses Initiator Node Names to perform authorization to iSCSI devices (iSCSI Targets). The iSCSI node names are values that are similar to the World Wide Names in Fibre Channel SANs and hostnames in CIFS/NFS NAS implementations. Each of these values is used to identify the machine, not the user, on the network. Based on authorization parameters on the storage device, certain iSCSI node names (machines) will be allowed to connect to the storage device. It is important to understand that authorization does not authenticate any user or any machine, but just allows or denies machines to make connections.

An iSCSI node name is called the iSCSI Qualified Name (iqn). The iSCSI Qualified Name consists of the following entities:

- iqn—Prefix for every iSCSI Qualified Name.

  For example: iqn.
- Date—Date in year-month format where the naming authority owned the domain name that is being used.

  For example, October 2002 would be 2002-10.
- Reverse domain name of the naming authority (iSCSI card/driver vendor).

  For example, the name authoring of Aum.com would be listed as com.Aum.
- A field that can list a variety of components such as product types, serial numbers, host identifiers, hostnames, or other identifying information.

  For example, a machine with the hostname of win2003 would be listed as win2003.

An example of an iqn of a machine called Exchange-backup from the domain Aum.com that obtained its registration in June of 1994 would be iqn.1994-06.com.Aum:Exchange-backup. See Figure 8.31.

Each iSCSI storage device will contain a logical list, referred to as an iGroup or iSCSI zone, in order to be a part of an iSNS domain on an iSNS server, both of which lists all the iSCSI Targets, iSCSI node names, and LUNs that may access each other. Similar to how VLANs are used on IP switches and zones are used on Fibre Channel switches, an iGroup/iSCSI zone and iSNS domains will group all entities that have the permission to connect to each other. The groups and domains are authorization values that are based on each entity's Initiator Node Name.

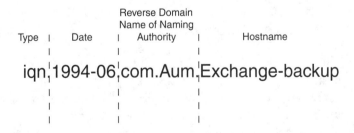

Figure 8.31 iSCSI Qualified Name format.

iSCSI LUN GROUPS (iGROUPS)

In order for an iSCSI client to connect to an iSCSI Target, the iSCSI node name should belong to an iGroup or an iSNS domain. If the iSCSI node name exists, the client will be allowed to connect. If it does not belong to the iGroup or iSNS domain, it will be denied. Once it is authorized, it will be asked to authenticate; however, if authentication is disabled, which is the default in most iSCSI devices, the client will be allowed to connect to the iSCSI Target and mount LUNs immediately after authorization. Figure 8.32 shows an example.

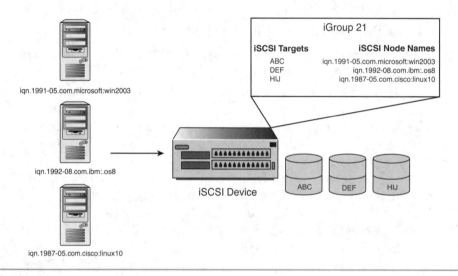

Figure 8.32   iSCSI authorization group.

In Figure 8.32, all the iSCSI node names in iGroup 21 are authorized to connect to LUNs ABC, DEF, and HIJ. This method logically organizes iSCSI node names and LUNs on the iSCSI network.

While iGroups, iSCSI node names, and iSCSI Targets are a great way to logically organize and allocate storage, they do not do much for security. The first issue is that iSCSI node names, the entities used to identify an iSCSI machine, can be changed (spoofed) to anything. Any value that is used for authorization should not be a value that can be changed. For example, your name can be legally changed to anything; therefore, it is not used by your bank to solely identify you. When you walk into your bank, they do ask you for your name, but they will ask you a few other questions as well as for a picture ID and maybe even a password to ensure you are who you say you are. With iSCSI authorization, there is none of that. It is the equivalent of someone changing their name to Bill Gates's (spoofing their iSCSI node name), walking into a bank (connecting to an iSCSI storage device), and getting access to all of Bill Gates' accounts (accessing the gigabytes of data). Any machine can change or spoof the iSCSI node name to be the value of another iSCSI node name. This allows any machine to impersonate another machine and get access to their data.

Another issue with iSCSI is the ability to guess an iSCSI node name. The iSCSI Qualified Name format can be guessed with relative ease. The first parameter will always be iqn. The next two parameters will be the date and the reverse domain name from the naming authority. The two entities can be identified easily by knowing the naming authority and their date of registration. For example, Microsoft, IBM, and Cisco iSCSI drivers will appear as com.Microsoft, com.IBM, and com.Cisco, respectively. Also, it is easy to look up when the naming authority registered with the IEEE, such as May of 1991 (1991-05), May of 1987 (1987-05), and August of 1992 (1992-08), respectively. This allows an attacker to enumerate 75% of the iqn without lifting a finger. The last section of the iqn is the optional section, which is the only true variable section of the iqn. The optional section can display a variety of items. For example, HP usually appends the hostname and a partition identifier. A Microsoft iSCSI driver appends the hostname of the machine. Since a machine's hostname can be enumerated easily from the network, this allows all parts of an iqn to be guessed or enumerated, which is not so good since it is the only entity required for security. An attacker can write a simple script that enumerates the network for all the windows hostnames, which is easily done through DNS or WINS, and append that information to `iqn.1991-05.com.Microsoft`. Eventually, the correct hostname and iqn prefix will be sent to the iSCSI storage device and allow the attacker to access the data. If the hostname is not being used for the optional section, it still can simply be sniffed over the network, as shown in the enumeration section, which is a severe problem. Authorization is the only entity that is required in iSCSI security; however, it is spoofable, and it can be captured by any attacker over the network in the clear. If security had a "three strikes and you're out" rule, this would be it. An entity that is spoofable, clear-text, and the only entity required for security does not fare well in terms of data defense. Furthermore, since iSCSI has the interconnectivity of IP networks, including internal and external networks, the primary attack threshold is significant. Complete the following steps to enumerate, spoof, and connect to an iSCSI Target.

ASSESSMENT EXERCISE

Figure 8.33 is the example architecture for the assessment exercise.

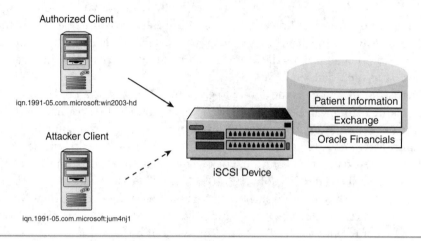

Figure 8.33   Example architecture.

1. Open Ethereal (Start -> Programs -> Ethereal -> Ethereal).
2. From the menu bar, select Capture -> Start.
3. Select the correct network card from the Interface drop-down box.
4. Under the Display Options, check Update list of packets in real time and Automatic scrolling in live capture. Select OK.
5. You are now sniffing all communications to/from the iSCSI device and the network. Once any iSCSI communication occurs over port 3205 or 3260, Ethereal will display the packet. In the Protocol column, you will see iSCSI for all communication over port 3205 and iSNS for all communication for port 3260. See Figure 8.34 for our captured iSCSI communication.
6. Now that we have sniffed and captured the iSCSI communication, we can double-click on the packet in Ethereal to view the contents. Because all the communication is in clear-text, all the contents of the communication will be readable to us.

7. Figure 8.35 shows the iSCSI Node Name from an iSCSI Packet, which is `iqn.1991-05.com.microsoft.:win2003-hd`. This iSCSI Node Name is the only required value needed to access the iSCSI Target.

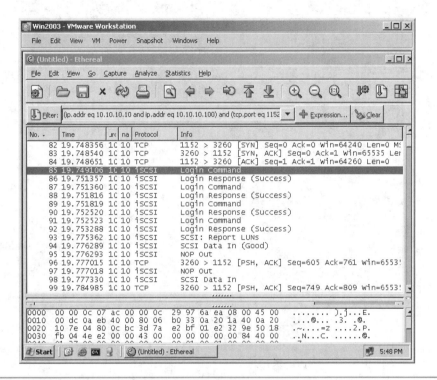

Figure 8.34 iSCSI communication.

8. Open the iSCSI Initiator:

   a. Start -> Programs -> Microsoft iSCSI Initiator -> Configure Initiator.

9. Click on the Initiator Settings tab. See Figure 8.36.

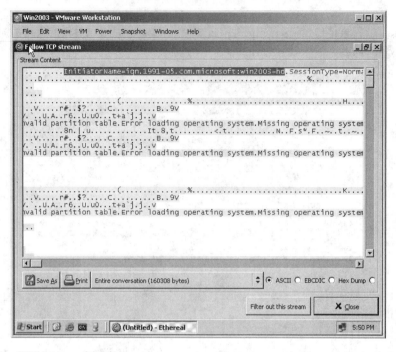

Figure 8.35   iSCSI Initiator Node Name.

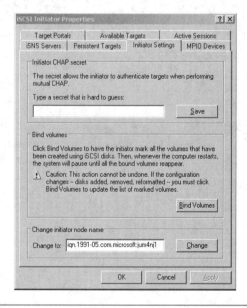

Figure 8.36   Initiator Settings tab.

10. At the bottom of the tab, change the initiator node name to the value captured in step 7 (`iqn.1991-05.microsoft.:win2003-hd`) and select OK. See Figure 8.37.

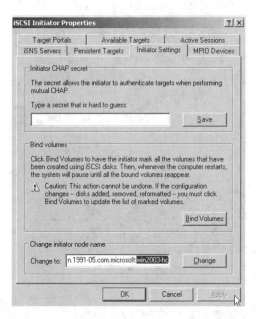

Figure 8.37 Changed iSCSI node name.

11. Click on the Target Portals tab and select Add.

12. Type the IP address of the iSCSI Target, which is **10.10.10.100**, and select OK. Note that this is the IP address of the iSCSI Target that was captured in step 6. See Figure 8.38.

13. Click on the Available Targets tab. Notice the iSCSI Targets that are now available. Note that this is only available due to the fact that the iSCSI client has the correct iSCSI node name. If the iSCSI node name was incorrect, no available targets would appear. Since the client has not initiated the connection yet, it shows up as inactive. See Figure 8.39.

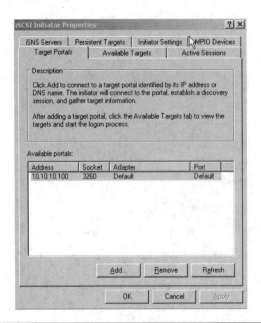

Figure 8.38   Target portals.

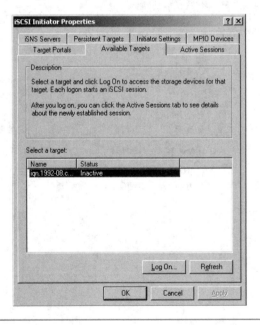

Figure 8.39   Available targets.

14. Highlight a target and select Logon and OK in the logon menu. Since the iSCSI node name is correct, the tab will now change from inactive to connect. See Figure 8.40.

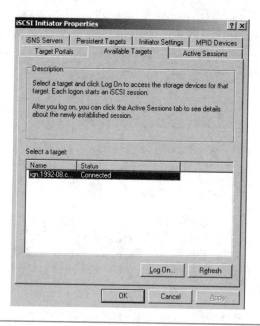

Figure 8.40 Connected targets.

15. Click on Active Session tab. Notice that the connection now appears as active. See Figure 8.41.

16. Done! You have now connected to the iSCSI Target by spoofing your iSCSI node name. Open up Disk Manager to see the new SCSI volumes:

a. Start -> Programs -> Administrative Tools -> Computer Management.

i. Select Disk Management from the left pane. See Figure 8.42.

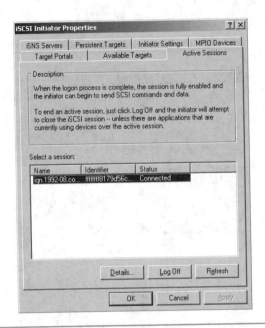

Figure 8.41   Active Sessions tab.

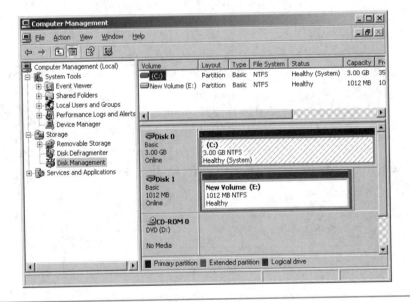

Figure 8.42   Disk management.

17. Double-click on My Computer from your desktop. If the volume (LUN) you just mounted is formatted for Windows (FAT, FAT32, or NTFS), the volume will now appear as another hard drive. It appears as "New Volume" in Figure 8.43.

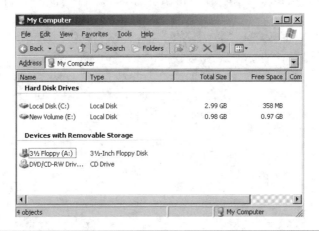

Figure 8.43 iSCSI volume.

At this point, there are two iSCSI node names—the original and now yours that is spoofed—trying to access the same volume (LUN). Some iSCSI target vendors will automatically drop the first connection in favor of the second, allowing the attacker who has spoofed the iQN to gain full control of the data and leaving the authorized client with nothing. This is supported in order to support failover in the case of a bad iSCSI Initiator. Some other iSCSI storage devices are not built to have two iSCSI node names connect to the same LUN at the same time. Unlike CIFS and NFS mounts where multiple users/machines can access the same mount point, Fibre Channel and iSCSI SANs are built to only have one machine at a time. At this point, both iSCSI clients will be unable to access the iSCSI volume, confusing the iSCSI storage device. This equates into a successful denial-of-service attack for the iSCSI volume. The legitimate iSCSI node name does not relinquish control of the volume; however, it doesn't maintain full control either. The original iSCSI node name will have intermittent access to the remote drive and possibly lose all real-time access to it. Furthermore, the spoofed iSCSI node name doesn't have full access to the drive either—only the ability to make it unavailable to the network. If this was an exchange server, this would be a severe problem since all mailboxes will suddenly disappear for the server. It most situations, the actual SAN administrator will troubleshoot the machine and possibly reboot or reinitialize the service. Once the legitimate server is rebooted or reinitialized, it relinquishes control of the iSCSI Target. After the original iSCSI client relinquishes control (via reboot or restarting the service), the spoofed iSCSI client captures full control of the volume since there are not two requestors anymore but just one. While this may only last 5 or 10 minutes until the legitimate machines reboots or attempts to reconnect, the attacker is given full access to the data drive and can browse the volume freely, as shown in Figure 8.44.

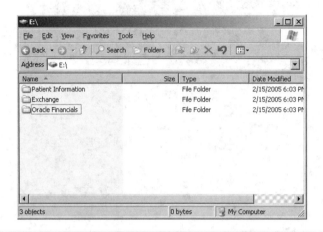

Figure 8.44   Full access to iSCSI volume.

The security issue with authorization and iSCSI is that it should not be used as the sole security control. It is probably good enough if it is used with some other proper security control, such as authentication or encryption. For example, CIFS uses IP addresses for authorization, which also can be spoofed; however, it requires authentication via Kerberos. Furthermore, since iSCSI uses existing IP networks, which is insecure no matter if it is the Internet or the internal network, the lack of required authentication and the implementation of poor authorization makes the default settings on iSCSI security an easy and extremely devastating target.

DOMAIN HOPPING ATTACKS

Another critical and devastating attack vector is the domain hopping attack, which follows the principals of VLAN hopping and zone hopping attacks. iSNS servers create discovery domains that are used to logically segment iSCSI node and targets in groups, similar to iGroup mentioned previously. The use of discovery domain is a great method to logically segment trusted groups for database, mail servers, file servers, or simply core applications from other nodes that should not have access to these trusted entities. Furthermore, certain iSCSI Targets (LUNs) will be grouped together with the correct iSCSI clients in order to ensure the right data store gets allocated to the right client. Figure 8.45 shows example discovery domains on an iSNS server.

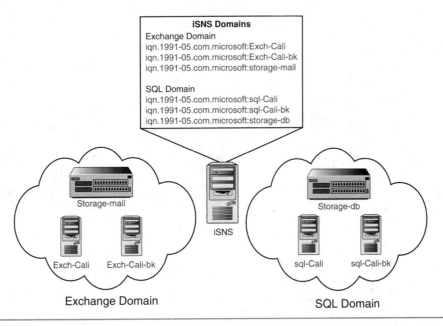

Figure 8.45 iSNS domains.

The issues with iSNS domains, similar to Fibre Channel zones, are that they rely on the iQN value of a node for identification. If a node simply spoofs the iQN value to match the iQN of their target, the iSNS server will automatically update and overwrite the legitimate node's information with the attacker's spoofed information. This allows any iSCSI client to simply hop across domains as he or she chooses by changing (spoofing) their iQN values. This attack is extremely devastating if iSNS domains are used for security purposes or if they are considered to be trusted. For example, separate domains can be set up for logical segmentation of nodes and targets. Furthermore, separate domains can also be set up to secure servers with critical access from servers with non-critical access. However, if one of the servers in a trusted domain is spoofed, not only is their data compromised, but the attacker can make the legitimate server disappear in the eyes of the iSNS server. It can also start enumerating information from other servers in this trusted domain to attack them at a later date. Domain hopping attacks can completely undermine the entire process of creating separate domains for security or segmentation purposes. The following example describes the process of a domain hopping attack.

EXAMPLE EXERCISE

Figure 8.46 is the architecture used for this example.

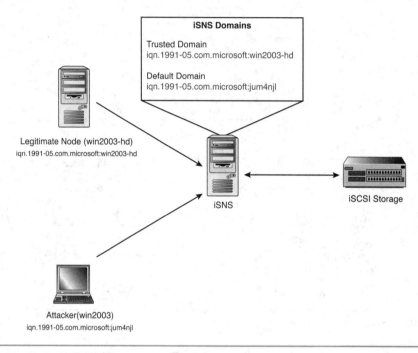

iSNS Domains

Trusted Domain
iqn.1991-05.com.microsoft:win2003-hd

Default Domain
iqn.1991-05.com.microsoft:jum4njl

Legitimate Node (win2003-hd)
iqn.1991-05.com.microsoft:win2003-hd

iSNS

iSCSI Storage

Attacker(win2003)
iqn.1991-05.com.microsoft:jum4njl

Figure 8.46   Example iSNS architecture.

1. Figure 8.47 shows the Trusted Discovery Domain section on the iSNS server, which consists of the iSCSI client of iqn.1991-05.com.microsoft:win2003-hd with the host name of win2003-hd (Entity column).

2. Figure 8.48 shows the Default Discovery Domain section on the iSNS server, which consists of the iSCSI client of iqn.1991-05.com.microsoft:jum4nj1 with the host name of jum4nj1 (Entity column).

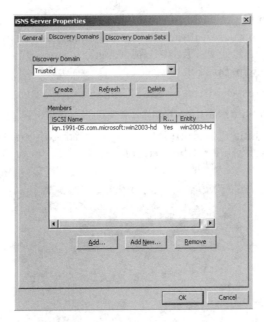

Figure 8.47 Trusted iSNS domain.

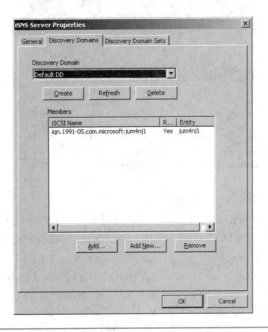

Figure 8.48 Default Discovery Domain (untrusted).

3. We will now open the iSCSI Initiator on the attacker's machine, which has the IQN of iqn.1991-05.com.microsoft:jum4nj1 and the hostname of jum4nj1, and change IQN value to the node in the Trusted node, which is iqn.1991-05.com.microsoft:win2003-hd.

    a. Start -> Programs -> Microsoft iSCSI Initiator -> Configure Initiator.

    b. Click on the Initiator Settings tab.

    c. Change the existing IQN from 1991-05.com.microsoft:jum4nj1 to 1991-05.com.microsoft:win2003-hd. See Figure 8.49.

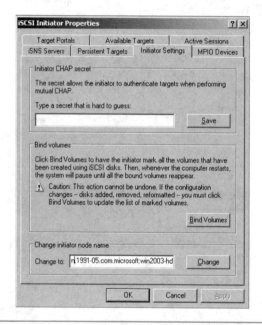

Figure 8.49   Attacker in Default Discovery Domain spoofing their IQN value.

    d. Reboot the attacker's machine.

4. After the attacker's machine is rebooted, we will go back to our iSNS server and open the Trusted Discovery Domain section, as shown in Figure 8.50.

    Notice that the entity (hostname) that is labeled as jum4nj1 is now being recognized in as iqn.1991-05.com.microsoft:win2003-hd, which used to belong to the real node with the entity (hostname) of win2003-hd. Also notice that there is only one entry now. After the attacker changed the IQN value, the iSNS server simply overwrote the information of the legitimate and trusted node with the spoofed information of the untrusted node. Additionally, since the original IQN of the attacker was changed, the iSNS server simply erased it from its table. Meanwhile the legitimate node has also virtually disappeared from the iSNS server. This attack not only hops across iSNS domains and allows an attacker to compromise data; it also performs a denial-of-service attack by completely removing the legitimate node of the storage network.

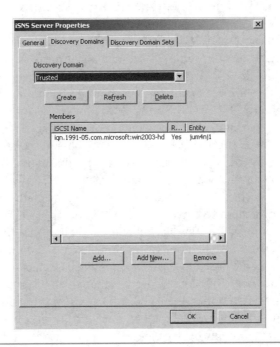

Figure 8.50 Attacker successfully hopping across domains.

5. Done! The attacker has just hopped across domains, compromised data belonging to the legitimate node, and performed a denial-of-service attack on the real node—all with one attack.

ENCRYPTION

Encryption is one of the best security features with iSCSI SANs. Unlike Fibre Channel SANs, iSCSI security supports IPSec encryption natively, which is a big win for security. The issues with iSCSI authentication become less of a problem if IPSec has been enabled from an iSCSI storage device to any iSCSI client.

IPSec is a layer 2 protocol that encrypts traffic before it gets to the upper layers. Unlike other encryption protocols like SSH or SSL, which work at layer 3 and above in the OSI model, IPSec can encrypt traffic at the lower levels before they move up the TCP stack. iSCSI packets, such as authentication or authorization communication, can still use the insecure clear-text methods; however, it will be encrypted at lower levels and unreadable to anonymous attackers sniffing the network. Since iSCSI security has numerous entities that pass the network in clear-text and are critical for data access, such as CHAP usernames, CHAP challenge messages, CHAP IDs, and iSCSI node names, the ability to encrypt the communication at lower levels dramatically improves the security model and mitigates many attacks discussed in this chapter. The key challenge of iSCSI and IPSec is the performance impact that it has, which might be too much to bear for most organizations with enterprise class iSCSI storage networks. For more information on iSCSI and IPSec, refer to Chapter 11, "Securing iSCSI."

Since iSCSI's implementation of IPSec relies on pre-shared secrets, it is very important that the key is protected. Since the iSCSI drivers produced by Microsoft, Cisco, IBM, and HP do not require any authentication to open the iSCSI software, the secret key that is held in the software needs to be secured. Unfortunately, this falls to the point made earlier about operating system security since the asterisks or blackened circles that hold the secret key information can be revealed by many security tools including Cain and Abel. Cain and Abel can be installed on any machine and contains a program called Box Revealer. Box Revealer can be used to show the hidden characters behind the blackened circles in the iSCSI software. The obvious point is that an attacker has to have the ability to control the operating system that the iSCSI software is running on since this attack cannot be executed over the network; however, this illustrates the earlier point on how operating system security for any device connected to the storage network is imperative. Complete the following steps to reveal the pre-shared secret for IPSec connections.

ASSESSMENT EXERCISE

1. Open the iSCSI Initiator.
   a. Start -> Programs -> Microsoft iSCSI Initiator -> Configure Initiator.
2. Click on the Target Portals tab.
3. Select Add and type the IP address of the iSCSI Target.
4. Select the Advance button.
5. Click on the IPSec tab.
6. Check the Enabled the IPSec settings checkbox.

7. Type the pre-shared string of **hackmeamadeus** in the pre-shared key textbox (leave the window open).

8. Now open Cain and Abel:

   a. Start -> Programs -> Cain -> Cain.

9. From the menu bar, select Tools -> Box Revealer.

10. Done! At this point, you should see the IPSec pre-shared secret that is being used by the iSCSI client. See Figure 8.51 for details.

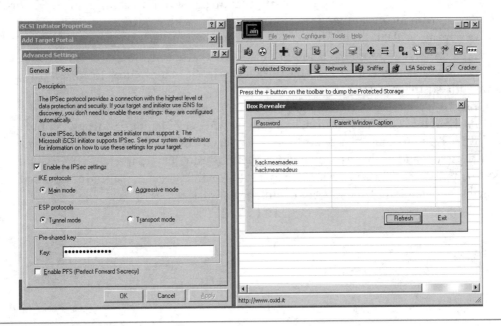

Figure 8.51 Revealed IPSec shared secret.

IPSec is definitely the ideal method to implement security inside iSCSI networks, but may have performance issues since each packet needs to be encrypted before being sent over the network. Also, while the complexity of implementing IPSec between two servers is minimal, implementing IPSec between 50 or 100 iSCSI clients and targets is not an easy thing to do since pre-shared keys will have to be set up and remembered for each one of those entities. Nevertheless, any storage device holding sensitive information or confidential data should strongly consider implementing IPSec for the iSCSI storage networks.

SUMMARY

In this chapter, we reviewed several aspects of iSCSI security. The basics told us that iSCSI has some strong security possibilities (CHAP and IPSec), but is vulnerable to some very common and trivial security attacks (such as clear-text communication, IQN spoofing, CHAP message challenges/offline brute forcing, and username enumeration). We were able to enumerate all types of information from iSCSI networks, including iSCSI communication, iSCSI Targets/devices, iSCSI LUNs, CHAP usernames, CHAP challenge messages, and iSCSI node names. This information allowed us to connect to iSCSI storage devices without any authentication and barely any authorization.

We were also able to see how the only entity required for security, which is authorization, can be easily subverted and compromised. The key idea from this chapter is that iSCSI does not come secure out of the box; however, it can be secured to an acceptable level with existing features.

This chapter wraps up our storage networking chapters where we discussed Fibre Channel SANs in Chapters 2 through 4, NAS networks in Chapters 5 through 7, and iSCSI SANs in this chapter. The next three chapters focus on defenses for each of the security issues and problems shown in Chapters 2 through 8. Chapters 9, 10, and 11 discuss best practices for securing storage to limit the ability for many of the attacks that are possible in default implementations of storage networks.

PART IV
STORAGE DEFENSES

Securing Fibre Channel SANs

Protecting Fibre Channel SANs from the security weaknesses, exploits, and attacks demonstrated in Chapters 2 through 4 is very important for a secure storage network. Additionally, a secure storage network is equally as important, if not more, for stable, functional, and highly available storage. This chapter is dedicated to the defenses and best practices for all attacks shown in Chapters 2 through 4. The primary focus will be on defenses and best practices for securing storage. The goal is to discuss and demonstrate the existing features, tools, and configurations available in storage networks that can mitigate the security weaknesses and attacks discussed earlier.

Now that we understand the security weaknesses and attack methods, we are better equipped and more knowledgeable to secure storage. In order to protect any entity, a deep understanding of the real attacks that malicious users perform should be known. The ability to understand the attacks and use the tools allows security architects and storage administrators to initially pinpoint popular attack classes first for proper defenses. This allows a strong defense for the entire environment as well as targeted defenses for the primary attack methods. For example, when parking a car in a mall parking lot, it is best to ensure that it has been locked, all valuables have been moved to the trunk or under the seat, and a "Secured By" sticker has been placed on the car to inform potential attackers that the car has an alarm. All these things help prevent a car from being targeted first. If there are two cars right next to each other and one has not locked the door and has a brand new laptop sitting on the backseat, an attacker will probably target that car first before the locked car with no valuables in sight. The same idea applies to storage networks. If an internal employee or attacker has targeted storage devices for data, it is best to ensure the storage network has covered the basics to motivate the attacker to move onto another target.

This chapter will discuss the defenses, best practices, and mitigating controls for SAN attacks. After each security defense is discussed, all the attacks it is protecting against will be listed. This will clearly define which security practices defend against which attacks. The following attacks were described in Chapters 2 through 4 and are the primary focus for this chapter:

SAN Attacks

- Session hijacking
- Man-in-the-Middle attacks
- Name server pollution
- LUN masking
- WWN spoofing
- Zone hopping (WWN)
- Zone hopping (routing)
- E-port replication
- Switch management

Securing SANs

As shown in Chapters 2 through 4, Fibre Channel SANs have plenty of security and data protection problems. The fact is that many SANs are often designed with the assumption that Fibre Channel networks are inaccessible, which is simply false. It is true that they are not as assessable as some other storage networks, including NAS or iSCSI; however, a storage management workstation, a SAN administrator's Windows XP machine, an IP interface on Fibre Channel switches, and especially a poorly configured (default) server with an HBA are more than enough avenues for attackers to get into a SAN. If any server or management station that is connected to the SAN has ever been infected with a virus or worm (for example, SQL slammer), then the SAN is probably more accessible to attackers. Additionally, with current and emerging regulations on data protection standards, data in a storage network must support several standard practices for security, where the obscurity of a communication medium (Fibre Channel) is not a legitimate security control. Often times security measures are used to protect against unauthorized users; however, security in Fibre Channel SANs are also essential in order to protect data from internal employees who can access the SAN very easily. Furthermore, accidental configuration changes, implementation mistakes, and incorrect modification for storage devices from authorized users are another critical aspect of SAN security. Remember from Chapter 1, "Introduction to Storage Security," that availability is a core aspect of security, which is extremely important for SAN administrators. From either perspective, SAN security is imperative for organizations. We will discuss Fibre Channel SAN security defenses according to the following areas:

- Fibre Channel Layer 2
- Authentication
- WWNs
- LUN masking
- Zoning and VSANs
- Port type security
- Port security
- Switch security
- Name server queries
- Securing storage tapes with encryption

FIBRE CHANNEL LAYER 2

The first set of defenses we will discuss are for layer 2 Fibre Channel attacks. Fibre Channel frames, specifically sequence control numbers, sequences ID, source/destination addresses, and FLOGI and PLOGI processes, are vulnerable due to the lack of authentication. Session exchanges, routing updates, and joining the fabric all are absent of one-way or mutual authentication between a client node and the SAN fabric. This leaves the stability and security of the fabric infrastructure open to weaknesses. The lack of authentication with a communication medium is nothing new to security architects. IP networks had the same problem for many years (and still do). The methods used to prevent these attacks in IP networks are with encryption, integrity checking, and authentication, which are also true for Fibre Channel networks. Fibre Channel SANs that can adopt authentication or encryption between nodes will be able to prevent layer 2 Fibre Channel attacks on a SAN fabric. Although the access profile is low, proper integrity checking and confidentiality of frames can mitigate security issues but can also create a higher level of availability for the SAN. The two methods of protection against the attacks are next and are specified in the Fibre Channel Security Protocol (FC-SP):

- Encapsulating Security Protocol (ESP): www.t11.org/ftp/t11/pub/fc/sp/03-149v0.pdf
- Authentication Headers (AH): www.t11.org/ftp/t11/pub/fc/sp/03-149v0.pdf

Encapsulating Security Protocol (ESP) can be used to provide encryption or authentication of Fibre Channel frames to and from switches, client nodes, and storage controllers. Authentication is also something to consider, but will not necessarily protect against network layer attacks; however, it will prevent other attacks discussed in the next section. In order for layer 2 Fibre Channel attacks to be protected, the session information, the route update process, and the PLOGI/FLOGI process should be encrypted to prevent attackers from gaining the correct information in the frame to execute an attack.

Another method to prevent attacks that will not have the performance hit of encryption (confidentiality) in Fibre Channel frames is Authentication Headers (AH), using MD5 or SHA1 hashes. AH can be used to provide integrity for each frame and a layer of virtual authentication. In each of the attacks described in Chapter 2, "SANs: Fibre Channel Security," most of the attacks involve the receiving entity requiring no form of authentication of Fibre Channel frames. The receiving entity simply trusts that the frames are being sent to it from a client node. The receiving entity does not perform any validation or authentication of the client node to ensure they are who they say they are. AH can be used to provide the level of integrity and authentication on the frame itself. (Note: Do not confuse authentication of frames with authentication of client nodes themselves.) AH allows a switch to ensure that it is speaking to the authorized host on the fabric and not a malicious node that has captured session information or spoofed port addresses. AH has the ability to create a hash for each frame and append it to the frame. If any modifications are conducted on the frame or if another frame is sent with the incorrect hash, the receiving entity will simply drop the frame and classify it as incorrect. Session Hijacking, Man-in-the-Middle, and Name Server Pollution attacks either modify an existing frame or actually create a new frame and send it to their target on the fabric. If AH were being used, all the attacks would be useless, preventing the attacker from compromising data or even creating denial-of-service attacks in the SAN. Additionally, since AH provide hash services for each frame; the performance impact would be quite small since no encryption is being conducted. An example of AH is shown in Figure 9.1.

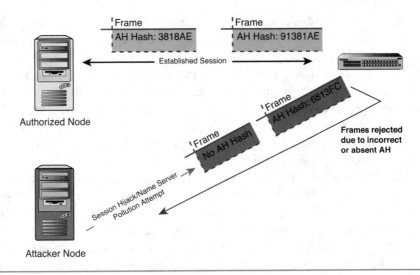

Figure 9.1 Headers.

The ability to implement Authentication Headers between Fibre Channel switches, client HBAs, and storage controllers is a significant security measure against Session Hijacking, Man-in-the-Middle attacks, and Name Server Pollution. Unfortunately, the adoption of AH in HBAs, Fibre Channel switches, or storage controllers is not widely adopted yet; however, many security issues have been making their way through T11 committees and product vendors, and it would not be surprising if they were supported by major vendors at the publication of this book.

LAYER 2 SECURITY

The use of frame integrity or frame encryption would mitigate the issues with Fibre Channel layer 2; however, the security weakness with session identifiers and the FLOGI/PLOGI process would still exist, but not be as easy to exploit. An ideal method to mitigate against these attacks is to actually improve the security of the Fibre Channel frame, which could start with the storage vendors implementing a stronger form of session management and improving the FLOGI/PLOGI process.

A stronger session management method in Fibre Channel communication would be to implement an unpredictable, random method for sequence control numbers. Instead of incrementing the Seq_CNT by one for each subsequent frame, it would be better to make the number a random and unpredictable number. Both the initial sequence number in IP packets and session identifiers in application cookies, both of which were also vulnerable to this attack, have prevented these attack types by implementing random, unpredictable session information for session management. Unlike the encryption solution, changing the Seq_CNT value would not have any affect on the performance of the fabric since the change is a value change to the existing communication, which does not add any types of additional overhead to each frame. In addition to making the Seq_CNT an unpredictable and random number, it would also be ideal for the sequence ID not to be a static number. Changing the Seq_ID to a non-static number would make it more difficult for an attacker to identify the session they want to tamper with. A non-static variable number would make the session management entities in the fabric harder to predict and, therefore, harder to compromise.

In addition to improving the state management values, the implementation of some type of validation in the FLOGI and PLOGI process would prevent Name Server Pollution attacks. For example, if a node that is joining the fabric performs a FLOGI, some type of validation (or authentication) that verifies the frame's header information (source address, destination address, WWNs) is correct would strengthen the security of the process. Furthermore, with the PLOGI process, taking some type of verification from the fabric that ensures the information in the PLOGI came directly from the fabric ACC frame would also improve the security. For example, a Fibre Channel node should not be able to perform a PLOGI without a previous FLOGI. Furthermore, the PLOGI information that is submitted by the Fibre Channel node should have the exact information that was sent by the fabric's ACC frame (the Fibre Channel switch) in response to the initial FLOGI frame. Any PLOGI frame without a corresponding FLOGI or without the same information that was granted by the ACC frame should be automatically discarded. Some IP solutions have implemented protections against similar attacks with the use of 802.1x, which can implement packet authentication that is invisible to the end user. Similarly, if there is some type of per-frame authentication, separate from Authentication Headers, that is invisible to end users, this could also prevent Name Server Pollution during the FLOGI and PLOGI without requiring additional overhead for the process.

Fibre Channel Layer 2 security, either with the use of encryption or frame-level changes, can mitigate the following attacks:

- Session hijacking
- Man-in-the-Middle
- Name server pollution

AUTHENTICATION

The lack of authentication is a major problem for storage fabrics. Unlike every other entity that stores large volumes of data, authentication parameters were initially overlooked for implementation and absent in most SANs. The problem became amplified when the authorization parameters used in the fabric were vulnerable to spoofing attacks, which equates to the ability for any node on the fabric to change their authorization values (their WWNs) and get access to LUNs. If authentication parameters were available, the ability to spoof a WWN would be less of an issue due to the fact that valid authentication must take place regardless of any WWNs that are sent by a potential attacker. Because entities don't need to be authenticated, but only authorized, attackers can become whomever they want in the storage fabric as long as no one chooses to authenticate them. This would be equivalent to a bank asking a customer only for their bank number and not a picture ID or PIN to access their funds. While one can assume that a person with the correct bank number is the right person to access the account, one can also assume that someone could have easily stolen that bank number. Without the bank asking for a picture ID or PIN, the account number would be the only entity required to steal all the money. In SANs, there are several methods that may be used for authentication. Many vendors have not fully supported one or the other; however, the ability to provide some type of authentication will be a significant security control for Fibre Channel SANs. The following are a few options that provide authentication for SANs:

- FC-SP
- DH-CHAP
- FCAP
- FCPAP
- CT authentication

FC-SP

Fibre Channel Security Protocols (FC-SP) are developed by the T11 committee (www.t11.org) to implement security in Fibre Channel fabrics. The standard involves authentication, which will be the primary focus of our discussion, the set up of keys, and to provide integrity and confidentiality to each Fibre Channel frame. FC-SP involves a variety of different security authentication methods, including Diffie-Hellman CHAP

(DH-DHCP), Fibre Channel Authentication Protocol (FCAP), Fibre Channel Password Authentication Protocol (FCPAP), and Common Transport (CT) Authentication.

Diffie-Hellman CHAP (DH-CHAP) can be used for authentication between Fibre Channel switches and is the standard for Fibre Channel Security Protocol (FC-SP). DH-CHAP will allow for the authentication between Fibre Channel client nodes and switches, or Fibre Channel storage controllers and switches. Similar to how iSCSI uses CHAP for authentication procedures, Fibre Channel infrastructures can use DH-CHAP for authentication. However, the use of DH-CHAP is also vulnerable to offline diction-ary attacks, which was described in detail with CHAP in Chapter 8, "SANs: iSCSI Security." In DH-CHAP, either a client node with an HBA, a switch, or a storage con-troller can be an authentication initiator or authentication responder. Depending on which entity initiated the authentication process first will determine which entity will be the initiator or the responder. If DH-CHAP were used, the following procedures would be required between any node on the SAN fabric:

1. An authentication initiator will send a Auth_Node message to the Authentication Responder to negotiate the hash functions. The Auth_Node message will contain the node_name, hash functions (SHA1 or MD5), and the usable Diffie-Hellman group identifiers.

2. The authentication responder will reply with a challenge message with their Node_name, hash function (SHA1 or MD5), and DH groups information.

  a. Note: It is possible for either the requestor or initiator to not send the DH infor-mation, leaving the authentication as CHAP only.

3. The authentication initiator will send a reply message with the response of the chal-lenge and the DH information. The response will be a combination of the challenge, shared secret, and the hash value (SHA1 or MD5).

  a. Note: The initiator can also send a challenge to the responder for mutual authen-tication.

4. If the response is correct, the responder will send a success message, which means the initiator has been authenticated.

5. Done!

Similar to CHAP attacks with iSCSI, DH-CHAP in Fibre Channel can potentially have security issues; however, enabling DH-CHAP for authentication is far better than relying on WWN for security. The first possible weakness is if the intervals on when a new chal-lenge message sent by the responder do not occur often enough. For example, if a chal-lenge message is sent once every 30 minutes by the responder, an attacker that captures the hash value from step 3 can simply replay that value to the responder and log in. The responder would accept it since it contains the correct hash value. If the responder sends out a new challenge message to the client, the old hash value obtained by the attacker would be incorrect; hence defeating the replay attack by the unauthorized user. The interval time where a new challenge is sent to the responder is key to defeating replay attacks with DH-CHAP.

The second weakness is the reflection of the CHAP message challenge existing across multiple connections. The message challenge is the key entity in the hash. As stated previously, a client would take its secret and the challenge from the responder and make an SHA1 or MD5 hash value. The value is sent to the authenticator over the network. The attack would involve an attacker beginning an authentication process. It will receive a challenge from the responder. The problem here is the attacker does not know the secret, so they cannot formulate the correct hash. However, the attacker can open a completely separate second connection to the responder. The attacker can send the challenge that was just sent to it by the responder back to the responder on the second connection as if the responder is trying to authenticate to the initiator, where the initiator is sending the challenge (step 2 in the previous steps). The responder would receive the challenge on the second connection (the same challenge it just sent to the attacker in the first connection), combine it with the secret, and make a hash value of it and send it to the attacker. The attacker now has the correct hash value that is made of the same challenge that is being used by the responder on the first connection and the real secret. The attacker can now present the hash value from the second connection to the client on first connection. The client would see the correct hash value on the first connection and authenticate the attacker without the attacker ever knowing the secret. The preceding steps have been outlined in Figure 9.2.

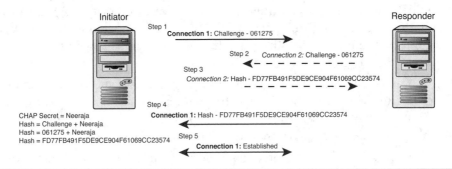

Figure 9.2   CHAP weaknesses.

It should be noted that if the challenge message does not become stale or if it is reflected across connections, DH-CHAP is a very secure method to perform authentication, especially over WWN authorization security.

The third weakness of DH-CHAP is that it is vulnerable to an offline dictionary attack, also mentioned in Chapter 8. Because the message challenge and hash can be sniffed over the network, an attacker can create hashes from a large dictionary of words and the message challenge. Once one of the hashes match the hash sniffed over the network, the attacker knows the dictionary word used to make the hash as the password. For more information and a sample tool, refer to Chapter 8's CHAP section.

FCAP

Fibre Channel Authentication Protocol is an optional method for authentication in a SAN based on digital certificates. Two Fibre Channel nodes must share a secret key that is used for digital certificates, at which time they can mutually authenticate each other and can communicate securely. If FCAP were used, the following procedures would be required between any node on the SAN fabric:

1. An authentication initiator will send an Auth_Node message to the Authentication Responder to negotiate the hash functions. The Auth_Node message will contain the node_name, FCAP signal, hash functions, and the useable Diffie-Hellman group identifiers.

2. The authentication responder with reply with a FCAP_Request message, which will include the responder's digital certificate of the responder, the selected hash function, the DH group, and a random nonce.

3. The initiator will verify the certificate with a Certificate Authority (CA) and generate a random number. After verification, it will send an FCAP_Acknowledge message that contains a random nonce, the generated random number, the initiator digital certificate, the DH group, and its signature.

4. The responder will receive the FCAP_Acknowledge message and verify the certificate of the initiator with the CA and its signature with its public key. It will also generate a different random number. The responder will then send an FCAP_Confirm message with the responder's signature and DH group.

5. The initiator will verify the signature with the responder's public key. After it verifies the signature, it now has all the entities to calculate the shared key used by the responder (stored nonce, DH group parameter, hash value). At this time, both sides have the shared key that is used for the digital certificates.

6. The responder will then send an FCAP_Confirm message with a signature and DH group.

7. The initiator will receive the FCAP_Confirm message and will verify the signature with the responder's public key and then use its stored nonce, the DH group, and the hash value to ensure they match.

8. The initiator will then send an Auth_Done message. This will indicate that FCAP has completed successfully.

FCPAP

Fibre Channel Password Authentication Protocol (FCPAP) is also another optional method for authentication in a SAN that uses SRP. FCPAP offers mutual authentication and key exchanges for SAN components based on a shared secret key. SRP requires a password, a salt, and a verifier. If FCPAP were used, the following procedures would be required between any node on the SAN fabric:

1. An authentication initiator will send a Auth_Node message to the authentication responder to negotiate the hash functions. The Auth_Node message will contain the node_name, FCPAP signal, hash functions, and the useable Diffie-Hellman group identifiers.

2. The responder will pick the salt and the verifier, and create a private key value in order to create a public key. It will reply to the initiator with an FCPAP_Init message that contains its name, a one-way hash function that was used to generate the verifier, the DH group parameter, the public key, and the salt.

3. The initiator will receive the FCPAP_Init message and also create a private key in order to create a public key. It will take both public keys (the responder and the initiator) to create a scrambled parameter. The initiator will then create another private key from the salt of the responder and its own password to create an exponential value. The initiator will then take this value, its public key, and the responder's public key, and create a hash. The initiator then sends an FCPAP_Accept message, which has its public key and this new hash.

   a. If a null salt is used, the unique verifier mode is used.

   b. If the responder's salt is used, it will be use the shared verifier mode.

4. The responder will receive an FCPAP_Accept message and will also compute the scrambled parameter, the exponential value, and the hash value. If all values agree, the responder will send an FCPAP_Complete message with the other hash that is derived from the public key of the initiator, the first hash, and the session key.

5. The initiator will receive the FCPAP_Complete message and also compute the second hash from its public key, the first hash, and the session key. If they match, it will send an Auth_Done message to the responder signaling successfully authentication.

Sounds simple, right? Actually, DH-CHAP, FCAP, and FCPAP are all invisible to the end user, but it is important to understand the level of security they bring when compared to using WWNs for authorization. For better reading on FC-SP, refer to the working draft by the T11 committee, specifically David Black, Craig Carlson, Jim Kleinsteiber, Claudio DeSanti, and Larry Hofer, which can be found at ftp://ftp.t10.org/t11/document.03/03-149v2.pdf.

DH-CHAP under FC-SP seems to be widely adopted by the major vendors to date, which will provide the necessary level of authentication to storage fabrics and also allow some type of interoperability from iSCSI SANs to Fibre Channel SANs. The standardization for authentication will be very important for end users to implement authentication within their SAN. Additionally, the interoperability between vendors will also be quite important for authentication to take place correctly.

CT AUTHENTICATION

Common Transport (CT) authentication can be used to authenticate communication that is usually performed for in-band management purposes developed by FC-GS-4. CT authentication provides a security header in the Fibre Channel frame request. The request and response also uses a secret key, unique hash functions, and digital signatures to secure the communication, as described earlier. The use of CT authentication will allow management functions to be secured by in-band communication without relying on out-of-band, which is usually IP, technologies.

The ability to implement authentication in Fibre Channel SANs will mitigate many of the LUN masking, WWN spoofing, zone hopping, and E-port replication attacks discussed earlier. Even if authentication is enabled, authorization parameters such as WWNs can still be spoofed. However, a spoofed WWN with the incorrect authentication does not give the attacker access to the SAN. This is an important concept to understand that is currently absent in many storage architectures. The ability to spoof an existing WWN becomes less of an issue if a valid authentication process is also required for LUN access. While the weaknesses of WWNs still exist, the strengths of authenticating a client node, such as an HBA, will mitigate many of these risks.

The lack of authentication in a storage fabric opens the door for many attackers on the SAN. The use of weak (spoofable) identifiers for authorization and the use of segmentation tools that fully trust the weak (spoofable) identifiers are more vulnerable without authentication being implemented. Using any one of the authentication options previously described will enable organizations to mitigate the following attacks:

- LUN masking
- WWN spoofing
- Zone hopping

WWNs

Although the ability to implement authentication in storage fabric is a great way to mitigate LUN masking, zoning, WWN spoofing, and E-port replication attacks, all SANs applications/devices might not offer the capabilities yet. It is important to understand and discuss what other methods can be used to help prevent these attacks, such as the use of port WWNs, port WWNs and node WWNs, hard zoning, port zoning, and VSANs.

The use of port WWNs can reduce the attack surface for WWN spoofing, but does not fully protect against it. Unlike node WWNs that can be spoofed, port WWNs cannot be changed in an HBA. If LUN masking or zoning tables are using the port WWN values of HBAs, the lack of ability to change the values reduces the ability to gain access to confidential data. However, if the LUN masking properties or zoning tables do not check if an HBA is sending its port WWN or node WWN value, certain attacks against entities using port WWNs are still possible. For example, while attackers cannot change their port WWN, they could change their node WWN to be the port WWN of another entity. Essentially, the attacker will have the port WWN of their own HBA and the port WWN of another HBA in their own node WWN field. When sending this information to a LUN masking entity or zone table, the entities that only check an HBA's port WWN would prevent this attack. Entities that check either an HBA's port WWN or node WWN for the correct WWN value would be vulnerable to this attack. As a best practice, port WWNs should only be used by LUN masking entities and zone tables; however, they should also have the ability to only check an HBA's port WWN value and ignore the node WWN value entirely for any type of authorization processes.

IDENTIFICATION WITH **WWNS**

Many SAN security problems exist due to the fact that WWNs are usually the only entity used for security, but they are spoofable to any value. Using a port WWN is better than using a node WWN, but both values can be spoofed from a node WWN and possibly subvert switch security controls. Another method that is stronger than using only port WWN values for security is the use of both the port WWN and the node WWN together for authorization. For example, every node in a Fibre Channel SAN contains a port WWN and node WWN. Some LUN masking and zoning methods use either port or node WWN for authorization; however, a few vendors are now beginning to use the entire value itself (node WWN plus port WWN) for authorization. If both the port and node WWN are to be used, the ability to spoof a node WWN is useless because that is only half the parameter required for authorization (similar to spoofing half a MAC address to subvert MAC filtering on a wireless access point). Furthermore, the ability to change a node WWN value to match the port WWN value of a target is also useless since that is also only half of the parameter required for authorization. Figure 9.3 shows the benefits of using both the port WWN and node WWN for authorization.

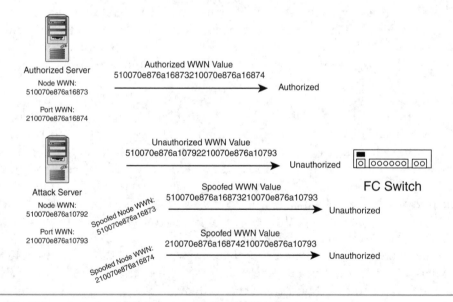

Figure 9.3   Using port and node WWNs together for WWN authorization.

Notice in Figure 9.3 that all the spoofed events fail. The first attempt is the incorrect value; therefore, it is rejected. When the attacker changed their node WWN to match the node WWN of the target, the attack also fails since the port WWN section of the WWN parameter is incorrect. Finally, when the attack changes their node WWN to match the port WWN of their target, the attack fails again because the port WWN field of the WWN parameter is still incorrect and does not contain the correct value. While the node WWN can be changed as often as the attacker wants, the port WWN cannot. If both the node and port WWNs are used for authorization, the WWN spoofing attack is not possible. Using both the port WWN and node WWN values for authorization security is the best and ideal method to use when WWNs are used as node identifiers.

The use of stronger WWNs can help mitigate against the following attacks:

- LUN masking
- WWN spoofing
- Zone hopping (WWN)

ZONING AND VSANS

Zoning is another great method to protect LUNs on a storage fabric. This statement may surprise some of the readers since it is directly opposite to prior statements I made about zoning in Chapter 4, "SANs: Zone and Switch Security." The fact is that there are secure methods of zoning, but they are rarely used and are off by default. The two types of secure zoning are hard zoning, which is enforcement base routing for Fibre Channel frames, and port zoning, which is segmentation of nodes on a fabric based on their physical port number on a Fibre Channel switch. The default method of zoning that is used by default on most switches is soft zoning with WWN zones. Chapter 4 discussed several ways to subvert soft zoning using WWN so we will not repeat the discussion at this time. Let's take a closer look at hard zoning and port-based zones to fully understand how a storage fabric can be more secure against one of the biggest attacks on a SAN.

HARD ZONING

Hard zoning ensures that frames that are routed between several nodes on a fabric are authorized to do so. For example, if a node in zone A wanted to send frames to a node in zone B but did not have permission to do so, hard zoning would not only not reveal any routing information to the node in zone A, but would also ensure that any frames coming outside of zone A are actively blocked from accessing zone B. The key difference between soft zoning and hard zoning is that soft zoning performs no active restrictions; it only refuses to pass along the route information to unauthorized zones, but does not block unauthorized frames. If a hostile node was able to enumerate the route to its target in zone B, it may attempt to send frames to that zone, which is essentially zone hopping. Under hard zoning, the frames are blocked since active monitoring/restriction is taking place, almost as if hard zoning performs as a Fibre Channel layer 2 firewall. Hard zoning not only helps mitigate zone hopping attacks, but enables stability and availability within the SAN by ensuring denial-of-service attacks, misconfiguration issues, or administrator errors don't allow the leakage from one zone to the other.

PORT-BASED ZONES

Another excellent method to block zone hopping attacks is the use of port-based zones. Port-based zones segment the SAN based on the physical port numbers on a Fibre Channel switch. For example, physical ports 1 through 8 on a Fibre Channel switch may belong to zone A, and physical ports 9 through 16 on the switch may belong to zone B. Let's say zone A and zone B do not have permission to access each other. If a node in zone A wants to communicate to a node in zone B, the node may attempt WWN spoofing attacks and attempt to trick the switch by spoofing a WWN that belongs to zone B. Under port-based zoning, all WWN spoofing attacks would be useless since the switch is not making any authorization decisions based on the node WWN, but rather the physical port number on the Fibre Channel switches. If the malicious node in zone A is connected to port number 2 and sends a WWN that belongs in zone B to the switch, the switch will simply ignore any WWN values because the request is coming from physical port 2; thus restricting all access to only nodes in zone A. Because port-based zoning does not rely on the insecure WWN value, but rather physical port numbers connected on the switch, all attacks involving WWN spoofing and the switch are not possible. Figure 9.4 shows an example.

Notice in Figure 9.4 that the node spoofing their node WWN to match the value of the real node in zone B is denied access because they belong on physical switch ports 1 through 8, which is in zone A, regardless of the node WWN value. In order to protect against zone hopping, WWN spoofing and hard zoning using port-based zones is the best security choice.

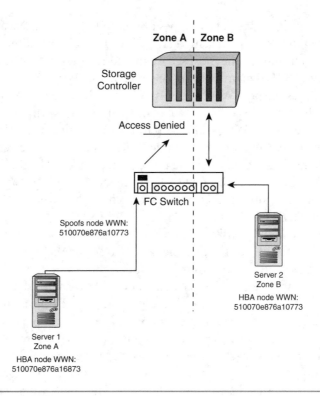

Figure 9.4 Port-based zones.

VSANs

Now that we understand how hard zoning and port-based zones dramatically improve security on a SAN, let's talk about Virtual SANs (VSANs), which is a technology developed and supported by Cisco systems. Most Fibre Channel switches, including Brocade, McData, and Qlogic, use the traditional types of segmentation described previously with hard/soft zoning and port/wwn zones. Cisco MDS switches also support these types of zones, but have introduced a new type of segmentation called Virtual SANs. Similar to Virtual LANs (VLANs), VSANs have the ability to create virtual domains with a SAN fabric. VSANs are a great security segmentation tool because VSANs are isolated from one another, including all routing information, name services, and zoning properties. For example, if four VSANs were created in a SAN, there would be four name servers, four fabrics, and four local routing groups. If further segmentation was desired with the VSAN, the zoning could be used with the VSAN itself.

VSANs can be configured using two types of methods: static VSANs and dynamic VSANs (supported in release 2.0). Static VSANs use physical port numbers on the Cisco Fibre Channel switch, and are the most secure method to deploy VSANs. The other method to deploy VSANs dynamically are called Dynamic Port VSAN Membership (DPVM). DPVM uses the port WWN or node WWN value. Because VSANs using WWNs can be vulnerable to spoofing attacks, use static VSANs where possible. If a DPVM is used and the same WWN shows up multiple times on a switch using different ports, the last port is remembered by dynamic VSANs, allowing an attacker to spoof their WWN, join the fabric, and overwrite the legitimate node. The use of port WWNs for VSAN membership can be acceptable if the switch only reads the port WWN section of the node's HBA (remember that an attacker can change their node WWN to be the port WWN of their target and get access to a zone/VSAN). VSANs using node WWNs should not be used in highly sensitive storage networks since a node can spoof their node WWN value to the value of their target and hop across VSANs.

By default, VSANs cannot route among each other; however, Inter-VSAN Routing (IVR) is now being supported by Cisco. Since static VSANs do not share infrastructure services between each other, such as routing and name services, the ability to hop across VSANs is extremely difficult when using static VSANs. For traditional SAN administrators, VSANs are similar to having a separate SAN fabric. If there were four separate SAN fabrics in a storage network, each of the fabrics would have their own names servers and routing information. While the security of having four separate SAN fabrics is great, the complexity level and overhead is dramatically worse. The ability to manage, support, and control four SAN fabrics in a single SAN is not an easy task to be taken lightly. The beauty of a VSAN is that it can exist within a single SAN fabric. VSANs can create a virtual domain independent of other VSANs without any shared services or even routing, but can also exist within one storage fabric. This allows administrators to deploy a single fabric but have the ability to have all the security of four different domains. Figure 9.5 shows an example of a SAN using static VSAN for segmentation.

Hard zoning, port-based zones, and VSANs can help protect against the following attacks:

- LUN masking
- WWN spoofing
- Zone hopping (WWN)
- Zone hopping (routing)

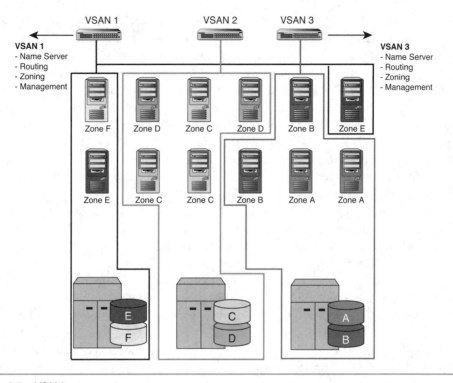

Figure 9.5 VSAN segmentation.

PORT LOCKING

Another method to prevent zone hopping and WWN spoofing attacks is the use of port locking on Fibre Channel switches. *Port locking* is a security option available on the secure versions of Fibre Channel switches that allows end users to bind a particular WWN to a specific port. For example, WWN 510070e876a16873 could be locked to physical port number 8. If an end user accidentally or maliciously changed the WWN value on the node that is connected to port number 8, the switch would ignore the new (spoofed) WWN since the value of 510070e876a16873 is locked to the port. Additionally, the use of port locking (sometimes called port binding) can be used with WWN-based zone membership. If zones are based on WWN but are also locked to physical port numbers on the switch, typical zone hopping attacks on WWN-based zones would not be possible. Hence, if zone membership must use WWN for ease of use or compatibility reasons, ensure that port locking is also used to prevent zone hopping or spoofing attacks. An important item to remember when using port locking is to ensure that all nodes are locked to their specific port. If a few nodes are locked and others are not, the ability to perform spoofing or zoning hopping attacks would still be possible. For example, if zone membership is based on WWNs, WWN 510070e876a16873 is locked to port 8, and WWN 510070e876a16091 is connected to port 9 but not locked, the node on port 9 could change their WWN to 510070e876a16873 (the WWN of port number 8). Once the node on port 9 sends their new WWN to the switch, the switch would be allowed to accept the new WWN since the original WWN on port 9 (510070e876a16091) was not locked. The only locking of WWN is on port 8, not port 9. Hence, when using port locking, it is important to understand that nodes that are not locked can still perform spoofing and zone hopping attacks.

Depending on the type of architecture of your SAN, you may want to implement port locking on servers that are considered to be less trusted. For example, if your SAN connects nodes from all parts of the network, such as the DMZ, the internal network, the partner network, the backup network, the extranet, and the management network, you may want to consider implementing port locking on nodes that are located in more hostile locations. For example, nodes in the DMZ, internal network, and management network should be considered less trusted since many unauthorized users or accidental changes can take place quite easily. If the backup network is considered isolated and trusted, implementing port locking may not be needed on those servers. By implementing port locking on DMZ nodes, compromised web and applications servers would not be a gateway into the SAN since WWN spoofing attacks would not allow the client node to change its zone or change is WWN value on the Fibre Channel switch. Figure 9.6 shows an example of using port locking to secure LUNs on a Fibre Channel SAN.

Port locking can help protect against the following attacks:

- LUN masking
- WWN spoofing
- Zone hopping (WWN)

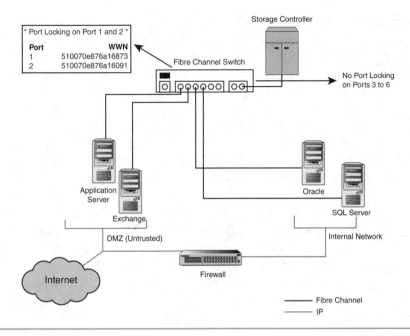

Figure 9.6   Port locking.

SWITCH-TO-SWITCH AUTHENTICATION

Unauthorized or accidental switch replication of fabric information, including name server information, zone information, routing information, and the entire logical topology of the fabric, is a severe problem for storage networks. While the unauthorized replication of SAN fabrics for Storage Service Providers (SSP) is a company-ending problem, the accidental replication of SAN fabrics from one SAN to the next may be a career-ending problem. Just like most network devices (IP or Fibre Channel), the idea of plug and play is very important for end-user acceptability. While plug and play is very nice, it may also be dangerous. If an SSP allows a customer to plug their switches' E-port (Expansion port) to the SSP's E-port, the entire SSP SAN, including all the customers of the SSP (which may be competitors of each other), has just been compromised. Furthermore, if two SAN fabrics are deployed in a single data center, the incorrect or accidental connection from an E-port on one SAN switch to an E-port on another SAN switch may create several routing, zoning, and possible performance errors on the SAN. To protect against incorrect, accidental, or malicious replication events in a SAN, the use of switch-to-switch authentication or port type locking can be implemented.

Switch-to-switch authentication allows SANs to ensure that any new switch that connects to a fabric is valid. Unlike node to switch authentication that is still emerging in Fibre Channel SAN, a switch may be required to authenticate to another switch before being allowed to connect to the SAN. Each switch would need to authenticate to a primary set of switches, which are usually the only switches in the fabric that are allowed to make any changes or add any new members, using a digital certificate and unique public/private key pair. If a switch connects to the fabric, it won't be given any information, such as fabric, zone, or routing information, until it has authenticated successfully. Using switch layer authentication, many SAN switches can protect against unauthorized or accidental E-port replication processes. These accidental or malicious processes may grant access to a switch that should not have any access or even combine two fabrics in a SAN that should actually be mutually exclusive of each other. Brocade switch-to-switch authentication is called SLAP (Switch Link Authentication Protocol) available in their secure fabric OS. Also, McData also has similar features in their SANtegrity OS. In addition, Cisco supports switch authentication in the MDS switches. E-port replication problems can be mitigated using any type of switch that supports switch-to-switch authentication. Figure 9.7 shows an example of switch-to-switch authentication to protect against accidental or malicious E-port replication.

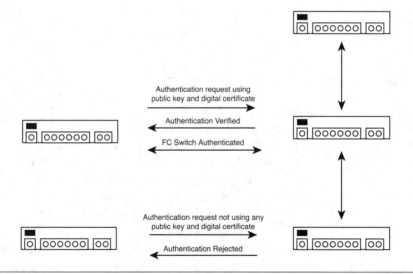

Figure 9.7 Switch to switch authentication.

Switch to switch authentication can mitigate the following attack class:

• E-port replication

PORT TYPE LOCKING

Another method to secure against accidental or malicious E-port replication is with the use of port type locking. *Port type locking* locks a type of port functionality, such as G-port, E-port, or F-port, to a single physical port. By default, most ports are G-port (general ports) that may interact with a connecting F-port, N-port, or E-port. G-ports are the most flexible since they can change to an E-port if they are connected to an E-port on the other side or they can change to an F-port if they are connected to an N-port on the other side. Although this is flexible, it is also a security risk as malicious or accidental connections to a G-port may compromise the security of the entire SAN. The ideal method of port type configuration is to lock each port to its specified port type. For example, most likely only one or maybe two ports will be needed as E-ports. It is best to lock the ports that will be used as expansion ports as E-ports. The rest of the ports should be configured as F-ports, since they will be connected to HBAs, which are N-ports. By locking all ports to F-ports and one or two to E-ports on a Fibre Channel switch, the likelihood of a malicious or accidental connection to another E-port is more unlikely. Furthermore, port type locking contains no penalties on performance since it does not affect any type of I/O interaction. Port type locking is offered by all major Fibre Channel switch vendors and should be used as the default rather than the exception. The ability to implement port type locking limits the attack surface for E-port replication. Figure 9.8 shows an example of port type locking.

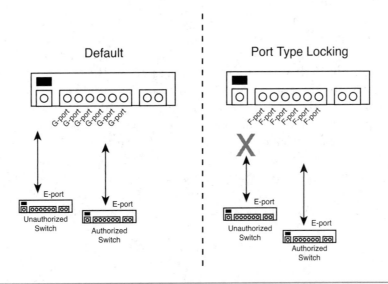

Figure 9.8 Port type locking.

Port type locking can mitigate the following attack class:

- E-port replication

LUN MASKING

Subverting LUN masking uses WWN spoofing attacks, as described earlier, as well as the implementation of LUN masking at the client node. Preventing LUN masking from WWN spoofing attacks can be completed by using port WWNs—or even better, using port and node WWNs—for node identification. Using both port and node WWNs remove the ability for any malicious or accidental change from subverting LUN maskings tables that rely on WWNs. If both the port and node WWN cannot be used or are not supported by the vendor, ensure that port WWNs are used for LUN masking and make sure that LUN masking software only checks a node's port WWN value and not either the port or node WWN value. If a LUN masking table checks either the node WWN or the port WWN, a malicious node can change their node WWN value to be the port WWN value of an authorized node.

In addition to using stronger WWN values, ensure that LUN masking is not implemented at the client node. It would be a trivial process for anybody who has access to the operating system (either a malicious attacker who has compromised the system or an authorized user who may make accidental changes) to simply change the values for the LUN masking properties. The operating system probably is part of a domain, which means all root or administrator group members also have the ability to change any LUN masking information. Because most LUN masking software does not contain any type of authentication to open or administer the software, any account, authorized or unauthorized, can change the information to whatever they choose. If LUN masking is implemented at the switch or storage controller, the ability for an authorized NT administrator accidentally making a change to the LUN masking software would be dramatically more difficult. The ideal method is to implement LUN masking at the storage controller since only authorized storage administrators have access to these machines, and the ability for a malicious attacker to get access to the storage controller is considerably less than getting access to an operating system on the network.

The most ideal method for LUN masking is to implement it at the storage controller using port and node WWN values for authorization. Proper LUN masking can mitigate the following attacks:

- LUN masking
- WWN spoofing
- Zone hopping (WWN)

NAME SERVER QUERIES

Name server queries are information requests from nodes on a SAN. Name service queries ask questions about the fabric, such as routing information, WWN information, LUN information, state change information, or general configuration information of the fabric. If name server queries grant information about the entire fabric to all nodes, including nodes in unzoned locations, then a node in a zone that wishes to get access to another zone it does not have access to can submit name server queries and potentially gain information regarding routing, LUNs, and general WWN information. Similar to our enumeration conversations earlier in the book, the more information a node can get regarding its target, the better chance it will succeed. Name server queries are a great resource for attackers to gain information that is leaked by the switch about a target. For example, if zone hopping attacks are possible but there is no way for a malicious node to know what LUN or WWN they want to target, then the attack is more difficult. The best method to deploy name server is to limit name server queries to only authorized nodes in a given zone. For example, if a node in zone A submits a name server information request to the switch about the location of LUN number 5, unless LUN number 5 belongs to zone A, the name server request should be rejected. By limiting name server queries within a zone or from zones that are authorized to communicate with each other, an attacker cannot find information easily about other zones that it should not have access to. Preventing name server queries from divulging information on the entire fabric is the best method to ensure any enumeration or information leakage by an attacker is prevented.

Limited name server queries can mitigate the following attacks:

- Name server pollution
- Zone hopping (routing)

SWITCH MANAGEMENT

Management access on Fibre Channel storage devices are key aspects to secure. The primary method to control the entire storage infrastructure are the management channels, which need to be secured from unauthorized users, attackers, accidental changes, or configuration mistakes. This idea is unfortunately overlooked. For example, since many storage devices are managed out-of-band using IP networks, access to them is quite easy. Furthermore, since many of the default passwords on the storage devices are never changed, gaining full control of the storage device can be easy. Finally, even if a complex password is chosen, many storage devices are still being managed by Telnet, HTTP, or SNMP, all of which are clear-text protocols allowing the username/password to be sniffed at any time. These methods make it easy for an attacker to compromise the management port of storage devices and reconfigure the SAN to give them access or just to delete/damage data (DOS attack).

Because many storage devices support out-of-band management using IP and in-band management using Fibre Channel SES or SNMP, ensure that Telnet for command-line access, HTTP for web management, and SNMPv1 for monitoring are disabled. Both Telnet and HTTP are clear-text protocols that can capture all authentication information over any network (as shown in Chapter 4). Instead of using Telnet or HTTP, implement SSH (secure shell) for the command line and SSL (HTTPS) for web management GUI. Both SSH and HTTPS will encrypt all communication to/from the client management station to the storage device. If an unauthorized user or attacker is sniffing the network connection, only encrypted traffic will appear to them if SSH and HTTPS has been installed and enabled. Be sure to disable Telnet and HTTP after SSH and HTTPS are enabled. Many environments install the more secure protocols, but often forget to disable the insecure ones. Figures 9.9 and 9.10 show an authentication packet that is using SSH and HTTPS. Notice that no username or password information could be captured.

In addition to SSH and HTTPS, ensure that SNMPv3 is used over the insecure and clear-text version, which is SNMPv1. SNMPv1 is clear-text where any attacker can sniff the public or private community strings over the network. SNMPv3 can be used with encryption, making it very difficult for an attacker sniffing the network to gain the correct SNMP information over the wire. It also prevents unauthorized nodes from making SNMP requests if the public community string has been changed to something else but "public."

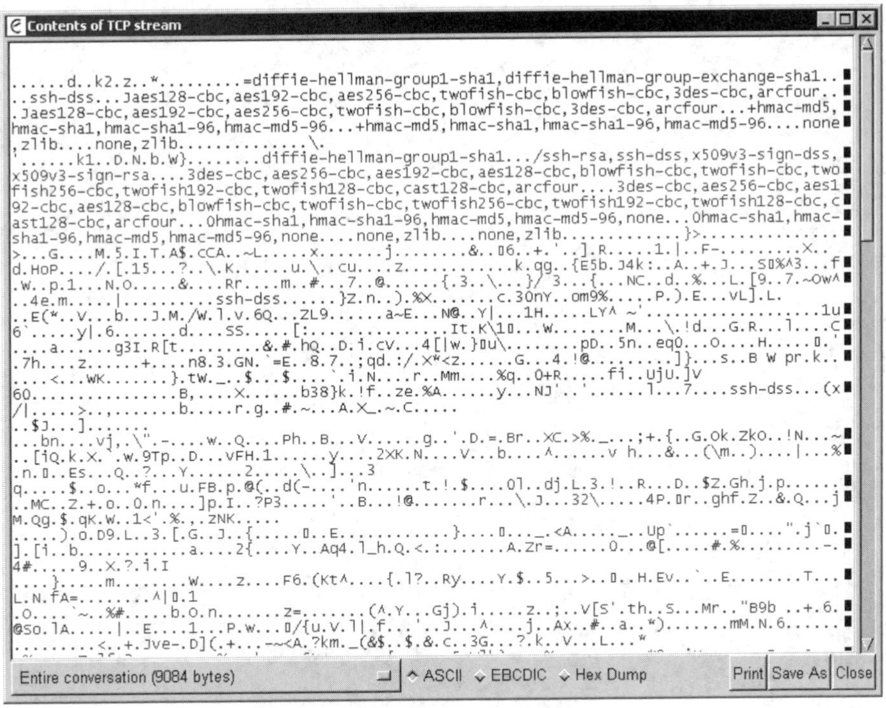

Figure 9.9   SSH usage.

Another method to secure switches is to prevent the ability for any anonymous enumeration of the fabric from the Fibre Channel switch. As stated in Chapter 4, many Fibre Channel switches give away information without requiring any type of authentication about the fabric. An attacker can connect to the IP management interface or make in-band management over the Fibre Channel connection to gather information. Limiting the ability to enumerate the SAN after a user has successfully authenticated to the management interface or after an HBA has authenticated within the fabric would significantly limit the ability of an attacker to enumerate information about a potential target. For example, without knowing any WWN to spoof, the attacker would only have the ability to brute force WWNs, which takes much longer to perform. Certain Fibre Channel switch vendors do not require authentication when connecting to its IP information for information gathering, but only when issues change commands. The ideal method is to require authentication before any access is granted, informational or change oriented.

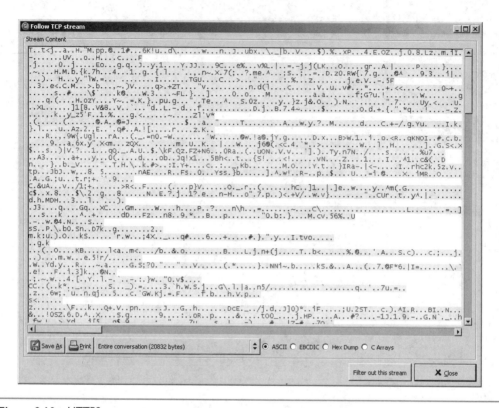

Figure 9.10 HTTPS usage.

The last message on security management is to deploy secure management software for storage networks. Storage management applications from Veritas, Computer Associates, IBM, EMC, and NetApp need to contain high levels of application security. Application security issues, such as buffer overflows, format strings attacks, input/output validation, cross-site scripting, weak session identifiers, authorization bypass, hidden field manipulation, and so on, are continuing to devastate all application vendors, where storage application vendors are not immune. In fact, in June of 2005, seven security vulnerabilities (five of which were severe) were released on Veritas software, many of which has a worm already targeting port 10000, which is the port that Veritas Backup-Exec uses (for more information on the Veritas issues, see http://www.storagepipeline.com/164904026). While the focus of the book has not been vendor specific and has not addressed specific issues with storage applications, the attack classes listed previously are apparent in many storage management applications and should be reviewed thoroughly by vendors. As end users, ensure that you are aware of the latest attacks and vulnerabilities on your storage management software, make sure your vendor has taken adequate steps to ensure their application is written securely, and confirm that weak management applications that are used to manage SANs are not being deployed in the network. Many security researchers now target storage management applications since they have the control of large amounts of data and are vulnerable to many application attack classes.

Secure switch management can protect against the following attacks:

- LUN masking
- WWN spoofing
- Zone hopping (WWN)
- Switch management

SECURING STORAGE TAPES WITH ENCRYPTION

Encrypting storage tapes (data at-rest) is a great method to ensure that the data on your storage network is not available to unauthorized eyes. By now you have probably read the media and news articles about the large data security/privacy issues from lost, stolen, or compromised storage tapes. The year 2005 alone saw major banks and organizations publicly embarrassed with large amounts of information lost. Bank of America, Ameritrade, Iron Mountain, and Citibank all had to admit the loss of storage tapes that contained sensitive information.

With government regulations such as California Senate Bill 1386 (as well a few others), organizations are now required to notify the public if any non-public personal information, such as credit card numbers or social security numbers, have been lost, stolen, or compromised. Although there are many procedural ways to ensure that data storage tapes are not lost while waiting for Iron Mountain or the UPS truck to pick them up (like not placing the tapes in the hallway for anyone to take), the technology solution is the use of at-rest encryption. It should be noted that although encrypting data at-rest is a very good security practice, it does not protect against everything, such as denial-of-service attacks that can leave data entirely unavailable, incorrect configuration changes, accidental data allocations, or compromised operating systems/applications servers with attached HBAs. Despite the fact that encryption does not protect against every attack, it protects storage tapes from growing legs and walking into the hands of unauthorized viewers. This chapter briefly discusses the tape storage security methods for SAN and NAS architectures next.

SAN TAPE SECURITY

Many storage security vendors, such as Decru, NeoScale, Vormetric, and Kastan-Chase, provide in-line appliances to encrypt data to and from a storage controller and tape devices for both SAN and NAS infrastructures. In SANs, the encryption appliances sit parallel to a Fibre Channel switch in a storage network. Instead of the switches communicating directly with the storage controllers, the switches would send traffic to the encryption appliance first. The encryption appliance would encrypt the data and then send it back to the switch. At that point, the switch would then send the data to the storage controller or the tape device. Once the storage controller or tape device receives the data, it stores it locally, oblivious to the fact that data is encrypted and not in clear-text. It should also be noted that any attack to subvert the security controls on the SAN would still work, but the data the attacker would receive would be encrypted and look like garbage; hence, being useless to the attacker. In addition to attackers, accidental changes that may grant a node access to a LUN is also protected when data is encrypted. If a Windows Exchange server accidentally gets connected to an Oracle database, the Windows server would see garbage data that cannot be written to, protecting the Oracle application and all of its data. Additionally, since storage controllers are connected to tape drives for offsite storage, any tape that is accidentally lost or maliciously stolen— such as the Los Alamos tapes storing nuclear data in New Mexico in 2004—the data is still protected because it is encrypted. Also, if an attacker chooses to get a job with the off-site tape library company or simply drive the truck that the tapes are transported in, then any physical hijacking of the tapes would also not be a security issue since the data the attacker would receive is already encrypted. Encrypting storage data at-rest adds a strong amount of security for offsite tape storage. Figure 9.11 shows an example architecture with an encryption appliance being used.

Encryption data at-rest can mitigate the following attacks:

- LUN masking
- WWN spoofing
- Zone hopping (WWN)
- E-port replication

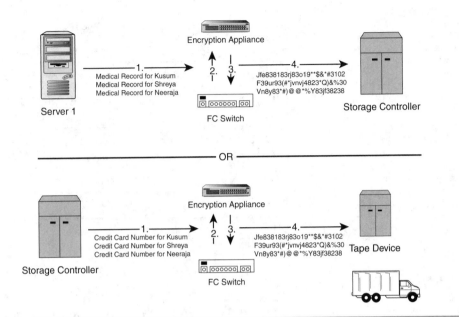

Figure 9.11 Storage encryption appliances.

SAN SECURITY SUMMARY

Next is a summary of the options that are available in most Fibre Channel SAN environments and their recommended security settings. An organization must choose the ideal setting that best fits their environment; however, the table demonstrates which security options are better than others.

Table 9.1 Fibre Channel SAN Security Options and Recommendations

Feature	Option	Ideal Security Option
Zoning (routing)	Soft or hard zoning	Hard zoning
Zone membership allocation	WWN or ports	Port-base zones
Port security	Port binding or no binding	Port binding
Port type security	Port locking or no locking	Port locking
Switch management	Telnet, HTTP, SSH, HTTPS, or SNMPv1	SSH, HTTPS, or SNMPv3

Table 9.1   Fibre Channel SAN Security Options and Recommendations (continued)

Feature	Option	Ideal Security Option
LUN masking	Client, switch, or storage controller	Storage controller
LUN masking identifiers	Node WWN, port WWN, or node and port WWNs	Node and port WWNs (if possible) or port WWNs
WWN zoning identifiers	Node WWN, port WWN, or node and port WWNs	Node and port WWNs (if possible) or port WWNs
Name server queries	All or zone only	Zone only
Encryption	None, in-transit, or at-rest	In-transit or at-rest

SUMMARY

This chapter discussed the methods to protect against many Fibre Channel SAN attacks described in Chapters 2 through 4. Secure storage is key for data protection and data availability. Although many issues exist in Fibre Channel SANs, there are several existing mitigations that can be deployed by organizations to safely and securely keep their data available and hold its integrity. As shown in this chapter, a few key settings and configuration changes might help protect the data volumes in your SAN from unauthorized access and unintentional damage. These settings will help mitigate the security risks without having a severe impact on performance. The next chapter focuses on security NAS environments, along with CIFS and NFS security.

Securing NAS

10

Protecting storage in CIFS and NFS devices (NAS) is core for data security. Although operating systems, both Windows and UNIX, seem to get the most attention in terms of security, the data is actually sitting on a NAS device, which is open to anyone. A NAS device should be regarded as another operating system on your network. Just like a Windows or Unix system, you need to ensure that your NAS devices have disabled unnecessary services, prevent information leakage, are patched and up to date, and use required authentication/authorization from NSF/CIFS clients.

Chapters 5 through 7 described many attacks on NAS devices, both CIFS and NFS. This chapter is the second of three chapters dedicated to showing all the defenses and best practices for each attack shown in the previous chapters. The primary focus will be on defenses and best practices for securing storage. The goal is to discuss and demonstrate the existing features, tools, and configurations available in storage networks that can mitigate the security weaknesses and attacks discussed earlier.

This chapter discusses the defenses, best practices, and mitigating controls for the following attacks types:

NAS Attacks

- Enumeration (CIFS usernames, share, and groups)
- Authentication
- Authorization

- Encryption
- NFS export enumeration
- Anonymous mounting of exports
- Authorization
- Encryption

Securing NAS

Securing NAS devices actually translates into securing the two primary protocols that are used for data access, including NFS and CIFS. Additionally, the security of the supporting entities of the network device, including user accounts, system services, and access management, is also part of the process. This section will discuss the various methods to mitigate all the attacks shown in Chapters 5 through 7 as they pertain to the listed categories:

- CIFS security
- NFS security
- NAS device security
- vFilers
- NAS tape security

CIFS Security

CIFS security is similar to securing any other type of protocol: limit enumeration, enable strong authentication, use good authorization, and implement encryption where possible. Let's begin with enumeration.

Enumeration

Limiting enumeration on NAS devices running CIFS means to limit the information leakage of the SMB protocol. Most devices (or even operating systems) running CIFS/SMB enable an IPC$ share that is used to transfer information from one CIFS device to the next. The problem is that it leaks information without authentication to the entire network, including unauthorized or malicious users. The information that is usually leaked from most NAS devices includes the following:

- Usernames
- Group names
- Group members
- Power groups (administrators)
- Open shares

In order to prevent the enumeration of anonymous information from a Network Appliance filer supporting CIFS, enter the following command on the system (see Chapter 13, "Auditing and Securing Storage Devices," for a comprehensive list of security settings):

```
options cifs.restrict_anonymous.enable on
```

This command will prevent unauthorized and malicious users from utilizing readily available tools and gaining sensitive information that fuels successful attacks. While the IPC$ share will still be enabled on the device, it will not relinquish information unless it is coming from an authorized and authenticated user. It is great how a simple one-line command can prevent several attacks described in Chapter 6, "NAS: CIFS Security."

Disabling anonymous access to the NAS device can mitigate the following attacks:

- CIFS usernames and group enumeration
  DumpSec
- CIFS share enumeration
  Winfo.exe
- CIFS power users (administrator accounts) enumeration
  Enum.exe

AUTHENTICATION

The core issues with CIFS authentication are the use of plain-text passwords, LM (LAN Manager), or NTLM (NT LAN Manager) for authentication. Plain-text passwords should never be used; hence, if you are using share-level authentication, ensure that you don't enable plain-text passwords (most NAS devices do not support share-level authentication anymore, so this should not be an issue for most environments). To disable plain-text passwords on Windows machines, complete the following steps:

1. Start -> Run -> Regedit.
2. Browse to HKLM\System\CurrentControlSet\Services\lanmanworkstation\Parameters\.
3. Edit -> New -> DWORD.
4. Name the new DWORD value EnablePlainTextPasswords.
5. Give the new DWORD value a value of 0.

The next couple authentication methods are LM and NTLM. Unlike the ability to disable anonymous enumeration on a NAS device, disabling LM or NTLM is not necessarily a NAS device setting but actually a setting on your Windows server operating system. Unfortunately, most NAS devices do not support the ability to disable LM or NTLM and force the strongest authentication method, which is Kerberos. Many other network devices in other markets, such as certain SSL VPNs, offer the ability to disable LM, NTLM, or even NTLMv2 in favor of Kerberos only. This would reject all authentication methods except for Kerberos, which is most ideal when in a Windows 2000/2003 domain. (It would be nice if that option was also available for NAS devices running CIFS.) While the use of Kerberos is automatic and the default option when a NAS device is joined to a Windows Active Directory domain, the ability to force LM or NTLM and downgrade the connection is possible, leaving all the attack vectors against LM and NTLM open. A NAS device using CIFS for authentication simply uses pass-through authentication for each user attempt. The NAS device does not contain the database of all usernames and passwords locally on their own system but simply passes the request to the nearest domain controller. If the domain controller says the authentication request is successful, then the NAS device will accept the request. It is acting as a proxy when it comes to authentication from clients. Hence, if LM or NTLM is disabled on the Windows 2000/2003 Active Directory domain, the ability to attack the LM or NTLM authentication methods becomes more difficult. The only available authentication methods will be Kerberos and NTLMv2. The following steps will disable LM and NTLM on Windows 2000 and Windows 2003 servers:

1. Start -> Programs -> Administrative Tools -> Local Security Policy.
2. Expand Security Settings -> Local Policies -> Security Options.
3. Double-click on Network security: Do not store LAN Manager hash on next password change.

4. Select the Enabled radio button. See Figure 10.1.

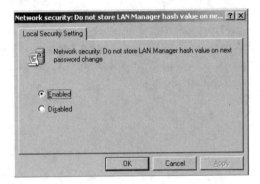

Figure 10.1 Remove the LM hash.

5. Select OK.

6. Double-click on Network security: LAN Manager authentication level.

7. Select "Send NTLMv2 response only\refuse LM & NTLM" from the drop-down box. See Figure 10.2. (Note: Any Windows 9x or NT machine without the appropriate hot fixes will not be able to communicate with the NAS device or the domain.)

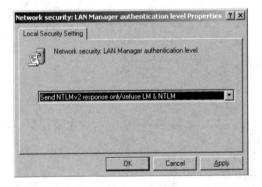

Figure 10.2 Disabling LM and NTLM.

8. Select OK.

9. Done! You have now removed the LM hashes and disabled LM and NTLM on the server.

10. You should now do this on the rest of the servers in the domain since the server that is closest to a certain NAS device may not be the closest to another. The best way to implement these settings on the domain server is to create a group policy file and attach it to the domain. Next are contents of a group policy file called DisableLM.NTLM.inf that can be attached to the domain. It can also be emailed to you by emailing the author at securingstorage@gmail.com or downloaded from www.isecpartners.com/securingstorage.

```
; Disable LM.NTLM.inf

[Profile Description]
%ProfileDescription%

[version]
signature="$CHICAGO$"
revision=1
DriverVer=10/01/2002,5.2.3790.0

[System Access]
[System Log]
[Event Audit]

[Registry Values]

MACHINE\System\CurrentControlSet\Control\Lsa\LmCompatibilityLevel=4,4
MACHINE\System\CurrentControlSet\Control\Lsa\NoLMHash=4,1

ProfileDescription = "Removes LM Hashes and disables LM/NTLM communication."
```

For Windows 2000 servers, the process is the same to enable NTLMv2 communication only, but a bit different to remove LM hashes from the machine. The following steps will remove the LM hash from Windows 2000 servers:

1. Start -> Run -> Regedit.
2. Browse to HKLM\System\CurrentControlSet\Control\LSA.
3. Edit -> New -> DWORD Value.
4. Name the new DWORD Value to NoLMHash.
5. Give the new DWORD Value a 1.
6. Done!

The following are the contents of a registry file called NoLMHash.reg that will create the key for you. It can also be emailed to you by emailing the author at securingstorage@ gmail.com or downloaded at www.isecpartners.com/securingstorage.com.

```
Windows Registry Editor Version 5.00

[HKEY_LOCAL_MACHINE\SYSTEM\CurrentControlSet\Control\Lsa]
"nolmhash"=dword:00000000
```

In addition to disabling LM and NTLM on Windows 2000 and 2003 servers, they should also be disabled on client machines. For example, if Kerberos and NTLMv2 are the only methods used for authentication, a client could still send its LM or NTLM hash over the network. Since the LM or NTLM hash will have the same information as the Kerberos or NTLMv2 information, that information sent over the network cancels out the strong authentication that is being used. For example, if you send your password in clear-text and also encrypted, the use of encryption is useless since the same packet has the password in clear-text. This idea also applies to LM and NTLM. You want to make sure that client machines are not sending LM or NTLM hashes over the network when they are attempting Kerberos and NTLMv2. The great thing is that if you are using Kerberos only, no LM or NTLM hash will be sent at all; however, if an attacker forces you to downgrade, your machine will send the LM or NTLM unless you have disabled them. The previous steps will also disable LM and NTLM on a Windows 2000 Professional and Windows XP machine. If you are using Windows XP, follow the steps for Windows 2003 listed earlier. If you are using Windows 2000 Professional, follow the steps for Windows 2000 Server listed previously.

Now that we have learned how to disable LM and NTLM to/from our NAS device, we can safely rely on Kerberos for authentication. Using Kerberos makes the authentication process on a NAS device using CIFS a lot safer.

Removing LM hashes and disabling LM and NTLM communication in favor of Kerberos can mitigate only the following attacks:

- Share-level password attacks
  Smbbf.exe, CIFShareBF.exe
- LM and NTLM attacks
  Cain and Abel (NTLM section only)
  L0pthCrack (LC2.5 to LC5)
  BeatLM

AUTHORIZATION

Unlike authentication on NAS devices using CIFS, the attack vectors and defenses for authorization values are not too deep. The primary authorization methods used on NAS devices using CIFS are IP addresses, IP subnets, or hostnames. The defenses to these attacks are to not rely on them for security. There is no method for NAS devices running CIFS to prevent client machines from changing their IP address, performing Man-in-the-Middle attacks, or changing their hostname. As with anything in security, if any entity cannot be trusted, don't use it as the sole security parameter. While enabling IP address/subnet or hostname filtering as the sole security parameter would not be ideal, enabling it with proper authentication methods is a good idea. Even though IP address spoofing and hostname spoofing can be subverted, it still requires an attacker to perform a particular attack in addition to any authentication attacks they will also need to perform. For example, we all know a car burglar could break the window of a car and then attempt to steal the car by hot-wiring the ignition; however, we still choose to lock our doors. We keep the doors locked despite the fact that we know there are simply ways to get around it; however, we want to force the burglar to break the window and then attempt to hot-wire the ignition (not make it any easier for them if they really want to steal the car). Now if we kept the keys in the ignition and felt that it was okay to do that because we have locked our doors, then we would be relying on poor security parameters because the car windows can be subverted easier than the ignition (this would be similar to disabling username/password authentication in favor of authorization only, despite the fact that IP addresses can be spoofed). Hence, when deploying NAS devices running CIFS, ensure you have enabled the strongest form of authentication; however, consider implementing IP address/subnet or hostname filtering on key shares.

The ideal method to secure against IP address/subnet and hostname spoofing is to implement file-level permissions on each CIFS share. For example, many CIFS shares are shared out to everyone by default. This allows anyone who can authenticate to the NAS device, which would be everyone on a Windows 2000/2003 domain, to have full access to the folder. The better method is to create CIFS shares and only allow authorized user accounts and groups to access those folders. For example, if a share is being made for the Oracle database application, you should limit the share to the administrator or backup group only. Furthermore, if a share is being created for the Finance department, you should limit the share to the finance group or users' accounts that belong in finance. The following method will demonstrate how to enable file-level permissions on CIFS shares on a Network Appliance filer.

1. Log into the filer:
   a. `SSH <ip address> 22`

2. Make a share called "Oracle" and limit it to the administrator account in the domain called "iSEC:"
   a. `cifs shares -add oracle /vol/vol0/oracle`

   b. `cifs access oracle iSEC\administrator Full Control`

   c. `cifs access oracle iSEC\everyone No Access`

3. Make a share called finance and give everyone in the finance group read access and everyone else no access:
   a. `cifs shares -add finance /vol/vol0/finance`

   b. `cifs access finance iSEC\finance Read`

   c. `cifs access finance iSEC\everyone no access`

Enabling IP address/subnet/hostname filtering on NAS devices as well as file permission on CIFS shares can mitigate the following attacks:

- IP address/subnet spoofing
  winrelay.exe
- IP hostname spoofing
- File permission subversion

ENCRYPTION

Encryption can be enabled between NAS devices running CIFS and NAS clients, whether they are server or client operating systems. Most NAS devices support IPSec encryption, offering authentication headers (AH) or payload encryption (ESP). Using encryption between a NAS device and an Exchange mail server can drastically reduce the attack surface by a malicious user. Unlike most IPSec implementations that are used between VPN clients and a VPN server for a virtual network, this type of IPSec implementation will be used between two individual nodes. A NAS device will not be acting like an IPSec VPN server (nor should it), but will be able to send and receive IPSec packets to any node that wants to communicate in an encrypted fashion. Figure 10.3 shows an example of a NAS device using encryption between server and client operating systems.

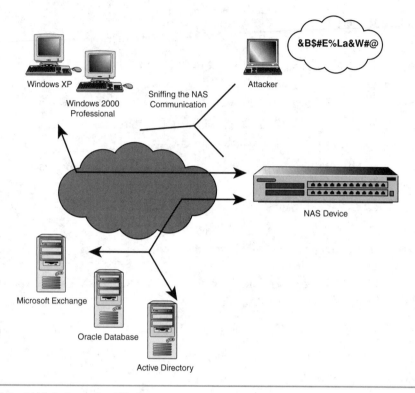

Figure 10.3   NAS devices using IPSec.

Notice in Figure 10.3 that the attacker is still able to sniff the communication from any node on the network to the NAS device; however, when the attacker actually views the packets he or she has captured, the information shows up as garbage data. In order to see what IPSec encryption would look like if it were sniffed over the network with any basic sniffer, such as Ethereal, refer to Figure 10.4.

Notice all the traffic is labeled as ESP, denoting that the traffic has been encrypted. In order to enable IPSec on a NAS environment, you must enable it all on a NAS device and on the node operating system. Therefore, there are two places to set up IPSec, not just on the NAS device itself. To enable IPSec on network appliance NAS devices, complete the following commands.

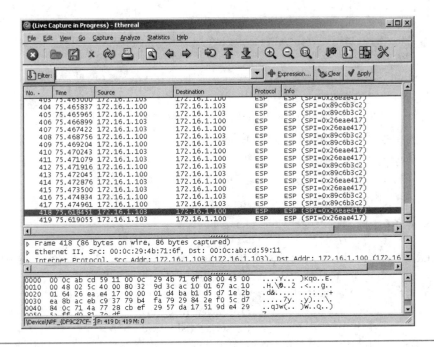

Figure 10.4 IPSec traffic.

1. Log into the filer:

   a. SSH <ip address> 22

2. The syntax for IPSec is

   a. ipsecpolicyadd –s {source ip} –t {destination ip} –p {esp|ah|none} –e {des|3des|null} - a{sha1|md5|null} –d {in|out} –f ip_protocol –l {restrict|permit}

   i. Source IP: The NAS device

   ii. Destination IP: The target client or server operating system

   iii. –P: Use payload encryption (ESP) or packet integrity (AH)

   iv. –E: If ESP, then choose type of encryption (DES, 3Des, or null)

   v. –A: If AH, then choose type of hash (SHA1, MD5, or null)

   vi. –D: In or out directions

   vii. –F: TCP (number 6) or UDP (number 17)

viii. –L: Restrict means communication is only allowed if it gets an SA. Permit means if it cannot get an SA, then there will be no security on the data.

3. To enable IPSec from the NAS device of 172.16.1.100 to all sources in the network using payload encryption with triple DES:

a. `ipsecpolicyadd -s 172.16.1.100 -p esp -e 3des -a sha1 -d in`

4. Create a pre-shared key file on the NAS device:

a. Browse to /etc.

b. Make a file called psk.txt.

c. Type the IP address(s) and shared key for each node:

i. **0.0.0.0/8 supersecretpre-sharedkey**

Now that IPSec is enabled on the NAS device using the pre-shared key of "supersecret-pre-sharedkey," ensure that it is also enabled on your Windows 2003 server using the IPSec Policy manager (ipsecpol.msc). Note that most NAS devices support IPSec and IKE with pre-shared keys or Kerberos authentication. Kerberos is only enabled mostly for Windows environments. Hence, if it is set up using pre-shared keys, the NAS device can use IPSec with both Windows and Unix clients (using the /etc/psk.txt file with the pre-shared key). Complete the following steps to set up IPSec on a Windows 2003 server that will be communicating with the NAS device:

1. Start -> Programs -> Administrative Tools -> Local Security Policy.

2. Highlight IP Security Policies on Local Computer.

3. In the right pane, right-click on Server (Request Security) and select Properties.

4. Highlight the first rule (All IP Traffic) and click Edit.

5. Select the Authentication Method tab.

6. Select Edit.

7. Select the "Use this string (pre-shared key)" radio button.

8. Enter **supersecretpre-sharedkey** for the pre-shared key.

9. Select OK and then select OK again.

10. Done! You have now enabled IPSec on the Windows 2003 server. Each time the server communicates with another node, such as the NAS device, it will attempt to use IPSec with the pre-shared key listed previously. If it is not communicating with the NAS device but some other machine on the network that is not IPSec-enabled, it

will continue to use whatever communication possible. The request security option allows nodes to use IPSec if possible, but to use other communication if both sides cannot use IPSec.

The use of IPSec between a NAS device and nodes on the network can help mitigate the following attacks:

- CIFS usernames, share, and group enumeration
- LM and NTLM sniffing
- Telnet, FTP, HTTP sniffing
- Kerberos pre-authentication sniffing
- General CIFS communication sniffing

NFS SECURITY

Securing NFS is very similar to the steps to secure CIFS. Both protocols have similar weaknesses that can be mitigated with appropriate settings on NAS devices. The key aspects we will discuss in securing NAS devices running NFS are the abilities to limit enumeration, enable strong authentication, use good authorization, and implement encryption where possible.

ENUMERATION

Enumerating NFS on NAS devices is primarily conducted with the retrieval of the /etc/exports file remotely over the network, which requires no authentication. The `showmount -e <IP Address>` command can be used to see what exports are available on the remote NFS server (NAS devices), including the following items:

- Exports
- Authorized hostnames
- Authorized IP addresses

Unlike CIFS where this is a simple command to disable enumeration, in order to prevent the enumeration of anonymous information from a NAS device supporting NFS, we must use a creative solution to mitigate the risk.

The easiest solution would be to reject the showmount request or only allow them by authorized nodes already in the /etc/export file. If your NAS device allows the show-mount request to be rejected or disabled, you should enable that setting. I have never seen the ability to reject the showmount request; however, the option could be available after the publication of this book. It is possible to limit NFS mount request over low numbers ports only. This will reject any showmount requests using high-number ports. On a Network Appliance filer, the command is as follows:

```
options nfs.mount_rootonly on
```

If there is not an option to disable the showmount request (aside from normal network filtering and firewalls), we can limit the type of correct information an attacker can get from showmount. The results of showmount will show the exports and authorized host-names. Let's say there is a server called oracle-db3, which has the IP address of 172.16.1.250 and is authorized to access the exported folder called /vol/vol0/oracle. In order to protect the hostname information, you can place an entry in the NAS device's host file for 172.16.1.250 to be referred to as server1. When you export /vol/vol0/oracle, you can export to the same name of server1. When a request comes in from the server, the NAS device will see the request from 172.16.1.250; however, it will then look at its local host file to see if there is an entry for 172.16.1.250. At that time, the NAS device will see that 172.16.1.250 is referred to as server1, which is allowed to mount the exported folder /vol/vol0/oracle. When an anonymous user attempts a showmount command, they will see that a node by the name of server1 has access to the exported directory. What they will not see is that server1 is actually oracle-db3 or the ip address is 172.16.1.250, thus limiting their ability to spoof their hostname and get access to the folder. Note that this is a classic example of security by obscurity, which is not a strong security practice. Because there are no other options available to prevent showmount responses on most NAS installations using NFS, this method can be used; however, note that this method does not actually secure showmount information—it just obscures it. Figure 10.5 shows this example.

The following steps show how to configure the architecture in Figure 10.5:

1. Architecture details:
   a. Exported file system: /vol/vol0/oracle
   b. Authorized node: oracle-db3 (172.16.1.250)
   c. Alias for authorized node: server1
2. Make the export:
   a. Open /etc/exports.

b. Enter the following in /etc/exports:

    i.   /vol/vol0/oracle   rw=server1

c. Type **exportfs -a.**

3. Make the alias:

  a. Open /etc/hosts.

  b. Enter the following in /etc/hosts:

    i. **172.16.1.250 Server1**

4. Done! Server1, which is 172.16.1.250 according to the NAS device, now has access to /vol/vol0/oracle without the showmount command telling anonymous users who server1 is or what the IP address actually is.

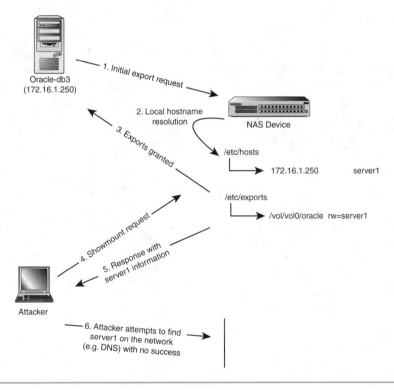

Figure 10.5 Protecting NFS enumeration.

Although we have limited the ability for anonymous users to enumerate the authorized hosts, we have not limited the enumeration of the exported directories, which is equally as important (if not more). If desired, symlinks could be used; however, they introduce other security issues. Furthermore, while they might obfuscate what path is being exported, a user who exports that directory will be able to retrieve that information automatically. The defense we would want is to prevent the attacker from knowing the path (symlinked or not) to export, which symlink does not do.

While limiting information on the exported file system is not possible, implementing protections on the enumeration of authorized hosts and IP address will prevent the following attacks:

- Authorized hostnames spoofing
- Authorized IP addresses spoofing

AUTHENTICATION

Authentication has been the key security problem for NFS. Authentication has been available with NFS in 4 via RPCSEC GSS. In fact, NFS supports Kerberos authentication, which is very good in terms of security. It should be noted that many NAS devices can work only with a single KDC; therefore, if your NAS device is pointing to a Windows Active Directory server for its KDC under CIFS, you cannot point it toward another KDC for NFS. The good news is that NFS clients can use a Windows Active Directory server for its KDC. In mixed environments where there will be CIFS and NFS clients, using Windows AD for the KDC works pretty well.

NFS servers and clients can support Kerberos under three different modes. It can be used for authentication only, which uses the sec=krb5 option in the /etc/exports file, authentication and integrity checking, which uses sec=krb5p as the option, or authentication, integrity checking, and data encryption, which uses sec=krb5p as the option. In order to enable Kerberos authentication on a Network Appliance machine running NFS, complete the following steps (this assumes you have already configured Kerberos for CIFS, described previously in this chapter):

1. Log into the filer:
   a. SSH <ip address> 22
2. Set up NFS authentication process on the NAS device (entered commands are in **bold**):
   a. setup nfs
   b. Enable Kerberos for NFS? **Y**

c. The filer supports these types of Kerberos Key Distribution Centers (KDCs):

1 - UNIX KDC

2 - Microsoft Active Directory KDC

d. Enter the type of your KDC (1-2): **1** (if NFS only) or **2** (Win-AD)

Kerberos now enabled for NFS.

NFS setup complete.

3. Open up /etc/exports and add sec=krb5 for Kerberos authentication, sec=krb5i for Kerberos authentication and integrity, sec=krb5p for Kerberos authentication, integrity, and privacy on each NFS export you want to require Kerberos authentication.

a. /vol/vol0/oracle   sec=krb5, rw=server1

As stated in Chapter 7, "NAS: NFS Security," enabling authentication on NAS devices using NFS can be simple from the NAS device perspective, the problem is that nfs clients need to support authentication in their commands. Solaris has provided the capability to use Kerberos authentication for NFS since version 2.6; however, in version 2.6, the Kerberos package needs to be downloaded on the machine since it does not have it enabled out-of-the-box. The following list shows which operating systems support NFS client authentication with Kerberos:

- Solaris 2.6 to 2.8

  SEAM 1.0 or 1.0.1 is required.
- Solaris 2.9 to 2.10 (fully supported)
- Partial support in the Linux Kernel 2.6 and above
- Red Hat Fedora core 2 (fully supported)
- FreeBSD 5.2
- AIX 5.3
- Windows with Hummingbird 7.0 or 8.0
- Windows Services for Unix

The syntax to mount an NFS export that is using Kerberos on a Windows client is as follows:

- `mount -u:<username> -p:<password> IP.address:export directory drive`
- `mount -u:neeraja -p:shreya 172.16.1.100:/vol/vol0/oracle x:`

The syntax to mount an NFS export that is using Kerberos on a Unix-supported client is as follows:

- `mount -t nfs -o username=<username>,password=<password> ip.address:export directory local directory`
- `mount -t nfs -o username=neeraja,password=shreya 172.16.1.100:/vol/vol0/oracle /mnt/oracle`

While preventing the information leakages for the exported file system is not possible, implementing protections on the enumeration of authorized hosts/IP addresses and enabling authentication on NFS NAS devices will prevent the following attacks:

- UID/GID authorization attacks
- Anonymous access to NFS exports
- File permission subversion on CIFS shares
- File permission subversion on NFS exports

AUTHORIZATION

Traditional authorization is the only security value required for NAS devices supporting NFS. Now that you understand how to enable authentication, hopefully authorization is the second level of security control on your NAS device.

Authorization can also be improved from NFS default settings. From Chapter 7, we saw the major problem of NFS authorization is the fact that the client UID and GID values are trusted. Similar to spoofing a WWN or an iQN, changing a UID value to match the value of the owner of a particular directory is also spoofing. In fact, many of the major attacks in NFS are due to the lack of authentication for NFS and the fact that UID and GIDs values are trusted.

As a defense, most NAS devices don't trust the root UID (UID=0) from any client machine. Therefore, you do not need to worry about a client submitting a request for a file access from the UID=0. A NAS device will take that request and transfer it to the nobody account (UID=65534), giving the remote root user guest access only. The problem is when a user changes their UID to match the UID of a file that is not owned by root. One method to disable UID/GID values of the requesting client is to use NFS version 4. NFS version 4 does not rely solely on the UID/GID value of the client, but also uses the user's username and domain (a NFS version 4 client must be used to support this new feature). For example, if a request is coming from the user Kusum from the domain called Aum.com, her UID and GID will be sent along with kusum@Aum.com. There are still issues with using the username and domain, since the malicious client can change their username and domain to anything; however, this is why you want to enable authentication with NFSv4 to mitigate against these attack classes.

A method to defend against UID/GID attacks against non-root accounts on a NetApp filer is to enable the setting to map each requester's UID and IP address to the usermap.cfg file. The usermap.cfg file is a file that maps Windows/Unix users together along with IP addresses (optional). This setting enabled would force a successful check with the usermap.cfg file that states the specific UIDs that can access the filer from a specific IP address only. For example, a sample setting could be that the user Shreya with the UID 1021 can only access the filer from the IP address of 172.16.11.17. If an attacker spoofs their UID to match Shreya's and attempts to access the filer with the security setting enabled, the attacker will be denied even though they contain the correct UID since they are not coming from the correct IP address. This setting could also be subverted if the attacker spoofs both the UID and their IP address, which is still very possible but requires the attacker to do extra work. In a large environment, this setting would be highly difficult to deploy since users and UIDs can come from many thousands of IP addresses; however, for powerful users (Windows administrators and root superusers) and accounts with sensitive information (executives), you may want to consider enabling this option. The setting on a NetApp filer to enable this setting is as follows:

```
options nfs.require_valid_mapped_uid on
```

A method to ensure that all the root UIDs (UID=0) from NFS clients are ignored and only given guest or nobody access is to add anon=65534 at the end of each export line. For example, if all clients come in as root and should not have access to the /vol/vol0/oracle export, then enter the following line in /etc/exports:

```
/vol/vol0/oracle        anon=65534
```

This setting would not protect the NAS device running NFS from the UID/GID attacks shown in Chapter 7 because those attacks were coming from another UID and not the root UID. In order to ignore all UIDs that are received from an NFS client and give them nobody access, you can export each directory with read-only access (ro). Exporting all directories with read-only access will still give every machine/user the ability to read all files; however, when an attacker changes their UID/GID to match the UID/GID of a file/folder owner, the file permission values will be ignored due to the fact that the directory is exported as read only. The read-only option overrides any file permission values. To export a directory as read only, add the -ro option in the /etc/exports file:

```
/vol/vol0/oracle        -ro
```

Another method to grant read-only access to exported directories while allowing authorized machines read-write access is using the rw=*host* option. This option will allow all host read-only access to the exported directories, similar to the previous setting, except the hosts listed. All hosts listed would be grated read-write access. To export a directory with read-only access to all exported directories and read-write access to listed hosts, use the following syntax:

```
/vol/vol0/oracle        -rw=exchange.us.aum.com
```

Any UID, whether it is the root UID of 0 or some account UID of 30, would only have read-only access. The user would hold low privileges on the NFS system, which means that any export that does not specifically allow the nobody (guest) account access to the export would deny the user. The only exports that allow the nobody account (UID=65534) by default are world-readable exports.

Several other methods to ensure that the UID of root (UID=0) is always mapped to the anonymous account is the use of the squash option. The root_squash option will always map any client with the UID=0 to the anonymous account. Also, the squash_uids option will mount all UIDs listed with read-only access. For example, -squash_uids=0,30,49, 50-239 would map all users with UIDs of 0, 30, 49, or 50 through 239 as anonymous users. The problem with that is the users could still change their UIDs to ones that are not squashed. The method to map all UIDs to squash would be to use the all_squash option. The all_squash option would map all UIDs from clients as the anonymous account. This setting is the same as mounting the file system as read only (ro). The following syntax are examples of the squash options with root, specific UIDs, and all UIDs.

```
/vol/vol0/oracle        -root_squash
/vol/vol0/oracle        -squash_uids=0,30,49,50-239
/vol/vol0/oracle        -all_squash
```

What if a certain user called Neeraja with the UID of 61276 on a host called brkgs.sd.aum.com needed full access to an export, but you don't want anyone else to have access? While all hosts can be limited to read-only access with the -ro or -rw option, unfortunately all users on the host called brkgs.sd.aum.com could still perform UID/GID attacks and get full access to the directory. Even if the squash commands were used, an attacker could still see that the UID of 61276 is allowed to mount the exported as read write and change their UID to that value. Additionally, remote hosts that are willing to perform DNS attacks or IP spoofing attacks along with UID/GID attacks could still subvert this security control. Using Kerberos authentication is the best and only true method to fully defend against UID/GID attacks.

It should be noted that not all NAS devices support all the export options listed previously. Contact your NAS vendor to understand what export options are supported. Table 10.1 shows some of the options for security as well as the NFS export setting.

Table 10.1 Security Options for NFS exports

Security Level	Option	NFS Export Setting
Root access only for Server1.	/vol/vol0/oracle	-root=Server1 anon=65534
Read-only access for all hosts.	/vol/vol0/oracle	-ro
Read-only access for all hosts except Server1.	/vol/vol0/oracle	-rw=Server1
Force all UID=0 to be mapped to the anonymous UID; however, this setting does not protect against any other UID.	/vol/vol0/oracle	-root_squash
Force all listed UID to be mapped to the anonymous UIDs.	/vol/vol0/oracle squash_uids=0-10, 20,25-30	-squash_uids=1-400, 405-65535
Maps all UIDs to the anonymous UIDs. Same as exporting a file system as read only.	/vol/vol0/oracle	-all_squash

ENCRYPTION

Encryption on NAS devices supporting NFS has the same benefit described earlier in the CIFS section

Because NFS is clear-text and transmits several entities that are important for attackers in the clear—such as UID/GID, exports, valid IP addresses/hostnames—the ability to encrypt the communication is very important. Using encryption between a NAS device and a Oracle database will reduce the attack surface by a malicious user. Figure 10.6 is an example of a NAS device using encryption between Unix operating systems.

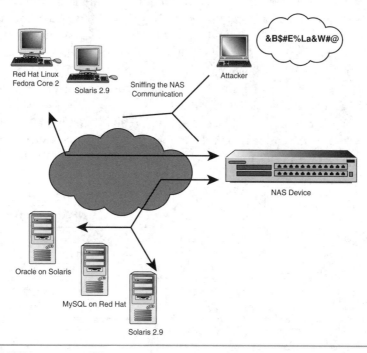

Figure 10.6   NAS devices using IPSec.

Notice in Figure 10.6 that the attacker is still able to sniff the communication from any node on the network to the NAS device; however, when the attacker actually views the packets he or she has captured, the information shows up as garbage data. In order to see what IPSec encryption would look like if it were sniffed over the network with any basic sniffer, such as Ethereal, refer back to Figure 10.4.

In order to enable IPSec on a NAS environment, you must enable it on the NAS device and on the node operating system. Therefore, there are two places to set up IPSec, not just on the NAS device itself. To enable IPSec on Network Appliance NAS devices, complete the following commands:

1. Log into the filer:

    a. SSH <ip address> 22

2. The syntax for IPSec is

   a. `ipsecpolicyadd –s {source ip} –t {destination ip} –p {esp|ah|none} –e {des|3des|null} – a{sha1|md5|null} –d {in|out} –f ip_protocol –l {restrict|permit}`

     i. `source ip:` The NAS device

     ii. `destination ip:` The target client or server operating system

     iii. `–p:` Use payload encryption (ESP) or packet integrity (AH)

     iv. `–e:` If ESP, then choose type of encryption (DES, 3Des, or null)

     v. `–a:` If AH, then choose type of hash (SHA1, MD5, or null)

     vi. `–d:` In or out directions

     vii. `–f:` TCP (number 6) or UDP (number 17)

     viii. `–l:` Restrict means communication is only allowed if it gets an SA. Permit means if it cannot get an SA, then there will be no security on the data.

3. To enable IPSec from the NAS device of 172.16.1.100 to all sources in the network using payload encryption with triple DES:

   a. `ipsecpolicyadd –s 172.16.1.100 –p esp –e 3des –a sha1 –d in`

4. Create a pre-shared key file on the NAS device:

   a. Browse to /etc.

   b. Make a file called psk.txt.

   c. Type the IP address(s) and shared key for each node.

     i. **`0.0.0.0/8 supersecretpre-sharedkey`**

Now that IPSec is enabled on the NAS device using the pre-shared key of "supersecret-pre-sharedkey," ensure that it also is enabled on your Solaris or Red Hat operating system. The /etc/ipsec.conf or the /etc/isakmpd.conf can be used to set up IPSec on Unix systems. The use of IPSec between a NAS device and nodes on the network can help mitigate the following attacks:

- Enumeration of exports
- Enumeration of authorized IP addresses/hostnames
- Lack of authentication
- UID/GID attacks
- Telnet, FTP, HTTP sniffing
- General NFS communication sniffing

NAS DEVICE SECURITY

Securing CIFS and NFS on a NAS device is significant, but other parts of a NAS device (or any network device) can also lead to data compromise or unavailability if ignored. Consider all the management aspects and monitoring protocols that are available for any network device. NAS devices include all of these items that can lead to compromises that can control the entire system, similar to any other devices and operating systems on the network. If you secure NFS and CIFS but are still using Telnet or RSH for management purposes, then an attacker can control the entire NAS device and all the data sitting inside it.

Additionally, there are other methods to mitigate NAS attacks using virtual segmentation technology deployed by NAS storage vendors. Due to the significant security issues combined with the fact that NAS devices often store data for various type of users, business units, and security zones, virtual domains on the same NAS device, similar to VSANs, is a great method to enable logical segmentation to mitigate security exposures.

This section will focus on the security of support entities of a NAS device, including the following topics:

- Management protocols
  SSH and SSL
- Monitoring protocols
  NDMP and SNMP
- Data security
  At-rest encryption
- vFilers
  Virtual filers on a single NAS device

MANAGEMENT PROTOCOLS

Stop using Telnet, RSH, Rlogin, or HTTP for anything security related, including management. Let's be very clear on this. Nobody would enjoy if their bank had an insecure web site for online banking, nor should we use weak protocols to access our critical network infrastructure. While many storage vendors never supported more secure protocols such as SSH or SSL, most of the major ones do now. As described in Chapter 6, "NAS: CIFS Security," using SSH or SSL (HTTPS) instead of Telnet, RSH, Rlogin, or HTTP adds in-line encryption to prevent sniffing attacks.

Implementing SSH is a great choice to protect command-line management. SSH version 2 should be used since version 1 has had security issues. If a NAS device only supports version 1, it should still be enabled over telnet or rsh. An SSH client is required to connect to the SSH service on a NAS device. Most Unix operating systems already have an SSH client and a Windows clients can download it from OpenSSH.org, SSH Communications (www.ssh.com), or Vandyke Software (www.vandyke.com).

Implementing SSL is another great choice to protect web management. Many NAS devices have used insecure HTTP management that allows a username and password to traverse the network in clear-text, which can be captured, stolen, and used to compromise the entire NAS storage system. Similar to SSH, SSL can used to replace HTTP entirely, ensuring that management functions and authentication methods are secure from remote attackers. Enabling HTTPS is a very simple task on a NAS device and does not require any changes on administrative workstations since all browsers can support the use of HTTPS.

In order to enable SSH or SSL on a Network Appliance filer, complete the following steps:

1. Download and install SecureAdmin. This will enable SSH and allow the administrator to set the key strength for the RSA key, ranging from 384 bits to 1024 bits:

   a. `secureadmin setup -f ssh`

2. Enter the following command to enable SSH:

   a. **`secureadmin enable ssh`**

3. Enter the following command to set up SSL:

   a. **`secureadmin setup ssl`**

4. Enter the following command to enable SSH:

   a. **`secureadmin enable ssl`**

5. Done! SSH and SSL have been enabled.

6. Now you should disable Telnet, RSH, and FTP, and disable HTTP access:

   a. `options telnet.enable off`

   b. `options rsh.enable off`

   c. `options ftp.enable.off`

   d. `options httpd.admin.access none`

7. Now that SSH and SSL have been enabled and Telnet, RSH, and HTTP have been disabled, ensure your NAS device is using strong passwords:

   a. `options security.passwd.rules.enable on`

MONITORING

The two major methods to monitoring a NAS device on a network is through the use of Network Data Management Protocol (NDMP) and Simple Network Management Protocol (SNMP).

NDMP

NDMP controls a significant amount of entities in a storage network, including backup systems, storage devices, and storage software. Similar to any other management entity, the use of this powerful protocol should be safe and secure. The first thing to do should be to enable strong authentication on NDMP devices. It is quite frightening how many NDMP connections are without passwords. Because NDMP is not a mainstream protocol like Telnet, it often gets overlooked. However NDMP has such a significant amount of control over data on a NAS device, it should not only be focused on, and it should have a strong authentication model to secure it. NDMP supports three types of authentication, including plain-text, challenge, or both. Challenge authentication should only be enabled, and plain-text authentication should be completely disabled. To enable NDMP challenge authentication on a Network Appliance filer, enter the following command:

```
options ndmpd.authtype challenge
```

The second thing that should be done is to limit the NDMP applications that can actually control the NDMP devices. Placing access control lists on NAS devices will ensure that any NDMP host cannot send commands to the NDMP agent located on a backup server of an NAS storage device. To enable NDMP access control lists to only the management server, such as 172.16.1.5, on a Network Appliance filer, enter the following command:

```
options ndmpd.access host=172.16.1.5
```

As best practice, you also want to enable logging on your NDMP connections. Connections that fail and succeed will allow administrators to understand if any attacker is attempting to access the storage device. Additionally, logging will also notify the administrator if an accidental change or misconfiguration has taken place that may affect data availability. All too often protocol auditing is ignored; however, when problems arise (which always do), they are the best and safest resource to understand what went wrong. Ensure you have enabled logging on your NDMP connections. In order to enable NDMP logging on a Network Appliance filer, enter the following command. The example command will log time, request, action, source IP, source port, and session ID into /etc/syslog:

```
options ndmpd.connectlog.enabled on
```

SNMP

SNMP may also control a certain amount of monitoring and management duties, but certainly not as many as NDMP. SNMP security involves three basic things: the use of SNMPv3 to utilize encryption, strong public and private SNMP community strings (passwords) to monitor or manage the NAS device, and SNMP trap filters to limit the number of hosts that can access an SNMP trap from a NAS device.

The first step is to enable strong public and private community strings. Public community strings are like passwords to allow read-only access to a NAS device. Several NAS devices support SNMP; however, most of them also leave the default community string of "public" on the device. When using public community strings, ensure that they have been changed to something else other than public. Many NAS devices don't support private community strings. Private community strings are also live passwords, but give a host read-write access to the storage device. If your NAS devices does not support private community strings, you are not at risk of someone changing the configuration of your storage via SNMP. If your NAS device does support private community strings, ensure it is a very difficult string and not the default value, which is "private." To enable a strong public community string on Network Appliance filer, enter the following command (be sure to enter the following command to delete the existing public community string):

```
snmp community add ro 06supersecret12communitystring75
snmp community delete ro public
```

The next entity to secure SNMP is to restrict SNMP traps to valid hosts. Because anyone on the network can request information from SNMP, it becomes a nice attack vector for information leakage. If SNMP has to be enabled, ensure you are limiting the SNMP traps (information that is sent about a NAS device to an authorized host) to only authorized management stations. In order to enable SNMP trap filters to the authorized workstation of 172.16.1.5 on a Network Appliance filer, enter the following command:

```
snmp traphost add 172.16.1.5
```

The last major security setting for SNMP is to enable SNMPv3. While SNMPv1 is used on most major NAS devices (most major devices in general), it is clear-text. This means that no matter how strong your public/private community string is, any attacker can access that information over the network in clear-text. Using clear-text protocols is such a bad thing, especially when it is used for monitoring or management activities. If your NAS device supports SNMPv3, enable it. If not, consider disabling SNMP altogether since it is a very big security target.

vFILERS

Virtual Filers (vFilers) is a segmentation technology developed by Network Appliance (NetApp). vFilers are used to logically segment a NetApp NAS device into completely domains, where one vFiler is not able to access any data, NFS exports, or CIFS shares from another vFiler. vFilers are similar to VLANs and VSANs, which was discussed in Chapter 9, where their purpose is to provide a single device to support various networks or groups without the use of multiple filers. For example, if a single NetApp filer needs to support the DMZ servers on an untrusted network security zone and also a few servers on the internal network, which is holds a higher level of trust, then the use of vFilers would be ideal. The filer can provide data resources for the DMZ servers and not expose any of that communication/access to the internal network or internal data resources (CIFS shares or NFS clients). Figure 10.7 shows an example.

vFilers can also be used for internal network resources. For example, if there are shares that should only be exposed to the finance department and other shares that should only be exposed to accounting due to confidentiality concerns (for example, government regulations to protect the integrity of financial data), virtual filers could also be used in internal environments. Furthermore, vFilers can be created per department to ensure that data is not damaged, tampered with, or compromised by unauthorized users.

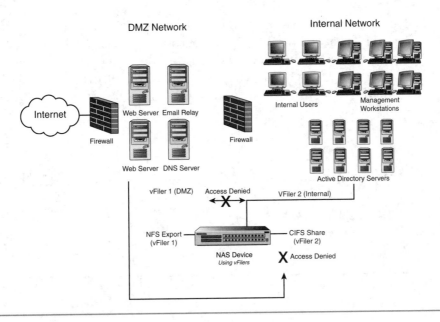

Figure 10.7 vFilers.

NAS TAPE SECURITY

Similar to SAN devices encrypting data at-rest, NAS storage networks can encrypt data at-rest before it hits the NAS device or tape devices connected to NAS devices. Encrypting data at-rest is a great method to ensure data on your storage network is not available to unauthorized users. It should be noted that encrypted data at-rest is a very good security practice, but it does not protect against denial-of-service attacks that can leave data entirely unavailable, incorrect configuration changes, accidental data allocations, or compromised operating systems/applications servers. Despite the fact that encryption doesn't protect against availability attacks, it protects against several other attacks in a storage network. Many storage security vendors, such as Decru, NeoScale, Vormetric, and Kastan-Chase, provide in-line appliances to encrypt data in NAS infrastructures also. Unlike SAN architectures, these encryption appliances would sit between the host operating system (Windows or Unix) and the NAS storage device or the NAS device and the tape device. The encryption appliances support both NFS and CIFS communication, encrypting the data for both of them before it reaches the NAS device or tape device. Once the NAS or tape device receives the data, it stores it locally as it would for any other type of data, but is oblivious to the fact that data is encrypted and not in clear-text. If an attacker were to compromise the data on the NAS disk, they would now receive encrypted information that they could not read or understand. Additionally, if the tape is accidentally lost or intentionally stolen, the information would not be at risk. Encrypting storage data adds a significant amount of security that will protect data against many attacks. Figure 10.8 shows an example architecture with an encryption appliance being used.

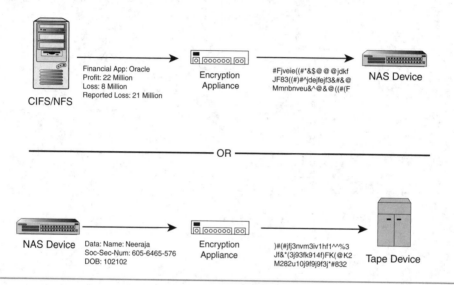

Figure 10.8   Storage encryption appliances.

Encryption data at-rest can mitigate the following attacks:

- Authentication attacks
  LM, NTLM, pre-auth Kerberos
- Authorization
  UID/GID
- Data sniffing (CIFS and NFS)
- Misplaced, stolen, or lost tapes

NAS SECURITY SUMMARY

Table 10.2 is a summary of the options that are available in most NAS environments and their recommended security settings. An organization must choose the ideal setting that best fits their environment; however, Table 10.2 will demonstrate which security options are better than others.

Table 10.2 NAS Security Options and Recommendations

Feature	Option	Ideal Security Option
CIFS enumeration	On or Off	Off
CIFS authentication	LM, NTLM, or Kerberos	Kerberos
CIFS authorization	Hostnames or IP addresses	Either with file-based permissions
CIFS encryption	None or IPSec	IPSec
NFS enumeration	None or hostnames/hostfiles	Hostnames/hostfiles
NFS authentication	None or Kerberos	Kerberos
NFS authorization	UID/GIDs or usernames	Usernames with Kerberos authentication
NFS encryption	None or IPSec	IPSec
Management	Telnet, RSH, Rlogin, HTTP, SSH, or SSL	SSH and/or SSL
Monitoring	NDMP and SNMP	Authenticated NDMP and SNMPv3
Segmentation	vFilers or IP subnetting	vFilers
Data encryption	None or at-rest encryption	At-rest encryption

SUMMARY

This chapter discussed the methods to protect against many CIFS and NFS NAS attacks described in Chapters 5 through 7. Secure storage is key for data protection and data availability. While many issues exist in NAS architectures, there are several existing mitigations that can be deployed by organizations to safely and securely keep their data available and secure. As shown in this chapter, a few key settings and configuration changes might help the data in a NAS from unauthorized access and unintentional damage. This mitigates the security risk significantly without having a severe impact on performance. The next chapter focuses on security iSCSI environments, as well as securing iSCSI storage devices.

Securing iSCSI

Protecting iSCSI storage is a hefty task. iSCSI storage is susceptible to all the attacks of IP and all the devastating flaws of block data. The security weaknesses, exploits, and attacks demonstrated in Chapter 8, "SANs: iSCSI Security," are important to mitigate in order for iSCSI to be a stable, secure, and highly available storage network. This chapter is the last of three chapters that discusses the defenses and best practices for securing storage. The goal is to discuss the existing features, tools, and configuration settings that are available in iSCSI storage networks. These settings will help mitigate the security weaknesses/attacks discussed earlier.

Understanding the security weaknesses and attacks from Chapter 8 will help us better secure our storage network. This allows a strong defense for the entire environment as well as targeted defenses for the primary attack methods. A good example of this is using The Club to secure your car. The company that made The Club obviously decided that car thieves will always be one step ahead of the car manufacturers. They will learn how to pick locks, bypass locked windows, use coat hangers, use hot-wiring, or simply capture signals from wireless remotes. Instead of always coming up with a technology that will be subverted by an attacker, they just make the car undriveable if broken into. Although thieves may be able to get the valuables from the car, they won't be able to steal the car itself (which probably holds the biggest value). It should be noted that picking the lock on The Club is another attacker vector, but let's focus on iSCSI networks.

This chapter discusses the defenses, best practices, and mitigating controls for iSCSI attacks. After each defense is discussed, a list of the attacks it protects against are listed.

This will clearly define which security practices defend against which attacks. The following attacks were described in Chapter 8 and are the primary focus for this chapter:

iSCSI SAN Attacks

- iSCSI targets, iQNs, devices, and LUNs enumeration
- iSCSI sniffing (Man-in-the-Middle)
- CHAP weaknesses
- iSCSI iQN spoofing
- iSNS spoofing
- Domain hopping attacks (iSNS servers)
- iSCSI challenge attacks

Securing iSCSI

As shown in Chapter 8, iSCSI SANs have plenty of security and data protection problems. iSCSI security is not assisted by the fact that important security items like authentication are disabled by default, even if it uses CHAP. In most modern networks, a user cannot do anything without authenticating to a domain, a firewall, or even a proxy server to access the Internet. It is somewhat amusing how some organizations will require users to authenticate to access the Internet, which holds data that is freely available to the world, but don't require authentication to protect terabytes of their own data. Requiring users to authenticate to use the Internet (via proxy servers or firewalls) is a great idea because penetrating networks via web viruses and worms are becoming the major attack method; however, more attention should be given to iSCSI storage than the defaults that are implemented during setup procedures. This chapter will focus on the following defenses to help organizations protect against the iSCSI attacks that can devastate a storage network:

- Authentication
  - Enable authentication
  - CHAP message challenges
  - Mutual authentication with CHAP

- iSNS security
  - Authentication
  - iSNS management
  - iSNS discovery domains
- Encryption
  - CRC checksums
  - IPSec
- Future security requests
  - Kerberos
  - Replacing iQN values
  - iSNS query authorization

AUTHENTICATION

The following sections describe the authentication options and strengths with iSCSI.

ENABLE AUTHENTICATION

Most iSCSI storage products have left authentication disabled by default. Although there are plenty of reasons for this, such as the ease of setup, the negatives (the complete compromise of your data) outweigh the positives (easy management of storage devices).

The first thing to do with iSCSI storage products is to enable CHAP authentication. Despite the fact that there are attacks on CHAP, as discussed in Chapter 8, having some type of authentication is rarely a bad thing. Enabling authentication will limit the impact of the authorization attacks involving iQNs. Furthermore, enabling authentication will force the attacker to perform real-time or off-line brute-forcing attacks on CHAP, which still can lead to successful compromise but can make an attack timeline significantly longer. Making an attacker work harder to compromise your iSCSI storage device might make them move to a different target since it would probably be easier to hack another iSCSI storage device that has left authentication off by default. In order to enable iSCSI authentication on a Network Appliance filer, complete the following steps.

Note that each iSCSI vendor, such as Lefthand or EqualLogic, has the ability to enable iSCSI authentication using different steps than shown next, but NetApp has only been shown as an example.

1. Log into the filer:

   a. `SSH <ip address> 22`

2. Enable CHAP:

   a. `iscsi security add -i <initiator> -s CHAP -p <password> -n <name>`

   b. Example: `iscsi security add -i iqn.test.com -s CHAP -p iscsisecurity -n iscsisecurity`

3. Generate a random 128-bit CHAP password for iSCSI authentication:

   a. `iscsi security generate`

Now that iSCSI CHAP authentication has been enabled on the iSCSI storage device, complete the following steps to enable it on the Microsoft iSCSI client. Note that each iSCSI client vendor, such as Cisco or IBM, also has the ability to enable iSCSI authentication using different steps than show next:

1. Open the iSCSI Initiator (Start -> Programs -> Microsoft iSCSI Initiator -> Configure Initiator).

2. Under the Target Portals tab, click on the Add button.

3. Type the IP address of the iSCSI target and select the Advanced button.

4. Check the CHAP logon information checkbox.

5. Type the username for the iSCSI client, which is the name option set on the iSCSI device (for example, iscsisecurity).

6. Type the secret for the iSCSI target, which is the password set on the iSCSI storage device (for example, iscsisecurity). See Figure 11.1.

7. Select OK on the Advance Settings window.

8. Select OK on the Target Portal menu. At this point, the iSCSI client will attempt to login to the iSCSI storage device using CHAP authentication.

9. After authentication has taken place successfully, the Target Portals tab will show the available portals. See Figure 11.2.

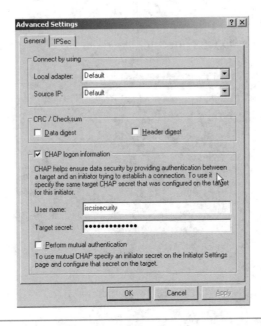

Figure 11.1 CHAP authentication settings.

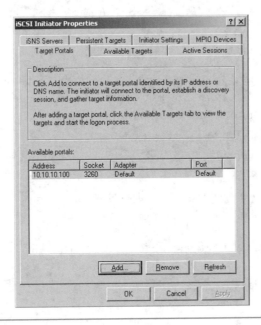

Figure 11.2 Target portals.

10. Click on the Available Targets tab to see the available targets.

11. Click the Log On button to connect to the target. See Figure 11.3.

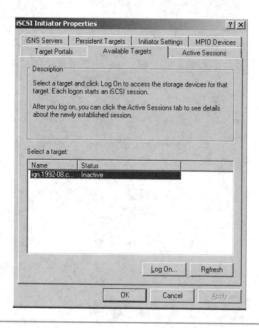

Figure 11.3   Available targets.

12. Click on the Advanced Tab. Notice that it is the same tab that we enter our username and secret information from in steps 5 and 6. You can re-enter that information or leave it as is if the information is correct.

13. Select OK in the Log On to Target window.

14. At this point, you will see "Connected" in the Status column in the Available Targets tab. See Figure 11.4.

15. Done! You have now logged into the iSCSI storage device (iSCSI target) using CHAP authentication.

Enabling authentication can mitigate the following attacks:

- iSCSI iQN spoofing
- iSNS spoofing
- Domain hopping attacks (iSNS servers)

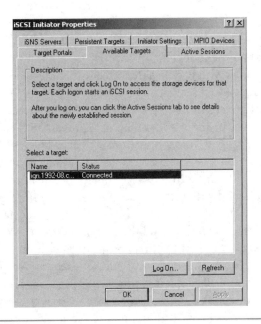

Figure 11.4 Connected status.

CHAP Message Challenges

Message challenges can be the strongest aspect for CHAP; however, it can also be the weakest link if not implemented correctly. If CHAP implementations follow the RFC closely and do not have large increments of time without a new challenge or do not allow challenges to be reflected across connections, then CHAP can be strong. On the other hand, if there are large time delays from when a new challenge is issued, replay attacks can occur. Furthermore, if challenge messages can be reflected across connections, then reflection attacks can occur. Let's address the defenses of each one separately.

iSCSI implementations (products) that have small time increments and do not repeat challenges will limit the opportunity for a replay attack. Simply put, if the challenge is always changing and never repeated, it cannot be replayed. As stated in Chapter 8, the issue with large time delays for new challenges or repeating a challenge is that the correlating hash that is generated is a password equivalent value. If any client shows the correct hash to an iSCSI target, they will accept it as valid regardless if the client actually generated the hash or just sniffed it over the network and replayed it. So how do you know if the iSCSI product you are using has implemented short time delays between challenges or no repeatable challenges? Unfortunately, there is no setting to check for this item. You can either have your security partner test for this attack or actually ask the vendor to see the results of all the independent security tests that were conducted on their product. From these results, you will be able to see if these tests were conducted and what successes any independent security team had. Many times vendors display these tests from independent groups on their web site.

iSCSI implementations (products) that have also prevented the ability for message challenges to be reflected across two connections will also prevent their storage products from reflection attacks. After a client receives a message challenge on one connection, it can take that challenge and send it to the target on a separate connection. If the target sees that it is being presented with a challenge, it forgets that it never asked for one and responds with the hash that will be generated from the challenge (the same challenge it gave the client in the first connection) and the real password; then, the malicious client gets the hash that it can now use on the first connection without ever knowing the password. This problem can be mitigated if the iSCSI nodes do not respond to challenges that they did not ask for, as well as not accepting challenges that they have already distributed. If an iSCSI node sends out a challenge and receives the same back, either on the same connection or a different connection, the node should immediately drop the connection. Similar to message challenge intervals, there is not a way to check if an iSCSI node will reject the same challenge they created from another connection. The best way is to have your local security partner verify this or ask for the independent security report that your iSCSI vendor has developed in order to ensure the product has been implemented in the most secure fashion.

Either of these scenarios still allows offline brute-forcing attacks to occurs, which is a significant CHAP security issue. Preventing message challenges from being reflected across connections or containing a small interval for new challenges is quite important for security, but the best way to defend against offline brute-forcing attacks of CHAP is to enable mutual authentication and/or IPSec, which is discussed later in this chapter.

Enabling strong message challenges and short intervals can mitigate the following attacks:

- iSCSI iQN spoofing
- iSNS spoofing
- Domain hopping attacks (iSNS servers)
- iSCSI challenge attacks

MUTUAL AUTHENTICATION WITH CHAP

CHAP authentication can be enhanced with the use of mutual authentication. Under mutual authentication, the client would authenticate the target, but the target would also authentication the client. If either part fails, the entire authentication process fails. Mutual authentication protects against several layer 2 and layer 3 attacks that IP networks are vulnerable to. For example, Man-in-the-Middle, CHAP replay attacks, spoofing, and CHAP message challenge attacks can all be prevented with the use of mutual authentication.

In order to set up mutual authentication, the iSCSI initiator would contain a secret that must be known by the iSCSI target. If the iSCSI target is unaware of the secret held by the iSCSI initiator (iSCSI client), then the connection will be refused by the client. Mutual authentication is designed specifically for Man-in-the-Middle attacks, as mentioned previously. For example, if an attacker is performing a Man-in-the-Middle attack, they can trick the iSCSI client into thinking they that are connected to the legitimate iSCSI target; however, they may be actually connecting to a malicious iSCSI target controlled by the attacker. The Man-in-the-Middle attack can trick the client into assuming that it is connecting to an iSCSI target of 10.10.10.100, where it may actually be connected to the iSCSI target 10.10.10.101, which is controlled by the attacker. Because the client natively has no way to confirm that it is connecting to its real destination, it sends in credentials (username/password) to the target that is consequently captured by the malicious attacker performing the Man-in-the-Middle attack. Using this example, if mutual authentication has been enabled, the client would ask the target for the secret that it should hold. If the iSCSI target is unable to present the correct secret, the client refuses the connection and assumes that the communication is not legitimate. Figure 11.5 shows an example.

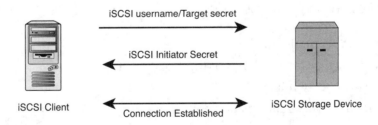

Figure 11.5 iSCSI mutual authentication.

In order to enable iSCSI mutual authentication, complete the following steps:

1. Open the iSCSI Initiator. In our example, we will use the Microsoft iSCSI Initiator (Start -> Programs -> Microsoft iSCSI Initiator -> Configure Initiator).
2. Click on the Initiator Settings tab.
3. Type the secret in the Initiator CHAP secret section, select Save, and then select OK. See Figure 11.6.

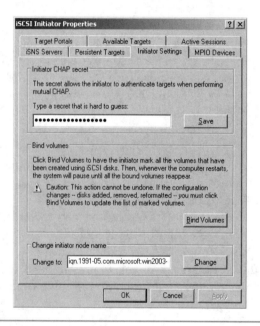

Figure 11.6   iSCSI mutual authentication with CHAP.

4. Select the Target Portals tab.
5. Select Add and type the IP address of the iSCSI target.
6. Select the Advance button.
7. Check the CHAP logon information box.
8. Type the username and target secret.
9. Select the Perform mutual authentication box. This is the setting to ensure mutual authentication will be enabled.
10. Select OK.

11. Select OK again.

12. Done! Mutual authentication has now been set up on the iSCSI client.

13. On the iSCSI target, in addition to setting the iSCSI username and target secret, ensure that you also add the client secret. The location of this setting or the syntax of the command-line option will vary between iSCSI vendors; however, most major iSCSI vendors do support mutual authentication.

14. Done! Once the iSCSI username, target secret, and client secret are set up, mutual authentication is ready on the iSCSI target.

15. Now go back to your iSCSI client and click on the Available Targets tab.

16. Select the target you just set up with mutual authentication and click Log On.

17. Done! Once the session is begun, the server will authenticate the client with the username and the target secret. Then the client will authenticate the target with the client secret. After both entities are successful, the connection will begin.

Enabling mutual authentication can mitigate the following attacks:

- iSCSI iQN spoofing
- iSNS spoofing
- Domain hopping attacks (iSNS servers)
- iSCSI challenge attacks

iSNS SECURITY

The following sections describe the security options with iSNS servers/services.

AUTHENTICATION

iSNS (iSCSI Storage Name Servers) hold a significant amount of information on the storage network. Similar to Fibre Channel name servers, an attacker can simply query the iSNS server in order to identify targets, LUNs, valid iQNs, domains, and domain groups for potential targets. If the iSNS server's information is not protected or if the iSNS server itself is spoofed, tampered with, populated with the incorrect information, accidentally misconfigured, or simply made unavailable, the entire iSCSI storage network can be at risk. Similar to the power and significance DNS servers have for Internet connectivity, an iSNS server holds a tremendous amount of responsibility for uptime and availability of the storage network, including security aspects.

One of the primary methods to secure iSNS servers is to authenticate broadcast and multicast packets within the iSNS protocol. Unlike iSCSI authentication that uses shared secrets with CHAP, iSNS communication can use authentication within its own protocol without end-user interaction. If iSNS servers can authenticate heartbeat messages (multicast) and broadcast packets, then the ability for a malicious attack, such as Man-in-the-Middle attacks, replay attacks, reflection attacks, and iSNS spoofing, is more difficult. In order to deploy authentication with broadcast and multicast iSNS packets, a PKI has to be implemented. If a PKI has been deployed, the authentication block of an iSNS broadcast/ multicast packet can be used to securely send messages and updated information from iSCSI nodes. The authentication block would contain a timestamp, a signature generated from the timestamp and message information, the hash type used to create the signature (such as SHA1), and initiator information of the key material and algorithm used.

By implementing authenticated heartbeats, which uses multicast, it will give iSNS clients the integrity and assurance that they are receiving information that is valid. If an iSNS client receives incorrect information from an iSNS server, it can equate to full compromise of the system because all of its data could be attached to a hostile target. You may be saying to yourself that DNS servers don't authenticate packets, so why should iSNS servers have to? Well, there are several reasons why. First, an iSNS server controls several hundred gigs of data; DNS only controls access to public web sites. Second, if your iSNS server is compromised, all your data could be compromised and high-end servers could be destroyed. (If you go to an incorrect web site, there is a different percentage of damage when compared to 50 to 300 gigs of data damage.) Third, iSNS servers are easier targets and have access to a lot more data than DNS. Most iSNS servers are located in the internal corporate network accessible to almost everyone. This make an attacker's job easier compared to targeting a DNS server in the DMZ. Fourth, DNS servers have a root chain process, so an attack would be quite extensive, whereas an iSNS server has no chain of trust. Fifth, DNS servers are not necessarily considered as trusted entity that have the right to allocated data, where iSNS servers do hold this false sense of trust in organizations. Sixth, think of all the DNS cache poisoning attacks that disrupt Internet communication. An attacker can update a DNS server with false information, causing a user who wants to browse to www.google.com to instead go to www.viruses.com. If the iSNS server were corrupted with incorrect information, it would do a lot more damage than simply taking a client to the wrong web site. For example, if an attacker spoofs the iSNS server that makes the client connect to a hostile iSCSI target containing viruses and worms, all the data on the client machine would be compromised and damaged. Finally, DNS servers are indirectly tied to data, whereas iSNS servers are directly tied to data. This makes an iSNS server a higher-risk device that requires more security. For example, the amount of money attached to your ATM card is significantly lower than the amount of money in your bank deposit box. While both deal with money, the security of your ATM card relies on a four-digit PIN number, and the security of your bank's vault relies on two keys from two different people, physical barriers, personal identification, and access codes. Figure 11.7 shows an example of authentication iSNS servers.

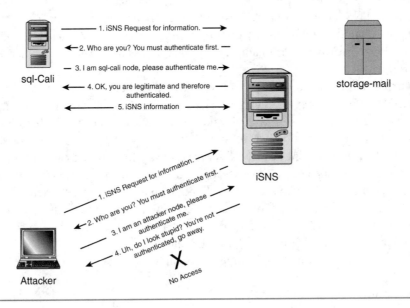

Figure 11.7 iSNS authentication.

While heartbeat messages uses multicast, iSNS uses unicast for query and response messages. These messages also need to be authenticated and secured since they contain valuable information of the iSCSI target and client over the clear-text network. iSNS relies on IPSec in order to secure unicast messages. IPSec can be used to provide integrity and confidentiality to iSNS unicast packets. IPSec is further described later in this chapter in the encryption section.

Enabling iSNS authentication can mitigate the following attacks:

- iSNS spoofing
- Domain hopping attacks (iSNS servers)

iSNS MANAGEMENT

iSNS servers can also be used to manage security within the iSCSI storage network, assuming the information is trusted, authenticated, and secure. For example, iSNS servers can be used to distribute security authentication, authorization, and encryption policies between requesting clients and targeted nodes. Two nodes that require IPSec can be given information via the iSNS server regarding AH or ESP. While iSNS servers are not required between an iSCSI client and target, using iSNS servers as the centralized policy manager can scale security policies very well, which can limit rogue attackers. For example, if an iSNS server contains a security policy that all clients need to use the correct IPSec pre-shared secret, then any unauthorized or accidental client that is attempting to connect to information they should not have access to will simply be denied by the iSNS server.

All security policy-related information, such as IKE/IPSec, AH, or ESP, can be kept and required by the iSNS server. It can act as a domain controller that will not give any entity access to any storage node or even information about a storage node unless the entity contains the correct information, such as certificates, pre-shared keys, or security associations. Additionally, since the iSNS server knows which devices are authorized (nodes with IPSec enabled or nodes with IPSec disabled), it can group all secure and trusted clients into one domain set and all clients who do not have IPSec enabled into another domain set. Therefore, if any node is accidentally or maliciously connected to the iSNS server, they would be grouped into a domain that is consider untrusted and not granted any access to iSCSI storage. Figure 11.8 shows this example.

Enabling iSNS management can mitigate the following attacks:

- iSNS spoofing
- Domain hopping attacks (iSNS servers)

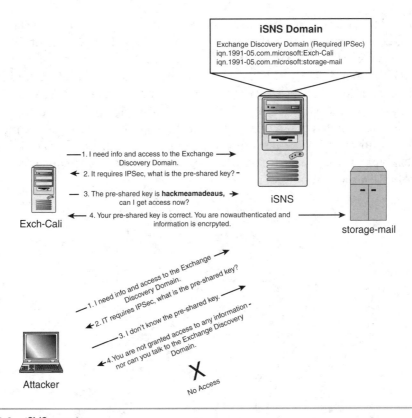

Figure 11.8   iSNS security.

iSNS Discovery Domains

Another method to secure iSNS servers is to create separate discovery domains for each class (type) of node. Instead of using the default discovery domain that groups all nodes together, separate domains can be created. The default domain on iSNS servers is a virtual domain that is used for all new registered initiators and targets. Think of it as the default zone or VLAN that all new iSCSI targets and initiators are grouped into. If there is no other domains (zones or VLANs) set up, each node will belong to this group and be able to retrieve information about any other node within the group (including the entire group itself). In order to prevent unauthorized or malicious iSCSI clients from connecting or enumerating information about a trusted iSCSI target, it is best practice to set up a separate domain for each class of node. If a separate domain is set up on the iSNS server, then only the targets and initiators that are in that same domain will be able to query information from the iSNS server. Furthermore, if a separate domain is set up for trusted nodes, all new nodes that appear on the network will be siphoned off into the default domain, which should not contain any nodes that are considered to be trusted. If the default domain is designed as a place for insecure or untrusted nodes to reside, then the attack surfaces for a malicious user are significantly smaller. An iSNS administrator needs to ensure that a separate domain is set up and all authorized and trusted nodes are moved. It should be noted that creating separate domains does not protect against spoofed iQNs; however, it would be more difficult for an attacker to find and target certain iQNs if separate domains have been set up. See Figure 11.9 for a good security example of iSNS domains.

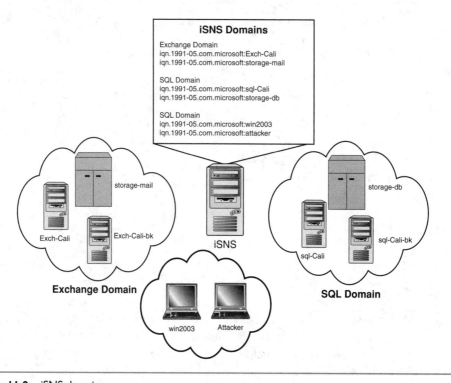

Figure 11.9 iSNS domains.

Enabling iSNS discovery domain security can mitigate the following attacks:

- iSCSI targets, iQNs, devices, and LUNs enumeration
- Domain hopping attacks (iSNS servers)

ENCRYPTION

IPSec offers two methods of security: Authentication Headers (AH) and Encapsulated Payload (ESP). AH is used for packet integrity and ESP is used for packet encryption. iSCSI implementation does not use AH for packet integrity; however, it does support packet integrity options using CRC checksums. CRC checksums is a method that iSCSI storage devices and clients can use to ensure the integrity of any iSCSI packet. A client sending a packet could create a checksum and append it to the packet. The receiving entity would receive the packet and also perform a checksum. If the checksums match, the receiving entity knows that the packet has not been modified. If they do not match, then the receiving entity knows that the packet has been tampered with. iSCSI communication can enable CRC checksums on the data portion of the packet, the header portion of the packet, or both. The header holds the routing information for the packet (source address, destination address) while the data holds the actual information. If performance is an issue, enabling CRC checksums on the Header portion is a lot better. To enable CRC checksums, complete the following exercise:

1. Open the iSCSI Initiator. In our example, we will use the Microsoft iSCSI Initiator:
   a. Start -> Programs -> Microsoft iSCSI Initiator -> Configure Initiator.
2. Click on the Target Portals tab.
3. Select Add and type the IP address of the iSCSI target.
4. Select the Advance button.
5. In the CRC / Checksum area, select Data digest and Header digest.
6. Select OK.
7. Done! CRC / Checksums have been enabled on the client.

iSCSI IPSec is implemented by Internet Key Exchange (IKE). IKE is a method to implement IPSec where both parties share pre-shared keys to encrypt the traffic between each other. Because IKE uses pre-shared strings, it is not the ideal method of IPSec since the security relies on the ability to protect that shared string, which is not always easy with insecure operating systems or attrition with employees knowing the secret. The optimal way to implement IPSec uses trusted third-party certificates; however, this architecture would be very difficult to implement in storage networks. Using IKE, both the iSCSI client and the iSCSI target (iSCSI storage device) would require a pre-shared key (a shared string). Using this shared key, both entities would set up an IPSec channel for all communication between the two parties. Although ESP is used for packet encryption, it can be set up in tunneling mode or transport mode. Tunneling mode is the more tradi-tional mode, where encryption is set up between gateways. Transport mode is usually between an end-station and a gateway or two end-machines only. Using either mode, IPSec connections between two entities create an encrypted channel for all traffic. For example, all iSCSI communication on TCP ports 3205 and 3260 would use the encrypted IPSec channel on UDP port 500. This channel creates an encrypted and secure method of communication for all other communication. Once the channel is set up between the iSCSI client and iSCSI storage device, all other traffic can communicate as usual without any changes between the entities. Figure 11.10 shows an example archi-tecture with IPSec enabled.

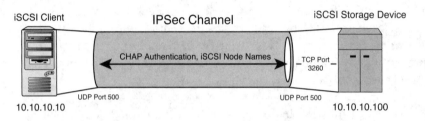

Figure 11.10   iSCSI IPSec architecture.

Once IPSec is set up correctly, a malicious attacker sniffing the communication between the two nodes in Figure 11.10 would see only encrypted data, as shown in Figure 11.11. Notice that Ethereal shows all the protocols used as ESP, denoting that all traffic has been wrapped with IPSec.

In order to set up IPSec between an iSCSI client with an iSCSI storage device using the pre-shared key of hackmeamadeus, complete the following steps.

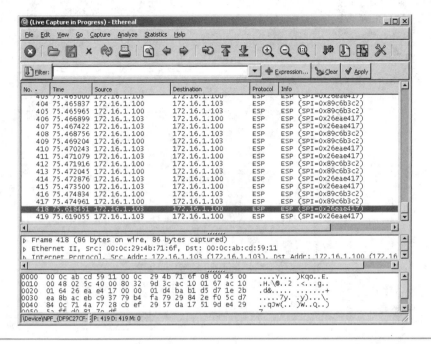

Figure 11.11   IPSec encrypted traffic for iSCSI.

ASSESSMENT EXERCISE

1. Open the iSCSI Initiator.

   a. Start -> Programs -> Microsoft iSCSI Initiator -> Configure Initiator.

2. Click on the Target Portals tab.

3. Select Add and type the IP address of the iSCSI target.

4. Select the Advance button.

5. Click on the IPSec tab.

6. Check the Enable IPSec settings checkbox.

7. Select Main mode or Aggressive mode for IPSec, depending on the configuration of the iSCSI storage device. (Note: Main mode is more secure than Aggressive mode.)

8. Select Tunnel or Transport mode, depending on the configuration of the iSCSI storage device.

9. In the Pre-shared key textbox, type the pre-shared key between the iSCSI client and the iSCSI storage device. In our example, the pre-shared key is hackmeamadeus.

10. Enable Perfect Forward Secrecy if required.

11. Select OK. See Figure 11.12.

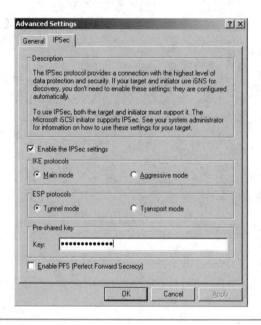

Figure 11.12 iSCSI IPSec settings.

12. Now log on to your iSCSI storage device using SSH:

    a. ssh <ip address> 22

13. Enable IPSec (NetApp gfiler support iSCSI):

    a. `ipsecpolicyadd -s {source ip} -t {destination ip} -p {esp|ah|none} -e {des|3des|null} - a{sha1|md5|null} -d {in|out} -f ip_protocol -1 {restrict|permit}`

       i. `source ip`: The NAS device.

       ii. `destination ip`: The target client or server operating system.

       iii. `-p`: Use payload encryption (ESP) or packet integrity (AH).

       iv. `-e`: If ESP, then choose type encryption (DES, 3Des, or null).

       v. `-a`: If AH, then choose type of hash (SHA1, MD5, or null).

      vi. -d: In or out directions.

     vii. -f: TCP (number 6) or UDP (number 17).

   viii. -1: Restrict means communication is only allowed if it gets an SA. Permit means if it cannot get an SA, then there will be no security on the data.

14. To enable IPSec from the NAS device of 172.16.1.100 to all sources in the network using payload encryption with triple DES:

    a. `ipsecpolicyadd -s 172.16.1.100 -p esp -e 3des -a sha1 -d in`

15. Create a pre-shared key file on the NAS device:

    a. Browse to /etc.

    b. Make a file called psk.txt.

    c. Type the IP address(s) and shared key for each node.

       i. **0.0.0.0/8 hackmeamadeus**

16. Done! You have now enabled IPSec between the iSCSI client and iSCSI storage device. At this point, all iSCSI packets on ports 3205 and 3260 will be channeled through the IPSec connection.

If all authorized nodes are using IPSec security, the following attacks can be mitigated:

- iSCSI targets, iQNs, devices, and LUNs enumeration
- iSCSI sniffing (Man-in-the-Middle)
- CHAP username enumeration
- iSCSI iQN spoofing
- iSNS spoofing
- Domain hopping attacks (iSNS servers)
- iSCSI challenge attacks

FUTURE SECURITY REQUESTS

Now that we have discussed the current iSCSI security measures that can defend against the attacks described in Chapter 8, let's discuss some security requests that would be ideal for iSCSI. Because iSCSI is accessible directly via IP and offers large blocks of data ranging from 30 to 300 gigs at one time, the ability to offer standard security measures needs to be designed. The following security measures will be discussed and why iSCSI should consider its implementation:

- Kerberos
- Replacing iQN values
- iSNS query authorization

KERBEROS

Kerberos has been widely accepted as a stable and secure authentication method for many years. Kerberos also has several authentication advantages over CHAP. While using CHAP is better than no authentication at all, using CHAP as an authentication model simply is not the ideal method when attempting to protect large amounts of data. We have discussed many CHAP attacks previously in the book, including CHAP username sniffing, CHAP replay attacks (CHAP hashes being password equivalents), offline dictionary attacks, and CHAP reflection attacks. Kerberos (version 5) authentication is not vulnerable to any of these attacks. Under Kerberos, no sensitive information is transferred in the clear, Kerberos tickets have lifetime expiration and source identification fields to protect against reply attacks, and service tickets are not password equivalents. There are working groups and researchers who have published information about using Kerberos with iSCSI. Unfortunately, no vendors support Kerberos at this time, but many of these workgroups have excellent ideas to ensure Kerberos authentication can be an option for end users who want to better secure their storage.

Kerberos has been implemented in most major applications, servers, and appliances that have data to protect. For example Unix and Windows environments both support Kerberos. Additionally, many appliances are Kerberos enabled (they contain a Kerberos client) to give the end user the option to use Kerberos. The use of Kerberos would require a Kerberos Distribution Center (KDC) in order to use the three-headed approach to authentication. Implementing a separate device as a KDC in iSCSI networks can be a cumbersome task, even it if does add to security. Another model is to implement KDC services on existing nodes on the storage network, similar to how every Windows Active Directory servers is also a KDC. An iSNS server that has been implemented on the network could also be used as a KDC. While existing iSNS servers do not perform any type of authentication, even if CHAP is enabled, it could be used as a KDC that is distributing service tickets to Kerberos clients (iSCSI clients) in order to allow them to authenticate to iSCSI storage devices. Authentication would introduce a new function to iSNS servers; however, since is already responsible for domain groups, name and LUN allocation, and general lookups, the ability to have an option to enable Kerberos would be significant.

Another location where Kerberos authentication could be used is at the storage controller itself. Many NAS devices, including NetApp filers and gfilers, offer the ability to use Kerberos for NFS and CIFS connections. I would imagine that providing Kerberos authentication for iSCSI clients, as well as NFS and CIFS clients, would be possible. The support of Kerberos at the storage controller would limit the administrative overhead since a separate entity, such as the iSNS server mentioned previously, would not be required. Because iSCSI clients have the ability to connect directly to iSCSI storage devices without the need of any other device, it would be ideal to offer the same model (two nodes only) with Kerberos (removing the dependencies of a separate node on the network).

Both models would require the iSCSI client to be Kerberos enabled. Similar to our discussion in Chapter 10, "Securing NAS," concerning NFS clients and their support of Kerberos, if an iSNS or storage controller was able to support Kerberos, the iSCSI client software would have to be Kerberos aware.

REPLACING iQN VALUES

The use of iQN values for authorization is a key security pitfall for iSCSI storage networks. iQNs, similar to WWNs and MAC addresses, are easy to change and spoof. Any value that is used as a trusted identifier should not be a changeable entity. Similar to how you cannot change your DNA code and simply re-invent who you are (as least genetically) or take the physical identity of someone else (aside from DNA and RNA cloning practices), you should not be able to change an iQN value, especially when iQN values are often the sole security control used in iSCSI networks.

A more ideal method for authorization values of iSCSI storage networks would be the use of static value that is not changeable. For example, some Fibre Channel storage controllers are using both the port WWN and node WWN values together to identify a node since an end user can't change both values. End users are able to change their node WWN value to whatever they want, but they can't change their port WWN value. Hence, if identification is based on the entire 32-character value and not a single 16-character value, the use of port and node WWNs is a good security identifier. Unfortunately in iSCSI, there are not two separate iQN values. There is a single value that is used, which makes things simple for implementation purposes, but not for security. iSCSI storage devices need to change the authorization values that are currently used so they become true static values that are unchangeable by a client system.

iSNS Query Authentication/Authorization

Another method to better secure iSCSI storage networks is the use of authentication and authorization for iSNS queries. Current implementations allow iSCSI clients to query the iSNS servers for storage information without any authentication. As mentioned previously in the book, limiting an attacker's enumeration ability significantly reduces their success. While the use of domain groups could limit enumeration, the ability to subvert the existing authorization values that rely on iQN values is not sufficient. Although it might take an attacker longer to enumerate the iSCSI environment, an attacker would still have the ability to do so if he wishes. A better method would be to require iSCSI clients to authenticate before they are allowed to query information from the iSNS server. While this would either require CHAP authentication to be enabled or some type of protocol-level authentication within iSNS, both options would be able to ensure that legitimate iSCSI clients and storage devices are granted information.

iSCSI SAN Security Summary

Next is a summary of the options in most iSCSI SAN environments and the recommended security setting. An organization must choose the ideal setting that best fits their environment; however, Table 11.1 demonstrates which security options are better than others.

Table 11.1   iSCSI Security Options and Recommendations

Feature	Option	Ideal Security Option
iSCSI authentication of client	CHAP or none	CHAP
iSCSI authentication of target	Mutual authentication or none	Mutual authentication
iSNS discovery domains	Default discovery domains or multiple discovery domains	Multiple discovery domains
Integrity checking	CRC checksums or none	CRC checksums
Encryption	IPSec or clear-text	IPSec

SUMMARY

This chapter focused on the protection of iSCSI storage attacks described in Chapter 8. Securing storage is a key part of data protection and data availability. Although significant security issues exist in iSCSI storage architectures, there are key mitigations that can be deployed in order to safely and securely keep data available with high levels of integrity. As shown in this chapter, a few key settings (enabling authentication) and implementing some configuration changes will help the data in iSCSI storage from unauthorized access or unintentional damage. These measures can mitigate the security risk without having severe impacts on performance.

This chapter is the last of three chapters regarding the methods to secure storage networks. The next chapter focuses on the affects of government regulations and information standards on storage, such as Sarbanes-Oxley, California Senate Bill 1386, Gramm-Leach Blily, and HIPAA. The chapter discusses how financial, personal, and medical data residing on the insecure storage networks will produce results that are non-compliant with regulatory bodies. Compliance and storage is a very important aspect of security, especially when auditors and regulator bodies have already begun to take a closer look.

PART V
SAN/NAS POLICIES, TRENDS, AND CASE STUDIES

Compliance, Regulations, and Storage

At what point is it possible to call data in storage secure, compliant, or meeting industry standards? This is one of a few thousand questions the storage industry and storage administrators have been facing for several years. For example, if your financial applications, operating systems running financial software, and networks that hold financial data are being audited due to Sarbanes-Oxley requirements, at what point does the NAS device or the FC/iSCSI storage controller come into play? The auditors are attempting to ensure that appropriate controls are in place to make sure the integrity of that data is not modified; however, if the data can be modified, tarnished, destroyed, or slightly tampered due to the lack of controls on the storage systems, will storage be the weakest link on the compliance chart?

This chapter will focus on the compliance and regulatory questions facing storage. It will discuss the importance of securing storage as it pertains to audit requirements. It will also focus on how the defenses discussed in Chapters 9, "Securing Fibre Channel SANs," 10, "Securing NAS," and 11, "Securing iSCSI," can meet certain control activities required for many of these regulatory acts. The chapter will begin with a description of each of the major regulatory acts and how they affect storage systems. An outline of the chapter is as follows:

- Government regulations and the impact on storage
- Auditing storage
- Regulations and storage
  Sarbanes-Oxley

HIPAA

Gramm-Leach Bliley

California Senate Bill 1386 (SB1386)

- Standards and storage

North American Electric Reliability Council—cyber security

- Regulatory themes
- Control activities and storage defenses

GOVERNMENT REGULATIONS AND THE IMPACT ON STORAGE

Government regulations have had their impacts on every industry or market, where storage is simply no different. Regulations always impact data in one aspect or another. For example, U.S. Senator Paul Sarbanes and Representative Michael Oxley probably did not intend for their regulation, which was designed to enforce strict control over financial information, to affect information technology so heavily. However, as people began to understand how financial information needs to be protected, many items covered IT areas, including the areas where the information is stored and accessed (NAS or SAN networks). Sarbanes-Oxley is just one of many major regulations that storage networks must adhere to. The first step is to understand what type of data is being stored and what requirements it may have. Table 12.1 shows the regulations that must be adhered to if the specified type of data is being kept.

Table 12.1   Government Regulations and Data Types

Type of Data	Government Regulation
Financial information	Sarbanes-Oxley
Medical (patient) information	HIPAA
Non-public personal information	Gramm-Leach Bliley
Personal information	California Senate Bill 1386

The impact of being non-compliant for any of these regulations can range from heavy penalties per incident to the complete closure of the organization's business. The impact to storage is that it needs to follow reasonable security practices just like everything else on the network that holds sensitive information (such as applications, operating systems, databases). This should not be a big surprise since the storage network controls most, if not all, of an organization's data. For example, many applications that run e-commerce programs need to follow standard security practices to ensure that non-public personal information of customers is not compromised. Furthermore, the same organization's NAS or SAN environment also needs to ensure that all non-public personal data in the organization is protected from both external attackers and internal unauthorized users.

One of the biggest impacts these regulations have had on storage is the removal from the false sense of security from the "external hacker," "storage is behind a firewall," or "storage is generally not a target" ideas. Many storage administrators know that there are significant security issues with storage, but rely on a false sense of security that an external hacker may not be able to "find" the storage network or they simply might not know about storage protocols such as iSCSI, NFS, CIFS, or even Fibre Channel. However, the government regulations listed in Table 12.1 do not differentiate between an external hacker and an internal employee. Both are subjected to the same requirements. This means that an internal employee, a storage administrator, or even an unauthorized finance or HR employee should not have access to a particular piece of storage even if they are employed by the organization. For example, if your NAS administrator has full access to data residing in a NAS device, which also happens to be financial information held by Oracle financials, then your storage network would not be in compliance. Furthermore, if your organization's e-commerce applications store data, such as credit card numbers, in the SAN and the SAN is not protected from internal employees, then you would not be in compliance. The examples can go on and on, but the fact is that these regulations have stated that an internal employee with millions of ways to access the storage network is as big of an issue as an external attacker tries to compromise data. Both can lead to the compromise of medical information, personal credit card numbers, or even financial information, all of which would make an organization storage network non-compliant.

Another aspect of data protection and government regulations is authorized and unauthorized data deletion. Several government regulations require that certain types of data (for example, email messages or audit log messages) must be stored and archived for up to seven years. While security is usually focused on unauthorized data access, it must also be used to ensure that malicious or illegal deletion is not possible, whether it is the CEO/CFO who wants to delete email or the storage administrator who has accidentally deleted a data block that contains sensitive Sarbanes-Oxley information—both translate to breaking a government regulation. In fact, remembering back to 1972 when President Nixon's secretary, Rose Mary Wood, accidentally recorded over 18 minutes of tape that destroyed critical information from the Watergate scandal. Protections are in place now in these regulations to ensure that strong controls will ensure the data (i.e., tape) cannot accidentally or intentionally be destroyed. One of the major parts of all these new regulations is a proper audit trail to show what, if any, malicious activity might have taken place if corporate entities are breaking the law. If storage data contains sensitive email messages or audit trails of illegal activities are not properly protected from malicious or accidental activity, the storage network would not be in proper compliance with the archive control.

A good method to protect against improper or accidental data deletion is using Write Once Read Many (WORM) devices. (Note: Do not confuse WORM storage devices with Internet worms.) WORMs are devices that are used specifically to ensure that data is not deleted or erased. Similar to how a CD-R or DVD-R works, where data cannot be deleted or overridden, WORM storage devices can be used to store data that should not be destroyed. Using WORM devices, information is written once and can be read many times, but is specifically designed not to be overwritten or erased. WORMs have been used for archival purposes in the past and are a viable solution to store data that must be kept for regulation adherence.

So what are the keys to storage and government regulations? Just like everything else, ensure that your storage networks and devices use reasonable authentication, authorization, auditing, availability, integrity, and encryption measures. Also ensure that there are activities for each of these items that adequately show the measures you have taken to secure the data in your storage network. Auditors are just like the legal system—a security control simply does not exist unless there is some written documentation/process/report that proves it.

AUDITING STORAGE

Block or file data in storage networks are an auditable entity. Auditors require data, in any form, to have formal, documented, and auditable controls for data protection. Controls are methods to ensure that trust, integrity, availability, and security exist for a given entity. For example, a control might be the use of authentication and access mechanisms. To ensure that controls are being followed, auditors look for control activities. Control activities are processes, procedures, or configuration settings that prove that the control is in place. There may be several activities for a single control. For example, the control activity for the authentication and access mechanisms control would be the use of CHAP authentication in an iSCSI storage network. Another control activity would be the use of SSH authentication for storage devices. The key thing to understand about government regulations and how they are proven with auditors is with the documentation of control activities. For example, a process that secures all the data in your storage network but has no documentation or auditable control activities does not exist in the eyes of the auditor, who can/will say you don't comply. All too often, operational groups within large organizations have several good security practices, but do not simply have a method or a tool to show how strong their security practices really are.

REGULATIONS AND STORAGE

There are many regulations, both international and domestic to the U.S., that affect storage. The following sections discuss selected government regulations and their requirements on storage. Furthermore, we will be able to draw out consistent themes from the regulations and show the core requirements that exist among most of them. The identification of themes will allow organizations to implement core requirements that can adhere to most of the regulations, ranging from Sarbanes-Oxley in the U.S. to BS17799 in Great Britain.

The following section discusses the regulations. Each section specifies a general purpose statement of the regulation, an example of its implementation, and another example on how it affects storage. The examples should not be viewed as an exhaustive list of possible affects, but one class of activity:

- Sarbanes-Oxley
- HIPAA
- Gramm-Leach Bliley
- California Senate Bill 1386 (SB1386)

SARBANES-OXLEY

Sarbanes-Oxley was signed into law July 30, 2002 and has had a profound affect on IT systems since then. The act came out of several financial scandals that devastated major companies and the U.S. economy. The high-level goal of the act is designed to protect the public (investors and employees) by ensuring accuracy and reliability of corporate disclosures of an organization's financial information. Of all the provisions in the act, three of them affect IT storage systems heavily:

- Independent annual audit reports on the existence, condition, and reliability of internal controls as they pertain to the financial reports of an organization.

- Section 404 states that management must make an assessment of the internal controls of the financial reporting process and state the effectiveness of the internal controls.
- All financial reports must be certified (signed) by the CEO and CFO for authenticity.

The first two provisions include IT systems that affect the financial reporting process, including applications, operating systems, and of course, storage systems. The last one is also quite important since corporate executives who fail to comply with the act might lose more than their jobs at the end of the year, but also may lose their freedom. Hence, with CEOs and CFOs being held responsible, CIOs and CISO/CSOs are required to ensure that the entire financial reporting process and technologies that support the process contain adequate controls and control activities, and are evaluated at the end of the year. Furthermore, organizations are not stopping at the executive levels. Many executives are requiring IT directors, managers, and even administrators to sign off on Sarbanes-Oxley standards. Executives are realizing the significance of a non-complaint outcome and want to ensure that everyone involved who can make a positive impact also has some skin in the game. In fact, many storage administrators and IT directors have been asked directly to report on their Sarbanes-Oxley status and legally sign off on it.

So, how do a company's financial reports affect storage networks? Simple. The data that is created and used by financial applications, running on the operating system, comes from NAS devices running CIFS, NFS, or SAN systems using iSCSI or Fibre Channel. Does the entire financial report process rely on the storage network? Of course not, but it certainly is a significant part of the process that cannot be ignored. Part of Sarbanes-Oxley is to report factual financial reports, but another hidden part is the ability to produce the report itself. For example, if storage devices have been tampered with and the data in the storage network no longer holds integrity, then the financial application using the data will not be able to show correct information. Furthermore, if the storage network is taken offline, damaged, or simply deleted of all its data, the ability to create a financial report will not be possible, which also would cause a non-compliant statement of Sarbanes-Oxley. Following are the specific sections of Sarbanes-Oxley that affect storage and how storage networks and devices that support financial systems are affected:

- **Section 302: Corporate Responsibility for Financial Reports.**

  Section highlights—The CEO and CFO must prepare a statement that certifies the appropriateness of the financial statements that reflect the operations and financial conditions of the company.

Affects on storage—If the storage network/devices do not contain a high amount of integrity due to insecure or unstable storage operations, the financial information that they hold will prevent a CEO or CFO from making a statement on the appropriateness of the financial information of the company.

Example—A NAS (NFS or CIFS) device is infected with a virus or an iSCSI storage device has been compromised, leading to the inability for the CEO or CFO to make a statement that the financial statement has not been affected due to security weaknesses.

- **Section 303: Improper Influence on Conducts of Audit.**

  Section highlights—Any officer/director of the company cannot influence, coerce, manipulate, or mislead any auditor regarding the financial statements of the company.

  Affects on storage—The CIO, CSO, Director of IT, or Security must state where the data actually resides, whether the auditor asks for it or not. The IT auditors who look at the entire financial reporting process must be told that financial data is residing in a NAS or SAN system and not an operating system and/or an application.

  Example—The IT director states that the security of all systems that support financial applications are secure, stable, and controlled. The auditor finds out that a NAS filer is holding all the data for the financial application (not the operating system) and has not been addressed in terms of security or controls. The auditor has the power to state that they have been mislead to the location of the actual data.

- **Section 404: Management Assessment of Internal Controls.**

  Section highlights—The company must issue an annual report about internal controls. The report should state the following:

  Management's responsibility to establish adequate controls across all aspects of the financial report process.

  Assess the internal controls at the end of the fiscal year, which must state the effectiveness of the internal controls procedures that are in place.

  Each company's auditor shall make a statement of the internal controls.

  Affects on storage—If the NAS or SAN network or devices do not contain standard methods for strong authentication, authorization, encryption, auditing, or availability parameters, they will not be considered to contain proper internal controls. Ensuring that each storage switch, storage controller, storage director, storage device, or storage client contains proper IT controls will be required.

Example—A SAN using WWNs does not contain strong internal controls since authentication or strong authorization is not enabled. Additionally, a NAS device using default NFS or CIFS does not contain strong internal controls due to the lack of authentication or the ability to subvert user permissions. Finally, an iSCSI storage device relying solely on iQN values does not contain strong internal controls since authentication or strong authorization is not enabled.

- **Section 409: Real-Time Disclosure.**

  Section highlights—A company must report material changes on the financial condition or operations of the organization on a quick and timely basis.

  Affects on storage—The storage network must be stable and secure in order to support the financial applications and operating systems quickly and consistently. An extended period of unexpected downtime, data loss, or data compromise would prevent the organization from issuing statements on proper financial conditions.

  Example—A storage LUN goes down that supports Oracle financials. The ability to produce financial statements at quarter end is delayed by three days, causing doubt to the SEC that operational conditions are fit and controlled.

- **Section 1102: Tampering with a Record or Otherwise Impeding an Official Proceeding.**

  Section highlights—Any person trying to alter, destroy, tamper, or hide information that will change the financial information of the company may be prosecuted for 20 years in prison and receive a fine.

  Affects on storage—If the storage system is insecure, unstable, or simply does not hold the proper security controls, it could be the method used to damage the core locations of the data, which would be the storage systems.

  Example—A malicious internal employee deletes, damages, tampers, or changes information directly on a shared volume on a NAS device. Furthermore, a malicious person simply overwrites a LUN on an iSCSI or Fibre Channel SAN with hopping or spoofing attacks, which allows him/her to reformat the LUN's file system.

For more information, consult your auditor and your information security partner. The list can go on indefinitely on how storage must comply with the previously listed provision of Sarbanes-Oxley. Similar to assessing the internal controls of your application, network, and operating system, your storage network and its devices need to contain proper internal controls also.

HIPAA

The Health Insurance Portability and Accountability Act (HIPAA) deals with information privacy rather than internal controls; however, the core procedures to ensure information privacy are similar, if not the same, as internal controls. The act was signed in 1996 but took affect in April 2003. The act requires entities to protect the health information of individuals. The major goal of HIPAA is to ensure that the health information of individuals is properly protected from unauthorized viewers. For example, in the Data Safeguards section, the act states that an entity must maintain reasonable and appropriate technical safeguards to prevent the intentional or unintentional use or disclosure of protected health information. The statement requires that Electronic Protected Health Information (EPHI) should be secured by IT systems.

Organizations that are regulated by HIPAA are required to keep personal health information secure. Information that needs to be protected is individual identifiable health information. The information is also referred to as Protected Health Information (PHI). PHI includes the following types of information:

- An individual's past, present, or future physical or mental health or condition
- An individual's provision of health care
- An individual's past, present, or future payment of the provision of health care
- Common identifiers of individuals, including name, address, birth date, and social security number

HIPAA contains many sections and rules, including a security rule that was its final rule. HIPAA's final security rule specifies standard security measures need to be in place for EPHI. It states that standards and safeguards need to be in place to protect the confidentiality, integrity, and availability of EPHI data. These standards require that proper measures are taken to protect the EPHI data while it is in custody of organizations, as well as while it is in transit from one organization to another.

Following are the specific sections of HIPAA that affect storage and how storage networks and devices that support financial systems are affected:

- **Section 164.306: General Rules.**

  Section highlights—Organizations need to implement security measures, including technical security mechanisms, to ensure that health information confidentiality, integrity, and availability are protected.

Affects on storage—Storage systems need to have proper security controls and settings implemented. Protection of data in the storage network includes the use of authentication, authorization, integrity, auditing, and availability standards.

Example—A SAN storage switch has been implemented with default settings, allowing any spoofed WWN to access a LUN in the storage controller.

- **Section 164.308(a)(4): Information Access Management.**

  Section highlights—Organizations need to implement access control methods to ensure that access to health information, and how access is granted and modified, is appropriate.

  Affects on storage—Access methods to storage systems need to be defined, documented, and implemented. A formal and technical procedure needs to be in place to access NAS and SAN systems.

  Example—An NFS or CIFS filer is accessed anonymously via NFS exports, exposing all sorts of EPHI data.

- **Section 164.308(a)(6): Security Incident Procedures.**

  Section highlights—Organizations need to implement security incident procedures for all systems that hold EPHI information. The technical solutions need to show all security violations on a potential entity holding EPHI data.

  Affects on storage—All storage systems need to have alerting methods when an unexpected issue occurs on the system. Alerts, logs, and incidents need to be specific and detailed to retrace any and all events that may have occurred.

  Example—A storage administrator mounts LUNs to a server he controls, viewing the EPHI data of every employee. Furthermore, no logs are kept or enabled on the storage system, leaving the incident without any traces.

- **Section 164.308(a)(7)(i): Contingency Plan**

  Section highlights—Organizations need to implement a contingency plan to respond to system emergencies. The plan would need to include the retrieval of all applications and their data, a data backup plan, a disaster recovery plan, an emergency mode operation plan, and testing and revision procedures.

  Affects on storage—All storage systems need to have a tape backup method or a site-to-site replication method in order to ensure that data can be retrieved despite system accidents, problems, or attacks.

Example—A LUN can simply get damaged by an attacker, and there is no tape backup method in place.

- **Section 164.308(1)(8): Evaluation.**

  Section highlights—Organizations need to periodically conduct an evaluation of their security in order to demonstrate/document their compliance with the security standards.

  Affects on storage—Storage systems need to be assessed for security, including storage device configuration settings, compliance, and general security scans.

  Example—All EPHI data resides a NAS filer or an iSCSI storage device, which has never been assessed for security. Attackers have access to the EPHI data on the storage device, but only operating system security has been focused on.

- **Section 164.312(a)(1): Access Control.**

  Section highlights—Organizations need to implement access control for unique user identification, text-based, role-based, and/or user-based access, and the use of encryption as a means of providing access control.

  Affects on storage—Storage systems need to have multiple roles for management users, not just a single administrator or root level user. Additionally, end users/systems need to have roles applied to them also, such as full access, partial access, or no access.

  Example—A storage administrator has full access to a NAS device or an iSCSI/Fibre Channel storage controller. While he or she can manage the system, they can also view, control, tamper, and delete all the data.

- **Section 164.312(b): Audit Control.**

  Section highlights—Organizations need to implement audit control mechanisms in order to record and examine system activity.

  Affects on storage—Storage systems need to have a standard amount of auditing in all aspects of the system, not just management authentication. System logs, activity logs, user logs, backup logs, in-band data access logs, out-of-band access logs, and other general event logs should be enabled.

  Example—A NFS NAS system is accessed by unauthorized users, and no systems logs are available or enabled to see that the correct UID was used to access data. The data that was accessed is EPHI from the HR tables in the Oracle database.

- **Section 164.312(c)(1): Integrity.**

  Section highlights—Organizations need to ensure that EPHI data has not been tampered with or destroyed in an unauthorized manner.

  Affects on storage—Storage systems need to have the ability to show the integrity of their data. File, folder, and LUN MD5/SHA1 hashes should be supported to show that the data has not been tampered with or modified.

  Example—An insider trader changes the information on a transaction she has submitted, which are all stored on an iSCSI storage controller. The changed transaction shows that an amount purchased of Pets.com was 10 shares and not 10 million shares.

- **Section 164.312(d): Authentication.**

  Section highlights—Organizations need to authenticate users or systems by using unique user identification, including biometric identification, passwords, PINs, telephone call backs, or physical tokens.

  Affects on storage—Storage systems need to implement both end user authentication and system authentication for any type of access. Authentication methods need to ensure that a user or system is actually who they say they are, both for management access and data access.

  Example—WWNs or iQNs are the only method used in a SAN to access EPHI data on a storage controller. At no point does the storage system actually know (authenticate) that the system is who they say they are since CHAP and DH-CHAP have not been enabled.

- **Section 164.312(2)(1): Transmission Security.**

  Section highlights—Organizations need to implement security mechanisms (encryption) to guard against unauthorized access to data that is transmitted over a communication network.

  Affects on storage—Storage systems need to use in-transit encryption of IP packets and Fibre Channel frames. Any EPHI data going to or from a storage system need to be encrypted.

  Example—An iSCSI storage device is communicating in the clear to an iSCSI client, revealing all iQNs, hostnames, and LUN information to any unauthorized user on the network.

For more information, consult your auditor and your information security partner. The list can go on indefinitely on how storage systems must comply with the previous sections of HIPAA. Similar to ensuring that proper security settings are implemented on applications, networks, and operating systems—such as authentication, authorization, auditing, availability, and encryption—a storage network and its devices need to support similar security standards.

GRAMM-LEACH BLILEY ACT

The Gramm-Leach Bliley Act (GLBA), also known as the Financial Modernization act, includes provisions to help individuals (consumers and customers) protect their personal information that is held by organizations. While the act was targeted at financial institutions, it is an actually a target for any company that holds consumer information, such as a company that sells goods online or over the phone. The act aims to protect non-public personal information (NPI) of individuals. For example, a social security number, a credit card number, a bank account, names, and home addresses would be considered NPI data.

There are two rules and several sections under GLBA, including the Financial Privacy Rule and the Safeguards Rule. The Financial Privacy Rule requires institutions to give customers privacy notices that explain their sharing practices. In return, customers have the right to limit some of the sharing of that information. For example, if you own a home and have a mortgage, you have probably received eight million letters from other financial institutions about their loans. The other institutions have probably listed the exact loan amount that you have in your home and all the financial details. This is because financial institutions have shared (sold) the information to other institutions. The Safeguards Rules states that organizations need to have a security plan in place to protect the confidentiality and integrity of personal consumer information. Title V in GLBA has a Privacy provision. The Privacy provision discusses how NPI data needs to be protected and secured. Following are the specific sections of GLBA that affect storage:

- **Section 6801: Protection of Non-Public Personal Information.**

  - **Section 6801(a): Privacy Obligation Policy.**

    Section highlights—An organization needs to protect the security and confidentiality of customer's non-public personal information.

    Affects on storage—Storage systems need to have proper security controls and settings implemented. Protection of personal information (file or block level) in the storage network includes the use of authentication, authorization, integrity, auditing, and availability standards.

Example—An iSCSI storage device has not enabled authentication; which leaves all data supporting e-commerce applications open to external and internal attackers.

- **Section 6801(b): Financial Institutions Safeguards.**

  Section highlights—An organization needs to ensure the following:

  The security and confidentiality of customer records/information.

  Protection against anticipated threats to the security or integrity of customer records.

  Protection against unauthorized access to customer records/information.

  Affects on storage—The storage affects are as follows:

  Storage systems need to have proper security controls and settings implemented.

  Storage systems need to proactively secure storage controllers, storage switches, storage clients (nodes with HBAs), NFS/CIFS NAS filers, and storage management applications using the least-privilege principal. This equates to securing in anticipation of any threat and enabling standard security settings. Configuration settings, product features, and storage architecture design all need to support authentication, authorization, encryption, auditing, and minimal extraneous services.

  Storage systems need to enable authentication and proper authorization methods.

  Example—The storage examples are as follows:

  An iSCSI SAN has disabled authentication and only relies on default iQN values for authorization, which can be spoofed and lead to data compromise.

  A Fibre Channel SAN using WWN zoning with no authentication and encryption, ignoring all possible threats to the SAN from both internal and external unauthorized users.

  An NAS device supports both CIFS and NFS, does not use any authentication for NFS, and only relies on UID/GID values for authorization.

For more information, consult your auditor and your information security partner. The list can go on indefinitely on how storage systems must comply with the previous sections of GLBA. Similar to ensuring proper security settings are implemented on applications, networks, and operating systems—such as authentication, authorization, auditing, availability, and encryption—a storage network and its devices need to support similar security standards.

CALIFORNIA SENATE BILL 1386

The California Senate Bill 1386 (SB1386) was signed into law in September 2002. The law states that personal information that is held by any organization must be protected against possible theft. The law also states that if an incident occurs that involves the compromise of personal information, which could be any internal unauthorized employee or external attacker, the organization must notify each individual whose personal information was compromised. Although the law resides in California, it covers any organization that does business in California. Also, many other states, such as New York and North Carolina, as well as the U.S. government, will soon pass similar laws as SB1386 (Senator Diane Feinstein of California is in the works of creating stronger legislation). The following is a non-exhaustive summary of NPI data:

- Credit card numbers
- Credit card account numbers, access codes, pins, or passwords
- Social Security numbers
- Driver's license numbers
- Telephone numbers
- Real estate records
- Credit reports

Simply put, organizations need to keep all personal information they hold of employees, customers, consumers, or any other individuals under strong security controls. These security controls need to protect against external hackers, but also malicious internal employees or even unauthorized internal employees, such as storage administrators who have authority to manage the storage system but do not have authority to view all the credit card numbers on a NAS or iSCSI device, which is granted to them by default under most administrative accounts. Following are the specific sections of SB1386 that affect storage:

- **SEC. 2 Section 1798.29 (a).**

  Section highlights—An organization that holds computerized data, including NPI, needs to inform any and all individuals if there is a possibility that a breach of the NPI data has occurred. Any unauthorized access that compromises the security, confidentiality, or integrity of NPI is considered a security breach.

Affects on storage—Storage networks need to enable authentication, strong authorization, and the use of encryption (when possible) to protect NPI data. Protection from unauthorized individuals, including internal employees or external attackers, must be implemented for all NPI data in storage systems.

Example—An internal employee spoofs the iQN value, gaining access to 250 gigs of data, all of which belong to the SQL Server database holding credit card numbers.

- **SEC. 2 Section 1798.82 (b).**

  Section highlights—An organization that holds computerized data, including NPI, needs to inform any and all individuals if there is a possibility that a breach of the NPI data has occurred in unencrypted (clear-text) format. Any unauthorized access that compromises the security, confidentiality, or integrity of unencrypted NPI is considered a security breach.

  Affects on storage—Storage networks need to ensure that NPI data is encrypted, when possible. The use of encryption will protect NPI data when an unauthorized person compromises the data.

  Example—An offsite tape storage facility loses backup tapes or has had them stolen. The tapes contain NPI data and the information is in the clear.

For more information, consult your auditor and your information security partner. The list can go on indefinitely on how storage systems must comply with the previous sections of SB1386. Similar to ensuring proper security settings are implemented on applications, networks, and operating systems—such as authentication, authorization, auditing, availability, and encryption—a storage network and its devices need to support similar security standards.

STANDARDS AND STORAGE

The following section discusses the various standards developed by organizations that focus on information protection.

NERC

The NERC Standard 1200/1300 is a board of trustees who voted to ensure that any items used to provide reliability and availability to electric utilities, including computers, software, and networks, should be protected from intrusion. The standard was voted on in

August 2003 and is called the "Urgent Action Standard 1200—Cyber Security." This standard will expire and transfer into a more exhaustive standard, which will be upgraded to the 1300. Many of the requirements are similar to the requirements previously stated in the regulation section. Organizations must create and implement security settings, features, programs, and perform assessments to ensure any entity that is used to ensure the availability and reliability of the electricity grid is protected.

REGULATORY THEMES

At this point, we have covered four regulations and how each of them affects storage systems, devices, and networks. However, all of the regulations that we have covered only concern the U.S. and are fairly recent—1996 and later. What about all the international regulations that have not been discussed or the other regulations locally in the U.S. that have not been covered? The fact is that an entire book could be written on how international and domestic regulations affect storage; however, after reading the descriptions of the four regulations, you probably noticed a theme among all of them, which is data security. Most regulations, domestic or international, require some form of the six basic entities of security, as described in Chapter 1, "Introduction to Storage Security," which are authentication, authorization, auditing, encryption, integrity, and availability. Considering the regulations and standards that were required for several types of organizations before 1996—such as SAS70, ISO17799, BS17799, and Financial Audits with General Computer Controls—if there is some effort made to implement the core security entities on the storage network, several different regulations can be adhered to at the same time. For example, if an organization contains an iSCSI SAN and they enable the iSCSI security entities listed next, they will be able to meet the regulations listed under the regulation section:

- **iSCSI security settings:**
  Authentication on an iSCSI client to iSCSI targets.
  Remove the sole reliance on iQN values for complete authorization.
  Enable IPSec for in-transit communication.
  Enable auditing on the iSCSI client and iSCSI target.
  Enables CRC Checksums or AH on the packets.
  Encrypt the data at rest.

- **Regulations mitigated:**
  Sarbanes-Oxley:
  Section 404: Management Assessment of Internal Controls.
  HIPAA:
  Section 164.308(a)(4): Information Access Management.
  GLBA:
  Section 6801(b): Financial Institutions Safeguards.
  SB1386:
  SEC. 2 Section 1798.29 (a).

If core security principles are followed, many regulations can be accomplished. This why the COBIT standards were developed by the Information Systems Audit and Control Association (ISACA). If an organization wants to implement the standard practices and controls for security, the COBIT framework is probably the best method to ensure that all aspects are covered correctly within an organization. COBIT is the generally accepted standard for good IT security practices. Following COBIT standards and controls can help organizations adhere to many government regulations, from Sarbanes-Oxley to GLBA. Although COBIT is great for security practices, it is important to understand that government regulations or auditors don't think solely in security terms, but in terms of controls and control activities, as mentioned previously in the chapter. Controls are generated by the auditing bodies that were granted permission by federal and statute agencies to ensure certain regulations are met. Controls are quite similar between regulations, but controls are not something that your organization should feel responsible for. On the other hand, control activities are something that an organization must contain. If there are no control activities for the protection of medical information sitting on a NAS device, then an audit or will consider that as non-compliant. Control activities, which can be a technical setting or even a human process, are very important when attempting to demonstrate the adherence to a particular control and its regulation. For example, in order to ensure that SB1386-regulated data is being protected adequately, a control might be "Ensure proper policies and procedure limit sensitive data to authorized users." The control activities could be DH-CHAP authentication, port zoning, or at-rest encryption. Any or all of these control activities can be used for the overlying control.

Now that we have addressed controls, control activities, and how they relate to security, the next section focuses on common controls among a variety of regulations and what storage security settings can be used to adhere to these controls.

CONTROL ACTIVITIES AND STORAGE

In order to understand how security settings on storage clients, targets, devices, controllers, and communication mediums can become control activities for regulatory controls, we must use the same format that an auditing body would use. The use of COBIT's control activities across the various regulations will help organizations meet demanding requirements on storage networks.

The first column in Table 12.2 is a list of the most prominent controls that a regulatory body would require. The next two columns include control activities and technical solutions that will help adhere to the specific control. In the last column is the specific regulatory act that can be mitigated by implementing the control activities and technical security solutions. Table 12.3 is a list of COBIT security guidelines that apply to storage. These tables will also show how technical solutions can adhere to specific COBIT guidelines that are often used by a variety of government regulations.

Tables 12.2 and 12.3 are not an exhaustive list and should not be used in that fashion; however, they can be used as a guide to begin the complex and often confusing process of making storage networks compliant to regulations. Although the tables are not exhaustive, they do cover most of the items an organization would need to address for any type of audit.

Table 12.2 Controls, Regulations, and Storage Security Control Activities and Settings

Controls	Control Activities	Technical Solutions	Regulations
Where network connectivity is used, appropriate controls, including network segmentation, exist and are used to prevent unauthorized access.	Segment network traffic appropriately using routers, switches, storage controllers, and other segmentation principles.	FC SANs: Hard zoning or VSANs using port-based zone allocation iSCSI SANs: Unique domain sets CIFS/NFS NAS: VLANs	Sarbanes-Oxley Section 404 HIPAA Section 164.312(a)(1) GLBA Section 6801(B)
Application software and data storage systems are properly configured to provide access based on the individual's demonstrated need to view, add, change, or delete data.	Access to storage data, devices, and configurations is appropriately restricted to authorized individuals.	FC SANs: Port binding and port locking iSCSI SANs: Unique domain sets CIFS/NFS NAS: File/folder-level permissions	Sarbanes-Oxley Section 404 HIPAA Section 164.312(a)(1) GLBA Section 6801(B)

Table 12.2   Controls, Regulations, and Storage Security Control Activities and Settings (continued)

Controls	Control Activities	Technical Solutions	Regulations
Procedures exist and are followed to maintain the effectiveness of authentication and access mechanisms.	The identity of users and systems (both local and remote) is authenticated to the system through passwords or other authentication mechanisms.	FC SANs: DH-CHAP authentication iSCSI SANs: CHAP authentication and mutual authentication CIFS/NFS NAS: Kerberos	Sarbanes-Oxley Section 404 HIPAA Section 164.312(a)(1) GLBA Section 6801(B)
Access to facilities is restricted to authorized personnel and requires appropriate identification and authentication.	Sensitive data is encrypted while being transmitted.	All: SSH, HTTPS, or SNMPv3	Sarbanes-Oxley Section 404 HIPAA Section 164.312(d) GLBA Section 6801(B)
Data integrity standards have been implemented to ensure data and data transactions have been verified.	Communication and data files are monitored for validity.	FC SANs: FC-SP iSCSI SANs: CRC Checksums CIFS/NFS NAS: IPSec with AH	Sarbanes-Oxley Section 404 HIPAA Section 164.312(c)(1) GLBA Section 6801(B)
Access to documents, data, programs, reports, and messages (incoming and outgoing) are appropriately protected, encrypted, and/or authenticated.	Access to the production environments is appropriately restricted.	FC SANs: At-rest encryption iSCSI SANs: IPSec or at-rest encryption CIFS/NFS NAS: IPSec or at-rest encryption	Sarbanes-Oxley Section 404 HIPAA Section 164.312(d) GLBA Section 6801(B)
Data storage systems are properly configured to prevent unauthorized or malicious deletion of data.	Unauthorized tampering with a record or deleting data should be restricted.	Implement Write Once Read Many (WORM) or Content Addressable Storage (CAS) storage devices	Sarbanes-Oxley Section 1102 HIPAA Section 164.312(c)(1)

Table 12.3 COBIT Controls, Activities, and Technical Solutions

COBIT Controls	Control Activities	Technical Solutions
2.4 Security Levels	Management should define, implement, and maintain security levels for each of the data classifications identified above the level of "no protection required." These security levels should represent the appropriate (minimum) set of security and control measures for each of the classifications and should be re-evaluated periodically and modified accordingly.	N/A (An organization must define and follow storage security process and procedures.)
5.2 Identification, Authentication, and Access	The logical access to and use of IT computing resources should be restricted by the implementation of adequate identification, authentication, and authorization mechanisms, linking users and resources with access rules.	FC SANs: DH-CHAP authentication iSCSI SANs: CHAP authentication and mutual authentication CIFS/NFS NAS: Kerberos
5.3 Security of Online Access to Data	IT management should implement procedures in line with the security policy that provides access security control based on the individual's demonstrated need to view, add, change, or delete data.	FC SANs: Port binding and port locking iSCSI SANs: Unique domain sets CIFS/NFS NAS: File/folder-level permissions
5.21 Protection of Electronic Value	Management should protect the continued integrity of all cards or similar physical mechanisms used for authentication or storage of financial or other sensitive information, taking into consideration the related facilities, devices, employees, and validation methods used.	FC SANs: FC-SP iSCSI SANs: CRC Checksums CIFS/NFS NAS: IPSec with AH

Table 12.3   COBIT Controls, Activities, and Technical Solutions (continued)

COBIT Controls	Control Activities	Technical Solutions
11.17 Protection of Sensitive Information During Transmission and Transport	Management should ensure that adequate protection of sensitive information is provided during transmission and transport against unauthorized access, modification, and misaddressing.	FC SANs: N/A iSCSI SANs: IPSec CIFS/NFS NAS: IPSec
11.25 Back-Up Storage	Back-up procedures for IT-related media should include the proper storage of the data files, software, and related documentation, both on-site and off-site. Back-ups should be stored securely.	FC SANs: At-rest encryption iSCSI SANs: IPSec or at-rest encryption CIFS/NFS NAS: IPSec or at-rest encryption
11.30 Continued Integrity of Stored Data	Management should ensure that the integrity and correctness of the data kept on files and other media is checked periodically.	FC SANs: FC-SP iSCSI SANs: CRC Checksums CIFS/NFS NAS: IPSec with AH

SUMMARY

The chapter's focus was on government regulations and how they affect storage systems, especially SANs and NAS. We learned how all government regulations and standards are designed, directed, or ultimately intended to ensure that various forms of data are protected from unauthorized users, available to authorized users, contain a high level of integrity, and are generally secured. Ultimately, various forms of data reside in the SAN or NAS network, which can be vulnerable to network attacks, authentication flaws, viruses/worms, and misconfigurations. Storage networks need to comply with regulations depending on the type of data they hold, which can be medical, financial, personal non-public, or credit card information. Since most SAN and NAS networks hold all types of sensitive data, requiring storage devices, storage nodes, and storage protocols to comply with government regulations concerning data protection, integrity, and overall security will be required.

The next chapter focuses on conducting security audits on storage networks and securing storage devices, including an example NAS device and SAN device.

Auditing and Securing Storage Devices

Auditing and securing storage devices are a major part of securing storage. We have discussed many aspects of securing storage, but how can you tell if the devices that make up a storage network have been secured? Auditing storage devices, identifying the gaps, and then implementing the solution is the best approach.

Auditing network and application entities has occurred for several decades. Unfortunately there has not been any resource to perform the same functions in a storage network. If a storage administrator or a security engineer does not know where their storage security gaps are, the steps to remediate the gaps and track the process will be very difficult. This chapter focuses on auditing of the storage network for proper security settings and controls. Additionally, the chapter will also discuss the process of securing storage devices based on the gaps that most storage networks contain. The chapter discusses the following items:

- Storage Network Audit Program (SNAP)
  Fibre Channel switches
  NAS storage appliances
  iSCSI storage appliances/applications
- Securing storage devices
  NAS: Network Appliance filers
  SAN: Cisco Fibre Channel switches

STORAGE NETWORK AUDIT PROGRAM (SNAP)

SNAP version 1.0 is a methodology created by the author in order to begin the process of developing a clear standard for measuring storage security. A standard will help organizations understand how well/poor the storage network actually is. Furthermore, it will create a baseline to start measuring storage. SNAP will be a methodology that the author will continue to update even after the publication of this book. In order to receive the most recent copy of SNAP, feel free to email the author at securingstorage@gmail.com. The program consists of the following categories:

- SNAP
  - SANs

    SAN storage networks and switches
  - NAS

    NAS storage appliances
  - iSCSI

    iSCSI storage appliances/applications

SNAP is organized like a typical audit program using a question/answer format with different levels of measurement, including meeting or not meeting expectations. The following tables reflect the contents of SNAP.

SAN—STORAGE NETWORK AUDIT PROGRAM

SNAP for SANs: Preliminary Questions

Audit Topic	Audit Questions
Fabrics	How many SAN fabrics exist?
Zoning	How many zones exist within each fabric?
Zone Method	How is zoning performed?
Zone Configuration	How are zones configured?
Device System Versions	What system versions are used on the storage devices?
Management	Where is management being performed?

Audit Topic	Audit Questions
Management Methods	What are the management methods in use?
LUN Masking	Where is LUN Masking being performed?
Servers	How many servers are connected to the SAN?
Networks	What IP networks are connected to the SAN?
HBA	What types of HBA are being used?

STORAGE NETWORK AUDIT PROGRAM

SNAP for SANs: Storage Network

Audit Topic	Audit Questions	Audit Compliance
Management Passwords should be rotated on a regular basis. Additionally, strong passwords should be used that are difficult to guess or brute force.	Are password changed often? Have the passwords set by the vendors been changed?	**Meets Expectations:** Passwords are changed 90 to 120 days. Additionally, all passwords are alphanumeric with at least one special character. **Does Not Meet Expectations:** No password rotation occurs. Additionally, weak or default passwords are used.
HBA-WWNs WWNs should be difficult to spoof or enumerate.	Which type of WWNs are used: port WWN or node WWNs? Additionally, how are the actual WWNs defined?	**Meets Expectations:** Port WWNs are used. Node WWNs are prohibited from use for authorization parameters. **Does Not Meet Expectations:** Node WWNs are used for authorization.
Zoning Fibre Channel switches should isolate and restrict unauthorized nodes from accessing each other. Zoning should be used to enforce route-based restriction parameters based on zone configurations.	What type of zoning is in use: hard zoning (enforcement of authorized routes) or soft zoning (no enforcement of authorized routes)?	**Meets Expectations:** Hard zoning. **Does Not Meet Expectations:** Soft zoning.

SNAP for SANs: Storage Network (continued)

Audit Topic	Audit Questions	Audit Compliance
Zone Allocation Fibre Channel zone-sets should be allocated based on physical port numbers on zones to prevent WWN spoofing attacks.	Are zone members identified using their physical switch ports or their WWNs?	**Meets Expectations:** Physical switch ports. **Does Not Meet Expectations:** WWNs.
Port Security Port binding should be used to lock a node's WWN to the physical switch port of the switch to prevent WWN spoofing attacks.	Is port binding in use (or some other method to lock WWN to a specific switch port)?	**Meets Expectations:** Port binding in use. **Does Not Meet Expectations:** Port binding not in use.
Port-Type Security Port locking should be used to lock port types on switch ports, specifically locking ports to an F-port type and preventing them from becoming an E-port or G-port type.	Are physical switch ports locked to a specific fibre channel port types, such as E-port, G-port, and F-port? Are all E-ports and G-ports limited to authorized nodes only?	**Meets Expectations:** E-ports are strictly controlled and all other ports are locked to F-port types. **Does Not Meet Expectations:** Port-type locking is not in use.
Switch Security Install and utilize secure versions of switch operating systems, such as Brocade's switch fabric OS or McData's SANtegrity. Additionally, enable fabric configuration server, fabric membership authorization, and switch-level-authentication-protocol (SLAP) where appropriate.	Are secure versions of switch operating systems used?	**Meets Expectations:** Secure switch OS versions are used. **Does Not Meet Expectations:** Default OS versions of switches are used.
SAN Management Management methods for SAN devices should be out-of-band and managed from a secure and trusted management network. SAN devices should not be managed from in-band Fibre Channel connections.	Are SAN devices managed out-of-band via an isolated management network? Are SAN devices managed in-band through an encrypted communication channel via an isolated management network?	**Meets Expectations:** Out-of-band via a management network. *or* Encrypted in-band via a management network. **Does Not Meet Expectations:** Out-of-band via an open internal network. *or* Clear-text over in-band networks.

Audit Topic	Audit Questions	Audit Compliance
SAN Management Storage management should be limited to authorized machines using IP address and hostname filters.	Are access filters placed on SAN devices, filtering access to only management and authorized nodes (via IP address filters or hostname filters)?	**Meets Expectations:** Access filters are used. **Does Not Meet Expectations:** Access filters are not used.
LUN Masking LUN Masking should be enabled at the storage controller or the switch for optimal use.	Is LUN Masking used? If so, where is LUN Masking implemented: at the client node, the storage switch, the storage controller, or a third-party device/application?	**Meets Expectations:** Lun masking is enabled on the Storage switch, Storage controller, or third-party device/application. **Does Not Meet Expectations:** At the client node.
HBA Configuration Host Bus Adapters (HBA) should be configured with unique, unpredictable WWNs.	Are WWNs using their default values? Do different WWNs contain unique values from one another?	**Meets Expectations:** Unique WWNs. **Does Not Meet Expectations:** Default WWNs.
Host Security All servers, including Windows, Unix, and Linux operating systems, should be secured before connecting to the SAN to ensure the server cannot be used as a gateway (attack point) for attackers.	Are all operating systems connected to the SAN above a standard (default) level of security (disabled services, strong passwords, updated patch levels, and strong file permissions)?	**Meets Expectations:** Advanced level of O.S. security has been implemented. **Does Not Meet Expectations:** Default O.S. settings are installed.
Device Passwords Passwords for switches, SAN management tools, and hosts connected to the SAN should be alphanumeric with at least eight characters.	Do all storage devices in the SAN contain alphanumeric passwords that are 8 to 12 characters?	**Meets Expectations:** Eight-character alphanumeric password in use. **Does Not Meet Expectations:** Eight-character alphanumeric password not in use.
Logging All SAN devices should log important activity to the SAN management software. Logs should be reviewed regularly.	Are critical, informational, and severed logs stored?	**Meets Expectations:** Logs are stored and reviewed on a regular basis. **Does Not Meet Expectations:** Logs are not stored or reviewed on a regular basis.

SNAP for SANs: Storage Network (continued)

Audit Topic	Audit Questions	Audit Compliance
Name Server Queries All switch name server queries should be limited to only those nodes in the same zone. The switch should not release any WWN information of nodes in different zones.	Are name server queries from storage nodes limited to per-zone basis?	**Meets Expectations:** NS queries are limited to zone members only. **Does Not Meet Expectations:** NS queries are not limited, but used in the default method.
Port Security Enable ports on switches that are in use are enabled. Any ports that are not in use should be disabled.	Are all ports and all switches used? If not, are ports that are not in use disabled?	**Meets Expectations:** All ports are used and/or unused ports have been disabled. **Does Not Meet Expectations:** All ports are not used and unused ports have not been disabled.
Data Encryption Sensitive, private, and confidential information should be encrypted.	Is any classified data ever held in the following types of places: public storage service provider, off-site tape-holding organization, or internal network accessible to contractors, consultants, business partners, and other non-employee personnel?	**Meets Expectations:** Data is encrypted on disk or not accessible to any unauthorized personnel or storage attacks. **Does Not Meet Expectations:** Data is not encrypted on disk and is accessible to off-site tape organizations in the clear, storage service providers, or contractors/consultants with digital access via the internal network.
Backup Architecture Backup methods should be segmented into zones where a single backup server does not span across multiple security zones.	Are backup and tape devices located on multiple networks?	**Meets Expectations:** A centralized tape device is used that does not connect to any other network except the backend storage controllers. **Does Not Meet Expectations:** Tape devices span network zones and are connected to the internal network and the backend storage controllers.

Audit Topic	Audit Questions	Audit Compliance
Authentication Switches joining the SAN should be authenticated using key authentication methods.	How do switch-to-switch (ISL) updates occur?	**Meets Expectations:** Authentication must take place between the primary switch and the new switching joining the fabric. **Does Not Meet Expectations:** Two e-ports are connected together from each switch.
Authentication SAN clients should authenticate to SAN switches using DH-CHAP authentication.	Is authentication enabled from the HBA to a Fibre Channel switch?	**Meets Expectations:** DH-CHAP is used between HBAs and Fibre Channel switches. **Does Not Meet Expectations:** No authentication is enabled.
Management Passwords authentication for management purposes should use encrypted protocols.	What protocols are being used for management and administration?	**Meets Expectations:** SSH, SSL (HTTPS), and/or SNMPv3. **Does Not Meet Expectations:** Telnet, HTTP, and/or SNMPv1.
SNMP The use of SNMPv1 is strongly discouraged. If it is a business requirement, use difficult-to-guess community strings and restrict access via a firewall or router access control lists.	Is SNMPv3 used or is SNMPv1 used via a secure network?	**Meets Expectations:** SNMPv3 is used or SNMPv1 is used in an isolated management network. **Does Not Meet Expectations:** SNMPv1 is used via an internal network.
Timestamp/Date Date and timestamp information should be current in order to ensure integrity of all log files.	Are date and timestamp information correct?	**Meets Expectations:** Date and time are correct. **Does Not Meet Expectations:** Date and time are not correct.
Error Level The error save level should be 3 or higher to ensure the logging of errors of Panic, Critical, Error, and Warning.	Are error level controls 3 and higher?	**Meets Expectations:** Error levels are 3 and higher. **Does Not Meet Expectations:** Error levels are 2 or below.

SNAP for SANs: Storage Network (continued)

Audit Topic	Audit Questions	Audit Compliance
Fabric Membership Only trusted, authorized, and production switches should be attached to the fabric domain.	Are fabric confirmation servers used to limit the access of rogue/unauthorized switches?	**Meets Expectations:** Fabric configuration services are used. **Does Not Meet Expectations:** Fabric configuration services are not used.
Cut-Through Switching Cut-through switching should not be enabled on Fibre Channel switches. Cut-through switching ignores the source 24-bit fabric address on the fabric and only views the destination 24-bit address. This can lead to subverting zone tables.	Is cut-through switching enabled?	**Meets Expectations:** Cut-through switching is disabled. **Does Not Meet Expectations:** Cut-through switching is enabled.

NAS–STORAGE NETWORK AUDIT PROGRAM

SNAP for NAS: Preliminary Questions

Audit Topic	Audit Questions
Support Nodes	What are the NAS devices used for, file servers, database servers, home directories, or all of the above?
Device System Versions	What versions are used on the NAS storage devices?
Management	Where is management being performed?
Management Methods	What management methods are in use?
Servers	How many servers are connected to the NAS devices?
Networks	What IP networks are connected to the SAN?
Data Protocols	What data services have been enabled on NAS devices, CIFS, NFS, or both?

STORAGE NETWORK AUDIT PROGRAM

SNAP for NAS: NAS Devices

Audit Topic	Audit Questions	Audit Compliance
Remote Management Administer all hosts locally or use secure methods to ensure that credentials and data are encrypted.	Is SSH used? If not, are Telnet and HTTP management methods restricted via IP address?	**Meets Expectations:** SSH is implemented or Telnet/HTTP methods are disabled or restricted to specific IP address only. **Does Not Meet Expectations:** SSH is not used and there is no restriction methods on clear-text protocols.
SNMP The use of SNMPv1 is strongly discouraged. If it is a business requirement, use difficult-to-guess community strings and restrict access via a firewall or router access control lists.	Is SNMPv3 used or is SNMPv1 used?	**Meets Expectations:** SNMPv3 is used or SNMPv1 is used via a secure network. **Does Not Meet Expectations:** SNMPv1 is used from the internal network.
Timestamp/Date Date and timestamp information should be current in order to ensure integrity of all log files.	Are date and timestamp information correct?	**Meets Expectations:** Date and time are correct. **Does Not Meet Expectations:** Date and time are not correct.
CIFS Share Enumeration The ability to enumerate CIFS shares on a filer should be restricted or disabled.	Is the enumeration of CIFS shares enabled?	**Meets Expectations:** Enumeration of CIFS shares has been disabled. **Does Not Meet Expectations:** Enumeration is possible with the default settings implemented.
Disable CIFS Guest Access Guest access to the filer should be disabled.	Is guest or anonymous access to the filer enabled?	**Meets Expectations:** Guest and anonymous accounts have been disabled. **Does Not Meet Expectations:** Guest/anonymous accounts have read access to the NAS device.

SNAP for NAS: NAS Devices

Audit Topic	Audit Questions	Audit Compliance
Trust Hosts Trusted hosts options should be disabled.	Are any hosts allowed to login without authentication?	**Meets Expectations:** Trusted hosts have been disabled. **Does Not Meet Expectations:** Certain hosts are listed in the trusted hosts file.
User Accountability Log all administrative access.	Are logs kept for administrative functions?	**Meets Expectations:** Audit logs have been enabled for all types of users. **Does Not Meet Expectations:** Audit logs have not been enabled.
CIFS and NFS Admins Administrators should not be able to override permissions unless they own a specific folder.	Do all administrators have complete override capabilities?	**Meets Expectations:** Administrator/root users cannot override file permissions settings. **Does Not Meet Expectations:** CIFS and NFS administrators can override permissions.
CIFS Share-Level ACLs Default shares on CIFS should not be open to everyone.	What are share-level ACLs set to?	**Meets Expectations:** Restricted to authorized groups/users. **Does Not Meet Expectations:** Open to anyone on the network.
Traverse Checking Ensure that permissions are checked from top-level folders.	Is traverse checking enabled?	**Meets Expectations:** Traverse checking has been enabled. **Does Not Meet Expectations:** Traverse checking has been disabled.
Anonymous FTP Access Ensure that anonymous FTP access is off.	Is anonymous FTP enabled?	**Meets Expectations:** FTP has been disabled. **Does Not Meet Expectations:** Anonymous FTP is enabled.

Audit Topic	Audit Questions	Audit Compliance
UID and GID Mappings NFS clients should not have their client UID and GID mapped to the filer but a filer-specific UID and GID.	How is authentication conducted for users under NFS?	**Meets Expectations:** Kerberos authentication has been enabled. Additionally, all users are mapped to a nobody account, regardless of their UID. **Does Not Meet Expectations:** All UID values, except root, are left intact by the NAS device.

iSCSI—STORAGE NETWORK AUDIT PROGRAM

SNAP for iSCSI: Preliminary Questions

Audit Topic	Audit Questions
Domains	How many domains exist in the iSCSI storage network?
iSNS Configuration	Are default domain sets used (default setting) or have unique domain sets or iSCSI zones been created?
Device System Versions	What system versions are used on the storage devices?
Management	Where is management being performed?
Management Methods	What are the management methods in use?
Servers	How many servers are connected to the iSCSI devices?
Networks	What IP networks are connected to the iSCSI SAN?

STORAGE NETWORK AUDIT PROGRAM

SNAP for iSCSI SANs: iSCSI Storage Devices and Applications

Audit Topic	Audit Questions	Audit Compliance
Authentication iSCSI initiator should be required to authenticate for all iSCSI communication.	Is CHAP authentication enabled?	**Meets Expectations:** CHAP is enabled. **Does Not Meet Expectations** CHAP is disabled.
Mutual Authentication iSCSI targets should be required to authenticate iSCSI clients.	Is mutual authentication enabled with CHAP?	**Meets Expectations:** Mutual authentication with CHAP is enabled. **Does Not Meet Expectations:** Mutual authentication with CHAP is disabled.
Authorization iSCSI initiators should be unique and unpredictable.	Are iSCSI node names using the reverse of fully qualified hostname information?	**Meets Expectations:** iSCSI node names have been changed to unique and unpredictable values in addition to CHAP authentication or IPSec encryption being enabled. **Does Not Meet Expectations:** Default values are being used for iSCSI node names.
Encryption iSCSI networks using sensitive information or connected to untrusted networks, such as the internal network, DMZ, or Internet, should use encrypted communication.	Is IPSec being used?	**Meets Expectations:** IPSec is enabled. **Does Not Meet Expectations:** IPSec is disabled.
iSNS Servers iSNS should be used to segment initiators and targets.	What iSNS domains are set up?	**Meets Expectations:** Unique domains have been set up on iSNS servers. **Does Not Meet Expectations:** Default domain sets are used for all iSCSI targets/initiator.

SECURING STORAGE DEVICES

The security of storage devices that formulate a storage network is quite important. Most NAS devices are distributed throughout the network while most SAN devices are centralized; however, they are all directly connected to nodes that are distributed throughout the network. In order to secure data, the devices that hold the data must be secured. Every network device, whether it is a router, an operating system, or a storage device, has a list of configurations and features that can be enabled or disabled. Many of the features and settings directly affect the security of the device, especially when it is connected to the network. For example, securing a Windows operating system involves enabling or disabling several options on the system. Similarly, securing storage devices requires administrators to enable security features and disable features that lead to weaknesses. The remaining portion of this chapter will focus on the security of NetApp Filers (NAS) and Cisco Fibre Channel Switches (SAN). Because there are hundreds of storage devices, the security configuration of each of them could not be listed in this chapter. For information on securing other various types of storage devices, such as Brocade, McData, QLogic, Lefthand, EqualLogic, BlueArc, and EMC, using automated tools, email the author at securingstorage@gmail.com.

NETAPP FILERS

The following section describes the security settings for a Network Appliance filer running Data ONTAP version 6.0 or above. Security settings are described for CIFS, NFS, and iSCSI. This section was written by both the author and Chris Odhner of Network Appliance (Chris can be reached at codhner@netapp.com). Also, the author has written a program to automatically assess the security of a NetApp Filer, which analyzes all of the settings in the next table within minutes. For the most recent version of the program, please email securingstorage@gmail.com. The program supports SSH and Telnet to remotely log in to a NetApp Filer and analyze the device for security. It also supports analysis from a local file that contains the filer's configuration information. A screenshot of the automated tool is shown in Figures 13.1 and 13.2.

ASSESSMENT EXERCISE

1. Install the NetApp Security Analyzer Program and execute the program.
2. Choose SSH, Telnet, or LocalFile for the analysis method.

3. If you choose SSH or Telnet, you will be prompted for the username and password

   a. Type the username and password of the filer and select Enter.

   b. Finished! The program will analyze the filer for security and display the results in a local HTML file.

4. If you choose LocalFile, you will be prompted for the following items:

   a. Name of the filer, which can be anything.

   b. File name that contains the filer's configuration information (output from the "options" command on the filer).

   c. Finished!. The program will analyze the filer for security and display the results in a local HTML file.

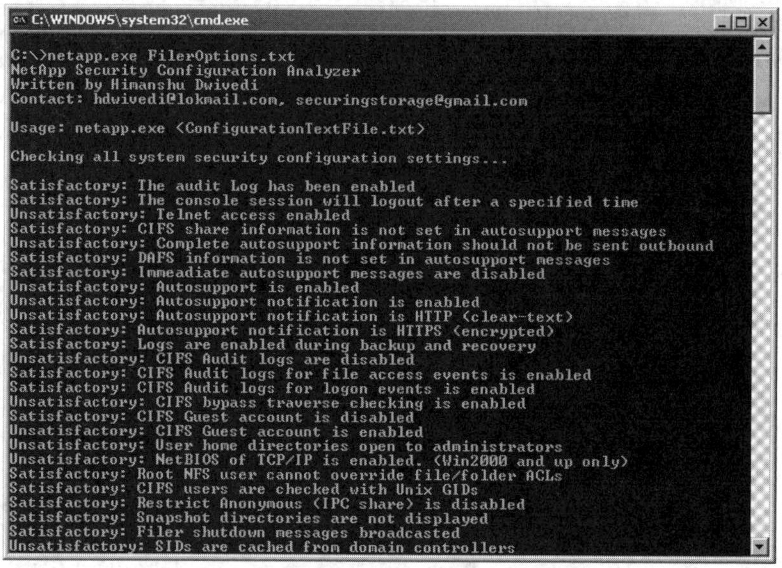

Figure 13.1 NetApp Security Configuration Analyzer.

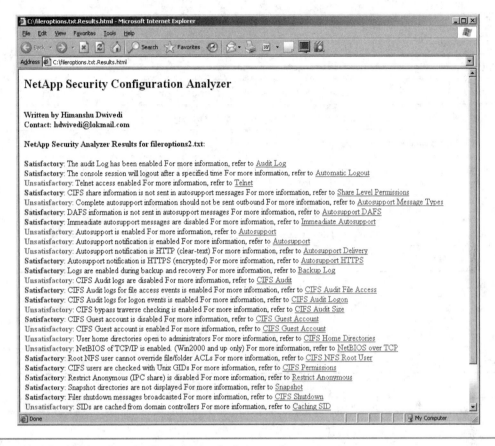

Figure 13.2 NetApp Security Configuration Analyzer results.

The configuration options to secure a Network Appliance filer are divided into the following areas:

- General options
- NFS
- CIFS
- Multiprotocol settings
- iSCSI
- Network configuration
- System services

NETAPP: General Options

Root Password

Option	Sets the password for the root account.
Secure Setting	Use a strong password for the root account.
Syntax	`filer# passwd root [password]`

Trusted Hosts Access

Option	Enables/disables the ability for certain hosts to access filers without authentication.
Secure Setting	Disabled the trusted host option.
Syntax	`filer# option trusted.hosts -`

Telnet Access

Option	Enables/disables Telnet access to the filer.
Secure Setting	Disable Telnet access.
Syntax	`filer# options telnet.enable off`

RSH Access

Option	Enables/disables RSH access to the filer.
Secure Setting	Disable RSH access. (Note: If using SnapDrive, DFM, or SnapMirror, RSH must be enabled.)
Syntax	`filer# options rsh.enable off`

HTTP Access

Option	Enables/disables HTTP (web) access to the filer.
Secure Setting	Disable HTTP (web) access.
Syntax	`filer# options httpd.admin.access none`

SecureAdmin

Option	Enables SecureAdmin for SSH and SSL security features.
Secure Setting	Install SecureAdmin.

SecureAdmin

Syntax	`filer# secureadmin setup ssh`
	`filer# secureadmin enable ssh`
	`filer# secureadmin setup ssl`
	`filer# secureadmin enable ssl`

Restrict SSH Logins

Option	Filters access to SSH to only authorized SSH clients.
Secure Setting	Limit access to the filer to authorized SSH clients only.
Syntax	`filer# options ssh.access host=[ipaddress],[ipaddress],[hostname]`

Password Quality Check

Option	Enables password quality check for non-root admin users.
Secure Setting	Ensure the password quality check is enabled for non-root admin users for strong password use.
Syntax	`filer# options security.passwd.rules.enable on`

Non-Root Users

Option	Creates additional accounts on the filer.
Secure Setting	Create non-root (low-rights) user accounts for each administrator and discourage usage of the actual root account.
Syntax	`filer# useradmin useradd [username]`

Automatic Logout

Option	Enables and sets an automatic logout for console and network sessions to the filer.
Secure Setting	Enable automatic logoff.
Syntax	`filer# options autologout.console.enable on`
	`filer# options autologout.telnet.enable on`
	`filer# options autologout.console.timeout 30`
	`filer# options autologout.telnet.timeout 15`

NETAPP: General Options (continued)

Logging Administrative Access

Option	Enables and configures logging for administrative sessions.
Secure Setting	Set logging procedure to high for administrative sessions.
Syntax	`filer#` options auditlog.enable on
	`filer#` options auditlog.max_file_size 49984

Host Equiv Access

Option	Allows trusted remote hosts access without authentication.
Secure Setting	Disable host.equiv access for web access. (Note: This does not affect RSH access.)
Syntax	`filer#` options httpd.admin.hostsequiv.enable off

NETAPP: NFS Options

Kerberos Authentication

Option	Enables Kerberos authentication for NFS. Requires NFS clients to support Kerberos.
Secure Setting	Enable NFS authentication with Kerberos.
Syntax	`filer#` nfs setup
	Enable Kerberos for NFS? **Y**
	The filer supports these types of Kerberos Key Distribution Centers (KDCs):
	1—UNIX KDC
	2—Microsoft Active Directory KDC
	Enter the type of your KDC (1-2): **1** (if NFS only) or **2** (if Win-AD domain)
	Kerberos now enabled for NFS.
	NFS set up complete.

IPSec

Option	Enables IPSec between NFS clients and the filer.
Secure Setting	Enable AH authentication and ESP payload encryption between filers and clients.
Syntax	`filer# ipsec policy add -s {source ip} -t {destination ip} -p {esp|ah|none} -e {des|3des|null}	{sha1|md5|null} -d {in|out} -f ip_protocol -l {restrict|permit}`

Exports File

Option	Lists of the file systems on the filer that are exported.
Secure Setting	Ensure that only data file systems are exports and no administrative file systems, such as /etc, are exported.
Syntax	`Filer# exportfs`

NFS over TCP

Option	Enables NFS session over TCP packets instead of UDP.
Secure Setting	Enable NFS over TCP. Additionally, consider using firewalls between filers and untrusted networks.
Syntax	**N/A**

NFS Mount Request

Option	Enables/disables NFS mount request over low-numbered ports.
Secure Setting	Enable NFS mounts over-low-numbered ports only.
Syntax	`Filer# options nfs.mount_rootonly on`

NETAPP: CIFS Options

Kerberos Authentication

Option	Enables AD authentication, which uses Kerberos by default.
Secure Setting	Use Active Directory authentication to support Kerberos.
Syntax	`<Join filer to the AD domain>`

NETAPP: CIFS Options (continued)

Share Level Permissions

Option	Sets the share-level permission on the filers' CIFS shares.
Secure Setting	Change the share-level ACL to authorized users only and remove "Everyone/Full Control."
Syntax	**N/A**

Audit CIFS Access

Option	Audits CIFS share-level access.
Secure Setting	Enables the auditing on CIFS access to the filer.

Syntax	`filer# options cifs.audit.enable on`
	
	`filer# options cifs.audit.logon_events.enable on`

Anonymous Connections

Option	Enables/disables enumeration of shares on the CIFS filer by anonymous users.
Secure Setting	Disable the ability to enumerate shares on the CIFS filer by remote anonymous users.
Syntax	`filer# options cifs.restrict_anonymous.enable on`

Guest Access

Option	Enables/disables CIFS guest access.
Secure Setting	Disable CIFS guest access.
Syntax	`filer# options cifs.guest_account ""`

NETAPP: Multi-Protocol Options

Ignore ACLs

Option	When on, ACLs will not affect root-level access from NFS drives.
Secure Setting	Disable this option to prevent administrator accounts from controlling files/folders on the NAS device that they should not have access to.
Syntax	`filer# options cifs.nfs_root_ignore_acl off`

CIFS Bypass Traverse Checking

Option	When on, directories in the path to a file are not required to have the X (traverse) permission.
Secure Setting	Disable traverse checking.
Syntax	`filer# options cifs.bypass_traverse_checking off`

CIFS GID Checks

Option	This option affects security checking for Windows clients on files with Unix security where the requestor is not the file owner.
Secure Setting	Enable CIFS GID checks.
Syntax	`filer# options cifs.perm_check_use_gid on`

Default NT User

Option	Specifies the NT user account to use when a Unix user accesses a file with NT security (has an ACL) and the Unix user would not otherwise be mapped.
Secure Setting	Set the option to a null string, denying access.
Syntax	`filer# options wafl.default_nt_user " "`

Default UNIX User

Option	Specifies the Unix user account to use when an NT user attempts to log in and that NT user would not otherwise be mapped.
Secure Setting	Set the option to a null string, denying access.
Syntax	`filer# options wafl.default_unix_user " "`

Root to Admin Mappings

Option	When on, an NT administrator is mapped to Unix root.
Secure Setting	Disable root to admin mappings.
Syntax	`filer# options wafl.nt_admin_priv_map_to_root off`

Change Permissions

Option	When enabled, only the root user can change the owner of a file.
Secure Setting	Allow only root access to change permissions to files.
Syntax	`filer# options wafl.root_only_chown on`

NETAPP: Multi-Protocol Options (continued)

Cache Credentials

Option	Specifies the number of minutes a WAFL credential cache entry is valid. The value can range from 1 through 20160.
Secure Setting	Set the minutes for 10 for cache credentials.
Syntax	`filer# options wafl.wcc_minutes_valid 10`

NETAPP: iSCSI

Default Security Method

Option	Sets the default security method to use.
Secure Setting	Set the default security method to deny, which denies access from any iSCSI client with no security method defined.
Syntax	`filer# iscsi default -s deny`

Initiator Security Method

Option	Sets the default security method to use for each iSCSI initiator.
Secure Setting	Require CHAP authentication for all iSCSI initiators.
Syntax	`filer# iscsi security add -I initiator -s CHAP -p [password] -n [name]`

Random CHAP Passwords

Option	Creates random CHAP passwords when using CHAP authentication.
Secure Setting	Enable random CHAP passwords.
Syntax	`filer# iscsi security generate`

iGroup Creation

Option	Creates logical groups to segment iSCSI nodes.
Secure Setting	Create several iGroups to support authorization, which will segment the nodes and limit access to data.
Syntax	`filer# igroup create -i -t [name of igroup] [iscsi node name]`
	`filer# lun map [lun name] [igroup name] [lun id]`

NETAPP: Network Settings

Incoming Packets

Option	Checks incoming packets for correct addressing.
Secure Setting	Enable packet checking for correct addressing.
Syntax	`filer# options ip.match_any_ifaddr off`

MAC FastPath

Option	Filer will attempt to use a MAC address and interface caching ("Fastpath") and send back responses to incoming network traffic using the same interface as the incoming traffic and (in some cases) the destination MAC address equal to the source MAC address of the incoming data.
Secure Setting	Disable this option. This increases the ability for ARP spoofing and session hijacking attacks.
Syntax	`filer# options ip.fastpath.enable off`

Logging Ping Flood

Option	Enables/disables logging of ping flood attacks.
Secure Setting	Enable logging of ping attacks.
Syntax	`filer# options ip.ping_throttle.alarm_interval 5`

SNAP Mirror Access

Option	Sets the IP address and hostname for nodes that can receive SnapMirror/SnapVault backups.
Secure Setting	Set IP address/hostnames to authorized users for backup.
Syntax	`filer# options snapmirror.access host=[ipaddress], [hostname]`

SNAP Mirror Source Access

Option	Enables IP address-based verification of snapmirror destination filers by source filers.
Secure Setting	Enable source address verification.
Syntax	`filer# options snapmirror.checkip.enable on`

NETAPP: Network Settings (continued)

NDMP

Option	Restricts control and data connections to authorized hosts.
Secure Setting	Limited backup using NDMP to authorized hosts only.
Syntax	`filer# options ndmp.access host=[ipaddress],[hostname]`

NDMP Authentication

Option	Sets the NDMP authentication type.
Secure Setting	Enable MD5 authentication for NDMP.
Syntax	`filer# options ndmpd.authtype challenge`

NETAPP: System Services

FTP

Option	Enables/disables FTP.
Secure Setting	Disable FTP.
Syntax	`filer# options ftpd.enable off`

PCNFS

Option	Enables/disables PCNFS.
Secure Setting	Disable PCNFS.
Syntax	`filer# options pcnfs.enable off`

SNMP

Option	Enables/disables SNMP.
Secure Setting	Enable SNMP since only read-only strings are supported (SNMP read-write is not supported on NetApp filers). Use a difficult-to-guess community string as well as IP address filtering for SNMP traps. Additionally, when adding a new community string, ensure the old one (such as public) has been removed.

SNMP

Syntax	`filer#` `options snmp.enable on`
	`filer#` `snmp community add ro [alpha_numeric_string]`
	`filer#` **`snmp community delete ro public`**
	`filer#` `snmp traphost add [hostnanme or ip address]`

RSH

Option	Enables/disables RSH.
Secure Setting	Disable RSH.
Syntax	`filer#` `options rsh.enable off`

Telnet

Option	Enables/disables Telnet.
Secure Setting	Disable Telnet.
Syntax	`filer#` `options telnet.enable off`

TFTP

Option	Enables/disables TFTP.
Secure Setting	Disable TFTP.
Syntax	`filer#` `options tftpd.enable off`

CISCO SWITCHES

The following section describes the security setting for Cisco MDS 9000 switches running version 2.0 or above. The author has also written a program to automatically assess the security of a Cisco switch, which analyzes all of the settings in the following table within minutes. For the most recent version of the program, please email securingstorage@gmail.com. The tool supports SSH and Telnet to remotely log into to a MDS switch and analyze the device for security. It also supports analysis from a local file that contains the switches' configuration information. A screenshot of the automated tool is shown in Figures 13.3 and 13.4.

ASSESSMENT EXERCISE

1. Install the Cisco MDS Security Analyzer Program and execute the program.
2. Choose SSH, Telnet, or LocalFile for the analysis method.
3. If you choose SSH or Telnet, you will be prompted for the username and password.
   a. Type the username and password of the switch and select Enter.
   b. Finished! The program will analyze the switch for security and display the results in a local HTML file.
4. If you choose LocalFile, you will be prompted for the following items:
   a. Name of the switch, which can be anything.
   b. File name that contains the switches' configuration information (output from the 'show config' command on the switch).
   c. Finished!. The program will analyze the switch for security and display the results in a local HTML file.

The configuration options are divided into the following areas:

- General
- Authentication
- VSAN
- IVR
- Zoning
- Port security
- iSCSI
- Security services
  IPSEC
  SNMPv3
  SSH
  SSL
- Logging

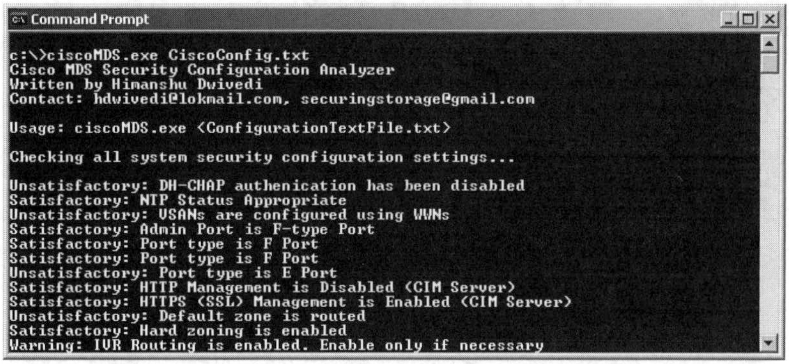

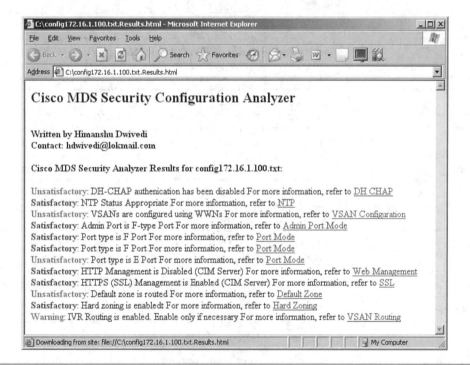

Figure 13.3   Cisco MDS Switch Security Configuration Analyzer.

Figure 13.4   Cisco MDS Switch Security Configuration Analyzer results.

Cisco MDS: General

AAA

Option	Enables authentication, authorization, and auditing.
Secure Setting	Enable AAA architecture with a third-party AAA device (RADIUS or TACACS+) for SSH, DHCP, and iSCSI.
Syntax	`switch#` aaa authentication login default `switch#` aaa authentication dhcp default `switch#` aaa authentication iscsi default

AAA Error Messages

Option	Enables logging for AAA services.
Secure Setting	Enable logging for all authentication, authorization, and auditing services.
Syntax	`switch#` show aaa authentication login error-enable

Password Type 5

Option	Enables a strong password storage method.
Secure Setting	Ensure password type 5 methods are used to store passwords in secure formats.
Syntax	`switch(config)#` username [user] password 5 [password]

Cut-Thru Mode

Option	Enables cut-through switching.
Secure Setting	Ensure cut-through switching is disabled, which helps prevent FCID spoofing.
Syntax	`Switch(config-if)#` no mode cut-thru

CallHome

Option	Calls home with system information.
Secure Setting	Do not enable the call home feature to prevent unwanted information leakage.
Syntax	`switch(config)#` callhome `switch(config-callhome)#` disable

Scheduler

Option	Sets up a schedule for the switch.
Secure Setting	Disable the schedule as a malicious command can be inserted by a low-rights user to gain access to a high-rights privilege.
Syntax	`Switch(config)# no scheduler enable`

Cisco Fibre Channel Analyzer (Sniffer)

Option	Enables the remote use of a Fibre Channel sniffer with the Ethereal application.
Secure Setting	Enable sniffing for security purposes, but limit the rights to authorized nodes (sniffers only) due the amount of information leakage.

Syntax	`switch(config)# fcanalyzer local write volatile: [nameoffile]`
	
	`switch(config)# fcanalyzer remote [ip.address] active`

Core Dumps

Option	Creates core dumps of important system information.
Secure Setting	Disable core dumps due to large amounts of sensitive information stored in the file.
Syntax	`switch(config)# no system cores`

Limit Broadcast

Option	Prevents broadcast traffic from moving between zones.
Secure Setting	Limits broadcast frames to nodes in the same zone. Prevents network enumeration and MITM attacks.

Syntax	`switch# config t`
	
	`switch(config)# zone broadcast enable vsan [number]`

IP Management

Option	Enables restriction of management services to authorized servers only.
Secure Setting	Restrict management of the switch from appropriate management subnets.

Cisco MDS: General (continued)

IP Management

Syntax	`switch# config t`
	`switch(config)# ip access-list management_net permit ip [management network subnet] 0.0.0.255 any switch(config)# interface mgmt0`
	`switch(config0if)# ip access group management_net`

VRRP Authentication

Option	Enables authentication for VRRP services.
Secure Setting	Enable authentication for VRRP communication between switches.
Syntax	`switch# config t`
	`switch(config)# interface vsan [number]`
	`switch(config-if)# vrrp [number]`
	`switch(config-if)# authentication md5 [password]`

Fabric Binding

Option	Limits authorized switches to VSAN group and prevents unauthorized switches from access.
Secure Setting	Bind specific fFbre Channel switches to a fabric domain. This will prevent unauthorized or unknown switches from joining VSANs without authorization.
Syntax	`switch# config t`
	`switch(config)# fabric-binding enable`
	`switch(config)# fabric-binding database vsan [number}`
	`switch(config-fabric-binding)# swwn [swwn] domain [domain number]`
	`switch(config)# fabric-binding activate vsan [number]`

Cisco MDS: Authentication

Enable Fibre Channel Security Protocol

Option	Enables security on the switch.
Secure Setting	Enable security options on the switch.
Syntax	**switch#** config t
	switch(config)# fcsp enable

DH-CHAP Authentication

Option	Enables authentication between switches and between a host and a switch.
Secure Setting	Require DH-CHAP authentication between host to switches, switch to switch, and storage controllers to switch.
Syntax	**switch#** config t
	switch(config)# fcsp enable
	switch(config)# interface [interface]
	switch(config-if)# fcsp on
	switch(config-if)# fcsp auto-active 60

DH-CHAP Hash Configuration

Option	Selects the hash method to be used with authentication.
Secure Setting	Enable SHA1 followed by MD5 hashes.
Syntax	**switch#** config t
	switch(config)# fcsp dhchap hash sha1 MD5

DH-CHAP Group Configuration

Option	Selects the group method to be used with authentication.
Secure Setting	Enable groups 2, 3, and 4.
Syntax	**switch#** config t
	switch(config)# fcsp dhchap group 2 3 4

DH-CHAP Password

Option	Configures the password to be used with DH-CHAP authentication.

Cisco MDS: Authentication (continued)

DH-CHAP Password

Secure Setting	Configure a strong password and ensure it is used with the password 7 command (not clear-text).
Syntax	`switch# config t` `switch(config)# fcsp dhchap password 7 [password]`

DH-CHAP Password Timeout

Option	Sets the password timeout length (in seconds) if a DH-CHAP message is not received on a timely basis.
Secure Setting	Configure a short interval for timeouts to ensure protection against CHAP message challenges attacks.
Syntax	`switch# config t` `switch(config)# fcsp timeout 30`

Cisco MDS: VSANs

VSAN Configuration (Static)

Option	Configures VSAN using physical port numbers (WWN are called Dynamic VSANs).
Secure Setting	Create static VSAN to segment the storage fabric.

Syntax	`switch# config t`
	`switch(config)# vsan database`
	`switch(config-vsan-db)# vsan [number]`
	`switch(config-vsan-db)# vsan [number] [name] update vsan [number]`
	
	Example:
	`switch# config t`
	`switch(config)# vsan database`
	`switch(config-vsan-db)# vsan 8`
	`switch(config-vsan-db)# vsan 8 Exchange update vsan 8`

VSAN Memberships

Option	Configures VSANs using physical port numbers.
Secure Setting	Use physical port numbers for VSAN instead of WWN to limit spoofing attacks.
Syntax	`switch#` config t
	`switch(config)#` vsan database
	`switch(config-vsan-db)#` vsan [number] interface fc[physical port number/number of ports on switch]
	Example:
	`switch#` config t
	`switch(config)#` vsan database
	`switch(config-vsan-db)#` vsan 8
	`switch(config-vsan-db)#` vsan 8 interface fc5/8
	`switch(config-vsan-db)#` vsan 8 interface fc6/8
	`switch(config-vsan-db)#` vsan 8 interface fc7/8
	`switch(config-vsan-db)#` vsan 8 interface fc8/8

Display VSAN Information

Option	Displays VSAN information.
Secure Setting	Ensure VSAN are configured using physical port numbers.
Syntax	`switch#` show vsan
	`switch#` show vsan membership

Display Isolated VSAN Membership

Option	Displays isolated VSAN membership.
Secure Setting	Ensure only authorized and known hosts appear in the isolated VSAN.
Syntax	`switch#` show vsan 4094 membership

VSAN Roles

Option	Creates roles for VSANs to enforce default deny or accept rules for nodes.
Secure Setting	Create a default deny rule for VSANs to selectively permit authorized nodes to the VSAN.

Cisco MDS:VSANs (continued)

VSAN Roles

Syntax	**switch#** config t
	switch(config)# role name VSANgroup8
	switch(config-role)# vsan policy deny
	switch(config-role-vsan)# permit vsan 8

Cisco MDS: IVR

IVR

Option	Enables Inter VSAN Routing.
Secure Setting	Disable IVR on switches unless absolutely required. If required, configure read-only zones with IVR.
Syntax	**switch#** config t
	switch(config)# no ivr enable

IVR NAT

Option	Enables Inter VSAN Routing with IP addresses with Network Address Translation.
Secure Setting	Disable IVR NAT on switches unless required. If needed, configure read-only zones with IVR.
Syntax	**switch#** config t
	switch(config)# no ivr fcid-nat

IVR Logging Level

Option	Enables logging wit Inter VSAN Routing.
Secure Setting	Set logging level to 6 (information, notification, warnings, errors, critical, and alerts).
Syntax	**switch#** config t
	switch(config)# logging level ivr 6

Cisco MDS: Zoning

Zone Configuration

Option	Creates zones based on interface (physical ports), IP address/subnet, domain ID/physical port, FC alias, FC ID, fabric port WWN, or port WWN.
Secure Setting	Create zones based on: • Domain ID/interface (physical ports) • Domain ID/physical port (compatible with other FC switches) • Local switch WWN Using IP address/subnets, port WWNs, FC ID, or FC aliases introduce greater attack surfaces.
Syntax	**switch#** config t **switch(config)#** zone name [zone name] vsan [number] **switch(config-zone)#** member [type] [value] Example: **switch#** config t **switch(config)#** zone name ZoneA vsan 8
	Domain ID/interface: **switch(config-zone)#** member interface fc6/1 domain-id 8 Domain ID/physical port: **switch(config-zone)#** member domain-id 8 portnumber 6 Local switch WWN: **switch(config-zone)#** member interface fc 6/1

Hard Zoning

Option	Enables hard zoning.
Secure Setting	Ensure hard zoning is enabled.
Syntax	**[Hard Zoning is enabled by default]**

Default Zones

Option	Limits communication of the default zone in VSAN 1, where all unknown or unallocated nodes are grouped.
Secure Setting	Deny traffic to the default zone members, which are a collection of nodes that have not been placed into any other zone (this would include nodes that have joined the fabric in an unauthorized fashion).

Cisco MDS: Zoning (continued)

Default Zones

Syntax	`switch# config t`
	`switch(config)# no zone default-zone permit vsan 1`

LUN Masking (LUN Zoning)

Option	Enables LUN Masking/zoning.
Secure Setting	Enable LUN Masking/zoning on switches. Ensure that all LUNs are exposed to appropriate nodes using their port WWN or their 24-bit Fibre Channel address (FCID).
Syntax	`switch# config t`
	`switch(config)# zone name [name] vsan [number]`
	`switch(config-zone)# member pwwn [port WWN value] lun [number]`
	Example:
	`switch(config)# zone name EmailLUN vsan 12`
	`switch(config-zone)# member pwwn 50:00:00:32:54:75:82:e3 lun 17`
	`switch(config-zone)# member fcid 0x81939 lun 17`

Read-Only Zones for Default Zone

Option	Enables read-only zones.
Secure Setting	Create read-only zones for the default zone in VSAN 1, where all unknown or unallocated nodes are grouped. This will prevent unauthorized nodes or accidental zone allocations from damaging the SAN and its data.
Syntax	`switch# config t`
	`switch(config)# zone name [zonename] vsan [number]`
	`switch(config-zone)# attribute read-only`
	Example:
	`switch# config t`
	`switch(config)# zone name default-zone vsan 1`
	`switch(config-zone)# attribute read-only`

Enhanced Zoning

Option	Enables enhanced zoning.
Secure Setting	Enable enhanced zoning when possible on all VSANs.
Syntax	**switch#** config t
	switch(config)# zone mode enhanced vsan [number]

Cisco MDS: Port Security

Port Security

Option	Enables port security (port locking), which locks a WWN to a physical port on the switch.
Secure Setting	Enable port security (locking).
Syntax	**switch#** config t
	switch(config)# port-security enable

Port Security (Port Locking)

Option	Enables port security (port locking), which locks a WWN to a physical port on the switch
Secure Setting	Enable port security (locking), which will lock a WWN to a physical port. This will help defend against WWN spoofing attacks.
Syntax	**switch#** config t
	switch(config)# port-security database vsan [number]
	switch(config-port-security)# pwwn [wwn] fwwn [fwwn]
	Example:
	switch# config t
	switch(config)# port-security database vsan 1
	switch(config-port-security)# pwwn 50:93:9e:38:81:66:41:2a swwn 20:00:00:0a:38:12:f3:90 interface fc8/1

Cisco MDS: Port Security (continued)

Port Security Activation and AutoLearning

Option	Activates port security and also enables AutoLearning.
Secure Setting	Activate port security and enable AutoLearning, which will allow the switch to learn all the WWNs and physical ports they are connected to in order to lock (secure) the configuration. After AutoLearning is complete, all new WWNs will not be allowed to communicate unless AutoLearning is conducted again.
Syntax	**switch#** config t
	switch(config)# port-security activate vsan [number]
	switch(config)# port-security auto-learn vsan [number]
	switch(config)# port-security distribute
	switch(config)# port-security commit vsan [number]

Set all Interfaces to F-Port

Option	Set interfaces on switch to be either F-port, E-port, G-port, or TE port.
Secure Setting	Ensure non-ISL ports are configured to be F-ports only.
Syntax	**switch#** config t
	switch(config)# interface fc8/8
	switch(config-if)# switchport mode F

Reject Duplication (Spoofed) pWWN

Option	Prevents duplicate WWN from registering or overwriting nodes in the SAN.
Secure Setting	Reject duplicated WWN to prevent against WWN spoofing attacks (both port and node WWNs).
Syntax	**switch#** config t
	switch(config)# fcns reject-duplicate-pwwn vsan [number]

Cisco MDS: iSCSI

iSCSI Zones

Option	Creates iSCSI zones for iSCSI SANs. Groups authorized iSCSI initiator and targets in the same zone.
Secure Setting	Create iSCSI zones to group authorized initiators/targets in the same zone, which will limit or prevent unauthorized or unknown servers from attaching to iSCSI targets. Use pWWN to identify members and only use IP addresses or IQN values if needed.
Syntax	**switch#** config t **switch(config)#** zone name iSCSI_Zone vsan [number] **switch(config-zone)#** member pwnn [pwwn] **switch(config-zone)#** member symbolic-nodename [iqn.Node.Name] **switch(config-zone)#** member ip-address [ip.address]

iSCSI AAA Authentication

Option	Enables authentication, authorization, and auditing services for iSCSI SANs.
Secure Setting	Enable AAA for iSCSI SAN access.
Syntax	**switch(config)#** aaa authentication iscsi default local **switch(config)#** iscsi authentication chap **switch(config)#** username [user] password [password] iscsi

iSCSI Local Authentication

Option	Enables authentication for iSCSI SAN.
Secure Setting	Ensure authentication is enabled for iSCSI targets.
Syntax	**switch#** config t **switch(config)#** iscsi authentication chap **switch(config)#** username [user] password [password] iscsi

iSCSI Initiator Authentication

Option	Enables authentication on iSCSI initiator targets.
Secure Setting	Ensure authentication is enabled for all iSCSI initiators.

Cisco MDS: iSCSI (continued)

iSCSI Initiator Authentication

Syntax	`switch# config t`
	`switch(config)# iscsi initiator name [iqn.node.name]`
	`switch(config-iscsi-init)# username [user]`

Mutual CHAP Authentication

Option	Enables mutual authentication in iSCSI SANs.
Secure Setting	Ensure mutual authentication is enabled on iSCSI SANs, which will allow iSCSI targets to authenticate iSCSI initiators.
Syntax	`switch# config t`
	`switch(config)# iscsi authentication username [user] password 7 [password]`
	`switch(config)# username [user] password [password] iscsi`
	`switch(config)# iscsi initiator name [iqn.Node.Name]`
	`switch(config-isci-init)# mutual-chap username [user] password 7 [password]`

Cisco MDS: Security Services

Implement SSH

Option	Enables SSH services on the switch.
Secure Setting	Ensure SSH is enabled and Telnet services are disabled.
Syntax	`switch# config t`
	`switch(config)# ssh server enable updated`

Enable SSH Public/Private Keys

Option	Creates public and private key pairs for SSH services.
Secure Setting	Create public and private keys for authentication to SSH service.
Syntax	`switch(config)# username admin sshkey ssh-rsa [key]`

Generate SSH Key Pairs

Option	Creates the SSH key pairs for SSH services.
Secure Setting	Create the SSH key pairs in order to use the SSH services.
Syntax	**switch#** config t
	switch(config)# ssh key rsa 1024
	switch(config)# ssh key dsa 1024

SNMPv3

Option	Enables SNMPv3.
Secure Setting	Enable SNMPv3, which supports authentication and encryption.
Syntax	**switch#** config t
	switch(config)# snmp-server user [user] network-admin auth [sha/md5] [password] priv aes-128 [encrypt string]
	switch(config)# snmp-server

SNMPv3 Message Encryption

Option	Enables encryption with SNMPv3.
Secure Setting	Enable encryption with SNMPv3.
Syntax	**switch#** config t
	switch(config)# snmp-server globalEnforcePriv

SNMP Traps

Option	Limits SNMP traps to authorized nodes only.
Secure Setting	Limit SNMP traps to authorized nodes only.
Syntax	**switch#** config t
	switch(config)# snmp-server host [ip.address] traps version 3 auth [user] udp-port 1163

IPSec

Option	Enables encryption with IPSec.
Secure Setting	Enable IPSec encryption between switches, host and switches, and storage controllers and switches.

Cisco MDS: Security Services (continued)

IPSec

Syntax	`switch# config t`
	`switch(config)# crypto ike enable`
	`switch(config)# crypto ipsec enable`
	`switch(config)# crypto ike domain ipsec`

IPSec Pre Shared Keys

Option	Creates the pre-shared keys for IPSec.
Secure Setting	Pre-shared keys are not the ideal method for IPSec encryption services, but must be used without a proper CA deployment. Ensure a long, alphanumeric pre-shared key is used with special characters.
Syntax	`switch(config-ike-ipsec)# key [key] address [ip.address]`

IPSec Policies

Option	Creates IPSec policies.
Secure Setting	Create IPSec policies for AES or 3DES using MD5 or SHA1.
Syntax	`switch(config-ike-ipsec)# policy 1`
	`switch(config-ike-ipsec-policy)# encryption aes`
	`switch(config-ike-ipsec-policy)# group 5`
	`switch(config-ike-ipsec-policy)# hash md5`

IPSec Transform Set

Option	Sets the IPSec Transform information.
Secure Setting	Use IPSec with 128-bit AES encryption with SHA1 HMACs.
Syntax	`switch(config)# crypto transform-set domain ipsec tfs-02 esp-aes 128 esp-sha1-hmac`

IPSec Peers

Option	Creates IPSec tunnels with peer devices.
Secure Setting	Create an IPSec tunnel with peer devices.

IPSec Peers

Syntax	`switch(config)#` crypto map domain ipsec cmap-01 1
	`switch(config-crypto-map-ip)#` set peer [ip.address]
	`switch(config-crypto-map-ip)#` set transform-set tfs-02
	`switch(config-crypto-map-ip)#` set security-association lifetime seconds 120
	`switch(config-crypto-map-ip)#` set security-association lifetime gigabytes 3000
	`switch(config-crypto-map-ip)#` set pfs group 5

IPSec Connections

Option	Sets up IPSec tunnels with iSCSI initiators.
Secure Setting	Create IPSec tunnels with iSCSI initiators.
Syntax	`switch(config-ike-ipsec)#` initiator version 1 address [ip.address]

SSL with CIM Servers

Option	Enables SSL (HTTPS) management.
Secure Setting	Ensure SSL (HTTPS) is used with all web management applications.
Syntax	`switch#` config t
	`switch(config)#` cimserver certificate blootflash:secure.pem
	`switch(config)#` cimserver enableHTttps

Cisco MDS: Logging

Console Logging

Option	Enables console logging.
Secure Setting	Enable console logging to log severity level 3 and above, which will print logs to the console that are error, critical, and alerts.
Syntax	`switch(config)#` logging console 3
	`switch(config)#` logging level kernel 4

Cisco MDS: Logging (continued)

Log File	
Option	Creates the log file for system information.
Secure Setting	Create a large log file for system information.
Syntax	**switch(config)#** `loggin logfile LOGFILE 3 size 4000000`

SUMMARY

Storage networks are a collection of storage devices. The first half of this chapter discussed a new standard audit program (SNAP) to consistently measure storage in terms of security. The audit program shows how to audit storage devices for standard security practices. Auditing SAN and NAS storage networks and devices is the best method to identify the gaps in a storage network, in terms of availability and security. It will allow end users to begin the process of mitigating any identified security gaps. Additionally, compliance bodies can use SNAP to demonstrate the strengths and weaknesses of a particular entity. Auditing storage networks will help storage administrators and security architects measure and secure storage. SNAP can be used as a consistent audit tool and will also be updated after the publication of this book.

The second half of this chapter showed how to secure two sample storage devices, including Network Appliance filers and Cisco MDS Fibre Channel switches. Step-by-step guidelines were provided to secure the storage devices and change many of their default insecure settings to an appropriate secure settings (tools to automatically assess the configuration of these storage devices and give recommendations are available from the author at securingstorage@gmail.com). Securing storage devices is a key process to ensure that storage networks remain available and prevent accidental downtime. Additionally, secure storage devices will help ensure that malicious users cannot attack these devices to gain access to sensitive or confidential data.

The next chapter is the final chapter of this book. It focuses on three real-world case studies and ties in many of the key ideas from the entire book. It discusses the various security gaps in storage networks and the best methods to mitigate the exposures.

Storage Security Case Studies

14

Secure storage is an important process for data availability, stability, compliance, integrity, and overall protection. In order to ensure that the data network, which runs an organization's critical infrastructure, is not vulnerable to malicious attackers or accidental mistakes, proper planning, design, and implementation of key security items are required. Throughout this book, we have discussed several items in order to secure storage, ranging from self-assessment steps to the implementation of specific security settings on storage devices. The focus of this chapter is to discuss case studies regarding the process of securing storage. We will take three real-world storage networks in a typical deployment and demonstrate how they can be secured while providing the same amount of capacity, availability, and performance. The following case studies will be discussed:

- PlayTronics: Financial Services (Fibre Channel SANs)
- Abhay Narayan Medical Center: Medical Services (NFS/CIFS NAS)
- Ace Tomato Company (iSCSI SANs)

In order to ensure that each case study meets all the storage and security requirements, each will consist of the following topics:

- Business requirements, security attacks, and regulations
- Security solution
- Results checklist

CASE STUDY #1: PLAYTRONICS: FINANCIAL SERVICES

PlayTronics, headquartered in Fremont, California, designs elevator button panels that light up when a selected button is pressed. The organization sells the elevator button panels to large high-rise buildings. A few years ago, they changed their sales channels to increase revenue. The first thing PlayTronics did was to stop selling their traditional models to high-rise office buildings. From noticing the habits of every small child in an elevator, PlayTronics decided to sell the elevator button panels to toy stores as a toy for children. Due to the overwhelming popularity and enjoyment children gain by pushing all the buttons in an elevator and seeing them all lit up, they were able to generate millions of dollars. PlayTronics also added a feature to all of their new elevator button panels that they still sell to large high-rise buildings. The new feature allows a particular floor to have first priority if its button is selected five times in a row. For example, if floors 2 through 10 are selected in an elevator and a person selects floor 8, but also hits the button 5 times in a row, the elevator would go directly to floor 8 first. This feature would only be shared to key individuals in the building.

Due to the improvements of its products and sales, PlayTronics was able to gain millions of dollars in revenue and expand its offering to financial services. The financial services business unit is called SETEC. SETEC offers traditional financial services, while the parent organization (PlayTronics) still sells elevator button panels to toy stores and office buildings. Although both business units offer different products and services, they share much of the same infrastructure and business applications. The shared infrastructure and countless applications have created an increasing demand for storage. Due to the overwhelming cost of storage, the organization decided to consolidate its storage into using a SAN. Figure 14.1 shows the architecture of PlayTronics and SETEC's SAN.

The type of data that is held in the SAN are external customer data from its online sales (front-end web servers), financial data for internally generated quarterly reports (database applications), source code and patents to the product's unique features (developer servers), market/sales reports (office applications), and sales numbers (SAP applications).

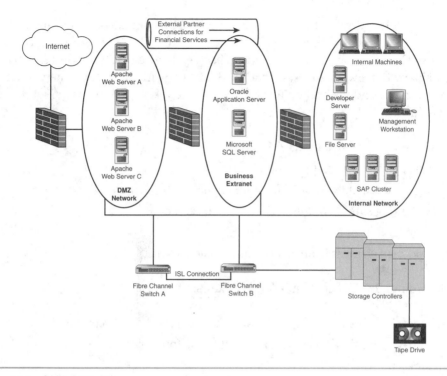

Figure 14.1 SAN architecture.

BUSINESS REQUIREMENTS, SECURITY ATTACKS, AND REGULATIONS

The business requirements provided by the PlayTronics/SETEC are listed next:

- Performance cannot be impacted.
- No storage downtime.
- Management control must be easy, scalable, and encompass the entire SAN network.
- Monitoring must be available.
- Applications supported by SAN should have low-to-minimal impact.
- The IT Director and CIO must be able to sign off on the stability and security of the SAN.
- Authorized users and/or systems should only have access to the SAN and its data.
- *Absolute requirement:* Zone allocation cannot use physical port numbers (port-based zones) due to management constraints.

The existing storage architecture for PlayTronics/SETEC contains several storage controllers, Fibre Channel switches, and client nodes holding HBAs. It also contains a management station and a tape library for offsite backup. Notice that the architecture also traverses many IP network zones, such as the DMZ network, the internal network, the business extranet, and the backup network. The current security threats in Figure 14.1 are the following:

- WWN spoofing from a DMZ web server
- Zone hopping from an application server
- Switch management compromise from any IP-enabled machine
- LUN Masking subversion on the application servers
- Data retrieval from tape devices
- In-band management from any node connected to the SAN

The PlayTronics/SETEC regulations are as follows:

- **Sarbanes-Oxley**—Financial information from being a public company.
- **Gramm-Leach Bliley**—Personal non-public customer data from direct online sales.
- **SB1386**—Information held by online sales.

In order to defend against the attacks, adhere to the government regulations, and also meet the business requirements, security must be designed and implemented in the most effective method. The first step is to understand the threat profile. For example, what is the likelihood that a server can/will be hacked and become a gateway to the SAN. The best way to determine that without endless hours of debate is to perform the self-assessment steps described earlier in the book. Also, if any server on the SAN has been infected with a virus, worm, or Trojan, then you know it could also be compromised by an attacker, if not done so already, and become a gateway into the SAN. If any of the web servers, application servers, or management servers have been infected by viruses, it means they have already been hacked and can probably be hacked again unless thorough host-hardening exercises of each server have been completed. PlayTronics/SETEC's web servers were vulnerable to the Slapper worm that targeted OpenSSL, the application servers were vulnerable to SQL Slammer and 997.dam worms as well as SQL injection attacks, and the management servers were infected with the Blaster worm that targeted RPC-DCOM on Windows environments. This information has led PlayTronics/SETEC to believe that the web servers in the DMZ, the application servers in the internal network, and the management servers in the internal network are verified attack targets and potential gateways.

SECURITY SOLUTION

The current network architecture contains the appropriate segmentation on the IP network using a three-tier architectural model with firewalls between each layer. Unfortunately, this model does not carry over to the SAN. The SAN fabric is completely flat where a compromised web server has direct access to the data of a backend application server. This essentially negates the segmentation designed/implemented on the IP network; therefore, the front-end web servers with an HBA need to be secured against hostile attacks. The areas for securing the storage network can be categorized as the front-end servers with HBA, the Fibre Channel switches, and the storage controllers. The settings for each category are listed next:

HBA on DMZ nodes

- Disable local LUN Masking on the HBA and move it to the Storage Controller.
- Harden the operating system and application on each node with an HBA.
- Enable DH-CHAP authentication on all HBAs.

HBA on business extranet nodes

- Disable local LUN Masking on the HBA and move it to the Storage Controller.
- Harden the operating system and application on each node with an HBA.
- Enable DH-CHAP authentication on all HBAs.

HBA on internal network nodes

- Disable local LUN Masking on the HBA and move it to the Storage Controller.
- Harden the operating system and application on each node with an HBA.
- Enable DH-CHAP authentication on all HBAs.

Fibre Channel switch A

- Enable hard zoning on the switch.
- Zoning:
  - Create a zone called web_server_zone and place the three web servers in that zone using their WWN.
  - Enable port locking using WWN of each HBA and locking in the physical port number it is connected to on the switch.
  - Enable zones using WWN base zone allocation.
  - Normally we would recommend using physical ports for zone allocation; however, one of the core requirements is that management software must be able to encompass all SAN nodes. Unfortunately, some SAN management software does not support physical port zones; therefore, the recommendation is to use WWN-based zones but also to enable port locking. Port locking will prevent WWN spoofing.
- Enable zoning with port WWN or both the port and node WWN (if possible).
- Require DH-CHAP authentication from node HBAs.
- Disable clear-text management on the Fibre Channel switch.
- Implement SSH for command-line access and SSL for web access.

Fibre Channel switch B

- Enable hard zoning on the switch.
- Zoning:
  - Create a zone for each type of server class, such as application servers, developer servers, file servers, and SAP servers.
  - Enable port locking using WWN of the HBAs and locking in the physical port number it is connected to on the switch.
  - Enable zones using WWN base zone allocation.
  - Normally, we would recommend using physical ports for zone allocation; however, one of the core requirements is that management software must be able to encompass all SAN nodes. Unfortunately, some SAN management software does not support physical port zones; therefore, the recommendation is to use WWN-based zones but also to enable port locking. Port locking will prevent WWN spoofing.

- Enable zoning with port WWN or both the port and node WWN (if possible).
- Require DH-CHAP authentication from node HBAs.
- Disable clear-text management on the Fibre Channel switch.
- Implement SSH for command-line access and SSL for web access.
- Enable SNMPv3 and disable SNMPv1.
- Disable in-band monitoring/management from unauthorized hosts and limit it to management workstations.

Storage controllers

- Enable LUN Masking using both the node and port WWN as the unique identifier for any HBA.
- Place an at-rest encryption device between the Fibre Channel switches and the storage controllers, encrypted on the data that resides in the SAN.
- Disable clear-text management on the Fibre Channel switch.
- Implement SSH for command-line access and SSL for web access.

Management workstation node

- Harden the operating system.
- Enable DH-CHAP authentication on all HBAs.
- Ensure that the management workstation is the only machine allowed to make an SSH or HTTPS connection to any storage node with TCP/IP filtering.

Using the same architecture in Figure 14.1, Figure 14.2 shows how the security of the SAN has improved with the settings described previously. The checkmarks in Figure 14.2 show where a security setting has been enabled.

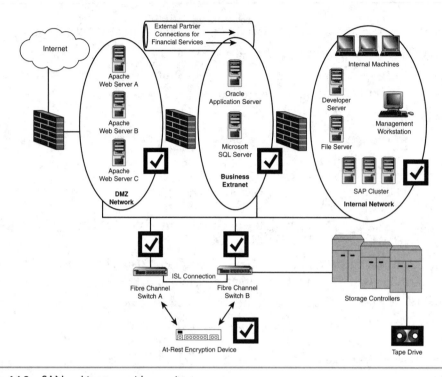

Figure 14.2   SAN architecture with security.

RESULTS CHECKLIST

Table 14.1 shows all the key requirements, security attacks, and regulations of the SAN network and how they were fulfilled or maintained with the security settings/features installed.

Table 14.1   Requirements, Attacks, and Regulations

Requirements, Attacks, and Regulations	Result
Performance cannot be impacted.	All security settings have not impacted performance from any SAN node to/from the storage controllers.
No storage downtime.	Several security controls have been implemented to prevent accidental mistakes or the misconfiguration of storage systems, leaving the storage environment more stable from incorrect actions from authorized users.

Requirements, Attacks, and Regulations	Result
Management control must be easy, scalable, and encompass the entire SAN network.	WWN base zone allocation was specifically used to adhere to this requirement. Due to the weaknesses of WWN-based zone allocation, port locking was enabled.
Monitoring must be available.	Monitoring is still available with SNMPv3 and to authorized management workstations only.
Application support by SANs should have low to minimal impact.	All applications are still connected to the SAN, but isolated from other applications that are not the same type.
The IT Director and CIO must be able to sign off on the stability and security of the SAN.	No unstable settings or features have been enabled.
Authorized users and/or systems should only have access to the SAN and its data.	Authentication (DH-CHAP), strong authorization (port/node WWN usage, or port locking on FC switches), and encryption (at-rest encryption device) have been enabled on the SAN.
WWN spoofing from a DMZ web server.	Using physical ports for zone allocation was not possible due to a previous requirement; however, port locking was enabled. Port locking locks the node's WWN to the physical port on the switch. Additionally, DH-CHAP authentication has been enabled.
Zone hopping from an application server.	Using physical ports for zone allocation was not possible due to a previous requirement; however, port locking was enabled. Port locking locks the node's WWN to the physical port on the switch. Additionally, DH-CHAP authentication has been enabled.
Switch management compromise from any IP-enabled machine.	Enable TCP/IP filters on IP networks in order to limit access to IP management interfaces from authorized management workstations.
LUN Mask subversion on the application servers.	LUN Masking has not been enabled on any client storage node. LUN Masking has been enabled on the storage controllers using both the port and node WWN for identity values.
Data retrieval from tape devices.	Encryption devices have been implemented between the Fibre Channel switches and storage controllers, encrypting all data at rest.
In-band management from any node.	In-band management should be discarded unless it comes from an authorized management server or authorized management switch.

Table 14.1   Requirements, Attacks, and Regulations (continued)

Requirements, Attacks, and Regulations	Result
Sarbanes-Oxley—Protect the integrity of financial information and reports.	Several security controls have been enabled to ensure that access to data in the SAN is protected from unauthorized users.
Gramm-Leach Bliley—Protect personal non-public customer data.	Several security controls have been enabled to ensure that access to data in the SAN is protected from unauthorized users. Additionally, encryption has been enabled of all data at-rest.
SB1386—Protect information held by online sales.	Several security controls have been enabled to ensure that access to data in the SAN is protected from unauthorized users. Additionally, encryption has been enabled of all data at-rest.

CASE STUDY #2: ABHAY NARAYAN MEDICAL CENTER

The Abhay Narayan Medical Center, headquartered in Belewa, Uttra Pradesh, is a health-care provider in India. The primary corporate offices are located in India; however, many of their hospitals are located in the United States. Additionally, the Center's call centers have been outsourced to Europe, the world's largest outsourcing location. Unlike traditional health-care providers that offer services to insured individuals, Abhay Narayan Medical Center offers health care to any individual who needs treatment. Due to the overwhelming number of individuals who need health services but do not have any type of insurance coverage, the data storage needs of Abhay Narayan Medical Center have increased significantly, but the operational budgets for storage have remained the same. In order to adequately fulfill the growing demand on storage, the organization decided to consolidate their storage into NAS devices and remove any storage demands from local operating systems. Consolidation of their storage will save the medical organization millions of dollars, which they will use to purchase medicine for sick individuals who cannot afford it. Figure 14.3 shows the storage architecture of Abhay Narayan Medical Center.

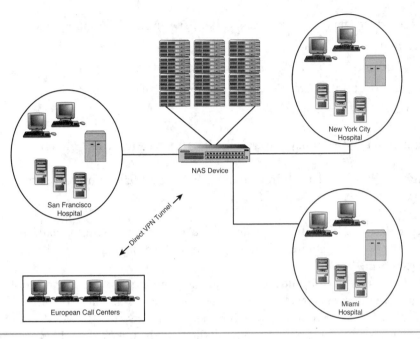

Figure 14.3 NAS storage architecture.

BUSINESS REQUIREMENTS, SECURITY ATTACKS, AND REGULATIONS

The business requirements provided by the Abhay Narayan Medical Center are as follows:

- User access should not be modified.
- The impact on the file servers supported by NAS devices should be minimal.
- Authorized users and/or systems should only have access to their own data on the NAS device.
- *Absolute requirement:* A single NAS environment must support all hospitals.

The existing storage architecture for the Abhay Narayan Medical Center contains several operating systems that make CIFS and NFS connections to NAS storage devices. The current security threats in Figure 14.3 are the following:

- Clear-text sniffing of all storage data
- Man-in-the-Middle attacks on IP networks

- Full access to data on NAS devices without any authentication required
- CIFS Enumeration attacks
- CIFS Authentication attacks (LM and NTLM)
- NFS Authorization attacks (UID/GID spoofing)
- Clear-text management

The regulation that the Abhay Narayan Medical Center must conform to is

- **HIPAA**—Protected Health Information (PHI) must have confidentiality and protection.

In order to defend against these attacks, adhere to the government regulations, and also adhere to the business requirements, security must be designed and implemented in the most effective method.

Similar to our SAN case study, the first step is to understand the threat profile of the storage systems. Because any client on the network—which includes the internal network, VPN users, extranet, or even the Internet—can access the IP NAS devices, the attack surface is quite large. Additionally, all the NAS devices have enabled NFS and CIFS by default, allowing access to data files from Unix or Windows operating systems, which doubles the attack vectors on the NAS device. The threat profile is quite large since basically any node (Windows or Unix) on the regular network (IP) is a possible attacker.

SECURITY SOLUTION

The IP network contains several applications that require authentication for access; however, due to the demanding storage needs, the data has been consolidated and centralized to a NAS storage system. Although appropriate authentication has been implemented on the application and the operating systems, it has been ignored on the NAS device. The poor security controls on the default installation of the NAS device negates the proper security settings in place on the applications and operating systems. The areas to focus on in order to fix the security issues are the NAS clients, the storage devices, and the protocols supported. The settings for each category are listed next:

NAS storage devices

- Disable enumeration of CIFS.
- Enable Kerberos with CIFS.

- If possible, disable LM and NTLM completely and strictly use Kerberos.
- Enable authorization parameters by limiting corporate shares to appropriate network subnets.
- Enable IPSec encryption.
- Require Kerberos for NFS communication.
- Do not rely on any UID/GID values from NFS clients.
- Enable VFilers, granting each hospital its own virtual filer in the NAS storage environment.

NAS clients (NFS and CIFS)

- Use Kerberos authentication only.
  - Both NFS and CIFS Authentication
- CIFS clients should disable the use of LM or NTLM.
- NFS clients should not use UID/GIDs; for access, use Kerberized NFS clients.
- Enable IPSec encryption.

Supported protocols

- Disable Telnet, RSH, Rlogin, and HTTP access for management.
- Enable SSH and HTTPS access for management.
- Enable SNMPv3 for monitoring.
- Enable IPSec for client-to-server communication.

Using the same architecture in Figure 14.3, Figure 14.4 shows how the security of the NAS environment has improved with the setting described previously. The checkmarks in Figure 14.4 show where a security setting has been enabled.

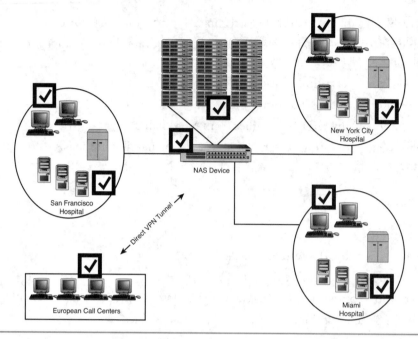

Figure 14.4 NAS architecture with security.

RESULTS CHECKLIST

Table 14.2 shows all the key requirements, security attacks, and the regulation for the NAS environment and how they were fulfilled or maintained with the security settings and features installed.

Table 14.2 Requirements, Attacks, and Regulations

Requirements, Attacks, and Regulations	Result
User access should not be modified.	Authentication was not modified. CIFS users are required to use Kerberos, which is invisible to the end user. Additionally, NFS clients must use a kerberized NFS client, which uses the same syntax but requires a username and password with the `mount` command.
The impact on the file servers supported by NAS devices should be minimal.	File servers have not been modified on the Windows or Unix servers. All security changes take place on the NAS device or the IP network.

Requirements, Attacks, and Regulations	Result
Authorized users and/or systems should only have access to their own data on the NAS device.	Authorization to network shares is limited to valid subnets that the departments reside in.
A single NAS environment must support all the hospitals.	vFilers have been enabled, which creates a virtual filer for each hospital. Data allocated to one Vfiler is not mixed with the data on any other Vfiler. Vfilers are not accessible to nodes on the other segments.
Clear-text sniffing of all storage data.	IPSec ESP has been enabled from NFS and CIFS clients to IPSec-enabled storage devices. All IP communication will be encrypted.
Man-in-the-Middle attacks on IP networks.	IPSec authentication headers have been enabled to ensure that authentication of IP packets is completed.
Full access to data on NAS devices without any authentication required.	Kerberos authentication is required between all CIFS and NFS clients and NAS storage devices.
CIFS Enumeration attacks.	All proper hardening steps to secure the NAS device has been completed, which disables anonymous enumeration of CIFS information.
CIFS Authentication attacks (LM and NTLM).	Kerberos has been enabled and is the default method for authentication. Due to the limitations of NAS devices, LM and NTLM cannot be turned off; therefore, CIFS clients have disabled the use of LM and NTLM with registry edits in the Windows registry.
NFS Authorization attacks (UID/GID spoofing).	Kerberos authentication is required for all NFS clients. Additionally, any UID = 0 is classified as a nobody account. Finally, UID/GID without any authentication parameters will be denied.
Clear-text management.	Telnet, Rsh, and HTTP have been disabled in favor of SSH and HTTPS.
HIPAA—Protected Heath Information (PHI) must have confidentiality and protection.	Several security controls have been implemented to required authentication and strong authorization in order to access PHI data. Additionally, all PHI data traverses the network from NAS clients to NAS storage devices over an encrypted communication channel.

CASE STUDY #3: ACE TOMATO COMPANY

Ace Tomato Company is a telecommunications organization. The regional offices are located in Fremont, California, Minneapolis, Minnesota, and Nashville, Tennessee. Additionally, two sales offices are located in Brookings, South Dakota and Columbus, Ohio. The organization runs many business applications, but the application used most often is the Exchange server for email and calendaring. The organization has tried several times to encourage end users to use different applications for file transfer or simply to delete some of their email messages (attachments); however, with the growing support of Exchange on remote handheld devices, such as PocketPC and BlackBerry devices, Exchange continues to be the application that contains the most flexibility for employees and the largest storage needs. Due to the increasing demands of all the Exchange servers across the organization and the monthly request to increase data capacities for email/ calendaring, Ace Tomato Company has decided to offload storage to iSCSI storage devices.

Figure 14.5 shows the storage architecture that Ace Tomato Company has implemented for the iSCSI environment.

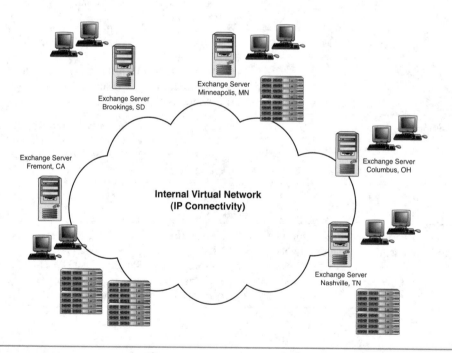

Figure 14.5   iSCSI storage architecture.

All Exchange servers will use iSCSI via the IP network, and the two sales offices (Brookings and Columbus) will use the iSCSI storage device in Minneapolis and Nashville, respectively. Each office has their own Internet feeds, ranging from fractional T1 connections to DSL connections in the smaller offices. Additionally, each office is connecting to the corporate network using site-to-site VPNs. Remote users are using client-to-site VPNs for remote email access.

Because all iSCSI storage devices are used for the Exchange servers, the type of data that is held in the iSCSI network ranges from personal information of customers to personal information of employees. Since all users store office files, notes, and emails on the Exchange server and never delete their mail, Ace Tomato Company is extremely worried about the compromise of any iSCSI storage device. Furthermore, since Ace Tomato Company does not deploy internal firewalls or access filters, a user in a coffee shop, an internal employee, a contractor/consultant, or a malicious attacker could access and target the iSCSI storage device from the IP network. Furthermore, a recent audit of the Exchange servers identified that HR groups were sending social security numbers to employees via email, IT users were sending passwords to employees via email, and sales employees were sending customer information to employees via email.

BUSINESS REQUIREMENTS, SECURITY ATTACKS, AND REGULATIONS

The business requirements provided by the Ace Tomato Company are listed next:

- User or application access cannot be impacted.
- Performance cannot be impacted.
- No storage downtime.
- User access should not be modified.
- Authorized users and/or systems should only have access to their own data on the iSCSI device.
- *Absolute requirement:* No IPSec encryption can be used due to the performance penalties.

The current security threats in Figure 14.5 are the following:

- Clear-text sniffing of all storage data
- Man-in-the-Middle attacks on IP networks
- Full access to data on iSCSI devices without any authentication required

- iSNS Enumeration attacks
- iSCSI Authentication attacks (CHAP)
- iSCSI Authorization attacks (IQN spoofing)
- Clear-text management

Due to the fact that social security numbers, passwords, and customer data is being sent to internal and external recipients via email, the type of data that is being stored on the Exchange servers could be under several types of government regulations. Therefore, Ace Tomato Company has decided to follow COBIT standards for information security. COBIT is the generally accepted standard for good IT security practices. See http://www.isaca.org/Template.cfm?Section=COBIT6&Template=/TaggedPage/ TaggedPageDisplay.cfm&TPLID=55&ContentID=7981 for more information.
In order to defend against the attacks, support the COBIT control activities, and also adhere to the business requirements, security must be designed and implemented in the most effective method.

The first step is to understand the threat profile of the storage systems. Because there are no internal firewalls at Ace Tomato Company, any client on the network—which includes the internal network, VPN users, and business extranets—can access any of the IP iSCSI devices, which makes the attack surface quite large. Additionally, since authentication is disabled by default and the authorization parameters in place are spoofable, the success ratio for any attacks is also quite high for any attacker.

SECURITY SOLUTION

The IP iSCSI network holds sensitive and confidential information, but does not deploy the basic security practices for data protection such as authentication and strong authorization. Additionally, the communication is not encrypted (clear-text) and is accessible to any user on the IP network, which is almost all users and nodes. The poor security controls on the default installation of the iSCSI devices negates many of the security settings that have been placed on the Exchange server or its underlying operating system.

The areas to focus on in order to fix the security issues are the iSCSI clients, the iSCSI storage devices, and the protocols in use. The settings for each category are listed next:

iSCSI storage devices

- Enable CHAP authentication (client to target).
- Create unique domain sets (iSNS servers) and ensure each iSCSI client belongs to a customized domain set.
- Enable CRC checksums on the communication processes between the client and target.

iSCSI clients

- Enable mutual authentication using CHAP (target to client).
- Enable CRC checksums on the communication processes between the client and target.

Supported protocols

- Disable Telnet, RSH, Rlogin, and HTTP access for management.
- Enable SSH and HTTPS access for management.
- Enable SNMPv3 for monitoring.

Using the same architecture in Figure 14.5, Figure 14.6 shows how the security of the iSCSI environment has improved with the security setting described previously. The checkmarks in Figure 14.6 show where a security setting has been enabled.

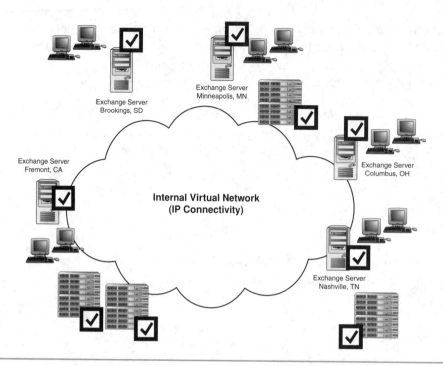

Figure 14.6   iSCSI architecture with security.

RESULTS CHECKLIST

Table 14.3 shows all the key requirements, security attacks, and the regulation of the iSCSI storage environment and how they were fulfilled or maintained with the security settings and features installed.

Table 14.3   Requirements, Attacks, and Regulations

Requirements, Attacks, and Regulations	Result
User or application access cannot be impacted.	All security settings have not impacted performance from any iSCSI client or device.
Performance cannot be impacted.	IPSec has not been enabled due to performance requirements. As a mitigating security control, mutual authentication and CRC checksums have been enabled, which do not impact performance.

Requirements, Attacks, and Regulations	Result
No storage downtime.	Several security controls have been implemented to prevent accidental mistakes or the misconfiguration of storage systems, leaving the storage environment more stable.
User access should not have to be modified.	iSCSI clients (systems) have to authenticate before accessing data; however, the authentication process is a one-time process and does not need to be repeated.
Authorized users and/or systems should only have access to the iSCSI devices and their data.	CHAP authentication and mutual authentication has been enabled to ensure that only authorized user/clients are accessing iSCSI devices.
Absolute requirement: No IPSec encryption due to the performance loss.	IPSec has not been enabled due to performance requirements. As a mitigating security control, mutual authentication and CRC checksums have been enabled, which do not impact performance.
Clear-text sniffing of all storage data.	IPSec has not been enabled due to performance requirements; however, in order to prevent Man-in-the-Middle attacks, CRC checksums have been enabled, which make Man-in-the-Middle attacks more difficult.
Man-in-the-Middle attacks on IP networks.	Mutual authentication and CRC checksums have been enabled to mitigate Man-in-the-Middle attacks.
Full access to data on iSCSI devices without any authentication required.	CHAP authentication and mutual authentication have been enabled.
iSNS Enumeration attacks.	Unique domains have been created for iSCSI clients and targets.
iSCSI Authentication attacks (CHAP).	Mutual authentication has been enabled to prevent CHAP (client-to-target) attacks.
iSCSI Authorization attacks (IQN spoofing).	CHAP authentication and mutual authentication have been enabled to remove the security dependencies of IQNs.
Clear-text management.	Telnet, Rsh, and HTTP have been disabled in favor of SSH and HTTPS.
COBIT—Standards for acceptable IT security practices.	Several security controls have been implemented to require authentication and strong authorization. These security protections will help protect data and access methods to iSCSI systems.

SUMMARY

This chapter discussed three case studies for securing storage. Due to the performance and capacity demands on storage networks, security controls and best practices are often overlooked. Many false assumptions exist about the impact a security feature has on the storage network, which prevents many administrators from implementing strong security controls. The purpose of this chapter was to show three real-world scenarios where existing Fibre Channel SANs, IP NAS, or iSCSI SANs were deployed but with poor or absent security controls. Each scenario had business requirements for the storage network that were non-negotiable. Each scenario also has plenty of security weaknesses due to its existing implementation and design. Finally, due to the type of data that was residing in the storage network, each scenario had a government regulation that it must comply with. With all of these requirements, the ability to support security, performance, and compliance is not always easy. Some risks must be accepted due to performance or functionality reasons. Conversely, some performance/functionality requirements might have to be modified in order to meet security or compliance requirements. Each scenario also had an absolute requirement, where no adjustments could be made. Storage requirements often have at least one of these absolute requirements mentioned in this chapter due to the availability requirements of storage. Finally, each scenario was able to demonstrate how enabling existing security settings and modifying certain storage designs can significantly improve the security of the storage network. Additionally, each solution was able to ensure that the data residing in the storage network (or its devices) are meeting industry standard regulations and requirements.

Index